THE
STRATEGIC
TRIANGLE

THE STRATEGIC TRIANGLE

China, the United States
and the Soviet Union

Edited By Ilpyong J. Kim

A PWPA Book

PARAGON HOUSE
New York

Published in the United States by

Paragon House
90 Fifth Avenue
New York, New York 10011

A Professors World Peace Academy Book

The Professors World Peace Academy (PWPA) is an educational organization of scholars
from diverse backgrounds. Paragon-PWPA books include topics in peace studies, international relations, area studies, education, and development.

Library of Congress Cataloging-in-Publication Data

The Strategic Triangle
  "A PWPA book."
  Bibliography.
  Includes index.
  1. World politics—1985–   . 2. China—Foreign
relations—1976–   . 3. Soviet Union—Foreign relations
—1975–   . 4. United States—Foreign relations—
1981–   .   I. Kim, Ilpyong J., 1931–   .
D849.S87 1987   327'.09'048   87–8897
ISBN 0–943852–20–X
ISBN 0–943852–21–8 (pbk.)

Second printing

Table of Contents

Glossary of Abbreviations, Acronyms and Initialisms

ABM	Anti-Ballistic Missile
ANZUS	Australia–New Zealand–U.S.
ASEAN	Association of Southeast Asian Nations
BAM	Baikal-Amor Mainland Railway
CCP	Chinese Communist Party
CDSP	Current Digest of the Soviet Press
CENTO	Central Treaty Organization
CINCPAC	Commander-in-Chief of Forces in the Pacific
CMEA	Council for Mutual Economic Assistance
COMECON	Council for Mutual Economic Assistance
CPSU	Communist Party, Soviet Union
CPSU CC	Communist Party, of the Soviet Union Central Committee
CPUSA	Communist Party, United States of America
DRV	Democratic Republic of Vietnam (North Vietnam)
FRG	Federal Republic of Germany
GPCR	Great Proletarian Cultural Revolution
ICBM	Intercontinental Ballistic Missile
INF	Intermediate Range Nuclear Forces
IRBM	Intermediate Range Ballistic Missile
KAL 007	Korean Airlines Flight 007
KMT	Kuomintang (Nationalist Party)
MARG	Marine Amphibious Ready Group
MBFR	Mutual and Balanced Force Reduction Talks
MFN	Most Favored Nation
Mig	Russian-built fighter aircraft
MIRV	Mobile Intercontinental Re-entry Vehicle
MRBM	Medium Range Ballistic Missile

NATO	North Atlantic Treaty Organization
NEATO	Northeast Asia Treaty Organization
NEP	New Economic Policy
OECD	Organization of Economic Cooperation and Development
OPIC	Overseas Private Investment Corporation
PLA	People's Liberation Party
PRC	People's Republic of China
RIMPAC	Rim of the Pacific
ROC	Republic of China
ROK	Republic of Korea
SALT I, SALT II	Strategic Arms Limitation Talks I and II
SEATO	Southeast Asia Treaty Organization
SLBMs	Submarine-launched Ballistic Missile
SS18	Russian missile
WEIS	World Events Interaction Survey

Introduction

ILPYONG J. KIM

A series of events in the early 1980s, among them the Soviet invasion of Afghanistan, the U.S. boycott of the Olympics in Moscow, and the cancellation of the Strategic Arms Limitation Talks (SALT), ushered in a new cold war. In contrast to the trends toward detente and a multipolar world in the 1970s, characterized by the Kissinger balance-of-power diplomacy which was designed to restructure the bipolar international system to a multipolar system, a shift in U.S. policy in the 1980s has yielded a new strategic triangle between the U.S., the Soviet Union, and China. Moreover, the normalization of relations between the United States and China in 1979, and the abrogation of the thirty-year treaty between China and the Soviet Union for Friendship, Cooperation and Mutual Assistance in April 1980, contributed to further changes in the relationships between these three powers.

The rise of China as a world power after the Cultural Revolution has created a new pattern of relations within the U.S.-Soviet-Chinese triangle in world politics. In the beginning of the 1980s the power triangle could be analyzed in terms of relative distance from each other, with these distances representing degrees of hostility or friendliness. Thus, the Sino-American relations following the normalization treaty have been increasingly friendly while the U.S.-Soviet relations were fairly hostile and the Sino-Soviet

1

relations have been very hostile until recent years. However, the Chinese-American relations began to cool off in 1982 as the result of U.S. arms sales to Taiwan and changes in the Chinese perception of U.S.-Soviet relations.

The Tashkent proposal on 24 March 1982 by Leonid Brezhnev, the late General Secretary of the Communist Party of the Soviet Union, for the improvement of Sino-Soviet relations, coupled with the Chinese adoption of "Independent Foreign Policy" in 1982, provided an impetus for the reduction of tensions on the Sino-Soviet border areas and enhanced the process toward the resumption of negotiations between the Chinese and Soviet leaders for normalization of relations. The vice-foreign ministers of China and the Soviet Union met in late 1982, their first conference since the fall of 1979 when the negotiations between the Chinese and Soviet foreign ministry officials were terminated as the result of the Soviet invasion of Afghanistan.

Negotiations for the normalization of relations between China and the Soviet Union in 1982, therefore, could be characterized as the resumption of temporarily halted talks. This was fueled to a large extent by the stresses and strains which had developed in the Sino-American relations over their differences in approach to the Taiwan issue and the technology transfer from the United States to China.

The increase in trade between China and the Soviet Union was another indication of their improved relations. Bilateral trade between the two countries expanded 26.4 percent in 1982 over the previous year, 218 percent in 1983, and 200 percent in 1984. Furthermore, the border trade between the two communist giants was stepped up in 1983 in the Heilungjiang province, Inner Mongolia Autonomous Region, Sinjiang Uighur Autonomous Region; which prompted Hu Yaobang, General Secretary of the Chinese Communist Party, to stress the necessity of open doors in the border regions when he visited Inner Mongolia in September 1984.

The representatives of China, the Soviet Union, Mongolia and the Democratic People's Republic of Korea (North Korea) also met on 23 March 1984 in Ulan Bator to discuss the improvement of the railway transport system among these four countries. Such a conference had not been held in the previous 18 years. Following the conference a direct line of railroad communication was set up among these four nations and, hence, the communication system was considerably improved. Thus, the train service between Sinjiang and the Soviet border area was resumed in August 1985 and the freight transport facilities along the river banks of the border area resumed their services in 1985. The improvement of communications between China and the Soviet Union facilitated the reduction of tensions and the improvement of inter-government relations.

The onset of adverse relations between the United States and China in 1981 prompted China to move towards the minimization of the Sino-Soviet conflict, since China cannot afford to maintain conflict with two superpowers. China, therefore, no longer considers the Soviet Union as its principal adversary and is able to maintain an equidistant relationship with the United States and the Soviet Union. This contributed to the reformation of the strategic triangle in U.S.-Soviet-Chinese relations. By improving its relations with the superpowers, China hopes to achieve its goal of "four modernizations" by the year 2000 and to become an equal partner with the United States and the Soviet Union in the arena of world politics.

Against the background of these developments a group of scholars specializing in U.S.-Soviet-Chinese relations attended a conference sponsored by the Professors World Peace Academy, in Los Angeles, California on 15-17 February 1985. Thomas H. Etzold, Thomas Robinson, Lowell Dittmer, Richard Thornton, Steven Levine, Parris Chang, Donald Klein, Peter Berton, Bernard Gordon, Michael Kau, Jane Shapiro Zacek, James Hsiung and Rudolf Rummel contributed research papers which were extensively discussed at the conference. Donald S. Zagoria contributed his paper on "The Superpowers and Korea" after the conference.

Tao Bingwei, Michael Blaker, Craig Etcheson, Edward A. Olsen, William Tow, and Allen Whiting served as discussants.

On the basis of suggestions made at the conference the authors revised their papers by the end of 1985. Finally, the revised versions were sent to an anonymous reviewer to evaluate their quality for publication. The reviewer enthusiastically recommended publication, saying that the volume "is significant in that it encompasses a range of theoretical models to explain and predict the triangular relationship, with special attention to China's role therein." The authors then made final revisions to their papers based on the reviewer's suggestions and recommendations. Morton A. Kaplan also presented his assessment of the triangular relationship and the prospects for the U.S.-Soviet-Chinese relations in the 1980s.

As editor, I extend my gratitude to all conference participants and to those who reviewed the proceedings. Hugh Spurgin, then secretary-general of the Professors World Peace Academy, and Gordon Anderson, current secretary-general, were always cheerful and helpful in their efforts to help me organize the conference. Nancy Farlow, director of publications, and Barbara Kubo, administrative assistant, were always willing to make their contributions toward finalizing this volume. My wife, Hyunyong, and two daughters, Irene and Katherine, have consistently encouraged my work, for which I am most grateful. As the editor, however, I assume sole responsibility for any omissions or errors in this volume.

On the Further Evolution of the Strategic Triangle

THOMAS W. ROBINSON

Depending on definition, the strategic triangle has been a central feature of the international system at earliest since 1950 and certainly since the early 1970s. Despite doubts in some quarters as to whether there really is any such entity (China has been thought to be too weak to qualify as a member) and other expressions of its early demise, it seems clear that the triangle has fundamentally configured international relations for a long time and that its existence and influence are assured for years to come. On the other hand, even now forces are at work that will lead to its eventual transformation. For these reasons, we need to know what the characteristics of the triangle are, how it forms the base of world politics, what its evolutionary history has been, and where the future is likely to lead it. These are the topics that this chapter addresses.

First, we need to get straight what we mean by the strategic triangle.[1] Its members, obviously, are China, the Soviet Union, and the United States. They share a set of qualities not characteristic of any other state: vastness of territory; hugeness of population; very large military forces; very large economies with at least some "highly modern" sectors; a tendency to dominate their regions of the globe; messianic ideologies; and a diversity of nuclear weaponry capable of being delivered at great distances. Consequently, each conducts a foreign policy under the assumption that the global future belongs to it and that it has an innate right (if not always the power) to have a say in events and situations far beyond its borders. It is true that China does not always fit this description, especially as concerns the degree of modernity of its economy and its comparable nuclear delivery capability. It is also true that two other states—Japan and India—and at least one other regional grouping of states—Western Europe—possess several of the same characteristics. India is more populous than the United States and the Soviet Union; and Japan is (depending on how one measures) the world's second economic power; while Western Europe, if it were to unite politically, would surely be in the same league as America, China, and Russia. Yet there is a sufficiently large number of characteristics shared by the three in common and by no other state that there is no doubt that the strategic triangle exists.

Moreover, all three members of the triangle act like they are its members, even if they sometimes declare that they are not. And other important states and competent observers also agree that there is a strategic triangle, whose corners are located in Washington, Beijing, and Moscow. This has been true since the emergence of the Sino-Soviet split in the late 1950s. Sometimes, it is true, decision makers in the three capitals have disclaimed the triangle or denigrated the influence of one of its members. The United States for too long tried to claim that China and the Soviet Union acted together under a single directorate or even at times asserted that China was too weak to be considered a member of the triangle.[2] Yet overall American policy for most of the period since about 1958 (the Taiwan Straits crisis) and perhaps even earlier (the Korean War) has regarded China as independent and powerful enough to warrant membership. It has accorded this status to no other nation outside the Soviet Union. The Soviet Union, too, occasionally argued that China was not a member of the triangle, either because Moscow presumed to speak for Beijing or because it attempted to deal with Washington as one superpower to another in a bipolar world or because it took China at its word as a Third World state and thus not a member of the triangle at all.[3] But for most of the last three decades, Moscow has devoted as much policy attention and foreign policy resources to dealing with China as it has with the United States, far beyond the attention and resources expended on any other third state. China, in its turn, also at times claimed that it was not a member of the triangle, as when it looked to Russian leadership in the early-mid 1950s, when it claimed to be independent of both Washington and Moscow in the early 1960s, and when it championed itself as a Third World leader in the late 1970s.[4] And yet the essence of Chinese foreign policy during the entire post-1950 period has been to pay attention first and foremost to relations with the United States and the Soviet Union and to derive most of its other policies from its status within the triangle.

Second, it is important to draw needful distinctions as a further way of specifying the strategic triangle. One is that the triangle is indeed "strategic." It is the principal set of relations in the international political system; change those relations, and the entire configuration of the system varies accordingly. It is also strategic in the strictly military sense; only these three states have the combined nuclear and conventional capability to wreak destruction on a regional and a global scale. It is true that China cannot project its conventional military power far beyond its borders and it is true that the British and French nuclear forces are at least the equivalent of the Chinese. Yet only China has the combination of ambition and potential to become a global military power. Neither European power can make that claim, and it is that combination that helps make China a member of the triangle. Finally, the triangle is strategic in the geopolitical sense; each power either dominates an important sector of the globe or has the potential to do so. No other state or group of states presently is in such a position.

Third, the strategic triangle, while exceedingly important to international relations, is not the only central structural aspect of the international system. There is, in addition, the whole international economic arena, which, although very much influenced by the policies and actions of the three members of the strategic triangle, is governed by a different set of operational regularities, is dominated by a different triangle composed of the United States, Japan, and Western Europe, and is linked to the strategic triangle principally through the common membership of the United States.[5] Another central structural feature of the international system is the existence of various regional configurations of power, in three regions of Asia, the Middle East, two regions of Africa, two of Europe, and two of Latin America. Each of these regions lives by a specific set of political and economic "rules" and is related in complex manners to the strategic and economic triangles.[6] Of note is that the United States and the Soviet Union are principal actors in all but one of these regions (East Europe and Latin America, respectively), and China is a principal actor in three of them (Northeast, Southeast, and South Asia). No other states can make claim to such widespread influence. The final additional central structural feature of the international system is global international organization, centered around the United Nations and its specialized agencies, regional international organizations of all kinds, transnational relations of diverse sorts (tourism, cultural and ideational flows, etc.), and global "issues—features of the system that affect states without regard for political and economic boundaries (pollution, resource availability, etc.)."[7] There are, of course, many connections between international organization, regionalism, transnationalism, and global issue, on the one hand, and the strategic triangle, on the other. The United Nations would not function without the support of the members of the triangle, its members participate in (and sometimes interfere in) the work of regional organizations, open and close their respective gateways to the flood of transnational interactions, and are as affected as most other countries by global problems (which by definition disregard national boundaries). But the important point is that the strategic triangle does not dominate this aspect of the broader system.

Having thus specified the strategic triangle and its place in the international system, the next task is to indicate some of its operational characteristics. The first is that it is heavily tipped toward the Soviet-American side, since the two superpowers are clearly more powerful than China and since Washington and Moscow have been at odds on most issues during the entire post-War period. It follows that, whenever America and Russia confront each other directly, an international systemic crisis ensues, and that, whenever relations between the two vary significantly, there are at least trembles at the base of the system.[8] However, despite this (or perhaps as a consequence—the reasoning supports both sides of the argument), the very enormity of power in the hands of the two superpowers, together with their competition for influence around the globe, has paradoxically supplied a good deal of stability to the international system. The system is a dynamic and changing one, but it is not the American-Soviet leg of the triangle that drives the larger system. It merely provides the backdrop for change, the impetus for which comes largely from elsewhere. International politics, like politics in general, is what happens at the margin, i.e., incremental changes to which the system must adjust. Were there to be a major change in Soviet-American relations, there would be a revolution in world politics, but that has not happened since the triangle was formed in 1950. It did happen in 1945 with the breakup of the wartime alliance, it could have happened in the 1960s and 1970s had detente had a firmer foundation, and it might happen if a major nuclear confrontation or war were to occur. But since neither detente nor war is likely,[9] and since the Soviet-American standoff is likely to continue for the foreseeable future (of which more below), we must look elsewhere to understand the dynamics of the triangle and also of world politics.

Dynamism within the triangle is supplied by the wide swings in Chinese policy toward the United States and the Soviet Union. This is the second operational characteristic of the triangle. Because China has always been the weakest of the three, it has been able to find security only by swinging from one extreme to the other, from Washington to Moscow and then again to Washington. The only other option for Beijing has been to balance between the two other members, but that possibility will be open only when China possesses reasonable innate strength of its own. It is now acquiring that strength, after frittering away nearly thirty years in false starts. It did attempt to choose a fourth option in the 1960s by pretending that it could escape the triangle altogether, first by setting itself against Washington and Moscow simultaneously and then during the Cultural Revolution by withdrawing entirely from international affairs. That was not viable, however, as sufficient power was not available, as the aftermath of the 1969 border incidents demonstrated. In such a manner, the inner history of the triangle can be traced through these variations in China's foreign policy.[10] It will continue thusly, so long as the **relative** power of the three remains approximately the same as during the last three decades.

A third operational characteristic of the triangle is that it is a balance of power system, the most primitive and vicious example of such a system because it contains only three states, but a balance of power system nonetheless. It therefore exhibits, in truncated but unmistakeable manner, all the distinctive features of such a system. These include: alliance of the weaker two against the third, strongest, member; reversal of alliances when power realities shift sufficiently; reasonably careful calculation of national interests as a basis of policy alignment within and outside the triangle; inability to judge with the necessary exactitude the power available to one's self and one's opponents; the expansion and contraction of national interests according to the judgment as to the relative power available; a tendency to negotiate differences where possible, to threaten force where necessary in the hope that it will not have to be used, and the willingness to use force in the end to ensure one's vital interests; and an interest in preserving the system itself and thus a disinclination to destroy another member through unlimited war.[11] The history of the strategic triangle reveals textbook instances of each of these rules of the balance of power. In that regard, the Sino-Soviet-American triangle is no different from many other earlier three-sided balance of power systems.

A fourth operational characteristic is complexity. The three states in question are really internal empires, each enormously variagated systems in their own rights. Each is also quite different from the others in terms of history, culture, geography, economy, level of modernization, and other determinants of foreign policy. Parallels with the European state system are therefore misplaced. Each tries, with varying degrees of success, to insulate its internal order from the actions of the others and each attempts, again with differential outcome, to make its policy toward the others stem from domestic *cum* national interest determinants alone. Domestic, foreign policy, and international levels are, however, linked in a complex systems dynamics manner. The history of the triangle is, in fact, the history of the connections and time-differentiated feedbacks between the various factors operating at these three levels. But merely because of their great size relative to all other states (size in the sense of the combination of defining characteristics noted on page 1), America, China, and Russia have had the comparative luxury of determining their respective foreign policies largely on the basis of domestic determinants. Thus, any considered understanding of the workings of the triangle must include, first and foremost, reference to what is happening domestically in each of the three entities. The arrow of causation in the foreign policies of the three members therefore points, basically, outward from a domestic base largely insulated from international influences. Hence, the latter should, as a first approximation, be looked on best as a set of disturbances to the internal determination of their respective foreign policies. No other three states in the postwar international system can make such claims.[12]

While the history of the strategic triangle is, in many ways, the history of postwar international relations and thus too complex and lengthy to reproduce here, it is useful to outline its evolution as a means of illustrating its structure and dynamics.[13] The Soviet-American leg was, of course, firmly in place even before 1950. The postwar alliance fell apart almost instantly, as it was no longer needed, while the diametrically opposed domestic orders in the two countries, the weakness of all other states of consequence, and American-Soviet sense of competition based on vast ideological differences and their great military power combined to set the two superpowers profoundly at odds. America and Russia theretofore had not had to grapple with each other as societies; inexperience thus compounded power competition and ideological warfare as causes of the ensuing Cold War. Under these circumstances, there would undoubtedly have been war between Washington and Moscow within a few years were it not for the additional factor of the nuclear weapon and its monopolistic possession over the short term by the United States, which, because it conducted a nonpredatory foreign policy, was reluctant to use such weapons in support of its goals.

Unwilling (in the case of the United States) and unable (in the case of the Soviet Union) to use direct military force against each other, both sides were constrained to turn to amassing as much internal power as possible and to constructing a vast alliance system (in the case of the United States) or a centrally-directed empire (in the case of the Soviet Union) in order to add to their respective sides as much as possible of the gross global political-military power. Bipolarity was the order of the day in the late 1940s and early 1950s, and states which otherwise had little or no interest in the Soviet-American conflict often had to choose one or the other side. The United States in particular felt it imperative to draw as many states into its own orbit as possible, mostly for geopolitical reasons. With Russia occupying such a large portion of the Eurasian land mass and with Europe, the cradle of Western civilization, so visibly threatened by Russian armies, Washington felt it necessary to begin a long effort to fashion a world *cordon sanitaire* around the new Soviet orbit. The result was NATO, CENTO, SEATO, and a host of bilateral treaties of guarantee in Asia. Later, the Russians responded with the Warsaw Pact and embarked on a series of blandishments to new nations in (what is now called) the Third World as a means of leapfrogging the American-centered system. It should be emphasized that zero-sum competition was largely forced on a reluctant America by a Soviet Union directed by a xenophobic totalitarian dictator who saw the world, at home and abroad, in Marxist-Leninist (i.e. Machiavellian) terms and thus was primed to treat the United States, the principal postwar capitalist state, as the Kremlin's principal enemy with whom no long-term compromise was possible.

The United States, if anything, was a reluctant superpower. That title and the responsibility that it entailed were accepted only out of necessity. America preferred to devote itself to perfecting its domestic order, one proof of which was the enormous speed with which it unilaterally disarmed itself after the war. It also tried to withdraw from areas, particularly in Asia, where it had found itself accidentally as a result of the war (Korea), where it once had a colonial relationship (the Philippines), or where it had chosen sides in a domestic conflict and had backed the loser (China). It was the result of the latter conflict—the coming to power of the Chinese Communist Party in 1949—that led to the formation of the strategic triangle. Mao Zedong and his associates deliberately associated themselves with Moscow, for ideological and security reasons, in a threatening anti-American alliance in early 1950. Such was the enormous potential of that combination (bringing into view the MacKinder fear of the direction of practically all Eurasian resources by one central authority) that the

United States, Western Europe, and Japan all took fright and banded together. Thus, when Stalin and Kim Il Sung perpetrated the Korean War, it instantly became an East-West contest and a test of the survival of the American-sponsored United Nations collective security system.

The Korean War had several outcomes of significance to the future configuration of the strategic triangle. First, above all other Soviet-sponsored actions (the Berlin Blockade, the communist insurgency in Greece, the overthrow of popular governments in East Europe and similar attempts in West Europe, and civil war in Vietnam and Malaya), the War demonstrated that America could no longer deal with the outer world on its own semi-isolationist terms. Second, the war so poisoned Sino-American relations (the American decision to defend Taiwan came as a result of the North Korean attack, and the direct Sino-American conflict cost each country dearly at the hands of the other) that little thought could be given to reconciliation, to say nothing of approaching Moscow with a common program, until many years had past. Third, the war drove Beijing and Moscow into each other's arms and at least the Chinese did not like what they perceived from such a close embrace. The seed of the Sino-Soviet dispute were thus sown during the Korean War. The immediate outcome, however, was a severe distortion of the triangle into a highly obtuse form, with the Russians and the Chinese clustered at one end and the Americans at the far corner, in which shape it was destined to remain until the late 1950s.

Formed in blood, misunderstanding, insecurity, and ideological opposition, the strategic triangle modified its form only slowly. Four processes were at work: the evolution of internal events in the Soviet Union; tests of strength between the United States and the Soviet Union; modification of the too-close relationship between Moscow and Beijing; and a search by Washington and Moscow for friends, allies, and clients outside the triangle. In the Soviet Union, the death of Stalin gradually unfroze the society, causing Moscow to take a somewhat less severe view of the West. Khrushchev soon was making trips to the Third World, formulating plans for economic reform, and initiating peace with the United States in Korea and Vietnam. The results were mixed: withdrawal of Soviet forces from Austria in 1955 and political relaxation in East Europe was followed by the brutal Soviet suppression of the Hungarian revolutionaries in late 1956. The most important ray of hope for Soviet-American relations was Khrushchev's denunciation of Stalin and his declaration that, in the nuclear era, wars are—contrary to what his communist predecessors had averred—no longer "fatalistically inevitable." That small crack in the door

led, in a few years' time, to the first American-Soviet arms control
agreements and, in the 1960s after the Cuban missile crisis, to a measure of
East-West detente.

The Khrushchevian initiative did, to be sure, make it plain that
competition with the United States would continue in most arenas,
including the military, and that the war of position would merely be
replaced by one of mobility. Thus, the Kremlin arranged a number of tests
of strength with the United States during the period down through 1963: a
new series of threats over Berlin, the 1960 summit fiasco, a forward policy
in the Middle East, and the Cuban events themselves. The upshot, of
course, was the realization by Moscow that it was not yet strong enough to
confront America directly and win. After Cuba, therefore, the Soviet
Union set in place a three-pronged strategy: selective detente in economic
and political relations with Washington, continued competition in the
Third World in order to whittle away at American strength throughout the
globe; and initiation of a long term arms buildup (particularly in the
strategic nuclear area) as the assumed best way to overcome the perceived
American advantage in raw power.

If the distance within the triangle between America and Russia was still
great, albeit decreasing slightly, the political space between Russia and
China on balance grew between 1953 and the early 1960s, due to the
Sino-Soviet split. While some separation was inevitable and desirable,
given the inequitable tie between elder and younger communist brothers
under Stalin, the lengths to which the dispute were carried evidence a
deliberate decision by Mao Zedong to regain China's independence from
Moscow. There had in fact been an improvement in the early post-Stalin
years, as Khrushchev successfully mended fences in Beijing. But events in
China, together with Chinese misperceptions of the nature of the strategic
triangle, combined to push Russians and Chinese apart. In China, it
gradually became clear that the economy could not be developed strictly
according to the Soviet heavy industry first model and that Soviet
economic assistance, however generous it was in Russian eyes, would not
suffice to modernize China. Beijing therefore departed economically from
Moscow, a move symbolized by the Great Leap Forward of 1958-59. It also
distanced itself politically from the Kremlin by making known Chinese
displeasure at Khrushchev's treatment of the Stalin issue and by setting out
an increasingly fulsome catalogue of ideological differences. These were
magnified by the Chinese into foreign policy issues, mostly differences over
how to deal, within the alliance, with the United States. The Russians
counselled caution while the Chinese wished to move ahead to confront
America at every turn, as in the 1958 Taiwan Straits crisis.

Not wishing to have its foreign policy made in Beijing, and suspicious that Mao was more interested in using Soviet economic assistance to build up Chinese political-military independence, the Russians in 1959 ripped up the atom bomb agreement and in 1960 withdrew economic advisors from China, thus deciding to cut their losses in China, on the one hand, and to gird for a long ideological battle for supremacy within the international communist movement, on the other. By the early 1960s, this process of accusation and counter-accusation was quite advanced and the stage was already being set for the direct military clashes and threats that were to follow later in the decade. By the beginning of the Cultural Revolution, therefore, the distance between the two communist members of the triangle had grown precipitously. And since in the meantime there had been no change for the better in Sino-American relations (despite furtive efforts from time to time—but never simultaneously—by both sides), the triangle had greatly changed its shape from the highly distorted configuration of the early years to a more nearly equilateral form. It also became a triangle of mutual enmity with only the faintest potential, as yet, for transformation into one of mutual advantage and assistance or, alternatively, for a reversal of alignments from those of the 1950s.

The triangle did not retain that shape, geometrically or politically, for long. No less than four forces, inside and external to its boundaries, worked to change it radically. The first was modification of relations between the United States and the Soviet Union. The test of strength represented by the Missile Crisis was followed quickly by a deliberated decision in Moscow first to build up its own national strength over the long run to prevent a repetition of the 1962 debacle. It also led, after a time, to Khrushchev's ouster and a new conservatism in the Kremlin's policy, at home and abroad, destined to last 18 years. The foreign policy component was seeking "detente" with the United States, i.e., avoiding the overt and direct test of force with Washington until Moscow would be strong enough to win a second direct confrontation, while still helping along the presumedly inevitable course of history through support of revolutionary movements and catering to anti-American governments wherever they could be found. The United States, for its part, was glad enough for the respite from the Cold War and many convinced themselves that permanent peace with the Russians had finally arrived. The string of arms control measures signed during the 1960s and early 1970s were, of course, the external measure of the success of detente.

America needed detente for another reason, which was the second force operating on the triangle. That was its participation in, and later its enormous investment in, the Vietnam War. That conflict diverted American attention from the Soviet buildup, caused a heavy outflow of blood and material from the body politic, and led (along with the purely domestic evolution of the civil rights movement into violence and political standoff) to a perceptible weakening of the country at home and abroad. For a time, from perhaps 1966 through 1974, American foreign policy, and with it most of world politics, centered on Vietnam. The United States had two choices: (1) either it could increase its degree of involvement to whatever extent was necessary and see the matter through to a victorious end (this means in effect national mobilization); (2) or it might progressively decrease its level of intervention, build up as best it could a native South Vietnamese government and army, and extricate itself progressively from the conflict. For better or worse, America chose the latter (the choice was, in fact, forced upon the government by popular opinion, expressed in the streets and at the polls). For the strategic triangle, the Vietnam War held several consequences. It kept Soviet-American detente from proceeding to its full length, since Moscow was adjudged (accurately) to be back of the North Vietnamese and since the Kremlin felt less compelled to compromise with the White House. It stretched out the time span of the progressive separation of Moscow and Beijing, thereby postponing final divorce. And it similarly postponed Sino-American detente, which thus had to wait for acute crisis in Sino-Soviet relations.

The third force was the series of events in China culminating with the Cultural Revolution. The Cultural Revolution weakened China even more in terms of its power position within the triangle. For that reason, it should have caused Beijing to meliorate its opposition to Moscow or at least to step back from its policy of the early 1960s of a "plague on both your houses" toward Washington and Moscow. It did neither. Instead, Mao decided the best attitude was to ignore the superpowers, to pretend that the universal spread of his own ideology would eventually transform world politics, and in the meanwhile to withdraw from active participation in normal diplomatic intercourse. For four years, therefore, China effectively excluded itself from the triangle. (It was that withdrawal, together with the harm the Cultural Revolution had caused China, that later caused some American decision-makers erroneously to conclude that China did not count and that the triangle did not in fact exist, even though it was at that very time, the early 1970s, that China had not only re-entered triangular politics but was working hard to secure the famous rapproachment with the United States, thus fundamentally recasting its shape.) Finally, the Cultural Revolution by 1969 had proceeded far enough that the leadership in Beijing felt it permissible (or imperative) to attack the Soviet Union directly with military force. That was done at Damansky Island early in the year, and that act, together with the Soviet military over-reaction, guaranteed that the triangle would quickly take on a very different shape.

The fourth force reconfiguring the triangle was a series of long-term developments outside Sino-Soviet-American relations. Other regions and states, hitherto areas where members of the triangle could play out their rivalries or reserve zones exclusively for themselves, now took on attributes of power and independence sufficient to make it progressively more complicated for the three to dominate them or to use their territories for intra-triangular purposes. Japan and Western Europe recovered from the war and became economic giants. NATO politics shifted to a balance between North America and Western Europe. Some East European states gradually slipped out from under complete Soviet domination despite the Russian invasion of Czechoslovakia of 1968. New middle powers began to appear: India, Brazil, Israel, and Iran. Wholesale decolonization occurred in the 1960s and was essentially complete by the middle 1970s. The multiplicity of new states thus created chose, for the most part, to stay away from triangular politics, although the concomitant "neutral and nonaligned movement" often was hardly that. Regional conflicts were usually the product of local rivalries rather than the politics of the strategic triangle, and its members were more likely to be drawn into such situations against their wills than to use them as the occasions for playing out their own struggle for influence. The principal examples of this trend were the Arab-Israeli and intra-Arab conflicts from 1967 to 1974. The United Nations and its associate specialized agencies came ever less under the domination of the triangle (China was not even a member until 1972 although the question of its membership was always a central issue) and evermore under the disparate leadership of the "Group of 77"—the underdeveloped and hence weak ex-colonies. There arose a set of international problems, the so-called global issues (pollution, population control, and the like) that by definition were supranational in scope and beyond the power of the strategic triangle to solve or even to use as means to conduct intratriangular affairs. Finally, trade among nonsocialist nations grew so rapidly that a high percentage of international activity took place in this sphere rather than in the political arena dominated by the strategic triangle.

The effect of these four forces—detente, Vietnam, the Cultural Revolution, and extra-triangular growth—was to change the shape of the triangle a bit over the short run and to set the stage for the major changes that came in the middle 1970s and beyond. Detente and Vietnam more or less offset each other in terms of the political distance between the United States and the Soviet Union. The former drew the superpowers together while the latter kept them apart, with the consequence that the American-Soviet leg remained much as it had been. The Cultural Revolution and Vietnam pushed Beijing and Moscow even farther away from each other and also served to keep China at arm's length from America. The emergence of extratriangular forces hemmed the triangle in with increasing restrictions on the scope of its activity. These, however, were not to achieve their full effect until later. The triangle thus attained a degree of equilibrium during this period, but it was an unstable equilibrium and, thus, was susceptible to the shocking force of otherwise small actions, inside and outside its boundaries. It was a system on the verge of major change, and the catalysts were soon to come.

The impetus within the triangle was the Chinese attack on Soviet border outposts in early 1969 and the Soviet diplomatic and military reaction that followed. By coercing Beijing into talks on the subject later that year and engaging in a massive and rapid buildup of its own forces arrayed against China over the succeeding three years, Moscow badly frightened the Chinese, causing them to shift the direction and pace of the Cultural Revolution and to begin meliorating their conflict with the United States. It was this latter process, which was reciprocated over the same period by the United States, that led to the transformation of the triangle from within by the middle of the 1970s. The story of the Sino-American reconciliation, from the Nixon *Foreign Affairs* article in early 1969 to the final establishment of diplomatic relations in 1979, has been oft-told. The point for our analysis is that enough momentum had been attained by 1971, the year of peak Soviet danger, that the secret Kissinger trip, so astonishing at the time, seems in retrospect to have been the inevitable result of the Soviet threat and the need by both China and the United States to respond to it. Momentum was continued, to be sure, by the American search for a way out of Vietnam, by the still-persistent ravages of the Cultural Revolution, and by the general instability of the international economic system stemming from the shocks of 1972 and 1974 noted below. But the establishment of a strong working relationship with the United States was a reality by 1974, symbolized by the organization of Liaison Offices in each other's capitals that year.[14]

The impulse from outside the triangle came largely from the economic sphere. The United States went off the modified gold standard in 1972, thus spelling the end of the Bretton Woods system that had been a principal reason for the success of post-war trade expansion. Nothing took its place immediately except short term *ad hoc* arrangements. The more important economic change came in 1974 with the OPEC embargo following the Arab-Israeli conflict in October. That definitively destabilized the entire international economy. Maldistribution of the international product followed, as did a severe world recession combined with inflation of a very high order. A shift in the balance of forces outside the strategic triangle occurred, as the United States and its associates in Western Europe and Asia struggled to maintain their economies and their previous degree of international influence. Petrodollar recycling led to the felt necessity to sell large amounts of arms to Middle Eastern countries, while the huge transfer of wealth to OPEC laid the foundation for the international debt crisis of the early 1980s.[15]

The United States was, of course, the most severely affected member of the strategic triangle. Its economy was weakened, its foreign policy necessitated restructuring, and its capability to lead the Western Alliance and to compete directly with the Soviet Union was considerably eroded. The Soviet Union was affected less economically, since it was self-sufficient in oil, but did not escape damage, mostly from the effects of high international inflation. Moreover, its influence in the Middle East, Africa, and South Asia did not increase, since an increasing percentage of international transactions took place in the economic sphere, where Moscow could compete least effectively. It could, and did, concentrate on its own arms production and thus further tip the military balance in its favor. But much of the augmented power was unusable, since nuclear weapons are useable only in nuclear war, which did not (and was not likely to) occur. The Russians could sell and give away much conventional military equipment around the world, and they could take advantage of American weakness and diverted attention to invade Afghanistan in 1979.[16] But the reduction of Soviet foreign policy to the military component also prompted many other nations to band together out of fright at the Soviet threat. China was one of these, which was driven more and more into the waiting arms of the Americans. And although Beijing was also not dependent on OPEC oil and stood to benefit in the long run from very high oil prices (if only it could find enough of that material of its own to export and thus finance imports for modernization), world inflation and recession negatively affected China perhaps as much as the United States, and just when post-Maoist development was beginning.

These two sets of new and strong forces, inside and outside the triangle, imparted an unprecedented degree of dynamism to the relations among the three. Soviet-American detente ended with Afghanistan and the failure of SALT II in the Senate. A new era of direct competition opened even before the Reagan election of 1980 and was given added push by the Olympic boycott, the American decision to rearm in order to re-establish a military balance, the KAL 007 incident (the Korean Airlines passenger plane that was shot down by the Soviet Union on 1 September 1983, killing all aboard), Soviet expansionist involvement in Southeast Asia and Central America, and continued competition for influence in the Middle East and the Persian Gulf. China felt it necessary to move very far over to the American end of the Moscow-Washington spectrum and to oppose the Kremlin at every turn. China also turned outward in terms of the degree of foreign influence it was willing to accept as a price for Western investment in the Four Modernizations, and undertook major reforms within its own society and economy. By the early 1980s, a radical transformation of China (the fourth, it should be noted, in thirty years) was well under way.[17] And although Beijing felt uncomfortable with too close a relationship with Washington, and also downgraded the immediacy of Soviet attack—thus causing Chinese foreign policy to attempt over the long run to balance between the superpowers—there continued a strong pro-American tilt in the Chinese capital. Needless to say, this was heartily reciprocated by the United States, which saw the opportunity to wean China once and for all of Soviet influence, to help shape the direction and the details of the new Chinese revolution, and to draw that country out into the modern, interdependent world from where it could never again withdraw and where it would have to become, at last, a responsible member of the international community. Thus, from the approximately equilateral shape of the 1965-1975 decade, the post-1976 period saw the triangle transmuted once again, this time into a severly isosceles form. China and the United States were reasonably close and each were equally distant from the Soviet Union.

I say that this was a dynamic set of relations among the three for reason that, not only was there nothing permanent in the forces causing the foreign policies of the three states to operate as they did, but also that new forces, inside and outside the triangle, were beginning to rise up and push it once again into some other shape. Within the Soviet Union, for instance, problems were accumulating that would have to be addressed directly instead of, as in the past, being ignored or pretending to be solved. These included political and generational succession within the Soviet Communist Party; coming to a head of the multiplicity of economic, technological, and managerial problems at the base of the Soviet inability to keep up with the West; an ideological crisis stemming from the declining belief in Marxism-Leninism by most Soviet citizens and the concomitant rise of religion; the Moslem nationality problem; and the progressively more serious lag behind East Europe and China in terms of societal and economic dynamism and ideological risk-taking. The cumulative effect of these separate, deliterious trends in the long run would be to cause the

Kremlin to turn its attention more and more inward, to say the least, and perhaps even to bring it to the edge of rebellion or, at the extreme, revolution. While things Soviet happen only slowly, the net influence of such trends was already apparent in the early 1980s: lack of confidence within the Kremlin, soul-searching throughout the society, and a greater degree of caution in foreign policy than would otherwise be necessary, given the enormous Soviet military machine. The upshot was that the Soviet Union's actions within the triangle turned hesitant and somewhat more cautious than normal, if not altogether relaxed, a syndrome characteristic of a regime unsure of itself, one that was playing for time, perhaps even muddling through the next several years.[18]

In China, things were quite a bit different. That country seemed finally to have shaken off Maoist negativism and to have embraced at last the gospel of modernization. Pragmatism ruled and Marxism-Leninism was redefined to include whatever was thought necessary to achieve rapid economic growth. Growth rates shot up (especially in the rural sector), attitudes and practices quickly departed from Maoist narrowness, the country opened itself to a large measure of foreign influence, and in general exhibited a positive and optimistic dynamism that exceeded by far the levels of the Cultural Revolution, the Great Leap Forward, and the original 1949 Revolution. Self-confidence and movement also infected Chinese foreign policy, as these qualities seemingly made up for much of the shortfall in raw national power as compared with America and Russia. Beijing thus dared to let in considerable American social influence along with massive amounts of Western technology and know-how, compromised severely on the Taiwan issue, and became an active participant in many of the international institutions and the global issues that it had hitherto shunned and deprecated. One might almost say that Chinese policy had been normalized were it not for past experience, which indicates that Chinese foreign policy, dependent mostly on the state of internal developments and on Beijing's role in the strategic triangle, was nearly always in motion. That would at least give pause to predictions that China would forever remain open to American influence and continuously keep out the Russians. Indeed, as the country gained confidence internationally on the basis of domestic success, there was already a movement, if not away from the United States, then surely still toward the Soviet Union in an effort to settle some disputes on their merits and to encourage renewed Soviet economic investment in China. China no longer claimed that it could, at its own discretion, stand outside the strategic triangle and no longer advocated a universal alliance against the Soviet Union. Instead, now it professed interest in achieving a rough balance in its relations with Washington and Moscow (albeit with a tilt, for insurance, toward Washington), and thus in improving ties with the Russians.[19]

As for the United States, dynamism was also the order of the day, internally and in foreign policy. At home, there seemed to be a new spirit of patriotism and optimism, as success (however superficial and at a large cost in human suffering) was achieved in controlling inflation, revamping industry, and increasing the rate of economic growth. An elderly and very conservative, if personally popular, President was re-elected for a second term in a landslide (although not necessarily a mandate), a novelty in American history. The United States undertook a massive rearmament program aimed at re-establishing balance in most defense sectors with the Soviet Union, and spent much diplomatic energy refurbishing its alliance structure. It also took the offensive in the international economic arena, for better or worse, in trying to limit domestic industry-destroying imports, financing the federal deficit through foreign borrowings, and averting a debt repayments collapse that, were it to occur, could spell disaster for many countries. America deliberately took a hard line toward Russia, particularily in the arms control talks, and deliberately professed friendship for China and spoke approvingly of the new, liberal, turn in Chinese domestic policy. The idea was to isolate Moscow within and outside the triangle, to construct a solid, hopefully longlasting relationship with Beijing, and thus leave Washington reasonably free to deal with other issues (Nicaragua, the Middle East, North-South questions, and trade issues, among others) reasonably free from the encumberances of the strategic triangle.[20]

Armed thusly with some notion of the operational characteristics of the triangle and also with an indication of how it has evolved during the past three decades and more of its existence, we are in a reasonable position to essay on its further development. In general, forces operating on the triangle are either internal or external to it. In terms of the former, it seems likely, with one important exception, that the four operational characteristics of the triangle noted previously will continue in effect. The triangle will still be dominated by the American-Soviet relationship, for the most part one of near total opposition and stasis. Dynamism will continue to be supplied by China, since it will still be relatively less powerful than the other two and since its domestic order tends to vary more than those of the United States or the Soviet Union. The triangle will continue to be a primative balance of power system, with all that that implies. And its operations will still be much dependent on what happens inside the domestic boundaries, and the respective spheres of influence, of America, China, and Russia. The exception that may modify, if not overthrow, the system that eventuates from the joint operation of these four characteristics is the growth in the relative power of China. *If* Beijing were to be able to maintain its early 1980s course of rapid modernization at home and a foreign policy of positiveness, openness, and a non-threatening posture toward its neighbors, and *if* neither superpower becomes so concerned about the raw increase in Chinese power as to take prophylactic action, the triangle could be transformed internally. It would revert to an approximately equilateral form, this time, however, of a mutually restrained and less tension-laden character. Such a triangle could well achieve a degree of stability unknown during its history so long as none of the three attempted to overcome the others and so long as equilibrating balance of power mechanisms were available outside the triangle to serve as means to adjust to the growth in relative Chinese power.

The chances of such a felicitous outcome, while not low, are still dubious enough to not assign too much hope in its occurrence. The reason (putting aside for a moment evaluation whether China will stay on its present course and whether Washington and Moscow will tolerate enormous growth in Chinese power without taking counteraction) is that Chinese foreign policy would, under the postulated circumstances, become expansionist in character. China is no more immune to the laws of international politics than are other states, and one of the principal regularities is that a nation's interests, and therefore its policies, vary with the relative degree of power at its disposal. China has claimed that it will never become a superpower in the sense of becoming imperialist. If it does attain its goal of enormous increases in gross power by the end of the century, however, it cannot help but look for ways to exercise that power. If Chinese gains come at the expense of the United States and the Soviet Union (i.e., in terms of relative power within the triangle), Beijing may move against one or the other first in Asia and then farther afield. If, as is more likely, Washington and Moscow counter such Chinese moves, Beijing may try to find outlets for its power outside the triangle, again principally in Asia (e.g., Taiwan and Southeast Asia) but also at greater distances from its border (most likely, the Middle East, by deploying a global sea-based nuclear missile force, and by providing itself with a blue-water navy and a concomitant land projection force.[21]

Here we encounter an interesting prospect. Would Washington and Moscow, in the name of intratriangular peace, allow (or even encourage) Beijing to exercise its newly developed power in areas outside the triangle proper? A strict balance of power analysis might answer positively. But that is hardly likely to take place because of the very nature of superpower policies: any situation in any region of the globe is of concern to them merely because each must demonstrate its all-encompassing reach. If China, the only third potential superpower, attempts to upset the status quo in some region (say Southeast Asia), where both Washington and Moscow already have heavy policy investments, it is unlikely that either will look with equanimity on Chinese power expansionist tendencies. They would move (undoubtedly separately) to limit the degree of enhanced Chinese influence or—an intriguing possibility—to insist on compensations of their own. In either instance, the result for the local states in question would not be palatable: they would have to accept increasing involvement of one or another member of the triangle or even the prospect of becoming a client to one of them. Divide and rule is, after all, a standard balance of power practice.

Of course, a China that appeared increasingly threatening, even indirectly, to either or both the superpowers would undoubtedly encounter more direct opposition. The United States, having invested so heavily in Chinese development, would at least possess the means to injure China by withdrawing its educational, economic, technological, and military assistance. It is also possible, on the other hand, that Washington would attempt to use its influence in Beijing to modulate or redirect China's power drive away from American interests and allies in Asia and beyond. Whether Moscow could do the same would depend on what instruments of policy then in the Kremlin's hands and its willingness to use them. If, as in the past, they were merely military, the Soviet Union would be left with an all-or-nothing choice, i.e., war or peace. Since Sino-Soviet war is highly unlikely under any circumstance, much less with a very powerful China, Moscow might have no choice but to acquiesce in greatly enhanced Chinese influence. In any event, an increasingly pugnacious China would (presuming Soviet-American relations and domestic trends in the United States and the Soviet Union remained as they are presently perceived) re-cycle the triangle back to its early 1960s form: an all-against-all system but with the significant difference that the relative power of the three would be more nearly equal than before so that intratriangular maneuverability would, correspondingly, decline. The obvious corollary is that all three members would seek to do battle against each of the others increasingly by resort to projecting influence into, and involving themselves in, areas and situations where the power of only one or two members now extends. The politics of the triangle would thus effectively be globalized and a great change, if not a transformation, would come over world politics as a whole.[22]

That analysis, however, leaves out two important factors, both of which militate in the opposite direction. The first is that it cannot be assumed that China will continue on its internal course of economic modernization *Uber alles* indefinitely. Twice before, post-1949 China has departed from what appeared a reasonable path to all-around modernization. There is no reason to believe that there will not be an enormous struggle within the Chinese Communist Party over the long term efficacy of the post-1976 reforms instigated by Deng Xiaoping (Teng Hsiao-P'eng). That appears all the more likely because the very essence of Party rule—the verities of Marxism-Leninism—has recently been subject to questioning by the Deng-led faction. And since political authority in Beijing depends very much on the personality of the top leader, Deng, since Deng will not live much longer, and since his putative successors are by no means firm in their positions, the likelihood of not merely a power struggle but of a halt to, if not a total reversal of, the pragmatic policies associated with Deng is relatively high. It cannot even be assumed that out-and-out military struggle will not take place in China. And since the United States and the Soviet Union will undoubtedly maintain their respective forward momentum in terms of power augmentation, China could once again find itself forced to adopt extreme foreign policy measures within the triangle (i.e., gyrate between Washington and Moscow as the only means to attain security) and postpone its dreams of intra-triangular equality and global influence.

The second is perhaps more important, as it is certain to occur and because it will affect not merely China but the United States and the Soviet Union as well. That is the growth in power of states and regions external to the triangle to such an extent as to modify severely the hitherto relatively impervious boundaries of the triangle. If allowed to continue unfettered, no longer would intratriangular events take place without being influenced, directly and importantly, by what goes on outside the triangle, and no longer would what transpires between America, China, and Russia configure the nature and outcomes of trends and situations in the rest of the world in measure equal to, or dominant over, the forces behind those trends and situations themselves. Japan and Western Europe are already partially outside the principal influence of the politics of the triangle in several areas, particularly those dealing with economic issues. India and Brazil are sure to continue their respective drives to become major powers. Medium powers will also exert their self-appointed perogative to exclusivity within their own regions or over ever-greater portions of their own foreign relations. These include South Korea and Vietnam in Asia, Egypt and Iran in the Middle East, perhaps Nigeria in Africa, and Mexico and Argentina in Latin America. This trend may even extend to the provision of greater degrees of autonomy within the Soviet sphere to some East European states, principally East Germany and Poland. Regional politics would thus take on a more exclusivist flavor, with the costs of strategic triangular intervention and/or participation rising faster than the capability of the triangle's members to do so. If such a trend were to continue, not only would the triangle and its politics eventually become an increasingly small factor outside its bounds but what happens between the three would itself be subject to increasingly strong external forces. Ultimately, the triangle would cease to exist as the center of international politics, to be replaced by a much more open, multipolar system exhibiting all the complexities that such systems have always possessed.

Such an eventuality does not spell the demise of the strategic triangle in the short to medium term, i.e., surely not for the years before 2000. And even after that time, some matters—questions of nuclear conflict and its avoidance being the principal one—will remain the principal concern of its three members. But, more and more, fourth, fifth, and even higher numbers of states will share increasingly in how central global political decisions are made. As the exclusivity of the triangle declines, in relative terms, with regard to an ever-larger range of issues, first Japan and West Europe, then other states will be drawn into triangular concerns, in the beginning on an *ad hoc* basis and then more regularly. The mechanism will probably be the need of one or more triangle member for augmentation of its own power on some issue or in a crisis, and thus the appeal for support to states or regional groupings outside the triangle. Such support will probably be given but at a price, in terms of autonomy or trade-off on some other issue in contention. It is true that, in some matters, a good measure of bipolarity between the United States and the Soviet Union will remain. And were Moscow to become too threatening in its military ambitions, it is possible that a grand alliance of America and China and their respective allies would be necessary. Overall, however, the tendency will be to replace the dangers of the often zero-sum operations of the triangle with the more liberal *modus operandi* of a global balance of power system of a more benign sort.

The trick is to move from the one system to the other with surety and care, avoiding too rapid a transition (which could lead to systemic breakdown and danger of war) while at the same time, at least so far as the

United States *and* its global associates are concerned, to deliberately move the process along as something in their best interests. Further study should, perhaps, center on how best to accomplish that transition.

Notes

1. The literature on this subject is large. Some of the better-known contributions are: Michel Tatu, *The Great Power Triangle: Washington-Moscow-Peking* (Paris: Atlantic Institute, 1970); William E. Griffith (ed.), *The World and the Great Power Triangle* (Cambridge, MA: M.I.T. Press, 1975); Gerald Segal, *The Great Power Triangle* (New York: St. Martin's Press, 1972); Raju G.C. Thomas (ed.), *The Great-Power Triangle and Asian Security* (Lexington, MA: D.C. Heath, 1983); and Lowell Dittmer, "The Strategic Triangle: An Elementary Game-Theoretic Analysis", *World Politics*, July 1981, pp. 485-516. See also the author's "Detente and the Sino-Soviet-U.S. Triangle", in Della Sheldon (ed.), *Dimensions of Detente* (New York: Praeger, 1978), pp. 50-83.

2. This was the basis of American policy toward China during the 1950s and 1960s, and one of the reasons for not recognizing Beijing diplomatically. See, *inter alia*, Foster Rhea Dulles, *American Foreign Policy Toward Communist China, 1949-1969* (New York: Crowell, 1972); Robert Blum, *The United States and China in World Affairs* (New York: McGraw-Hill, 1966), and Roderick MacFarquhar (ed.), *Sino-American Relations, 1949-71* (New York: Praeger, 1972).

3. O.B. Borisov and B.T. Koloskov (pseudonyms for M. Kapitsa and V. Rakhmanin), *Soviet-Chinese Relations, 1945-1975* (Bloomington, IN: University of Indiana Press, 1976).

4. A. Doak Barnett, *Communist China and Asia* (New York: Knopf, 1960); Alexander Dallin (ed.), *Diversity in International Communism, A Documentary Record, 1961-1963* (New York: Columbia University Press, 1963); Charles Neuhauser, *Third World Politics: China and the Afro-Asian People's Solidarity Organization, 1957-1967* (Cambridge, MA: Harvard University Press, 1968); and Lillian Craig Harris, *China's Foreign Policy Toward the Third World* (New York: Praeger, 1985).

5. Joan Edelman Spero, *The Politics of International Economic Relations* (New York: St. Martin's Press, 3rd ed., 1985). See the extensive bibliography contained therein.

6. See, in a surprisingly small literature, Louis J. Cantori and Steven L. Spiegel, *The International Politics of Regions* (Englewood Cliffs, N.J., 1970).

7. Harold K. Jacobson, *Networks of Interdependence* (New York: Knopf, 1979); Robert O. Keohane and Joseph S. Nye, Jr. (eds.), *Transnational Internation-*

al Relations and World Politics (Cambridge, MA: Harvard University Press, 1973); Dennis Pirages, *The New Context for International Relations: Global Ecopolitics* (North Scituate, MA: Duxbury Press, 1978); Richard W. Sterling, *Macropolitics* (New York: Knopf, 1974).

8. Adam Ulam, *The Rivals: America and Russia Since World War II* (New York: Viking, 1971), and his *Dangerous Relations: The Soviet Union in World Politics* (New York: Oxford University Press, 1983).

9. Richard A. Melanson (ed.), *Neither Cold War Nor Detente: Soviet-American Relations in the 1980s* (Charlottesville, VA: University of Virginia Press, 1983).

10. Thomas W. Robinson, "Political and Strategic Aspects of Chinese Foreign Policy", in Donald C. Hellmann (ed.), *China and Japan: A New Balance of Power* (Lexington, MA: D.C. Heath, 1976); "Restructuring Chinese Foreign Policy", in Kal J. Holsti (ed.), *Why Nations Realign: Foreign Policy Restructuring in the Postwar World* (London: Allen and Unwin, 1982), pp. 134-171, and "China's New Dynamism in the Strategic Triangle", *Current History*, September, 1983, pp. 241ff.

11. See, in a very large literature, Martin Wight (Hedley Bull and Carsten Holbraad, eds.), *Power Politics* (London: Holmes and Meier, 1978); E.H. Carr, *The Twenty Years' Crisis, 1919-1939* (London: MacMillan, 1956); Inis J. Claude, *Power and World Politics* (New York: Random House, 1966); and Dina A. Zinnes, "Coalition Theories and the Balance of Power", in Sven Groennings et al. eds., *The Study of Coalition Behavior* (New York: Holt, Rinehart, and Winston, 1970), for exposition.

12. Take, for instance, three representative samples: India, Israel, and Great Britain. The direction of Indian foreign policy has been set by the configuration of power between America, China, and Russia. During the 1950s, it was Washington and Beijing that most influenced New Dehli; in the 1960s and 1970s, it was Beijing and Moscow; and during the 1980s, it was Washington and Moscow. Israel's policy was a function of its regional security environment, and swung from attention to Cairo to Damascus and back, depending on whence the threat eminated. It was also determined by comparative Soviet success in penetrating the Middle East and Israel's success in penetrating the American in influencing the American foreign policy establishment. England, once a superpower, had shrunk by the 1970s to a regional power, where its security was determined by the American-Soviet nuclear balance and by the conventional balance on the Central Front, either of which London controlled. And its economy was largely structured by external forces, such as Common Market politics, world financial conditions, and the rates of growth of American and Asian economies. Only North Sea oil enabled England to avoid even greater dependence.

13. The following depends, in general, on: John Lucacs, *A New History of the Cold War* (New York: Anchor Books, 1966); Paul Y. Hammond, *The Cold War Years: American Foreign Policy Since 1945* (New York: Harcourt, Brace,

Jovanovich, 1969 and subsequent editions); Andre Fontaine, *History of the Cold War* (New York: Pantheon, 1969); George Liska, *Russia and the Road to Appeasement: Cycles of East-West Conflict in War and Peace* (Baltimore: Johns Hopkins University Press, 1982); Michael Mandelbaum, *The Nuclear Revolution: International Politics Before and After Hiroshima* (New York: Cambridge University Press, 1981); Mohammed Ayoob, *Conflict and Intervention in the Third World* (New York: St. Martin's Press, 1980); Carsten Holbraad, *Superpowers and International Conflict* (New York: St. Martin's Press, 1979); Strobe Talbott, *Endgame: The Inside Story of SALT II* (New York: Harper, 1979); Barry Blechman and Stephen S. Kaplan, *Force Without War: U.S. Armed Forces as a Political Instrument* (Washington: The Brookings Institution, 1978); Stephen S. Kaplan, *Diplomacy of Power: Soviet Armed Forces as a Political Instrument* (Washington: The Brookings Institution, 1981); A. Doak Barnett, *China and the Major Powers in East Asia* (Washington D.C.: The Brookings Institution, 1977); Robert W. Tucker, *The Inequality of Nations* (New York: Basic Books, 1977); Stanley Karnow, *Vietnam: A History* (New York: Viking, 1983); Henry Kissinger, *White House Years* and *Years of Upheaval* (Boston: Little-Brown, 1982 and 1983); and John Lewis Gaddis, *Strategies of Containment* (New York: Oxford University Press, 1982.)

14. Michael Oksenberg, "A Decade of Sino-American Relations", *Foreign Affairs*, Fall 1982, pp. 175-195.

15. C. Fred Bergsten and John Williamson, *The Multiple Reserve Currency System* (Cambridge, MA: M.I.T. Press, 1983); Ralph C. Bryant, *Money and Monetary Policy in Interdependent Nations* (Washington D.C.: The Brookings Institution, 1980); Richard Dale, with Richard P. Mattione, *Managing Global Debt* (Washington D.C.: The Brookings Institution, 1983); Christopher Kojm (ed.), *The Problem of International Debt* (New York: H.W. Wilson, 1984); Henry C. Wallich *et al*, *World Money and National Policies* (New York: Group of Thirty, 1983); Hollis B. Chenery, "Restructuring the World Economy: Round II", *Foreign Affairs*, Summer 1981, pp. 1102-1121; Øystein Noreng, *Oil Politics in the 1980s: Patterns of International Cooperation* (New York: McGraw-Hill, 1978); Joan Pearce (ed.), *The Third Oil Shock: The Effects of Lower Oil Prices* (London: Royal Institute of International Affairs, 1983); Robert Stobaugh and Daniel Yergin, *Energy Future: Report of the Harvard Business School Energy Project* (New York: Random House, 1979).

16. Henry Bradsher, *Afghanistan and the Soviet Union* (Durham, N.C.: Duke University Press, 1983).

17. Peter R. Moody, Jr., *Chinese Politics After Mao: Development and Liberalization, 1976 to 1983* (New York: Praeger, 1983); Stuart R. Schram, "Economics in Command? Ideology and Policy Since the Third Plenum", *The China Quarterly*, September 1984, pp. 417-461; Immanuel C.Y. Hsü, *China Without Mao: The Search for a New Order* (New York: Oxford University Press, 1982); Dorothy J. Solinger, "The Fifth National People's Congress and the

Process of Policymaking: Reform, Readjustment, and the Opposition", *Issues and Studies*, August 1982, pp. 63-106; Richard D. Nethercut, "Leadership in China: Rivalry, Reform, and Renewal", *Problems of Communism*, March-April 1983, pp. 30-46; Parris H. Chang, "Chinese Politics: Deng's Turbulent Quest", *Problems of Communism*, January-February 1981, pp. 1-21; and Kenneth Lieberthal, "China's Political Reforms: A Net Assessment", *The Annals*, November 1984, pp. 19-33.

18. Erik Hoffman (ed.), *The Soviet Union in the 1980s, Proceedings of the Academy of Political Science*, 1984, No. 3; Archie Brown and Michael Kaser (eds.), *Soviet Policy for the 1980s* (Bloomington: Indiana University Press, 1982); Robert F. Byrnes (ed.), *After Brezhnev: Sources of Soviet Conduct in the 1980s* (Bloomington: Indiana University Press, 1983).

19. James C. Hsiung (ed.), *U.S.-Asian Relations* (New York: Praeger, 1983); Jonathan D. Pollack, *The Sino-Soviet Rivalry and China's Security Debate* (Santa Monica, CA: The Rand Corporation, 1982); Samuel S. Kim (ed.) *China and the World: Chinese Foreign Policy in the Post-Maoist Era* (Boulder, CO: Westview Press, 1984); Harry Harding (ed.), *China's Foreign Relations in the 1980s* (New Haven, CT: Yale University Press, 1984); Thomas W. Robinson, "America and China in the New Asian Balance of Power", *Current History*, September 1985.

20. See the annual articles in "America and the World", *Foreign Affairs*, generally under the title "The Conduct of American Foreign Policy", 1979ff; Dennis L. Bork (ed.), *To Promote Peace: U.S. Foreign Policy in the Mid-1980s* (Stanford, CT: Hoover Press, 1984); Alexander M. Haig, Jr., *Caveat: Realism, Reagan, and Foreign Policy* (New York: MacMillan, 1984); Kenneth A. Oye *et al*, *Eagle Defiant: United States Foreign Policy in the 1980s* (Boston: Little-Brown, 1983); Kevin P. Phillips, *Post-Conservative America: People, Politics, and Ideology in a Time of Crisis* (New York: Random House, 1982).

21. See the author's recent elaboration of this theme (all forthcoming): "How Chinese Military Modernization Could Affect the Asian and Global Balances of Power"; "China as an Asian Pacific Power"; and "Should—And If So, How Can—The United States Influence Chinese Military Modernization?".

22. Students of international relations have not yet addressed this possibility. Most instead seem to think in terms of interdependence, political economy, transnationalism, or dependency. See, *inter alia*, Robert O. Keohane, *After Hegemony: Cooperation and Discord in the World Political Economy* (Princeton, N.J.: Princeton University Press, 1984); Robert O. Keohane and Joseph S. Nye, *Power and Interdependence: World Politics in Transition* (Boston: Little-Brown, 1977); and *International Studies Quarterly*, special issue on World Systems Debates, March 1981, with extensive bibliographies in the first and last of these.

The Strategic Triangle:

A Critical Review[1]

LOWELL DITTMER

From the time Richard Nixon announced his bold diplomatic opening to China in 1971, Sino-Soviet-American relations have been discussed in the language of "games."[2] The most common reference is to some sort of card game—the United States is "playing the China card," or China is "playing the American card" or the "Soviet card."[3] What do we mean when we discuss international relations in such terms? And does the "strategic triangle" qualify to be so discussed?

When international relations is referred to in the language of games this underlines two different features. First, a *fictive* quality is alluded to, a certain "boundedness." Specific aspects of international relations seem to have no immediate consequences in the "real" world, referring as they do only to contingencies—strategic nuclear deterrence, for example. A player may seem to be moving "tokens" around some sort of game board with the expectation that other players will respond appropriately without calling for actual performance of the action that is symbolically suggested—in which case the "game" illusion would of course be broken. Second, the language of games brings out the *conventional* aspects of international relations. Some aspects of international relations seem to have fairly clearly defined conventions—rules, stakes, contingencies—so that players may communicate implicitly with one another with some degree of accuracy, and plot their moves with provisional rationality.

By these criteria, I would argue, the "strategic triangle" qualifies as an international game—although both criteria must be qualified somewhat. It is "fictive" insofar as its "strategic" aspect is concerned because it is limited (or has hitherto been limited) to the shuffling of different prewar contingencies without actually engaging in full-scale warfare. On the other hand, the boundaries that set this fiction off from reality are permeable, in the sense that one or another pre-war coalition may give rise to diverse real-world ties (e.g., trade, cultural relations, military aid) with real-world implications. It is "conventional" in the sense that relations among the three players conform to a logic inherent in the fact that there are only three players engaged in the game, that the possible relations among them are finite, that these relations tend to become provisionally patterned into a limited number of structures or configurations, that each configuration has necessary implications for each position in that configuration. It should be clear that the "rules" that obtain are rules in the logical and not the normative sense—any player may break the rules, the only consequence being that calculable penalties must be paid.

The following paper consists of three parts. The first will reconsider the "rules of the game." The empirical basis for this reconsideration consists of the experience of the three participants in the triangle since it became explicitly recognized as such in 1971. The second section provides a broad overview of Sino-Soviet-American relations since World War II from a triangular perspective. The final section discusses recent American foreign policy in particular, attempting to adduce policy recommendations from the logic of the triangle.

Rules of the Game

There are two types of "rules of the game": the first are "rules of entry," the second are "rules of play." The first define who may compete in the game; the second denote which moves are possible, with what consequences, for what stakes.

Rules of entry may consist of either objective criteria as stipulated by the analyst, or of subjective criteria as defined by the participating players. Objective criteria refer either to the possession of various material assets, or to the successful performance of some functional role.

In terms of material assets, such as geographic and demographic resources, natural resource base, economic vitality, military strength, and scientific-technological capabilities, it has been (quite plausibly) argued that China does not qualify for inclusion in the game. Only the Soviet Union and the United States can fully qualify as "superpowers," and the structure of the international system is hence essentially bipolar.[4] In terms of the performance of a functional role, too, it has been argued that China cannot qualify. A superpower must by definition fulfill a "managerial" role in the world, which means that it must have the power to affect the foreign policy calculations of all other players in the game, in all international theaters. Again, only the Soviet Union and the United States have the international power-projective capability to play this role, it is argued.[5]

While cogent, each of these arguments might be controverted on its own terms. China is undeniably less economically developed than either the Soviet Union or the United States (although by the same token whether the Soviet Union deserves to rank with the U.S. might be questioned, for its economic output is only about 60 percent as large, according to CIA estimates). Much of its military weaponry is obsolescent. Yet in terms of simple mass, China has the largest army in the world and the third largest air force. If population is an asset (as it should be considered, in a "people's war" scenario), China is many times richer than either the U.S. or the USSR. Even in economic terms, although China has a per capita national income of only a few hundred dollars per year, in absolute terms it has the sixth largest economy in the world, and if the most recent growth trends continue will have the fourth largest by the end of this century. It is second in world grain output, third in strategic nuclear forces, space satellites, cotton, and raw coal output; fourth in steel and total commercial energy output, sixth the production of crude oil.

By functional criteria, China could be said to have more successfully qualified for a global role during the Mao Zedong era than today—not by dint of its global military projective capability, which was if anything even more limited than it is now, but through the power of its ideology, which inspired many Third World leaders and gravely concerned the leadership of the two "superpowers." Similarly, estimates of the Soviet Union as a major strategic actor certainly antedated its power-projective capabilities, which did not approach those of the United States until the 1960s (in strategic terms) or mid-1970s (in conventional military terms). In the post-Mao period China seems to have retreated to more strictly national concerns (including border issues and irridenta), but in view of Chinese diplomatic skills and continuing international ambitions, it is conceivable that it may again exert an international impact transcending its material resource base and power-projective capability in the future.

More compelling in my view than these "objective" considerations is the fact that the three "players" take one another to be engaged in a triangular "game." If the players themselves act on this assumption, who are we mere analysts to belie them?[6] "That which is perceived as real is real in its consequences," as W. I. Thomas once put it. Neither the Soviet Union nor the United States deals with China strictly in bilateral terms; for both powers, the importance of China depends on its relationship to the third power. Thus the Soviet Union devotes an estimated 25 percent of its military budget to the "China factor," fifty-two of its 184 divisions are along the Sino-Soviet (including the Outer Mongolian) border, and 135 of its 378 SS-20 IRBMs are based in the Far East, putatively with Chinese targets. The United States at one time considered installing an ABM defense to counter a prospective Chinese nuclear attack. Since the early 1970s the configuration of the triangle has led the U.S. to discount such threats and to think of China as a potential strategic asset against the Soviet Union; although American attempts to "play the China card" have certainly proved no panacea, the prospect of losing that "card" is still sufficiently disturbing for the U.S. to place higher value on Chinese "friendship" than that country's objective assets would otherwise warrant.

The methodological difficulty with such subjective criteria, it might be objected, is that they deal with perceptual or motivational factors in the minds of the actors that cannot be directly evaluated. How do we know what value each actor assigns to the participation of the other two, and why? To some extent this question is however susceptible to empirical treatment: the war planning literature of the three actors may be examined, to the extent that it is publicly available, and policy planners may even be interviewed. Barrett and Glaser, employing such techniques, found for example that Soviet war planners anticipate that a nuclear exchange between the two superpowers might be protracted, leaving the motherland devastated and hence highly vulnerable to Chinese intervention with conventional forces in the postnuclear phase.[7] It would not be realistic under such circumstances to bank on "swinging" large force contingents from one theater to another, and for the Soviet Union to deter China's conventional arms capabilities with nuclear weapons would prerequire a considerable list of targets. It is, to be sure, quite conceivable that such contingency planning may deal in vastly inflated, even "paranoid," estimates, which an "objective" analysis might tend to discount. National security planners may arrive at inflated estimates on the basis of prudential "worst case" assumptions, inadequate information, ideological biases or even stereotyped national images—but the history of arms races suggests that the fact that such estimates are inaccurate or even paranoid does not mean that they are not operational. In fact, the aim-inhibited, game-like quality of the competition allows players to proceed indefinitely on the basis of faulty assumptions. There is, no doubt fortunately, limited opportunity for "reality-testing" under conditions of nuclear deterrence.[8]

Thus, so far as the present analysis is concerned, a strategic triangle may be said to be operational if three conditions obtain: (1) All three players must demonstrate, via contingency planning and corresponding behavior, that *each takes into account the third player in managing its relationship with the second;* (2) If any player's political/military power is sufficient for its "defection" from one side to the other to *shift the strategic balance* (or for this presumption to be tenable), that player is a full participant in the game; (3) In order for such a shift in alignment to be plausible, none of the players may have stable and enduring alignments with any of the others. (Thus we do not consider the Soviet-American-European relationship to be "triangular," although the defection of Western Europe would certainly shift the strategic balance fundamentally, because we regard such a shift to have been precluded by formal alliance.) Based on these three conditions, the Soviet Union, the People's Republic of China, and the United States may still be considered participants in a strategic triangle. This is not necessarily to say that they are all superpowers or that they have equivalent resources or play comparable international roles—only that their relationships *with one another* are necessarily triangular.

The "rules of play" are, first, each player will prefer at a maximum to have positive relations with both other players, and at a minimum to avoid negative relations with both other players (i.e., to have positive relations with at least one other player.) Each player will try to prevent collusion between the other two players, under the apprehension that such collusion might be hostile. Abstractly considered, there are four possible configurations of triangular relationships. These are the *ménage à trois,* consisting of positive relationships among all three players without negative relationships; the "romantic triangle," consisting of positive relationships between one "pivot" player and two "wings" but negative relationships between the two wings; the "marriage," consisting of positive relationships between two "spouses" and negative relationships between each spouse and a third "pariah"; and a "unit-veto" triangle,[9] consisting of negative relations between each player and the other two. Graphically depicted in figure 1.1.

While all of these configurations are logically conceivable, each is not equally probable. The unit-veto triangle is included only for the sake of logical completeness: if there were enmity between all three players, there would be nothing to hold the triangle together and it would disintegrate. The *ménage à trois* is most ideal for all three players if the possibility of

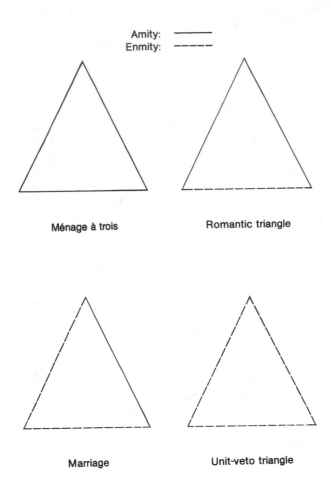

cheating or collusion can be foreclosed, and although relatively rare is empirically extant *(vide* the Trilateral Commission). But it is relatively "introverted" and tends not to be "strategic," given the lack of negative relations among its members (unless it is simply a defense alliance against some outside player, in which case it is not really a triangle but at least a quadrangle).

Thus for practical purposes the two most common configurations are the marriage and the romantic triangle. And the romantic triangle is inherently less stable than the marriage, in view of the difficulty in retaining the pivot position. The reason for this difficulty is that the pivot is systemically privileged, deriving advantages from its position within the triangle that would not accrue from its bilateral relationship with the other two players. In view of the structural advantages and liabilities inherent in the various positions, any rational player's first preference would be to play pivot in a romantic triangle; second choice would be partner in a marriage; third choice, to be a wing player in a romantic triangle; and the least preferred option would be a "pariah" facing a marriage of the other two players.

The practice of triangular diplomacy has exposed several theoretical ambiguities in the triangular "game" since I first ventured a systematic exposition a few years ago.[10] First, in a given triangle between A, B, and C, how should C be expected to respond to the formation of a "marriage" between A and B? (This question was raised by the formation of such a relationship between China and the U.S. between 1975 and 1979, excluding the Soviet Union.) As pariah, C might be expected (by the marriage partners) to intensify its suit for either A or B, hoping to pry loose a defection. It may however also *defy* AB and allow relationships to polarize, hoping to compensate either by unilateral self-strengthening measures (e.g., higher military budgets, accelerated growth), reinforcing solidarity with traditional allies (e.g., Warsaw Pact, NATO), and/or by seeking extratriangular gains (e.g., Afghanistan). Recent political experience suggests that the choice between these options will depend primarily on whether the AB marriage is perceived to be essentially "anti-C" in nature.[11] If it is, then the prospect for an intensified suit of either A or B would be foreclosed; if not, the suit should be plighted.

Second, in a given romantic triangle between A, B, and C, in which A plays the pivot, how may A be expected to respond to a reconciliation between the two wings? (This question is raised by the prospect of such a reconciliation between China and the Soviet Union in the post-1981 period.) On the one hand it might be argued that this is quite compatible with A's interests in that it obviates the possibility of warfare between B and C, which would obviously disrupt the triangle, and in any case an unnecessarily intense enmity between the two wings tends to make A's intermediate position untenable, creating irresistable pressure to "choose sides." On the other hand it might be argued that this constitutes collusion, depriving A of assured access to either B or C and implicitly threatening A with ostracism. Once again the key variable would seem to be whether the BC reconciliation is anti-A in character: if not, it is theoretically possible for the triangle to undergo a transformation from romantic to *ménage à trois*.

Third, how may a partner in a marriage, or a wing player in a strategic triangle, most intelligently play those positions? This question was raised by the prospect that the United States might have gravitated from the first of these roles into the second, and third, in the 1975-1981 period and the post-1981 period, respectively. For partners, the basic problem is how to deter one's counterpart from defecting to the pariah, and if this should occur, how to respond to it. For wing players, the main problem is how to avoid betrayal by the pivot in collusion with the other wing, and how to respond should that occur.

Fourth, what rules define the relationship between players in the triangle and extratriangular (e.g., nonaligned) actors? (This question was raised for the U.S. by Soviet inroads in Angola, the horn of Africa, and Afghanistan between 1975-1979; and perhaps for the Soviet Union by the dealignments of Yugoslavia, Austria, and Egypt.) The threat implied by such defections, provided they are on sufficient scale, is that one player may shift the strategic balance through the acquisition of clients outside of the triangle. The solution to this problem that suggests itself on the theoretical level would be to preclude extra-triangular relationships from taking precedent over valued triangular relationships, thus imposing a clear hierarchy of importance on each player's commitments. On a practical, diplomatic level such a solution would no doubt pose insuperable difficulties.

Triangular Permutations

Since World War II, the relationship between China, the United States, and the Soviet Union has undergone five historical permutations. From 1949-1959 was a relatively stable "marriage" between the Soviet Union and China, confronting an American pariah as an apparently monolithic "Communist Bloc." Although China was not even diplomatically addressed during this period as if it had an autonomous foreign policy, evidence has subsequently come to light suggesting that the Sino-Soviet relationship was never as amicable as it seemed from the outside, raising the question of a "lost chance in China" (in this case, a chance to turn the flank of the Soviet Union). Certainly the CCP made overtures to the U.S. in the late 1940s, and whether this might have been a harbinger of detente or was merely a tactical feint remains tantalizingly unclear. Assuming that the overture was serious, this may be categorized as a Chinese "bid" to play the role of pivot, which however failed because of rejection by both the Soviet Union and the United States. What is usually neglected in discussions of the plausibility of such a bid is some realistic consideration of the political options open to the U.S. As an established bourgeois order, it is perhaps fair to say that the United States harbors an innate tendency to be suspicious of communism, and has never been able to preserve friendly relations with a communist nation while the latter undertook "socialization of the means of production," which is usually interpreted by the capitalist press in terms of officially condoned terrorism and mob violence.

The period from roughly 1960 to 1969 was one of Soviet-American *rapprochement* (i.e., a somewhat spasmodic, competitive-collusive liaison in which economic and diplomatic rivalry were meant to displace force as a means of competition), during most of which China occupied a pariah position. The Sino-Soviet dispute, initially rhetorical but then territorial and finally even military, replaced the tight Sino-Soviet alliance, but China did not pursue friendship with the U.S., no doubt mainly due to ideological commitments, opting instead to pursue a revolutionary policy of support for National Liberation Movements in the Third World (and for the few established Third World governments who were pursuing a sufficiently radical line). Nor did the United States seriously attempt to woo China away from the Soviet Union, assuming (probably correctly) from the Chinese rhetoric that any such overtures would be spurned. The Chinese suspected that the Soviet-American relationship was adversely collusive (indeed they retained this suspicion until the late 1970s, frequently enveighing against negotiations for strategic arms limitation on this basis), but not until 1969 did they see sufficiently serious danger to their own position to try to pretermit this collusion.

According to one interesting recent reconstruction,[12] Sino-Soviet-American relationship during this period comprised a romantic triangle. In the 1960s, the Soviet Union began moderating its foreign policy, seeking a middle road between the PRC and the U.S., and by virtue of the fact that it was the only great power to have viable relationships with both wing powers, the Soviet Union qualified as pivot. The main problem with this interpretation is that if the Soviet Union was opting for the pivot position, it was the only player to take its own candidacy seriously. While it is possible that the Soviet Union had better relationships with each wing than either had with the other, neither wing actively courted the pivot, depriving the configuration of any triangular dynamic. There is little indication that the fitful and ambivalent Moscow-Washington flirtation was orientated around anti-Chinese collusion. Nor did China pursue reconciliation with the Soviet Union—in fact, quite the contrary. This period remains difficult to classify into any of the four configurations, presenting an odd mixture of Soviet-American marriage and a unit-veto triangle.

From a triangular perspective this may perhaps better be characterized as an unsuccessful Soviet bid to play pivot than a full permutation.

The period from 1969-1971 was transitional. The reasons China sought to break out of the Communist Bloc have been explored in great detail elsewhere,[13] and a brief review will suffice at this point. The Soviet Union had invaded Czechoslovakia in August 1968 and more to the point had enunciated in that context the right to intervene in any other Bloc member's domestic affairs if socialism became endangered there. The armed clashes on the Sino-Soviet border were followed by rumors that the Soviet Union was considering a preemptive strike against Chinese nuclear installations, then by Soviet efforts to build a noose of friendship treaties and bases around China's periphery. Fortification along the Sino-Soviet border proceeded apace.[14] Meanwhile, President Nixon had articulated in his Guam Doctrine the American intention to withdraw forces from Asia, and was actively seeking a politically acceptable exit from the Vietnam involvement. The U.S. seemed to be a declining threat to Chinese interests and an eligible alliance partner to waylay the vigorously burgeoning Soviet threat.

The 1972-1975 period may be characterized as a romantic triangle in which the U.S. played pivot. Washington had a better relationship with Moscow and Beijing than either wing had with the other, and this seemed, at least in the early period, to have a favorable impact on both bilateral relationships, as each wing intensified its courtship of the pivot. From the Soviet Union the U.S. gained SALT I and detente; from China the U.S. gained the leeway to reduce forces in the Pacific and along the Asian rimland (only one-and-a-half war contingency planning would now be deemed necessary, instead of two-and-a-half) and perhaps some marginal help in disengaging from Vietnam (at the expense of future Sino-Vietnamese relations). Later, however, toward the end of this period, the repercussions of the triangular arrangement seemed more adverse, as the Soviet Union broke out into the "arc of crisis," becoming involved in a series of episodes in the Third World that jeopardized this "wing" of the dual-detente policy in terms of American public opinion.

In 1975-1981 the triangle permuted to marriage between China and the U.S., leaving the Soviet Union in an isolated pariah position. In terms of intra-triangular relationships, this implied a provisional Chinese victory in the competition between wings for the hand of the pivot. Certainly Beijing was actively interested in a consolidation of the Sino-American realignment, and more to the point sought to place that relationship in an anti-Soviet context. As in its peace treaty with Japan (signed in August

1978), China insisted on inserting an "anti-hegemony" clause into the communique (signed 2 February 1979) announcing normalization of Sino-American diplomatic relations. The Chinese side seems to have accelerated normalization negotiations in the fall of 1978 in order to facilitate their successful conclusion prior to scheduled completion of Soviet-American negotiations on SALT II, thereby stealing the show from Brezhnev and prompting postponement (and eventual cancellation) of his visit as well as complicating ratification of the treaty. As the subsequent memoirs of Carter administration officials make clear, Deng Xiaoping privately indicated during his visit China's intention to "teach a lesson" to Vietnam, and the fact that China promptly invaded Vietnam upon his return suggested that China was "playing the American card." The hesitant Soviet response to this pedagogical war may perhaps be attributed to their reluctance to call the Chinese bluff.[15] It was during this period that the PRC was making an anti-Soviet stance virtually the sole touchstone of its foreign policy, opting on that basis to support the conservative parties in Great Britain and West Germany, the Pinochet regime in Chile, the Greek junta, and other strange bedfellows.

The Americans were initially reluctant partners in China's united front against "hegemonism," still harboring some interest in strategic arms negotiations and otherwise trying to resuscitate the dying embers of detente. But following the Soviet invasion of Afghanistan in December 1979, the Americans quickly adopted the more anti-Soviet Chinese construal of their relationship. Though both sides steered clear of a formal alliance, they agreed to pursue "parallel interests," toward which they pledged an expansion of trade and cultural exchanges. Based on the argument that the Chinese had after all turned to the U.S. for protection against the USSR, American arms aid to China was escalated gradually, particularly after the Mondale visit to China in August of 1979—in early 1980 the U.S. agreed to export "dual use" (i.e., both civilian and military) technology, and then, following issuance of Special Directive no. 81 in March, thirty types of military-related technologies and "nonlethal military" equipment was made available for purchase. Finally, in June 1981, during the visit of Secretary of State Haig to Beijing, the US agreed to sell specific categories of lethal weapons (perhaps thereby hoping to dissipate Chinese opposition to continued arms sales to Taiwan). Haig also promised that the administration would seek amendments to existing laws which would remove China from the trade restrictions placed upon members of the Communist Bloc, and indeed by 1981 China had graduated from Category Y to Category P, in June 1983 (following Secretary of Commerce

Baldridge's visit the previous month) rising to the category of "friendly and nonallied" nations such as Yugoslavia or India. The PRC began receiving special treatment denied the Soviets, such as most-favored nation treatment for Chinese imports, Export-Import Bank credits (up to $2 billion through the mid-1980s), Overseas Private Investment Corporation insurance coverage for American investors in China, and so forth. The U.S. and the PRC signed a trade agreement on 7 July 1979, calling for $8-10 billion dollars in trade through 1985. In late 1980 an electronic intelligence-gathering station was installed by the U.S. in Xinjiang, near the Soviet border, to replace facilities lost during the Islamic Revolution in Iran —thus giving the PRC a tacit veto over SALT accords, by making verification contingent upon Chinese collaboration.

And yet the final period, from 1981-1984, has witnessed the permutation of the triangle from marriage back to romantic triangle, this time with China attempting to move into the pivot position. As the Reagan administration allowed its relations with both players (but most conspicuously with the Soviet Union) to deteriorate in the context of an anti-Communist crusade, China began to back away from the U.S. embrace. Beginning in October 1981, the U.S. was first described as hegemonistic, in December 1981, as imperialistic.[16] The gravest threat to world peace no longer derived simply from the Soviet Union, but from the risk involved in the hegemonistic competition between the two superpowers, various Chinese representatives explained during their trips abroad.[17] China quietly dropped its 1979-1980 emphasis on development of a "long-term strategic relationship" with the U.S. as the centerpiece of an international united front. In September 1979, the first indication in fourteen years appeared (in an academic journal published in Heilongjiang, quickly withdrawn from circulation after this *contretemps)* that the Soviet Union could once again be considered a "socialist" country, a clue that was officially confirmed by Vice Premier Li Peng during his visit to Moscow for the Chernenko funeral in the spring of 1985. In the fall of 1979 China also agreed to participate without preconditions in "normalization" talks with the Russians. The first round took place in Moscow between September and November 1979; both sides agreed to a second round in early 1980, but this was postponed until the fall of 1982 in the wake of the Afghanistan invasion. The Soviet Union reportedly proposed a nonaggression treaty and mutual troop pullback, to which the PRC responded that no such agreement was possible so long as Soviet forces threatened Chinese security in Cambodia, Afghanistan, and Outer Mongolia; the Soviets refused to discuss such military activities, claiming that this involved sovereign third countries. Yet both sides have toned down internecine polemics, and bilateral trade has risen from a low point of $150 million in 1981 to $300 million in 1982 to an estimated $800 million in 1983 and a projected $1.8 billion in 1984 (in 1980 constant dollars).[18] Bilateral trade could be further expanded indefinitely without the dangers of "spiritual pollution" that attend trade with capitalist economies. Whether Sino-Soviet trade is complementary remains moot, but there would probably be a market for textiles (which seems to have been saturated in the West), and China could benefit from the adequate, less expensive, and more labor-intensive machinery of the socialist economies, particularly in those plants already constructed with Soviet assistance. Finally, China seems to have reassessed its nuclear defense policy, having concluded that its shift from an ICBM to exclusive concentration on MRBM development (which would be useful only against relatively proximate targets) in 1973 resulted in an excessively one-sided deterrent posture. There has since been a resuscitation of ICBM development, leading to the deployment, beginning in May 1980, of the CSS-X-4, a solid-fuel MIRVed weapon comparable to the Titan II or the SS-9, and beginning in October 1982 to the deployment of SLBMs on China's few nuclear submarines.[19]

There are a number of discernible reasons for this latest permutation of the triangle. One of these of course is the issue of Taiwan, which China suddenly escalated to top priority early in President Reagan's first term, partly in response to Reagan's campaign promises to upgrade Taiwanese-American relations, partly to preempt the prospect of "Taiwanization" following the death of the mainland refugee generation there. China discovered that a close relationship with the U.S. stood to jeopardize its relationship with the Third World, where there was clear evidence of a decline of Chinese influence following abandonment of Mao's more revolutionary international stance. At the September 1979 summit of nonaligned countries in Havana, only Pakistan rose to China's defense in the face of Castro's attacks on the United States and China as the two "arch-enemies" of the Third World; no doubt the American friendship became increasingly embarassing in the wake of Reagan policies in Central America and the adamant American stance *vis-à-vis* the Law of the Sea and a series of other North-South issues. From a fiscal perspective, moderation of Sino-Soviet border tensions probably made even more sense than the purchase of more sophisticated weaponry from the U.S. Defense expenditures consumed 17.5 percent of China's budget in 1979, 15.6 percent even in 1981 (i.e., after termination of the pedagogic war); if an amelioration of Sino-Soviet relations permitted further reductions in arms expenditures, these funds could more profitably be invested elsewhere. Finally, though Chinese foreign policymakers are least apt to admit this, there is reason to believe that the attractions of the pivot are fully apparent to them. The Chinese were evidently disturbed by reports from Washington that discounted their strategic maneuverability on the assumption that Sino-Soviet hostility forced them willy-nilly into reliance on American support. It was apparently considered that the pivot position, if subtly managed, might improve China's relations with both antagonistic wings while enhancing her attractiveness to each. Certainly in the light of the Soviet-American polarization China had no immediate apprehension of collusion, while polarization also reduced the dimensions of the Soviet threat in the East.

Conclusions

With regard to American national interest, from which perspective these brief concluding comments will be written, the period since the first Shanghai communique (1972) has witnessed a steady decline, from the high point of pivot in a romantic triangle to senior partner in a marriage to the current phase of partial recovery from the position of wing in a romantic triangle. Yet the United States alone among the three players involved disposes of the full complement of powers and resources to play the role of pivot in a triangle, attracting the courtship of both wings by dint of the intrinsic value of these resources and not merely relying on the ambiguity of the pivot position.[20] If the pivot is to be regained, the following policies seem advisable.

First, the restoration of reasonably amicable relations with the Soviet Union is necessary for any triangular advantage to be gained in the Sino-American relationship. It is the unnecessary deterioration of this relationship more than anything else which has facilitated the latest permutation of the triangle to American disadvantage. This deterioration meant that China could freely improve its relationship to the Soviet Union without fear of being thrust into a pariah position. If Soviet-American relations deteriorate further, this will create an incentive for the Soviets to offer further concessions to China for an improvement in their relations (in which they have shown a most active interest). This recommendation, it should be noted, derives purely from the logic of the triangle; an assessment of the relative merits of the two sides on the range of bilateral issues dividing them is beyond the scope of this paper.

Second, the United States must probably reconcile itself to a somewhat cooler and more distant stance toward the People's Republic of China, thereby lowering the level of expectations on both sides and reducing the prospect that any Chinese sense of dependency should develop (from which the Chinese have historically been inclined to rebel). This need not entail the rescission of concessions already granted nor the imposition of artificial burdens on the relationship, and indeed it should be made clear that Sino-American friendship is still valued. It should however be made clear (as had been emphasized in the early 1970s and subsequently lost sight of), that neither American-Chinese nor American-Soviet relations should be understood as being antagonistically oriented toward a third party; each "wing" of the triangle is intended to motivate an *improved relationship* with the other wing, not to exert leverage *against* it. Trade, cultural exchange, and arms limitations negotiations should be promoted toward both wings with an eye toward cultivating positive bilateral relations; although troublesome demands cannot be altogether precluded in view of the persisting ideological rivalry, they should be advanced with all due diplomatic finesse. For example, although the unification of China and Taiwan should not be opposed and indeed should be welcomed if it can be achieved voluntarily and through peaceful means, the United States need not accept an obligation to induce this outcome.

Third, if the United States succeeds in regaining the pivot, it should encourage collusion between the two wings, maintaining that this would be to the advantage of all three players. This would vitiate the prospect of blackmail by either wing threatening to form a marriage with the other wing. Above all, the U.S. should publicly renounce any interest in a marriage that is hostile to a third pariah, or in playing the position of tertius gaudens (viz., the spectator who sits on the mountain watching the tigers fight). Either of these positions would be a bluff anyhow, for the U.S. could not hope to provoke conflict between China and the Soviet Union unless the latter deem it in their own vital interests. It remains true that the logic of the romantic triangle presupposes better relations between the pivot and each wing than those between the two wings, but it is also empirically true that the ability of the pivot to affect interwing relations is extremely limited, and any such intention should therefore be disavowed to avoid jeopardizing pivotwing relationships. The antagonism between the USSR and the PRC developed quite without American contribution for strictly bilateral reasons, and it may be expected either to continue or not to continue for the same reasons. Nor should the United States panic at the emergence of a closer Sino-Soviet relationship should this come to fruition, for such a reaction would lead to a breakdown in Sino-American ties, and thereby precipitate permutation of the American position into that of pariah.

Finally, the relationships of the three players to extratriangular actors pose the most sensitive and difficult issue, for which no fully satisfactory solution is perhaps available. The Soviet Union would have at one time reportedly welcomed a superpower agreement segmenting the world into spheres of influence, as in the post-Napoleonic Holy Alliance, but the problem with this arrangement is that it would negate the autonomy of the national actors included in such spheres. From the perspective of the logic of the triangle, the optimal solution might be for the three players to agree that triangular relations must take priority over relations with non-triangular powers, at least in the sense that the former alone concern questions of the immediate survival of the three players involved. This need not entail sacrificing the interests of existing alliance partners, which it should be the policy of each player to honor (if not to guarantee). Although mutual suspicion remains too high for any actor or combination of actors in the current triangle to function in a peacemaking capacity, some understanding might possibly be reached not to become competitively engaged in Third World disputes without some attempt at prior consultation. Defections from one bloc to another may be anticipated, but should not be actively promoted or unduly exploited.

Notes

1. I wish to thank Avery Goldstein, Harry Harding, and Kenneth Waltz for their detailed comments and criticisms on an earlier draft of this article; I am also indebted to the discussants and other participants in a conference on "Triangular Relations of the United States, China and the Soviet Union" held 15-17 February 1985 at Marina del Rey, California, for their oral suggestions.

2. The recent popularity of the "game" analogy may perhaps be traced to Ludwig Wittgenstein, whose discovery that philosophizing could fruitfully be considered as a "language game" revolutionized Anglo-American academic philosophy and had a wide-ranging effect on post-war social science as well.

3. The earliest (and still one of the best) such discussions is Michel Tatu, *The Great Power Triangle: Washington-Moscow-Peking* (Paris: Atlantic Institute, 1970), which discussed the options open to the U.S. with startling prescience. See also Thomas Gottlieb, *Chinese Foreign Policy Factionalism and the*

Origins of the Strategic Triangle (Santa Monica, CA: Rand Corporation, November 1977); Roger Glenn Brown, "Chinese Politics and American Policy: A New Look at the Triangle," *Foreign Policy,* no. 23 (Summer 1976), pp. 3-24; Michael Pillsbury, "U.S.-China Military Ties?" *Foreign Policy,* no. 20 (Autumn 1975), and "Future Sino-American Security Ties: The View from Tokyo, Moscow and Peking," *International Security,* 1 (Spring 1977), p. 142; Banning Garrett, "China Policy and the Strategic Triangle," in Kenneth A. Oye, et al., eds., *Eagle Entangled: U.S. Foreign Policy in a Complex World* (London: Longman, 1979), pp. 228-264; William E. Griffith, ed., *The World and the Great Power Triangle* (Cambridge, Mass.: M.I.T. Press, 1975); and Raju G. C. Thomas, ed., *The Great Power Triangle and Asian Security* (Lexington, MA: Lexington Books, 1983). Other recent contributions to this voluminous literature will be cited in the course of this article.

4. See for example John Franklin Copper, *China's Global Role: National Power Capabilities in the Context of an Evolving International System* (Stanford, Calif.: Hoover Institution, 1980).

5. This seems to be the position of Michael Ng-Quinn, "International Systemic Constraints on Chinese Foreign Policy," in Samuel Kim, ed., *China and the World: Chinese Foreign Policy in the Post-Mao Era,* (Boulder, Col.: Westview Press, 1984). See also Jonathan Pollack (who does not, however, take this position), "China's Potential as a World Power" (Santa Monica, CA: Rand Corp., Paper no. 6524, July 1980).

6. That the Soviet Union and the United States deem themselves and each other to be major strategic actors probably requires no argument. The Chinese self-concept is somewhat more ambiguous. According to Mao's conceptualization of "three worlds," China is not a member of the "first world" consisting of "superpowers" but of the "third world." In a similar vein, Chinese foreign policy spokesmen have discredited the concept of a strategic triangle: "China upholds principles, and what China says counts," announced Deng Xiaoping, for example, during the visit of the new UN Secretary-General. "It never plays with politics or words, nor does it play 'cards.'" *Beijing Review,* no. 35 (30 August, 1982), p. 7. Yet China always seems to have regarded itself as occupying a special status within this category. During the Maoist era, China competed vigorously with both superpowers for the leadership of the Third World, engaging for example in an ambitious foreign aid program (which reached its peak of about $256 million in 1973). Whereas in the post-Mao era China has dropped some of these pretensions, now for example competing with other Third World countries for multilateral aid and drastically cutting foreign aid (to $64 million in 1983), it still engages in Great Power politics and reacts indignantly against any tendency to dismiss its strategic potential. See for example Zhang Jialin, "The New Romanticism in the Reagan Administration's Asian Policy: Illusion and Reality," *Asian Survey,* XXIV: 10 (October 1984), pp. 997-1012. Huan Xiang delivered an academic report to a meeting in Wuhan on 7 June 1984, in which he said that

"What now determines the development of the international situation is the so-called 'great trilateral relationship' between China, the USSR and the USA." Reported in *Wen hui bao* (Hong Kong), 22 June 1985.

7. Banning N. Carrett and Bonnie Glaser, *War and Peace: The Views from Moscow and Beijing* (Berkeley, CA: Institute of International Studies, Policy Paper in International Affairs no. 20, 1984).

8. One such opportunity for reality-testing in the use of conventional arms was provided by China's punitive expedition against Vietnam in February 1979. Although all participants in this brief incident could plausibly claim to have benefited, Chinese troops did not really acquit themselves well. The PLA probably achieved its geographical objectives, capturing five provincial capitals within a zone fifty kilometers deep at its farthest penetration. But the putative goal of inflicting a punishing defeat of forcing Vietnam to reconsider its invasion of Cambodia was not achieved. Despite mobilization of 500,000 troops and some 800 aircraft, the Chinese absorbed losses of 28,000 killed and 43,000 wounded in less than a month (while inflicting perhaps three times that number of casualties against Vietnam), failing to engage, let alone destroy, a single main force Vietnamese division.

9. Taken from Morton Kaplan's "unit veto system," in *System and Process in International Politics* (New York: John Wiley, 1957), pp. 50-52.

10. L. Dittmer, "The Strategic Triangle: An Elementary Game-Theoretical Analysis," *World Politics,* 33: 4 (July 1981), pp. 485-516.

11. There is actually a repertoire of anti-C moves, of varying intensity. One analyst for example distinguishes between "tilting," which involves a slight leaning toward B to offset C, and is accomplished by a subtle and sophisticated process of signalling; and actually "playing a card," which would include such steps as military cooperation or major economic arrangements between A and B. See Gerald Segal, *The Great Power Triangle* (New York: St. Martin's, 1982), pp. 6-7. Other analysts make a distinction between "playing a card" and "having played a card."

12. C. Segal, *Great Power Triangle.*

13. See Thomas Gottlieb, *Chinese Foreign Policy Factionalism and the Origins of the Strategic Triangle;* also see John Garver, *China's Decision for Rapprochement with the United States, 1968-1971* (Boulder, CO: Westview Press, 1982).

14. The Soviet military buildup in Asia has gone through two phases. The first began shortly after Khrushchev's purge, when the new Brezhnev leadership began to increase Soviet ground forces deployed against China from a little more than 12 divisions in 1965 to more than 40 a decade later. The second stage was initiated publicly in late March 1978 when Brezhnev toured industrial and military facilities in the Soviet Far East with Defense Minister Ustinov. Following that trip, a series of military developments oriented toward neutralizing U.S. forces in Asia proceeded. A new generation of mobile IRBMs was deployed in the Siberian and Transbaikal Military Districts—the SS-20s and the "Backfire" bomber—which could threaten all

of China as well as American bases in Japan and the Philippines. Attention was given to construction of the second major land supply route to Soviet Asia, the Baikal-Amur Mainland (BAM) railway. Concurrently, the Soviet Pacific Fleet was provided with significant new assets for anti-submarine warfare and force projection—notably the 1979 deployment of the carrier Minsk and the amphibious assault ship Ivan Rogov. See Richard Solomon, "East Asia and the Great Power Coalition" (Santa Monica: Rand, Paper no. 6733, February 1982).

15. The Americans made it clear enough at the time that it was a bluff. A State Department spokesman indicated that a Soviet strike on China's northern border the most logistically feasible response to China's demarche—"would not be of direct concern to the US." See *Christian Science Monitor,* 29 February 1979.

16. BBC, SWB/FE, no. 6930/A1/2.

17. For example, Zhao Ziyang took this position during his visit to North Korea in December 1981, as did Foreign Minister Huang Hua, during his visit to Nigeria and Ghana in November.

18. *Far Eastern Economic Review,* 25 April 1983, p. 26, and 24 March, 1983, p. 80; *Christian Science Monitor,* 12 March 1984, p. 23.

19. See Clemens Stubbe Oestergaard, "Multipolarity and Modernization: Sources of China's Foreign Policy in the 1980s," *Cooperation and Conflict,* 18 (1983), pp. 245-267, at p. 255.

20. There is already reason to question the tenability of China's role in the pivot for precisely this reason. In 1972, Richard Nixon could proceed from Beijing to Moscow even after bombing Haiphong harbor, in which Soviet supply ships were docked. In May 1984, Moscow however abruptly postponed the visit of first deputy premier Ivan Arkhipov to Beijing in the wake of President Reagan's visit the previous month. The Soviets apparently do not intend to allow Beijing to play pivot, preferring "pariah-dom" to the uncertainties of a wing position.

Strategic Change and the American Foreign Policy:

Perceptions of the Sino-Soviet Conflict

RICHARD C. THORNTON

American strategy toward the Eurasian landmass has been governed by the application of the general principle of promoting and maintaining a stable equilibrium of states, the objective being to ensure that no single power, the Soviet Union, could ever come to dominate the hemisphere. Within this context, U.S. policy has been a function of the Soviet-American strategic military balance. Operationally, this meant that when American leaders perceived that the Soviet Union was moving into a position of relative strength *vis à vis* the United States, Washington attempted to fortify positions around the Soviet periphery in Europe, the Middle East, South Asia, the Far East, or whatever area or areas could conceivably come under pressure. The assumption was that an improvement in Moscow's strategic position would be accompanied by attempts at geopolitical probe and advance in hopes of enlarging Soviet power, prestige and position. What I propose to do in this essay is to analyze American policy behavior toward China in light of this general thesis. I will examine two cases of U.S. policy toward China—the rapprochement of

1969 and the normalization of 1979—in an effort to illustrate the relationship between strategic change and American foreign policy.

Before proceeding with the analysis, however, some definitions of terms as well as explanation of intellectual purpose are in order. The term "strategy" is of course one of the most bedevilling of words in the international affairs lexicon. It is indiscriminately and inconsistently used to mean end, means, policy and plan. In this essay I use the term "strategy" to mean "end." More specifically, I take strategy to include the concept of "structure." Thus, in distinguishing between strategy and policy, strategy involves the determination of future structural ends toward which a state moves through employment of concrete policy means. Policy is to means what strategy is to ends.

My purpose is to suggest that neither U.S.-China rapprochement, nor normalization was an isolated bilateral question settled without reference to external influences affecting the two nations. While that may seem obvious with regard to the Soviet Union, it is much less so as far as Vietnam is concerned. It is the argument of this essay that the disposition of the structure of Indochina was very much in the minds of American and Chinese policymakers as the two states moved first toward rapprochement, then to normalization of their relations.

The Sixties' Rapprochement

President Nixon assumed office at an historic moment when the momentum of the Soviet Union's missile buildup would for the first time carry Moscow to the numerical lead in land based ICBMs. Much would yet have to occur in terms of qualitative improvements before the Soviet Union would be in position to threaten a first strike against the U.S. landbased force, Minuteman. Nevertheless, the day when the Soviet Union would achieve this capability was more clearly visible than ever before and countering this emerging threat lay at the heart of the President's policy calculations.

If the growing Soviet missile capability did not yet present the United States with a direct homeland threat, it did counterpose and to an increasing extent neutralize the U.S. ability to project its power to areas of interest and concern, particularly on the Eurasian landmass in support of friends and allies. Growing Soviet strategic weapons power would soon enable Moscow to play a much more forceful role than hitherto in probing the U.S. containment structure. Thus, the basic thrust of U.S. policy was to consolidate those geopolitical positions which could be expected to come under Soviet pressure. The consolidation effort would consist of three complex sets of policies: extrication of the nation from the debilitating conflict in Vietnam in as honorable a manner as possible, reinforcement of positions of strength around Moscow's periphery and the revitalization of the American role within the western alliance. Rapprochement between the United States and the People's Republic of China would occur within this context.

The war in Vietnam was the President's most immediate problem, but, shortly after his entry into office, also became his most challenging opportunity. The opportunity lay in the outbreak of open warfare between Soviet and Chinese forces along their common border, which laid bare the split between the two communist powers and raised the possibility of a genuine coincidence of interest between the United States and the People's Republic of China involving the growth of Soviet power and a mutually acceptable solution to the problem of Vietnam. Both Washington and Beijing each faced the question of how to deal with growing Soviet power. For President Nixon the problem was how to counter Soviet strategic weapons power and also to buttress the crumbling containment structure —both of which would take some time. Mao Zedong's needs, on the other hand, were more immediate. The Soviet military buildup along the Chinese border had reached significant proportions by the spring of 1968 (between thirty and thirty-five divisions). At that point Mao had terminated the tumultuous "cultural revolution" which had been wracking the country for three years and begun to reinforce China's northern defenses for what now appeared to be an inevitable showdown.

At the same time on China's southern border in Indochina the Tet offensive brought about a major increase in U.S. troop strength in South Vietnam to an authorized level of 549,500. In other words, Mao was faced with a major confrontation on the northern border with the Soviet Union and the possibility of the same on the southern border, if the United States were drawn to invade North Vietnam, tempted while Chinese and Russian forces were engaged in the north. In any case, the Chinese, caught in the tightening vise of a two-front conflict situation, sought to extricate themselves from it by neutralizing the southern front.

The United States from the beginning of its major troop deployment into South Vietnam had conveyed assurances to the Chinese that Washington would not invade North Vietnam. The policy of graduated escalation was designed in part to reinforce this conception. Still, Beijing was forced to construct its defenses on the basis of likely contingencies and not professions of intent on the part of one of its major enemies. Accordingly,

Beijing's major defensive deployments were along the northern border with the Soviet Union, the southern border with Vietnam and the east coast across from Taiwan.

When the Tet offensive produced a U.S. determination to negotiate rather than retaliate, fundamental signals were conveyed to both Beijing and Moscow that the United States would begin to move toward a settlement of the conflict one way or another. In November of 1968, after the presidential elections, the Chinese indicated their interest in exploring U.S. attitudes further by requesting the resumption of the Warsaw talks which they had broken off six months earlier. Moscow, on the other hand, hastened preparations to deter any Sino-American rapprochement by the use of force if necessary. In other words, by the time that Richard Nixon had become president the basis for a coincidence of interest between China and the United States over Vietnam and the Soviet threat was already in embryonic existence. The question was: could the new president bring it to fruition?

The importance of China to the war in Vietnam was impossible to overestimate. Chinese territory constituted a secure and invulnerable logistical base in itself and, more importantly, a safe if not always secure railroad corridor for the transit of Soviet and Chinese supplies to Hanoi. Including the Chinese corridor there were but three logistical routes into North Vietnam by which to fuel Hanoi's war effort. The other two were by sea to Haiphong and Sihanoukville, Cambodia, both highly vulnerable to U.S. interdiction. Between 1965 and 1968, despite the fact that Sino-Soviet relations worsened precipitously and the Cultural Revolution periodically disrupted the flow of Soviet material across Chinese territory, the Chinese corridor was the principal supply route for the Vietnamese war effort. During this period Soviet and Chinese material shipments were roughly of equal quantity and significance as Moscow sought to use support for Hanoi as a means of exerting leverage on Beijing for reconciliation.

The threat of conflict with the Soviet Union combined with the beginning of U.S. peace negotiations with Hanoi altered the equation for Mao Zedong. It now became manifestly in China's interest to improve relations with Washington from both the perspectives of countering the Soviet threat and resolving the Vietnam conflict on satisfactory terms. An improvement in relations would have both immediate and long-term benefits. Neutralizing the danger in the south, Beijing could redeploy its forces northward to meet the immediate Soviet threat. Over the longer term relations with Washington would at a minimum serve Beijing's strategy in Indochina.

Since 1954, when the Geneva conference divided Vietnam and established neutral status for Laos and Cambodia, Beijing's strategy displayed a remarkable consistency, seeking to maintain a fragmented structure to permit dominance of the region. Even during the Vietnam conflict, Beijing's policy under Mao was to support North Vietnam sufficiently to prevent defeat, but not enough to bring victory. Objectively, U.S. strategy in the conflict was similar. Washington had done enough to prevent Saigon's defeat, but not enough to defeat Hanoi, which would have required an invasion. The graduated U.S. war fighting policy suggested that Washington, too, sought to maintain the fragmented structure of Geneva and thereby a foothold on the southeast Asian mainland. Thus, from Beijing's point of view, too, the potential basis for a coincidence of interest existed between itself and Washington.

Moscow was acutely conscious of the possibility that China and the United States would attempt to counter the Soviet Union through rapprochement with each other. In the hope of forestalling that possibility, the Soviet Union generated intensive military pressure on China along the border from early 1969, while at the same time offering broad cooperation with Washington on a wide range of foreign policy problems. On 2 March, Soviet and Chinese forces clashed at Damansky (Chen Bao) Island in the Ussuri River on the Manchurian border, marking the beginning of what would become a protracted, six-month long crisis between the two countries.

Subsequent clashes would occur along the Manchurian border on 15 March; 12-15, 25 and 28 May, and in the west in the Sinjiang sector on 16, 25, April; 2, 20, May; 10 June; and 13 August. In addition, a noticeable heightening of tension was also evident along the border between Inner and Outer Mongolia as the Soviets reinforced their presence there, too. Although Moscow mounted a major propaganda campaign to assign the initiative and blame for the military confrontation to China, the U.S. leadership soon concluded that the Soviets were the responsible party.[1] If the Soviets calculated that these tactics would somehow forestall the movement of Beijing and Washington toward cooperation, it was a grievous error; the reverse happened.

Soviet military pressure against the Chinese and North Vietnamese attacks against U.S. forces in South Vietnam formed the crucible in which the initial links were forged between Washington and Beijing. In this context the first substantive move was made by Mao Zedong when he began to delay and then reduce the volume of Soviet supplies traversing the Chinese railway to Hanoi. Indeed, it would be no exaggeration to observe that the Chinese decision to close off the hitherto invulnerable supply route into Vietnam was without exception the single most important act affecting the tripolar relationship for the next several years. It raised for Washington the possibility of parleying a mutually acceptable Vietnam settlement into a Sino-American rapprochement, which would also help to offset the growth in Soviet power as well.

In retrospect, it would appear that a working understanding between Washington and Beijing had developed by mid-1969 (over two years before Henry Kissinger's celebrated trip to Beijing made Sino-American rapprochement public). President Nixon's initial substantive signal to Beijing came on 14 March against the backdrop of the first major clash between Soviet and Chinese forces on the Manchurian border following the skirmish of 2 March. His signal was imbedded in criteria discussed for determining the rate of American troop withdrawals from Vietnam. These were the state of the Paris peace talks, the rate of Vietnamization and the level of enemy combat activity. It would be some time before the Vietnamization process would begin to take hold and the Paris talks were stalemated, but the remark about the level of enemy activity was directed at Beijing and Mao's indicated willingness to slow down Soviet supplies to Vietnam.

Nixon's second signal, this a discreet proposal edged with a subtle threat, also came during heavy fighting on the Manchurian border in mid-May. Fighting had broken out on 12 May at Hu Ma on the Ussuri River and continued until the 15th. On the 14th, in a television address, the President proposed an eight-point program to reestablish the *status quo ante bellum* according to the Geneva agreements of 1954. Ruling out both the imposition of a "purely military solution," which implied an invasion of the north, and a "disguised defeat," Nixon proposed the mutual withdrawal of all non-South Vietnamese forces from South Vietnam over a twelve-month period to be supervised, as would future free elections, by an international supervisory body.[2] The President and his key advisors had already reconciled themselves to the fact that Hanoi would not agree to any genuine mutual withdrawal scheme, therefore the President's proposal was in actuality directed toward a different audience—in Beijing.

The subtle threat was that if mutual compromise were rejected the United States would achieve a unilateral settlement through the Vietnamization program. As the President put it: "the time is approaching when South Vietnamese forces will be able to take over some of the fighting fronts now being manned by Americans."[3] In effect, the President was asking for Mao Zedong's concurrence to cooperate in the reestablishment of the 1954 political structure of Indochina. The alternative was also clear.

Mao could either cooperate or forego the opportunity to gain the support of the United States against the Soviet Union and any hope of ensuring that China's interests would be served in Indochina. Following the 14 May speech, the President instructed Secretary of State Rogers to establish a channel of communications to Beijing through Pakistan.[4] Whether it was through this particular venue or some other, sometime in late May the Chinese appear to have conveyed to President Nixon their willingness to cooperate on a resolution of the conflict in Vietnam.

The next stage in the evolution of the initial working understanding with China came during President Nixon's earth-girdling trip in July which began with a stop at Guam to welcome the Apollo astronauts back from their successful flight to the moon, and thence to the Philippines, Thailand, South Vietnam, Indonesia, India, Pakistan and Rumania. On Guam, 25 July, he gave an informal briefing to newsmen. In the course of his remarks, in response to a question about Beijing's capability of inspiring wars of national liberation, Nixon replied: "Red China's capacity is much less than it was because of internal problems," of which a good indication was the "minimal role" that Peking was then playing in Vietnam compared to the Soviet Union and the role that it had been playing a few years earlier. "Three years ago, Red China was furnishing over 50 percent of the military equipment, the hardware, for the North Vietnamese. Now it is approximately 80-20 the other way around," meaning that it was the Soviet Union that was presently providing the bulk of Hanoi's supplies.[5]

In these brief remarks, the President revealed his understanding and expectation of the reduced Chinese role in the Vietnam conflict. The initial formulation of what eventually would become the "Nixon Doctrine" then followed. "The United States," he declared, "will keep our treaty commitments . . . but . . . problems of internal security . . . except for the threat of a major power involving nuclear weapons . . . will be increasingly handled by . . . the Asian nations themselves."[6] In the sensation generated by this remark, first dubbed the "Guam Doctrine," what was perhaps the most intriguing question was left unanswered. What had the President meant by the phrase "except for the threat of a major power involving nuclear weapons"? The only major power capable of making a credible nuclear threat against any Asian nation aside from the United States itself, was, of course, the Soviet Union. Did the President mean to convey, however obliquely, that the United States would extend its nuclear umbrella to cover China in case of a Soviet nuclear threat? Given the deepening crisis between Moscow and Beijing and the emerging understanding between Washington and Beijing, that—certainly in retrospect —is precisely what the President meant to do. It was by no means explicit at this point. It would only become so in November when the President reformulated his "doctrine."

The Soviet context makes this evolution unambiguous. From the outbreak of hostilities on the Ussuri River the Soviets had raised the threat of nuclear retaliation against China as they strove to marshal the support of communist party leaderships around the world.[7] In meetings of the Warsaw Pact countries and preparatory meetings for the coming world congress of communist parties, the Soviets sought the endorsement of their position against the Chinese—an effort in which they were largely successful, but the exceptions were notable. Nicolae Ceausescu of Romania and Josef Tito of Yugoslavia pointedly resisted Soviet demands for unity and condemned the "Brezhnev Doctrine" which had evolved publicly in the aftermath of the Soviet invasion of Czechoslovkia, because of its implications for themselves.

When the world congress of communist parties did convene in June, speculation was rife that the outbreak of full-scale war between the Soviet Union and China was imminent. Reports were circulating in Moscow of a possible Soviet preventive strike against Chinese nuclear installations in Sinkiang.[8] Brezhnev's sharp denunciation of the Maoist regime at the congress, his proposal to create an Asian Collective Security System, and insistent demands for international solidarity fed those fears. After the congress, in July, Chinese officials, uncharacteristically also spoke of war as "definitely imminent," possibly by October.[9] This, then, was the context within which President Nixon cautiously advanced his views on the island of Guam. Undoubtedly, Rumania's staunch objection to blanket condemnation of China at the congress was the main reason the President included Bucharest on his itinerary even though he protested that his visit should not be interpreted either "as an affront to the Soviet Union or as a move toward China."[10]

The President's oblique offer of support came just as the Sino-Soviet conflict was nearing its crisis point, which was reached in mid-September. That Mao understood and responded to this latest signal also seems beyond reasonable doubt. As American combat forces were withdrawn, Beijing began to pull out Chinese forces for deployment northward, including "service forces" in North Vietnam of between 40-50,000 men. The withdrawal of Chinese forces from North Vietnam was completed by early September.[11] It was accompanied by publicly expressed concern that the Soviet Union was about to execute a nuclear strike against China and increasingly visible war preparations on both sides.[12]

In mid-September the Sino-Soviet crisis reached its peak as Moscow moved to the brink of executing a nuclear strike. Amid armed conflict and tension all along the frontier from Manchuria to Sinkiang, test firings of missiles and the lofting of reconnaissance satellites, Moscow issued what appeared to be an ultimatum to China, although its public aspect was of an indirect sort. On 11 September on his way back to Moscow after attending the funeral of Ho Chi-minh, Soviet premier Alexyi Kosygin held a brief meeting at Peking airport with Chinese premier Zhou Enlai, but the substance of their discussion was not revealed. Then, on 16 September there appeared an article in the *London Evening News* by one of Moscow's KGB "channels" to the West, Victor Louis. Entitled "Will Russian Rockets Czechmate China?" the article moved the Sino-Soviet confrontation to its crisis-point. Mr. Louis declared that the Soviet Union was prepared to go significantly further against China than it had gone against Czechoslovakia, which it had invaded a year earlier. There was no reason, he asserted, why the Brezhnev Doctrine should not be applied to China. Furthermore, Soviet rockets stood aimed and ready to destroy China's nuclear center at Lop Nor, Sinkiang. Finally, he said that there was evidence that anti-Maoist forces were emerging and "could produce a leader who would ask other Socialist countries for fraternal help."

As Moscow increased pressure in the north, Washington relaxed pressure in the south. On the day the Louis article appeared President Nixon announced a further withdrawal of American troops from Vietnam, reducing the authorized ceiling from 549,000 to 484,000, in addition to accelerating the actual withdrawal of forces. Sixty thousand would be withdrawn by mid-December. Behind the scenes, Washington also applied unspecified diplomatic pressure on Moscow throughout the second half of September.[13] Whatever the effect of U.S. diplomatic pressure, the tension began to ease and in early October both sides withdrew their forces out of direct contact. On the 7th, Beijing announced that it had agreed to enter into negotiations if only to placate the "handful of war maniacs" in Moscow.[14]

Did Moscow suspect that the U.S.-China connection had already been made? Was the decision to terminate the crisis a reflection of that realization? Subsequent Soviet policy behavior suggested that that is indeed what Moscow suspected and brought the Soviets to attempt to improve Soviet-American relations to avoid being "odd man out" in the three-way combination. Soviet policy would attempt to move in lockstep with China's. Any improvement in Sino-American relations would be matched by similar improvements in Soviet-American ties—even while Moscow pursued the larger goal of moving toward overall supremacy. The shift in Soviet policy came through clearly in an *aide-memoir* to President Nixon dated 20 October the same day that Sino-Soviet border talks began.

Only a fragment of the note has been published, but it is sufficient to indicate the Soviet interpretation of events, even if only negatively.

> Moscow feels that the President should be frankly told that the method of solving the Vietnam question through the use of military force is not only without perspective, but also extremely dangerous. . . . If someone in the United States is tempted to make profit from Soviet-Chinese relations at the Soviet Union's expense, and there are some signs of that, then we would like to frankly warn in advance that such line of conduct, if pursued, can lead to a very grave miscalculation and is in no way constant with the goal of better relations between the United States and the USSR.[15]

From the juxtaposition of the subject matter alone, it is evident that the Soviet leadership linked the Vietnam conflict and the improvement in U.S.-Chinese relations. Despite the bluster about profiting "at the Soviet Union's expense" Soviet ambassador Dobrynin informed President Nixon when delivering the note that Moscow was now ready to begin strategic arms talks with the United States (which incidentally would begin 17 November 1969).

President Nixon's reaction to the Soviet note was to make explicit a U.S. guarantee to shield the People's Republic of China from any Soviet nuclear threat. On 3 November in a major speech, the President set forth the "Nixon Doctrine." Describing the long road to American involvement in Vietnam from President Eisenhower's initial commitment to the present, Nixon pointedly noted that "the Soviet Union furnishes most of the military equipment for North Vietnam" and refused to assist in bringing about a settlement. Nor had there been any progress with Hanoi, which remained intransigent. Since neither Moscow nor Hanoi showed any inclination to work for a peaceful settlement, the President declared:

> I, therefore, put into effect another plan to bring peace—a plan which will bring the war to an end regardless of what happens on the negotiating front.[16]

This was the Vietnamization plan which was public but also included the broad-gauged effort to close off the main logistical routes leading into North Vietnam, which was not. This part of the plan required Chinese support, which the President believed he was already receiving and for which he now reciprocated.

In line with what he termed "a major shift in U.S. foreign policy" the President referred to his press conference at Guam. He then proceeded to develop the "two commitments" made on Guam into "three principles" as guidelines for future American policy toward Asia. The first and third principles were the same as those set forth on Guam, that the United States would keep all of its treaty commitments and furnish military and economic aid to threatened nations, who would, in turn, provide the manpower for their own defense. But it was with the second principle that the President, in effect, replied to Moscow's warning expressed in the 20 October *aide memoir*. The United States, he said "shall provide a shield if a nuclear power threatens the freedom of a nation allied with us or of a nation whose survival we consider vital to our security."[17] That country, given the Sino-Soviet crisis and all that it implied, was of course, the People's Republic of China.

Thus, three essential elements comprised the *Sino-American quid pro quo* as it emerged in 1969. First, was the reestablishment of the 1954 Geneva structure for Indochina, a solution which would leave North Vietnam divided with a U.S.-supported South Vietnam and an overall fragmentation of the region which would present no threat to Beijing. Second, in return for Chinese cooperation in forging a mutually acceptable settlement in Southeast Asia, the United States would "provide a shield" against Moscow. Finally, the fruits of rapprochement would later include U.S. assistance in China's development, facilitation of China's entry into the western economic and diplomatic world, and ultimately the establishment of full diplomatic relations. Most of this, naturally enough, was not visible in 1969 or even in 1970. It would not be until mid-1971 that the broad dimensions of the subtle interchanges that took place in 1969 would begin to be realized.

The Seventies' Normalization

Early in the incoming Carter administration, U.S. officials learned that the Soviet Union had begun to develop a sharply improved guidance system for intercontinental ballistics missiles. This significant technological breakthrough, partially the result of the accelerated transfer of western technology during the "detente" era of the seventies, brought unexpectedly and uncomfortably nearer the day when the Soviet Union would be capable of launching a preemptive attack against the United States' land-based force, Minuteman, with a high damage expectancy. Intelligence estimates had predicted that Soviet achievement of an improved missile guidance capability would not come until the early or mid-eighties. Although it would take some time (perhaps several years) to perfect and install the new guidance system and, even though increased ICBM accuracy would represent a threat primarily to the U.S. land-based force and not to bombers or submarines, the new development signaled a major change in the strategic weapons balance. The Soviet force improvements would have an undoubted impact on world leaders' perceptions of the global strategic balance and, indeed, sparked immediate debate within the Carter administration over the proper response. Internally, administration officials agreed that the prospect was for "a prolonged period of wide-spread, turbulent upheaval."[18]

The impact of the new intelligence findings on President Carter was revealed in two major public statements on arms control, the first on 9 March and the second on 17 March 1977. They indicated the decisive period of the internal policy debate and suggested that the administration had been taken by surprise by the new intelligence. On 9 March President Carter called for adherence to the principal of equal numbers of missiles that had been established in the Vladivostok agreement of 1974 as well as for maintenance of the sublimit figure of 820 for missiles in the heavy MIRV category. Yet eight days later, on 17 March 1977, he shifted position dramatically, now calling for "deep reductions" of existing heavy missile launchers and a "freeze" on all new construction of strategic weapons.

The issue was whether to continue to seek security through arms control, or adopt a more secure basing mode for the now more vulnerable land-based system? The President's choice was to try the negotiating route first, but with a twist. In what former Secretary of State Vance described as "a radical departure from Vladivostok," President Carter sent the Secretary to Moscow on 27 March to present a "comprehensive proposal" for deep cuts in strategic weaponry which, if accepted, would resolve the danger posed by the missile guidance system breakthrough.[19] The essential components of the U.S. offer were, first, to reduce the total ceilings and sub-ceilings agreed to at Vladivostok. The overall aggregates were to be reduced from 2400 to between 1800 and 2000; MIRV launchers were to be reduced from 1320 to between 1100 and 1200. A new sub-ceiling was proposed for land-based MIRVs of 550 and a further sub-ceiling asked for the heavy missiles of 150. This last would require the Soviet Union to dismantle roughly one-half of the 308 heavy SS18 missiles it had already deployed and which had been agreed to in SALT I and at Vladivostok. The proposal also called for a ban on construction of new ICBMs, including mobile missiles, and limits on testing of existing weapons.

Moscow harshly rejected the comprehensive proposal, insisting instead upon commencing SALT II negotiations based upon the Vladivostok accords. The United States assented to Moscow's demand, but U.S.

leaders were now reasonably certain that the arms control negotiations would fail to meet minimum requirements for preserving national security. Thus, from early 1977 onward, even as U.S. leaders continued to dispute the significance of the strategic weapons developments among themselves, they proceeded to devise and implement plans to consolidate U.S. positions on the Eurasian landmass to minimize the impact that was expected to come from an intensified Soviet geopolitical offensive, as Moscow once again sought to reap the political gains of military advantage.

The Geopolitical Background

Soviet rejection of the comprehensive proposal cleared the way for Washington to begin actively to consolidate its geopolitical positions on the Eurasian landmass. The three principal regions of concentration were Western Europe, the Middle East and East Asia. In Western Europe, the United States attempted to gain agreement to increase the defense capacity of the region, an effort that culminated in the dual track NATO decision of December 1979. In the Middle East, Washington sought to bring about an Israeli-Egyptian peace agreement, thus defining the basis for a strategic consensus in that region. In the Far East, Washington moved to normalize its relationship with the People's Republic of China and establish the possibility of strategic cooperation between Washington and Beijing, and perhaps also Tokyo.

Meanwhile, the situation in and around China was in flux.[20] Several months before his death, Mao Zedong had attempted to determine his own succession and decisively influence the outcome of the continuing policy debate within the leadership. He did this by purging Deng Xiaoping a second time and a few days later designating Hua Guofeng as his successor. This latter action, however, had the unfortunate effect, from Mao's point of view, of splitting his own ruling coalition into two groups, one led by Hua and the other by the Chairman's wife, Jiang Qing. A third group, led by Defense Minister Marshal Ye Jianying, included several of Deng's supporters and, with Deng out of power for the time being, functioned as a swing group in the succession struggle which ensued immediately upon Mao's death in early September 1976.

In the immediate post-Mao succession crisis the Hua and Ye groups joined forces to defeat and oust the so-called Gang of Four led by Jiang Qing. The upshot of the first phase of the struggle was the appointment of Hua as Chairman of the Party to succeed Mao, but the price which the new Chairman had to pay for the support of the Ye group was agreement to rehabilitate Deng Xiaoping. Although Hua was able to delay acting on his commitment for several months, Deng was eventually restored to all of his previous posts in the party, state and military hierarchies at the Third Plenum of the Tenth Party Congress in July 1977. Ye Jianying, as Minister of National Defense, commanded the military hierarchy. In the uneasy coalition which emerged afterwards, Hua and Deng sought to outmaneuver each other by organizational and policy means, while Ye strove to maintain a rough equilibrium in the leadership as a whole. It was under these unstable internal conditions that the decisions for normalization of relations with the United States and war with the Socialist Republic of Vietnam were taken.

In Indochina, as both the Kampuchean and Vietnamese regimes moved to consolidate their respective territories after coming to power, initially cool relations soon deteriorated so that by the spring of 1976 border clashes were commonplace. Hanoi mounted two large, but inconclusive, punitive expeditions against Kampuchea the following year, the first in April 1977 and the second in December, which carried over into January of 1978. During this period Hanoi also sought to gain China's acquiescence to its domination of the region by diplomatic means, to no avail. By the early spring of 1978 it was clear that although the Socialist Republic of Vietnam had succeeded in strengthening its position in Laos, a treaty of peace and friendship had been signed the previous July, incorporation of Kampuchea into Vietnam's sphere of influence would be more difficult and require a substantial application of force. This, in turn, would most certainly provoke Chinese counteraction in support of Beijing's client. A major military effort to topple Pol Pot would thus require Soviet assistance both as arms supplier and to deter Beijing from taking action to frustrate Hanoi's objectives in Kampuchea.

The shift in the strategic weapons balance discussed at the outset of this section had as much impact on China and Vietnam as it had on the United States, but it came later. It was gradually perceived that the favorable shift in the strategic weapons equation had led to the adoption of a general Soviet foreign policy decision to seize the initiative and Soviet-sponsored moves in the Middle East, Afghanistan and Southeast Asia heightened that perception.

This last shift seemed to reflect a larger decision regarding China. Soviet leaders had assumed that, having consistently opposed Mao Zedong, Deng Xiaoping was the one leader with whom it would be possible to reach some sort of understanding and anticipated his return to a top position after Mao's death. Unfortunately for Soviet concerns, in ensuing months, even though extensive reshuffling of top leadership cadres had occurred, and even though Deng's position had visibly strengthened, he had not assumed a top post. When the Eleventh Party Congress of August 1977 confirmed Hua Guofeng as Party Chairman, Moscow decided to forego further efforts to reach a diplomatic accommodation with Beijing for the time being and instead to apply greater pressure through support of Hanoi's drive to conquer Kampuchea. Moscow's choice was reinforced in February 1978 when the Fifth National People's Congress reconfirmed Hua's position as Premier, while Deng, despite obvious popularity and political strength, was still excluded from any formal position of power.

Moscow's decision to support Hanoi in an attempt to conquer China's client state ran directly counter to Beijing's long-term strategy in the region. A Vietnamese invasion of Kampuchea would leave Beijing no recourse but military intervention to protect its ally. The unacceptable alternative was to stand idly by and witness the emergence of a Hanoi-dominated Indochina closely allied to Moscow, a region in which Beijing would have little influence and which would constitute a continuing threat to China's southern flank. It was therefore a foregone conclusion that Beijing would take military action against Hanoi once all other options to maintain Kampuchean territorial integrity had been foreclosed.

What were Moscow's motives in adopting this course of action? Aside from possible disruption of the Sino-American negotiations on normalization, then just getting under way in mid-1978, Moscow's longer-range objective was evidently to create the basis on which future efforts could be made to reach some kind of accommodation with Beijing, or, failing that, to lock the People's Republic into the vise of a vastly more threatening two-front conflict situation, which would enable the Soviet Union to strengthen its containment structure around China.

In retrospect, Moscow's plans probably crystalized sometime in the early spring of 1978 when the Soviet Union established a major new military command structure for the Soviet Far East and, at about the same time, Hanoi began to crack down on Chinese activity in Vietnam relocating Vietnamese citizens with any "taint" of Chinese heritage (amounting to several hundred thousand people) from urban areas to so-called "new economic zones" in the countryside. Nationalization of all property in May also hit the overseas Chinese community especially hard and led to a sharp deterioration of relations with Beijing as the Chinese media mounted a vituperative propaganda campaign excoriating Vietnam's domestic policies.[21]

Later that summer both sides withdrew their ambassadors and Beijing shut down its side of the border to all but official traffic. The movement toward conflict between Hanoi and Beijing quickened now as the Vietnamese intensified their military operations in Kampuchea from mid-June onward. The Vietnamese began openly training ethnic Khmer soldiers as part of a Kampuchean United National Front for National Salvation. June also saw Hanoi's entry into the Soviet-controlled Council for Economic and Mutual Assistance, reportedly to bolster a sagging economy. Finally, commencing in July, Vietnam moved to upgrade air and air defense positions in the north, strengthen border fortifications and conduct a campaign of repeated provocations along the Chinese border.

The first week of August saw Vietnamese military units step up operations against Kampuchea bolstered by a massive, new Soviet airlift of material and advisors. A *Pravda* commentator noted that Soviet-Vietnamese relations were "becoming filled with new content."[22] The Chinese responded with the charge that Moscow was "pushing" Hanoi into a "large-scale invasion of Kampuchea,"[23] and sped up preparations for conflict with both Hanoi and Moscow. From Beijing's side, final arrangements for normalization of relations with the United States paralleled stepped-up activity in preparation for war with China's northern and southern neighbors. China's interest in normalization was thus sharply defined by the contours of the impending conflict. Beijing needed some means of countering Soviet pressure and in fact, China's extremity seems to have forced a softening of its bargaining position in negotiations with Washington, particularly on the issue of Taiwan, as will be discussed below.

In the meantime, in September 1978, Deng Xiaoping traveled to Pyongyang, North Korea, and took an inspection tour of Manchurian defenses. His trip to North Korea was undoubtedly to ascertain Kim Il Sung's position should hostilities between Moscow and Beijing occur. That accomplished, Beijing began the deployment of what would eventually total twenty-seven divisions as well as hundreds of fighter aircraft to south China. The September deployments clearly indicated that China's decision to take military action against Hanoi had already been made and its size suggested a major campaign. The exact nature and timing of the strike, however, would ultimately depend upon Peking's success, alone or in concert with allies, in neutralizing the Soviet Union.

At this point, Moscow signed a treaty of peace and friendship with the Socialist Republic of Vietnam on 3 November 1978.[24] The treaty put Beijing on notice that any military move against Vietnam would have to reckon with Moscow's public pledge to support its ally. At the same time and for the same reason of Moscow's more forthcoming support, Hanoi redoubled its efforts to topple the Pol Pot regime in Kampuchea. In early December Hanoi intensified pressure on both the Kampuchean and

Chinese fronts. On the third, Hanoi announced the formation of the Kampuchean National United Front for National Salvation, theoretically offering the prospect of legitimizing its presence in Kampuchea, and at the same time sharply escalated military clashes on both fronts.

The U.S. Opening to China–Deja Vu 1969?

Structurally, the situation as it was evolving in the summer of 1978 was remarkably similar to that of ten years' earlier when the United States made its first attempt at improving relations with China. The Beijing regime then was facing intensifying conflict on both its northern and southern fronts just as it faced now. The major external differences were that in the former instance the primary threat came from Moscow, while this time the direct threat of conflict came from the south in Hanoi's attack on China's ally. Also, in the former case the United States and China had had no substantive relationship at all and Washington was mired in conflict against Hanoi, while in the latter instance the United States was no longer involved in any major way on the mainland of Southeast Asia and had an ongoing diplomatic relationship with the Chinese regime.

The impending conflict in Southeast Asia which foreshadowed not only a Chinese attack on Vietnam, but also some kind of Soviet action to deter China from defeating its ally, was thus both a challenge to the United States and an opportunity. The challenge lay in how to prevent the expansion of a Sino-Vietnamese conflict into a larger confrontation between Russia and China at a time when the U.S. position *vis à vis* the Soviet Union was perceived to be unfavorable. The opportunity lay in the Chinese leadership's own perception, or misperception, of Washington as a potential source of support to deter Moscow while it attempted to protect its own ally.

The U.S. response was to move to normalize relations with Beijing and through that act attempt to forestall the escalation of Sino-Vietnamese hostilities from spiralling into Sino-Soviet war. Upon reflection there seems little question that in the minds of U.S. policymakers the issues of impending war in Asia and normalization of relations with China were connected. Following the unsuccessful Vance trip in August 1977, President Carter sent his national security advisor Zbigniew Brzezinski to Beijing in early May 1978 to initiate the process. Brzezinski informed the Chinese leadership that the United States was ready to begin serious discussions regarding the terms of normalization.[25] The United States government presented its draft of a joint Sino-American communique announcing the normalization of relations on 4 November which was accepted after a month of internal deliberation and the announcement itself made on 15 December.

By this time Chinese preparations for war with Vietnam were in an advanced stage and the decision to normalize relations with the United States would play its part. In the context of Beijing's impending attack on Vietnam, the advanced preparations for which U.S. intelligence could observe, the timing of the decision to normalize relations was designed from both Washington's and Deijing's respective points of view to function as a form of deterrence diplomacy whose purpose was to forestall any direct Soviet-Chinese hostilities when Chinese forces attacked Moscow's ally Hanoi.

This is suggested strongly by the terms of normalization as they were worked out, particularly the issue of Taiwan's status. The issue of Taiwan, the historical stumbling block to the opening of relations, was in fact finessed at this time in order to establish Sino-American ties. Despite Deng Xiaoping's earlier objections to compromise on that issue, and insistence that the U.S. derecognize the Republic of China, abrogate the mutual defense treaty and withdraw all troops from the island, he agreed to a compromise which was in fact not a compromise but a concession. The U.S. further insisted that its defense treaty with the ROC be terminated in accordance with the treaty's provisions, that is, that one year's notice be given of intent to terminate. In other words, the treaty was not in fact abrogated, but terminated according to its own terms.

Finally, the U.S. indicated its intention to continue sales of defensive arms to Taiwan following termination of the Treaty. While the United States acknowledged the Chinese position that "there is but one China and Taiwan is part of China," Washington reaffirmed and Beijing formally but quietly acquiesced in the expressed U.S. intention to "maintain cultural, commercial, and other unofficial relations with the people of Taiwan,"[26] even while informally denying that part of the communique. In fact, U.S. relations with Taiwan changed very little, except in form. While Washington withdrew formal recognition from Taipei and reduced its military position on the island (which in 1979 in any case numbered only a few hundred personnel) it also continued to provide military support for the Taiwan government. Beijing, in other words, in return for recognition by the U.S. would have to remain content with the short-run *status quo* and only the future *prospect* of integration of the island.

Given the impending military conflict between China and Vietnam, the

15 December announcement of the decision to normalize relations on 1 January of the coming year was all but explicitly directed at Moscow and Hanoi. The communique emphasized that both the U.S. and the PRC "wish to reduce the danger of international military conflict," and that "neither should seek hegemony in the Asia-Pacific region or in any other region of the world and each is opposed to efforts by any other country or group of countries to establish such hegemony." But if the communique was intended as an exercise in deterrence diplomacy, the normalization announcement simply advanced Hanoi's timetable for attack on Kampuchea, which began on 25 December, one week before formal recognition between Washington and Peking was scheduled to occur.

The Struggle for Hegemony in Indochina and the Asia-Pacific

Vietnam invaded Kampuchea in force on 25 December 1978. On the same day *People's Daily* carried the headline: "Hanoi has gone far enough . . . Don't complain that we didn't warn you in advance." The Vietnamese invasion, with the prominent involvement of Soviet and Cuban "advisors," was a multi-pronged effort which carried along all of the major routes of access into Kampuchea. Within two weeks, by 7 January, Phnom Penh had fallen to the Vietnamese invaders and the west coast port of Kompong Som (formerly Sihanoukville) was under heavy attack. In the east, by 19 January, Hanoi's forces had secured the Mekong River between Phnom Penh and the Vietnamese border.

Hanoi's armies had overrun most of Kampuchea in a blitzkrieg-like operation lasting little more than a month, but which also left Vietnamese forces strung out and overextended at many points. Despite Hanoi's insistent claims of victory, Pol Pot's forces had been staggered but not routed and had reverted to guerrilla warfare tactics after initial heavy setbacks. Concentrating on cutting Hanoi's lines of communication, Pol Pot's scattered forces were still actively engaging the enemy although clearly on the defensive by late January and in danger of total collapse.

It was under circumstances of the imminent collapse of Peking's client, Kampuchea, that Deng Xiaoping visited the United States following the normalization of diplomatic relations. His trip, spanning the week of 28 January-5 February 1979, was intended, at least in part, to elicit from the U.S. leadership the extent of support that Beijing could expect to receive when it moved into action against Vietnam. In an important speech, shortly after his arrival in Washington, Deng declared that "our two countries are duty-bound to work together to maintain the peace," giving the clear impression that he expected U.S. support for the coming strike at Hanoi.[27]

Deng's visit precipitated another round of the seemingly interminable disputes within the Carter administration over the proper policy course to pursue. For Brzezinski the continuing Soviet buildup transformed Deng's trip "from what initially was conceived of as a formal diplomatic act into a summit meeting of global significance."[28] For the national security advisor "the very fact of Deng's visit . . . brought to a head the question of how far the United States should go in developing the new relationship with China," and he saw it as "a strategic opportunity . . . to off-set the Soviet military buildup."[29] Secretary of State Vance, as he did on most issues, strongly objected, recommending to the President that "he make it clear to Deng that we would not permit any disruption of our policy toward the Soviet Union."[30] The Chinese must not be allowed, said Vance, "to influence us to take a harder public line against the Soviets."

The most important and indeed self-evident question Deng wished to put to the U.S. leadership was: would Washington act to neutralize Moscow in the event the Soviet Union actively threatened intervention against China, while Beijing's forces were engaged in Vietnam? Washington's reply, resolving the internal dispute in Secretary Vance's favor, but casting a pall upon the just-established formal relationship with China, was that the United States would extend diplomatic support for China against Vietnam, but would take no action to deter the Soviet Union. Indeed, the U.S. response helps explain the curious nature of the "lesson" that Beijing then attempted to teach Hanoi.

Although the United States called for "two withdrawals" after the conflict had begun—withdrawal of Chinese forces from Vietnam and the withdrawal of Vietnamese forces from Kampuchea—the U.S. government made it clear that it would not attempt to deter the Soviet Union from pressuring China. In fact the opposite was true. During the conflict in late February, amid reports of Soviet troops and armor movements toward the Chinese border, a U.S. state department spokesman declared that a Soviet strike on China's northern border "would not be of direct concern to the United States."[31] This was, of course, a one hundred and eighty degree turn from the public stance the United States had adopted during the 1969 Sino-Soviet confrontation!

Even if Deng had anticipated a negative U.S. response, he nevertheless expressed bitter disappointment after his departure. In Japan, on the way back to Beijing, Deng was highly critical of U.S. policy. He said that he could not complain while a guest in the United States, but having left, he could say what he thought. "The Soviet Union," he remarked with characteristic acerbity, "will never be impressed by half-way positions."[32] On the other hand, the United States "is allowing the Soviet Union to place a lot of pawns on the world's chessboard . . . things cannot be allowed to go on this way."[33]

Chinese strategy in Southeast Asia for a generation was to promote fragmentation in order to preserve domination of the region. Given the imminent prospect of the utter failure of that strategy in the Soviet-supported Vietnamese invasion of Kampuchea, the last remaining area of significant Chinese influence, the only type of "lesson" which would have been consistent with long-term Chinese strategy was one which forced Vietnam to withdraw from Kampuchea. Yet the Chinese offensive against Vietnam, 17 February to 16 March 1979, did not come remotely close to accomplishing that objective. Despite the mobilization of over five hundred thousand troops and eight hundred aircraft and an initial attack on twenty-three points along the border from the Laotian frontier to the Gulf of Tonkin, no objective commensurate either with Beijing's long-term strategy, or the size of the military buildup, was achieved.

If the Chinese objective was simply a spoiling action with no other "lesson" than to demonstrate the capability to inflict punishment, as some have suggested, then it was extremely costly and produced a worse situation than existed prior to the attack. In less than a month of actual fighting the Chinese absorbed combat losses of some 28,000 killed(!) and 43,000 wounded, while exacting perhaps several times that combined figure against Vietnam. Even so, Beijing's forces failed to engage, let alone destroy, a single main force Vietnamese division, encountering only regional forces during the month-long campaign. Worst of all, from Beijing's point of view, the Soviet Union moved quickly to reinforce Hanoi as well as to increase its own presence in Vietnam with expanded air and naval facilities.

At the decisive moment in the conflict, Moscow commenced extensive military movements along the Sino-Soviet border, while providing Vietnam with air and seaborne assistance to redeploy three main-force combat divisions from South Vietnam to the Hanoi area in early March following the Chinese breakthrough at Langson. Although Secretary Vance asserted that there was "no . . . evidence" of a "Soviet buildup taking place on the Sino-Soviet border," his statement evaded the critical question of whether or not the Soviets moved what was already there.[34] Another source claimed that the Soviets "mobilized and moved about their military formations . . . on their side of the Sino-Soviet border. On the Soviet side of the Heilungkiang border alone, the Chinese perceived eleven such large-scale movements . . ."[35]

The Chinese breakthrough at Langson on March 5th after a fierce week-long battle opened the way for a direct attack on Hanoi itself, which explains in large part Soviet movements at this time. Indeed, with the transfer of three Vietnamese main force divisions to the Hanoi area it appeared that China's main objective of forcing a withdrawal from Kampuchea was coming within reach. Yet at this moment the Beijing leadership declared that its military objectives *had already been met* and announced that Chinese forces would withdraw. Clearly, the Chinese leadership chose not to undertake an offensive powerful enough to achieve the strategic objective, even when, following the battlefield success at Langson, that objective became a realizable possibility. What had happened, of course, was that in the absence of a countervailing U.S. posture toward the Soviet Union, Moscow's subtle saber rattling proved sufficient to deter Beijing's advance. Beijing would not tempt a Soviet strike and involvement in a two-front conflict and so withdrew.

Conclusion

Comparing U.S. policy behavior toward China in the two instances raises some apparent contradictions. For example, why did the United States support Beijing against Soviet pressures in 1969, but not in 1979? This would appear to invalidate the thesis set forth in the introduction of this essay that the United States moved to improve relations with China when it appeared that the U.S.-Soviet strategic weapons balance was becoming adverse. But a broader focus indicates that U.S. policy behavior was in fact consistent with the thesis, for Washington did move to improve relations with Beijing (normalization) prior to the Sino-Vietnamese war. It was only after normalization and during that conflict when Moscow threatened Beijing's advance in Vietnam that Washington declined to support the People's Republic. Yet that too, was consistent with the general structural objective of attempting to maintain a stable equilibrium of states on the Eurasian landmass. U.S. support for the People's Republic during the attack on Vietnam would only have encouraged Peking's march on Hanoi in disregard of the Soviet threat, increasing the probability of a Sino-Soviet conflict, which the United States sought to avoid. Thus, the

Carter leadership chose to decline support to Beijing in order to further the larger objective of regional stability, although at China's expense.

Notes

1. Henry Kissinger, *White House Years* (Boston, MA: Little-Brown, 1979), pp.174-5.
2. *Background Information Relating to Southeast Asia and Vietnam,* U.S. Senate Committee on Foreign Relations, June 1970 (Washington, D.C. 1970) pp.295-302 (hereafter referred to as *Vietnam Background.)*
3. *Ibid.,* p.296.
4. Tad Szulc, *The Illusion of Peace* (New York: Viking Press, 1978), p.116.
5. *Vietnam Background,* pp.319-320.
6. *Ibid.* p.315.
7. Joseph Whelan, *World Communism, 1967-1969: Soviet Efforts to Re-establish Control,* a study prepared for the Internal Security Subcommittee at the Senate Judiciary Committee, 11 June 1970 (Washington, D.C., 1970) p.127f.
8. *Ibid.,* p.152.
9. *New York Times,* 6 July 1969.
10. *Vietnam Background,* p.315y.
11. *New York Times,* 3 September 1969.
12. *Ibid.* 7 September 1969.
13. John Haldeman, *The Ends of Power* (New York: New York Times Books, 1978), pp.88-94.
14. *New York Times,* 8 October 1969.
15. Richard M. Nixon, *R.N. The Memoirs of Richard Nixon* (New York: Grosset and Dunlap, 1978), p.405.
16. *Vietnam Background,* p.326.
17. *Ibid.*
18. Cyrus Vance, *Hard Choices* (New York: Simon & Schuster, 1984), p.164.
19. *Ibid.,* p.52n.
20. See the author's *China, A Political History, 1917-1980* (Boulder, CO: Westview Press, 1982), pp.386-440.
21. See John Newman, "Soviet Strategy in Asia, 1977-1979," *Asian Affairs* (May-June, 1980)
22. *Pravda,* 2 September 1978.
23. *People's Daily,* 17 September 1978.
24. *Pravda,* 4 November 1978.
25. Zbigniew Brzezinski, *Power and Principle* (New York: Farrar-Strauss, 1983), p.209f.

26. *New York Times*, 16 December 1978.
27. *Wall Street Journal*, 30 January 1979.
28. Brzezinski, p.403.
29. *Ibid.*, p.404.
30. Vance, p.121.
31. *Christian Science Monitor*, 29 February 1979.
32. *New York Times*, 8 February 1979.
33. *Washington Star*, 8 February 1979.
34. Vance, p. 122.
35. Thomas Robinson, "What Policies Should the United States Adopt to Counter the Soviet Military Threat to Northeast Asia?" *Asian Perspective* (Spring-Summer 1983), p.77.

Soviet Perceptions of Chinese–U.S. Relations

STEVEN I. LEVINE

Like the well-known progression of economic development from agriculture through industry to the service sector, the primary field of Sino-Soviet-American relations has given rise to secondary and tertiary intellectual enterprises. If official as well as scholarly analyses of this tripartite relationship constitute the secondary sector, then analysis of how the parties to the relationship and their retinue of scholars themselves analyze the relationship in whole or in part may be called the tertiary sector. Such tertiary analysis, then, is frankly derivative and perhaps might even be viewed as a parasitical genre.

There is even more to this than meets the eye, however. Working in Washington, one quickly becomes aware of the diplomat China specialists (in such places as the Soviet Embassy, for example) whose job, inter alia, is to monitor the views of American scholars like ourselves who monitor Sino-Soviet-American relations. We, of course, try to keep tabs on those who keep tabs on us. The possibilities are endless. Everything we say or write becomes the subject for yet another level of analysis! I am reminded of Harold Rome's song written at the time of the Truman loyalty-security

72

probes which asked, "Who's gonna investigate the man who investigates the man who investigates me?"[1]

Like all genres tertiary analysis has its own formal or informal rules that vary from place to place, however. In the Soviet Union, a fundamental rule is that tertiary analysis must point out the distortions and errors of bourgeois scholars (presumably most of us gathered here including myself) who lack the light of Marxism-Leninism to illuminate their analyses. Even the very best of us—what the Soviets call the sober-minded (a peculiarly poignant phrase given what we know of alcoholism in the USSR)—even the very best of us, I say, are like the righteous pagans in Dante's *Inferno,* consigned to a kind of Limbo in the ideological struggle. The aforementioned rule is itself based on the assumption that most of us Western bourgeois falsifiers—a phrase we are supposed to understand as a scientific description rather than a mere term of opprobrium—are motivated by a singleminded determination to do our bit for the cause of anti-Sovietism and the exacerbation of international tension. Of course, by no means all Soviet scholars subscribe literally or even figuratively to such creedal articles. All of us who have spoken candidly with Soviet-China specialists have found among the best of them—the sober-minded, I am tempted to say—an appreciation of the contribution of Western scholars to the common sinological enterprise.

In the West, tertiary analysis is based, I think, on the implicit belief that a greater understanding of how our presumptive adversaries and friends themselves perceive Sino-Soviet-American relations will somehow enhance the capacity of decisionmakers to manage the politics of the strategic triangle. In particular, insights into Soviet views of U.S.-China relations may be relevant to the question of Soviet-American relations insofar as both superpowers include a China factor in their political and strategic calculations. Soviet threat perceptions, their views of the strategic environment, and their willingness to engage in dialogue, enter into compromises, and so forth are all related in some measure to their reading of the U.S.-China relationship since Moscow sees Washington and Beijing as its major adversaries.

The views of Soviet academic as well as bureaucratic specialists —whether on China, the United States, or Sino-American relations—are germane to our purposes, of course, because along with statements in the press, they form the primary material on which most analyses of Soviet perceptions of U.S.-PRC relations are based. Explicit statements on the subject by ranking Soviet leaders have been rare in recent years, and the virtual political interregnum of the post-Brezhnev era coupled with slow progress toward partial Sino-Soviet detente has further limited the flow of authoritative statements on the subject.[2] Soviet reticence on the subject of U.S.-China relations continued throughout 1984 and into the present year.

The influence of Soviet China specialists on the Kremlin's policy towards the PRC is a topic perhaps even more opaque than the influence of American China specialists on U.S. China policy, and suggests the appositeness of a comparative study of these subjects. A recent student of Soviet China-watchers has opined that by virtue of their "political/ administrative positions" and "their intellectual power", it may be said that "the main-stream Soviet scholars . . . continued to exert influence on the political leadership throughout the 1970s, thus contributing to the highly inflexible Soviet China policy of the last decade."[3] In his careful cataloging of Soviet China specialists, another student of the subject has differentiated between "the defenders of the status quo" and "the voices for change." He notes that only a relatively small number of senior Soviet academic specialists—either in the institutes or directly in government service—write on general themes relating to China, to Soviet-Chinese relations, and to triangular politics.[4] Incidentally, although our system is different in most respects, we also tend to have a kind of unofficial *genro* of prominent China specialists—at least several of whom are present at this conference—who contribute regularly to what passes for debate on China policy and who are consulted by officialdom on important occasions.

In the Soviet Union, the subjects of China, Chinese-Soviet, and Sino-American relations have been politically sensitive since at least the late 1960s. The reorganization of Soviet China studies in 1966 by decree of the Academy of Sciences to meet the long-term ideological and political challenge of a hostile Maoist China resulted in the ascendancy of the newly created Institute of the Far East (Institut Dal'nego Vostoka) headed by M.I. Sladkovsky, a veteran Ministry of Foreign Trade official specializing in Soviet-Chinese economic relations. Rozman correctly identifies Sladkovsky as one of the handful of leading "defenders of the status quo"—a kind of academic-apparatchik brain trust advising the Soviet leadership on China policy. (Other members of the group include Rakhmanin, Tikhvinsky, and Kapitsa who work directly within the Party and state apparatus.)[5] These hardliners on China policy contributed to and were themselves sustained by a bleakly negative view of PRC domestic and foreign policies articulated publicly in the Institute's quarterly *Problemy Dal'nego Vostoka* (published in English with a three month time lag as *Far Eastern Affairs*). Meanwhile, most of the more sinophile Soviet specialists remained in the Institute of Orientology (Institut Vostokovedenia), a haven for historians, literary specialists, linguists, and other herbivorous scholars.[6]

The tasks of Soviet sinology, set forth in two national conferences of Soviet-China specialists in 1971 and 1982, were first to criticize Maoism and lay bare its social and ideological roots, and secondly, to investigate the character of post-Mao Chinese political and social developments while at the same time criticizing the anti-Soviet character of Chinese foreign policy.[7] The subject of Sino-American relations, of course, is not the exclusive preserve of Soviet China specialists. It engages the attention of Moscow's America-watchers in the Institute of the USA and Canada which publishes *SShA* (USA), as well as general commentators on international relations in the Soviet press.

V.P. Lukin, himself a frequent contributor to the genre and a scholar at the Institute of the USA and Canada, has noted a certain repetitiveness in Soviet studies of U.S.-China relations. "In the best cases," he writes, "each subsequent work supplements with new information that temporal segment which separates it from the preceding edition."[8] The remedy he suggests is in-depth monographic treatment of particular aspects of Sino-American relations such as the study by A.A. Nagornyi and A.B. Parkanskii on economic and scientific-technological elements in the US-China relationship. Indeed, Soviet scholarly work, particularly on the American side of Sino-American relations, shows an increasing appreciation for the complexities of American policy making with respect to China. For example, a recent study entitled *Motive Forces of U.S. Policy toward China* (Dvizhushchie sily politiki SShA v otnoshenii Kitaya) by E.P. Bazhanov examines such factors as the role of the Congress, the press, the President and the Executive Branch, commercial and economic interests, public opinion, scholars, etc., in the making of China policy.[9] Within the framework of an argument that posits the class interests of American monopoly capital as the underlying motive force of American China policy—a position of unimpeachable Soviet orthodoxy—Bazhanov presents a fairly nuanced discussion of U.S. China policy that manifests a sophisticated understanding of the American political process. Of course, the journalistic and periodical press upon which this paper's analysis relies for the most part are considerably less detailed or differentiated in their approach to U.S.-China relations.

Western analyses of Soviet perceptions of China and of Sino-American relations have also probed for differences within the Soviet view. In addition to the work of Chi Su and Gilbert Rozman already cited above, one may mention Gretchen Ann Sandles' dissertation "Soviet Images of the People's Republic of China, 1949-1979," which relates six different Soviet images of China to the state of Sino-Soviet relations at particular periods since 1949. This diachronic approach is useful for understanding the continuing efforts of Soviet scholars to come to grips with the intellectual and political task of comprehending a China whose peculiar path of development appeared to challenge the laws of Marxism. A complementary method is the synchronous approach recently employed by William deB. Mills in his comparison of Soviet civilian and military views of China.[10] Starting with the hypothesis that Soviet civilian views of China as expressed in the Party newspaper *Pravda* differed from Soviet military views as expressed in the Army newspaper *Krasnaya Zvezda* (Red Star), Mills concludes his examination by suggesting a functional rather than an institutional basis for the differences he found. *Pravda's* more moderate, flexible, and hopeful view of China, he suggests, may have derived from its status in part as an international propaganda organ of the Soviet regime while *Krasnaya Zvezda's* uncompromising, bleak pessimism with respect to China may reflect its status as a domestic organ for the most part unconcerned with foreign reactions, and the latter may therefore be a more accurate barometer of Soviet elite perceptions of China.[11] This intriguing interpretation is probably unprovable, however, since there is no independent way to confirm what are "authentic" Soviet elite perceptions of China.

What *is* clear from the work of earlier analysts is that Soviet views of China, and of Sino-American relations too, are not monolithic. Within permitted boundaries demarcated by authoritative Soviet political and institutional leaders, lively discussions proceed about the character of contemporary China, about Chinese foreign policy, and about the significance of Sino-American relations and their implications for the USSR. The limited scope and character of the present paper, however, precludes an attempt to examine the full range of Soviet views of U.S.-China relations that a larger scale research effort might uncover. The much more modest objective I have in mind—of the sort noted in the remark of Lukin cited above—is to update the work of earlier scholars in a manner akin to the periodic revision of Congressional Research Service Briefs. After a summary review of earlier writings on the subject, I shall focus on Soviet commentary concerning U.S.-China relations during the last couple of years or so.

Soviet Views of U.S.-China Relations 1971-1982

Since the epochal breakthrough of 1971-1972, Soviet observers have followed the trajectory of U.S.-China relations with unflagging interest.

Until 1978, Soviet suspicions concerning the possible negative impact of Sino-American relations on Soviet political and security interests was allayed by two factors. The first was Washington's determination to achieve better relations with Moscow across a broad range of issues at the same time that it pursued normalization with Beijing. This was read in Moscow as an indication that American leaders recognized the primacy of superpower relations in the nuclear age. The second was the continuing inability of Washington and Beijing to consummate their quasi-official relationship through the establishment of formal diplomatic ties. Prior to 1978 the intercourse between China and the United States resembled a series of acts of coitus interruptus.

However, the growing ascendancy within the Carter Administration of advocates of a decisive pro-Beijing tilt (personified by National Security Advisor Zbigniew Brzezinski) culminated in the breaking of the Sino-American impasse by the end of the year. Viewing the rapidly burgeoning Sino-American relationship with increasing distaste, Moscow now believed that Washington was responding with alacrity to Beijing's anti-Soviet machinations. To be sure, Soviet commentators noted the continuing contradictions between the United States and the PRC, particularly over the Taiwan issue, but the trend lines were disquieting. The darkest Soviet suspicions were confirmed by the acceleration of Sino-American military-security cooperation commencing with Secretary of Defense Brown's visit to Beijing in January 1980 and culminating in Secretary of State Haig's journey of June 1981.[12] From a Soviet perspective, particularly disturbing was the enhancement of Chinese access to U.S. defense-related technology, Sino-American cooperation in regional conflicts, and intelligence-sharing.[13]

It may be appropriate at this point to raise one of the major questions of this paper? What is the correlation between Soviet perceptions of Chinese-U.S. relations and the actual trend of those relations, at least as described by non-Soviet observers? On the whole, I think, Soviet writers have rather accurately registered both the main trends as well as the short-term shifts in the relations between Beijing and Washington. They have noted the underlying concern in both capitals for the security dimension of the relationship within the context of global politics. To be sure, through mid-1981, apart from easily discounted ritual denials, Chinese and American leaders themselves acknowledged that their mutual interest in containing the Soviet Union was the driving force of their relationship. Not surprisingly, many Soviet analysts have tended toward worst case scenarios. They interpreted the emerging Sino-American security relationship as the core of an anti-Soviet alliance in Northeast Asia into which Japan was also allegedly being drawn.[14] In reality, the intensification of Sino-American security consultations, and movement toward providing China with advanced technology, equipment, and even arms provided ample grounds for Soviet perceptions even though the notion of an emerging alliance was premature at the very least. Needless to say, playing the injured innocent, Soviet analysts never admitted that Moscow, as a result of its interventionist policies in Afghanistan and its alliance with Vietnam, bore any responsibility for the Washington-Beijing entente.

Expressed Soviet anxiety over Sino-American security ties crested in mid-1981 when Secretary of State Haig announced the partial lifting of U.S. restrictions on arms sales to China. Soon thereafter, however, Beijing clouded the Sino-American atmosphere by harping on a series of irritants in the relationship, the most important of which was the issue of continuing U.S. arms sales to Taiwan. The Soviet barometer quickly registered this change in atmosphere, noting that the headlong rush towards a Peking-Washington axis had been halted by such apparently insoluble contradictions between the two countries as the issue of Taiwan, rivalry between Beijing and Washington for influence in Asia, and continuing ideological discord arising from the fundamental differences in the American and Chinese social systems.[15]

By early 1982 this perception of a rocky road ahead for Washington and Beijing was one of two key factors leading to a significant easing of expressed Soviet concern about the security implications of Sino-American relations.[16] The other factor, of course, was the resumption in October 1982 of Sino-Soviet talks at the vice-ministerial level that the Chinese had suspended in January 1980 after Soviet military intervention in Afghanistan. Of course, Beijing's willingness to resume the dialogue promised no early resolution of the outstanding issues, but it did complement the PRC verbal shift away from the formulas of the anti-Soviet united front —the rationale for the Beijing-Washington security relationship up till then.

By 1983, then, Soviet analysts were expressing views of China and the United States that stressed each country's individual hostility to the USSR, but that voiced doubts about their ability to link forces in any way that might significantly jeopardize Soviet interests. For example, one analyst, describing the Asian component of President Reagan's allegedly aggressive global policies, paid scant attention to the China factor, instead emphasizing American reliance on its traditional alliance partners, Japan and South Korea in the pursuit of its militarist aims.[17] Another essay on the same subject depicted the PRC as an object of Washington's malevolent courtship rather than an equally culpable partner in anti-Soviet machinations.[18]

As earlier students of the subject have noted, around this time Soviet views of China were beginning to show signs of divergence concerning the question of whether significant opportunities existed for improving Sino-Soviet relations. The "defenders of the status quo," represented at the Second Conference of Sinologists in January 1982 by O.B. Rakhmanin of the CPSU's International Liaison Department, presented a harshly negative view of post-Mao China as a system in which the essence of Maoism—national chauvinism, hegemonism, anti-Sovietism—is merely being repackaged, as it were, in order to promote an alliance with reactionary imperialism led by the United States.[19] The policy implications of such a view was that Soviet initiative to improve relations with the PRC would be in vain and might actually be counterproductive.[20] The alternate view, articulated by M.S. Kapitsa, head of the Far Eastern Department of the Soviet Foreign Ministry—equivalent to the U.S. Assistant Secretary of State for East Asia and the Pacific—was cautiously optimistic. While condemning "the ethnopsychological stereotypical thinking of the Chinese rulers and their geopolitical and hegemonic ambitions," Kapitsa contended that in China, "an ever greater number of working people, intellectuals and politicians" were freeing themselves from Maoist dogmas and realizing the need to establish better relations with the Soviet Union and the socialist bloc.[21] In policy terms, Kapitsa's critical insight was that the further consolidation of the Washington-Beijing leg of the strategic triangle in the form of a security alliance was not a foregone conclusion. The greater flexibility in post-Mao China's foreign policy created a competitive situation in which Moscow might achieve better relations with Beijing even as the latter responded to Washington's pressures and enticements. PRC articulation of its independent foreign policy line in the early 1980s suggested that even if the affair between Washington and Beijing was likely to be protracted, Beijing was not going to "move in" with Washington. The old socialist wife still had a fighting chance.

A glance at the American-Soviet-Chinese Communist relationship in the late 1940s may shed some light on the current triangular relations.[22] At that time, U.S. failure to pursue limited opportunities for establishing relations with the CCP contributed toward the establishment of a full-blown Moscow-Beijing alliance. At this time, some CCP leaders might have welcomed diplomatic, commercial, and even cultural links with the United States as a supplement to rather than a substitute for the links with the socialist "elder brother." The logic of Kapitsa's position was that modest, discrete improvements in Sino-Soviet relations—such as were already underway—might pay important long-term dividends in the form of ameliorated Sino-Soviet relations, and a less hostile China that abjured exclusive dependence upon the United States.

Soviet Views of U.S.-China Relations 1983 to the Present

The resumption of high-level U.S.-PRC contacts beginning with Secretary of State George Shultz's visit to Beijing in February 1983 and including subsequent trips by Premier Zhao Ziyang, President Reagan, Foreign Minister Wu Xueqien (Wu Hsiu-Chuan), Chairman of the Joint Chiefs of Staff General John Vessey and others provided the pegs on which Soviet commentary concerning U.S.-China relations was hung. Soviet analysts focused on several interconnected questions in their discussions of Sino-American relations: (1) What factors were producing closer U.S.-PRC ties? What were the limiting factors in the relationship? (2) How and to what degree did Sino-American relations threaten Soviet interests? (3) Did relations between Washington and Beijing preclude the resumption of the Soviet-American dialogue or jeopardize progress towards the normalization of Soviet-Chinese relations?

Initially, Soviet commentators were somewhat slow to recognize the significance of Secretary Shultz's China visit which took place with little of the ballyhoo of earlier trips.[23] A TASS report hinted at Chinese dissatisfaction with U.S. policy on technology transfer, cultural and economic exchanges, and Taiwan among other issues.[24] An *Izvestia* commentary by N. Nikitin concerning the meeting of two Sino-American joint commissions noted ongoing frictions despite the signing of various agreements. Nikitin wrote:

> Observers note in all of this, a desire to 'smooth over' long-standing problems in commercial and economic relations that reflect even deeper divergences and conflicts of interests is readily discernible behind the patently inflated trumpeting of achievements in bilateral relations, especially on the part of the American representatives.[25]

Secretary of Defense Caspar Weinberger's September 1983 visit to Beijing evoked little commentary in the central Soviet press. Brief reports in *Pravda* and *Izvestia* noted the significance of the trip for expediting the transfer of American technology to China, but refrained from criticizing the Chinese or warning about the dangerous implications of Sino-American military relations.[26] Soviet restraint may have been related to the timing of Weinberger's visit which was sandwiched between Soviet Deputy Foreign Minister Kapitsa's discussions with Wu Xueqien and the start of the third round of Soviet-Chinese talks on 6 October.

V.P. Lukin, writing in *SShA* (USA), took the occasion of Weinberger's visit to offer a current assessment of Sino-American relations. His analysis typifies that of those Soviets who downplay the threat to Soviet interests posed by Washington-Beijing ties. Lukin's point of departure is the fundamental divergence between Chinese and American objectives. While Washington's aim is to subordinate U.S.-PRC relations to its "global military antisocialist course," Beijing, "according to its official statements" is not interested in strategic cooperation but "simply in mutually beneficial relations with the United States *as with other countries.*"[27] Lukin correctly observed that Weinberger's visit was an effort to overcome the period of "friction and roughness" that characterized Sino-American relations between mid-1981 and Spring 1983. Noting the further development of trade, investment, cultural relations, military contacts, and so forth between Peking and Washington, Lukin nevertheless stressed the conflictual elements, particularly the Taiwan question. The United States, he said, was willing to pay in technology and economic aid for China's adherence to an anti-Soviet line, but engaged in recriminations, threats of sanctions, and other such bullying behavior whenever PRC foreign policy threatened to diverge from Washington's purposes.[28]

Lukin's thesis—that Washington rather than Beijing was the aggressive, dominant partner in the relationship—has been the leitmotif of Soviet commentary recently. Two points derive from this position. First is that as the subordinate party to the relationship, Beijing is probably less committed to it than is Washington. Second is the implicit suggestion that an astute Soviet policy towards China might be able to take advantage of the tensions between Washington and Beijing to enhance Soviet leverage in the triangular relationship. This latter point, of course, was already intimated by Kapitsa as has been observed above.

The exchange of high-level visits between Premier Zhao Ziyang who visited Washington in January 1984 and President Reagan who journeyed to Beijing in April constituted prima facie evidence that the period of "friction and roughness" had been surmounted, yet Soviet commentary on the visits continued to emphasize the underlying divergence of Chinese and American interests. Vsevolod Ovchinnikov, a hardline *Pravda* commentator, echoed Lukin's comments about Weinberger's trip, saying that:

the efforts of U.S. ruling circles have the primary goal of using China's interest in the development of scientific and technical ties with the United States in order to tie that country to Washington's global anti-Soviet course and to draw it into a 'strategic partnership' that would be in the interests of imperialism.[29]

However, Ovchinnikov observed that Zhao Ziyang rejected the notion of such strategic partnership and that the Chinese leader pointed out differences as well as similarities in Beijing's and Washington's views on international issues.

If the United States was supposedly trying to make anti-Soviet capital out of China's need for technical and economic assistance, PRC purposes were no less manipulative. I. Alexeyev and F. Nikolayev, writing in the monthly foreign affairs journal *International Affairs,* said:

the Chinese side, judging from everything, intends to draw top dividends from the existing tensions in the relations between the USSR and the USA and the pathological anti-Sovietism of the present U.S. government in order to gain maximum benefits in trade and economic relations, obtain credits and the latest technology from its overseas partner.[30]

The Soviet writers faulted Zhao for his failure to criticize Reagan's anti-socialist crusade, but they did not accuse the Chinese themselves of anti-Sovietism or hegemonistic aims. They summed up his visit as pointing to a "new stage of more active cooperation between China and the USA in political, and especially in the trade and economic fields . . ."[31] However, they did not assert that such cooperation endangered the USSR or Soviet bloc interests. The United States, not China, was identified as the enemy of peace and socialism. Chinese leaders, it was implied, viewed their relations with the United States in a purely instrumental fashion. The Soviet interpretation in effect saw the Chinese engaged in the time-honored technique of exacting squeeze from the foreigners while making no binding political-strategic commitments.

Soviet commentary on President Reagan's April 1984 trip to Beijing evoked the same harsh condemnation of U.S. policy with an ambivalent view of China's role in the "contradictory partnership" of Washington and Beijing, as the veteran political observer Alexander Bovin termed it.[32] Bovin saw Reagan's trip as motivated both by a desire to gain domestic political advantage and as part of the ongoing search for a Sino-American *modus vivendi* consistent with Washington's attempt to shore up the U.S. position in Asia and the Pacific. Contrary to ex-President Nixon's call for the United States to welcome improvement in Sino-Soviet relations—cited approvingly by Bovin—Reagan's aim in going to China was to "spoil the normalization of Soviet-Chinese relations and to nail the PRC to its anti-Soviet course by hook or by crook."[33] Bovin wrote that "For him [Reagan] the 'China card' has meaning only when it is in an anti-Soviet deck."[34] Beijing, for its part, refrained from publicly supporting Reagan's anti-Soviet remarks, but despite signs of change in Chinese foreign policy, "the desire [of the Chinese] to play the 'American card' in order to pressure the USSR can hardly be considered over."[35] Sounding a familiar note of warning, Bovin claimed that China was taking a considerable risk in "handing the keys to the modernization of China to the other side of the Pacific," because American aid would be used as a lever to force Chinese adherence to American policy objectives in Asia and elsewhere. An unfortunate side-effect of improved Sino-Soviet relations, Bovin suggested, was that insofar as it frightened the United States, it tempted Beijing from a position of greater advantage to play both a "Soviet card" vis-à-vis Washington and an "American card" vis-à-vis Moscow.[36] On the whole, however, Bovin's criticism of the Chinese was muted. He reserved his harshest words for the American side of the Washington-Beijing leg of the triangle, reflecting the Soviet desire not to jeopardize the process of Soviet-Chinese detente by goading Beijing.

A TASS statement printed in both *Pravda* and *Izvestia* sounded many of these same themes, but took a somewhat harsher tone towards Beijing for failing to condemn U.S. military preparations in Asia and for "equating the imperialist, militaristic policy of the U.S. and the peace-loving and fundamentally anti-war policy of the countries of the socialist commonwealth."[37] If such a view represents the actual position of the Kremlin leadership rather than merely public propaganda, it would mean that anything less than a Chinese tilt toward the USSR—a new "lean to one side" policy—would not satisfy Moscow.

As Sino-American relations recovered their momentum in the first half of 1984 with the further expansion of trade and technology transfer and the intensification of exchanges between the Chinese and American military establishments, Soviet observers noted these developments in a surprisingly dispassionate tone. I. Ilyin and F. Likin, writing in *International Affairs,* observed that Reagan's

> visit has shown that the material base for U.S.-China relations has consolidated further and that conditions have been created for their expansion in a number of fields. It has also revealed continuing differences

between Peking's and Washington's political and strategic interests on the international scene as well as their mutual mistrust and suspicion.[38]

The military dimension of Sino-American cooperation was not emphasized in most Soviet media reports from 1984. Brief low-level reports on American Asian policy in *New Times* (Novoe Vremya) in the second half of the year briefly mentioned Washington's purported hopes of entangling Beijing in its militarist net, but targeted Tokyo and Seoul as the major elements in American strategy in the Asian-Pacific region.[39] The most critical view of Chinese foreign policy was provided at second hand by Gus Hall, the veteran pro-Moscow leader of the CPUSA, in an abridged version of an article from *Political Affairs*. Hall, not noted for his analytic subtlety, purported to see in the foreign policy of the Chinese leaders, "an identity of views and interests with the Reagan Administration."[40] This was quite at variance, of course, with Soviet writings that stressed the continuing differences of views and interests between Beijing and Washington.

The fullest treatment of Sino-American military cooperation published in 1984 was by V. Biryukov in *Problemy Dal'nego Vostoka* (Far Eastern Affairs). Descrying a U.S. view of China that oscillated between perceiving Beijing as "an ideological and possible military opponent" on the one hand and "a factor which could contribute somewhat to the implementation of American global military and foreign policy strategy" on the other, Biryukov wrote that:

> By the beginning of the 1980s, as a result of the interaction between these tendencies what could be called a structure of U.S.-China military contacts within the framework of general U.S.-Chinese relations had developed.[41]

As elements in the developing Sino-American military relationship, Biryukov cited exchanges between the two military establishments, the liberalization of U.S. regulations concerning technology transfer, Chinese delivery of strategic minerals to the United States, intelligence-sharing, and so forth.[42] In a curious formulation that straddled the question of Chinese culpability, Biryukov wrote that Chinese approval of the American military buildup demonstrates that "China has not completely abandoned the concepts of mutual relations between the great powers characteristic for the 1960s and the 1970s on which the Beijing leaders based their ungrounded strategic calculations of setting the USA and the USSR against each other."[43] Biryukov stops short of accusing the Chinese of any malevolent intentions or objectives and interprets PRC defense modernization as merely one element of the Four Modernizations rather than as their alpha and omega. He interprets the quickening of Sino-American military cooperation as "apparently linked to the mounting apprehension in the USA that China might scale down its cooperation with Washington."[44] Downgrading of expressed Soviet concern with U.S.-PRC military cooperation is evident most recently from the minimal attention paid in the central Soviet press to recent high-level military exchanges including the mid-January visit to China of General John Vessey, Chairman of the Joint Chiefs of Staff. Both *Pravda* and *Krasnaya Zvezda* (the Defense Ministry organ) accorded just a few scant lines to Vessey's meetings with top Chinese military officials providing little detail or interpretation to their readers.

Conclusion

Earlier tertiary analysts such as Chi Su and Garrett and Glaser have already noted the easing of expressed Soviet concerns regarding Sino-American relations in general and Sino-American military-security ties in particular.[45] To be sure, underlying Soviet suspicions about the United States and China separately and together have not vanished and it is probable that Soviet leaders (like Americans) are given to worst-case scenarios when they contemplate Sino-American relations.[46] But by now several factors have emerged to allay Soviet anxieties.

First is that Chinese leaders have explicitly dissociated their country from adherence to an American-led bloc designed to oppose the Soviet Union. As Soviet observers repeatedly note, Chinese-American political and military-security relations are taking place in a more fluid environment containing conflictual as well as harmonious elements. Secondly, the pace of U.S. technology transfers, including military technology and weaponry, to the PRC is too slow and the task of modernizing the PLA so complex that Soviet superiority in the Moscow-Beijing military balance is not seriously jeopardized by China's American connection. Thirdly, the incremental improvement in Sino-Soviet relations, although it has thus far not resolved any of the core foreign policy disputes between Moscow and Beijing—and is not likely to in the near future—has significantly expanded areas of cooperation in trade, science and technology, education, culture, sports, etc. It is interesting to note that the central Soviet press treated the China visit of Soviet Deputy Premier Arkhipov in December 1984 very circumspectly, alloting minimal space to this important trip. The objective may have been to minimize internally the generation of any overly optimistic false expectations regarding the future of Soviet-Chinese relations and externally not to jeopardize in any way further incremental improvements in relations with the PRC nor to cloud the atmosphere for Soviet-American talks.

Recent Soviet analyses of Sino-American relations appear to be grounded in a view that the Chinese are genuinely preoccupied with their domestic modernization program rather than intent on threatening Soviet interests via a military bloc with the United States. Repeated Chinese expressions of interest in a more peaceful international environment and China's welcoming of Soviet-American talks on strategic arms limitations may have encouraged Moscow to believe that Sino-American relations are less likely to be directed by Beijing against the USSR. Any amelioration of Soviet-American relations would almost certainly further reduce the level of expressed Soviet objections to U.S.-China ties. As indicated by Arkhipov's trip and the agreements signed in December 1984, Soviet leaders apparently realize by now the potential advantage in participating along with the United States in the modernization of China. This is, of course, a tacit recognition that Beijing has adroitly positioned itself between the two superpowers and that Chinese foreign policy has by now advanced beyond the either-or, zero-sum politics of the past *vis-à-vis* Moscow and Washington. Soviet emphasis on the continuing limits of Sino-American relations as a result of both specific and general differences between the two countries suggests the utility to Moscow of bidding for Beijing's favor, at least through politically inexpensive means such as trade and exchanges. Of course, Soviet observers have noted the incremental growth of multidimensional Chinese-American military ties, but the Kremlin may have learned that explicit Soviet objections to such cooperation may actually enhance their value in the eyes of American and Chinese hawks. It is clear, in any case, that the current Chinese leadership has rejected what might be called the *machomodernization* typical of American client states like the Shah's Iran, involving the rapid acquisition of imported military technology in large quantities, in favor of a more balanced developmental program responsive to popular needs.

There is one conspicuous area of Sino-American relations that has received even scanter attention from Soviet writers—the area of cultural relations, broadly defined to include Chinese interest in American society, education, management, popular culture, values, and so forth. The Soviet writers who have commented briefly on this aspect of the relationship point to culture as an arena of conflicting Chinese and American values, and take comfort in the concerns of Chinese cultural conservatives about "spiritual pollution" and "bourgeois decadence." The real significance of culture as a vital element of attraction, particularly for better-educated younger urban

Chinese, either escapes the Soviet observers or is a point they prefer to pass over in silence. Certainly nothing in contemporary official Soviet culture can compete with the dynamism, vibrancy, and appeal of America. If Soviet observers have noted the revitalization of ties between the older generations of American-educated Chinese and their old friends and colleagues in the United States, it must give them pause when they consider the numerous links that are being forged today between new generations of Americans and Chinese. It is difficult to imagine that the thin stream of Soviet and Chinese official exchange students and cultural intercourse can remotely rival the phenomenon of Sino-American cultural links, particularly insofar as the latter are structurally imbedded in China's open door economic policy.

As noted above, Soviet perceptions of the evolving Sino-American relationship—leaving aside the cultural aspect on which I have just remarked—have been quite consistent with recent American accounts with respect to charting major developments, evaluating trend lines, and so forth. Of course, Soviet interpretations, deriving from a political perspective that views both the United States and China as hostile states, differs substantially from those of most American scholars. In the years since Leonid Brezhnev's death, his successors have reaffirmed their interest in the improvement of Sino-Soviet relations and have made modest progress in that direction. They have not commented directly on U.S.-China relations as Brezhnev himself did on several occasions. However, from the analyses of Soviet writers, scholars, and journalists, one may perhaps infer that the Soviet leadership itself takes a somewhat more relaxed view of Sino-American relations than it did in the years immediately following U.S.-PRC normalization. If this is indeed the case, then it may marginally improve the prospects of success in the difficult and protracted Soviet-American negotiations on strategic arms, space, and related issues that may mark the mid-1980s. Of course, deep-seated Soviet phobias about China will not vanish, but resumption of the Soviet-American superpower dialogue may encourage Soviet leaders to view Sino-American relations in perspective once again.

Notes

1. "The Investigator's Song," *The People's Songbook*, ed. Waldemar Hille (New York, 1959), p. 103.

2. Banning N. Garrett and Bonnie S. Glaser, *War and Peace: The Views from Moscow and Beijing* (Institute of International Studies, University of California, Berkeley, Policy Papers in International Affairs, no. 20, 1984), p. 15.

3. Chi Su, "Soviet China-Watchers' Influence on Soviet China Policy," *Journal of Northeast Asian Studies,* II, 4 (December 1983): 26-27.

4. Gilbert Rozman, "Moscow's China-Watchers in the Post-Mao Era: The Response to a Changing China," *The China Quarterly,* no. 94 (June 1983): 224-236.

5. *Ibid.,* 226-231.

6. For a much fuller exposition of the organization and characteristics of Soviet China specialists see the articles by Chi Su and Gilbert Rozman cited above.

7. Chi Su, *op. cit.,* p. 35; O. Borisov, "The Situation in the PRC and Some of the Tasks of Soviet Sinology," *Far Eastern Affairs,* no. 3, 1982: 3-14; M. Ukraintsev, "Soviet-Chinese Relations: Problems and Prospects," *Far Eastern Affairs,* no. 3, 1982:15-24.

8. "Foreword," to A.A. Nagornyi and A.B. Parkanskii, *SShA i Kitai: Ekonomicheskie i nauchno-technicheskie aspekty kitaiskoi politiki Vashingtona* (The USA and China: Economic and Scientific-Technological Aspects of Washington's China Policy), Moscow: Nauka, 1982, p. 3.

9. This book was published by Nauka in Moscow, 1982.

10. William deB. Mills, "Comparing Soviet Civilian and Military Views of China," *The Korean Journal of International Studies,* XV, 3 (Summer 1984): 285-305.

11. *Ibid.,* 305.

12. For discussions by U.S. scholars of this period see, inter alia, Jonathan Pollack, *The Lessons of Coalition Politics: Sino-American Security Relations* (The Rand Corporation: Santa Monica, 1984: R-3133-AF); Robert Sutter, *The China Quandary: Domestic Determinants of U.S. China Policy, 1972-1982* (Westview Press Boulder, CO:, 1983; Steven I. Levine, "China and the United States: The Limits of Interaction," in Samuel S. Kim, ed., *China and the World: Chinese Foreign Policy in the Post-Mao World* (Westview Press Boulder, CO:, 1984), pp. 113-134.

13. Chi Su, "U.S.-China Relations: Soviet Views and Policies," *Asian Survey,* XXIII, 5 (May 1983): 566.

14. *Kommunist,* July 1980, cited in Garrett and Glaser, *op. cit.,* p. 31.

15. Garret and Glaser, pp. 33-37.

16. *Ibid.*

17. V. Denisov, "Some Aspects of the US New Far Eastern Strategy," *Far Eastern Affairs,* no. 2, 1983: 10-23.

18. V. Petukhov and G. Ragulin, "Escalation of US Aggression in East Asia," *Far Eastern Affairs,* no. 3, 1983: 79.

19. See note 7 above. Borisov is the pen-name of Rakhmanin.

20. See Chi Su's analysis in his *Asian Survey* article cited in note 13 above.

21. See note 7 above. Ukraintsev is the pen-name of Kapitsa.

22. See the essays by Steven Goldstein, Michael Hunt, and Steven Levine in Dorothy Borg and Waldo Heinrichs, eds., *Uncertain Years: Chinese-American Relations, 1947-1950,* and Nancy B. Tucker, *Patterns in the Dust: Chinese-American Relations and the Recognition Controversy, 1949-1950.*

23. See Jonathan Pollack, *The Lessons of Coalition Politics,* pp. 105-107 for an assessment of the trip.

24. TASS report in *Pravda,* 8 February 1983, p. 5, in *Current Digest of the Soviet Press* (hereafter CDSP), 33:6 (9 March 1983): 19.

25. *Izvestia,* 5 June 1983 in CDSP, 35:23 (July 6, 1983) :15.

26. *Pravda,* 27 September 1983, p. 5; *Izvestia,* September 29, p. 4; *Pravda,* September 30, p. 5, in CDSP 35:39 (October 26, 1983) : 20.

27. V. P. Lukin, "SShA-KNR: Novyi tur vizitov," [USA-PRC: A New Round of Visits], *SShA,* 1, (169) January 1984 : 76.

28. *Ibid.,* 73-75.

29. *Pravda,* January 20, 1984, p. 5, in CDSP 36:3 (15 February 1984: 13).

30. I. Alexeyev and F. Nikolayev, "PRC State Council Premier Visits the USA," *International Affairs,* No. 4 (1984) (April 1984): 51.

31. *Ibid.:* 50.

32. A. Bovin, "Vashington-Pekin: Protivorechivoe partnerstvo," *SShA,* No. 8 (176) 1984, (August 1984): 17-27.

33. *Ibid.,* 20.

34. *Ibid.*

35. *Ibid.,* 21.

36. *Ibid.,* 24.

37. TASS statement in *Pravda,* May 4, 1984, p. 5, CDSP, 36:18 (30 May 1984) : 1-3.

38. I. Ilyin and F. Likin, "Some Results of the U.S. President's Visit to China," *International Affairs,* no. 6, 1984 (June 1984) : 95.

39. Dmitry Volsky, "Pacific Strategems," *New Times,* No. 31, 1984 (July) : 11; V. Grishin, "Dangerous Alliance," *New Times,* no. 36, 1984 (September) : 13.

40. Gus Hall, "The Reagan Trip to China," *New Times,* No. 32, 1984 (August): 18-19.

41. V. Biryukov, "China in US Strategic Schemes," *Far Eastern Affairs,* no. 4, 1984 : 69.

42. *Ibid.,* 69-73.

43. *Ibid.,* 75.

44. *Ibid.,* 76.

45. Garrett and Glaser, *op. cit.,* pp. 33-45; Chi Su, "U.S.-China Relations . . .", pp. 572-573.

46. Garret and Glaser, p. 45.

Peking's Perceptions of the Two Super Powers and of American-Soviet Relations

PARRIS H. CHANG

Introduction

For over two decades after 1949, the leaders of the People's Republic of China (PRC) had been vehemently anti-American. They perceived the U.S. as China's archenemy; they accused the U.S. of occupying Taiwan and colluding with the Chinese Nationalist regime to invade the mainland, attacked the U.S. for reviving Japanese militarism, and called U.S. imperialism "the chief bulwark of world reaction" and "the most vicious enemy of peace."[1] In July 1949, three months before the PRC government was set up in Peking (Beijing), Mao Tse-tung (Mao Zedong) openly called for China's alliance with the USSR to struggle against the Western imperialists. In February, 1950, Mao and Stalin concluded a 30-year Treaty of Friendship, Alliance and Mutual Assistance, which was directed against the United States and Japan.

However, the alliance did not last long as the two communist giants differed on the strategy to handle the U.S. By the late 1960s, most Chinese leaders had come to see the USSR, instead of the U.S., as China's principal enemy. Peking's leaders have perceived Soviet social imperialism as "even more deceitful" and "more dangerous" than "the old imperialist countries." China's strategic responses since the 1970s have been opening to the West, reconciliation with the U.S. and Japan, and a concerted effort to forge a global united front against Soviet hegemonism.

What has been said above implicity acknowledges that human actions are not merely accidents, but are rather events flowing from human thoughts, i.e. from the images, perceptions and considerations of the actors. The decisionmakers' images of the world and perceptions of their national and international milieu are not simply passive intellectual appreciations of the external environment: such images and perceptions do have important policy implications as they frequently constitute the major premises, whether articulated or not, by which to exercise choice and make decisions. It is true that perceptions alone do not determine policy, for a policy is often the product of a multiplicity of "conditions"; nonetheless the perception of decisionmakers does constitute one of these conditions.

The purpose of this paper is to analyze Chinese leaders' perceptions of the world, of their relations with the two superpowers, of the U.S.-Soviet relations, and explore the policy implications for the future. True, perception does not often conform to reality, as it contains a mixture of truth, half truth, distortion, and hopes and fears; nonetheless, it is an important clue to detecting and understanding policymakers' views and actions.

The U.S. as China's Major Enemy

China's foreign policy, like that of other nations, is shaped by a complex of factors and forces. Ideology clearly exerts a considerable influence on the Chinese Communists' image of the world and shapes their actions. For a long time they appeared to have uncritically accepted Lenin's theory of a bipolar world divided into two diametrically opposing camps (a socialist camp and an imperialist camp) and had sought alliance with the Soviet Union against the imperialists. As far back as 1926, for example, Mao stated that "the present world situation is such that the two major forces, revolution and counterrevolution, are locked in final struggle."[2] This two-camp world view was forcefully articulated by Mao in his 1940 essay "On New Democracy" in which he wrote:

> Once the conflict between the socialist Soviet Union and the imperialist powers grows sharper, China will have to take her stand on one side or the other. This is an inevitable trend . . . The whole world will be swept into one or the other of these two fronts, and neutrality will then be merely a deceptive term.[3]

Mao also asserted that "all the imperialist powers in the world are our enemies," China cannot possibly gain her independence "without the assistance of the land of socialism and international proletariat."[4]

Viewing the world through the Communist ideological lens, Mao thus considered the United States and other Western nations as enemies and hostile to his cause, and an alliance with the socialist camp as necessary to the success of revolution in China. Such assumptions were to condition Peking's foreign policy in the 1950s. On 30 June 1949, three months before the establishment of the Communist regime in China, Mao enunciated the celebrated "lean to one side" policy of alliance with the Soviet Union and declared: "Internationally, we belong to the side of the anti-imperialist front headed by the Soviet Union, and so we can turn only to this side for genuine and friendly help, not to the side of the imperialist front."[5] To secure such help, in December 1949, Mao travelled to Moscow and, two months later, forged a formal alliance with Stalin.

The Chinese perception of the American threat, no doubt, helped reinforce Peking's tilt toward Moscow. For one day after the PRC was established, a Chinese publication warned:

> They (the American imperialists) will not only send their running-dogs to bore inside China to carry out disruptive work and to cause trouble, they will not only use the Chiang Kaishek bandit remnants to blockade our coastal ports, but they will send their totally hopeless adventurist elements and troops to raid and to cause trouble along our borders . . .[6]

One must point out that Chinese leaders' anti-American view was not based on ideology alone: undoubtedly it was also strengthened by the reality of U.S.-China relations before and after the 1949 Communist takeover of power in China. As we recall, American involvement in Chinese politics throughout the Second World War appeared to support the Nationalists against the Communists. Despite the inconsistency of subsequent U.S. policies in the Chinese Civil War, which at times were opposed to the Nationalist interests, the over-all impression of American support for Chiang seemed to confirm CCP expectations of U.S. imperialist hostility.

Misperceptions between the Chinese communists and the U.S. produced disastrous effects on policy decisions and set in motion the mechanism of self-fulfilling prophecy. Many Communist actions provoked negative reactions from the U.S., which exacerbated their relations which in turn strengthened CCP perception of American imperialist hostility and the need for Soviet support. For instance, in 1948, American consular officials in Mukden were put under house arrest, tried, and expelled from China. Moreover, the seizure of Economic Cooperation Administration stocks in 1949, and inflaming of public-opinion against U.S. diplomats in China all served to arouse hostile Congressional and public opinion in the U.S., leaving the Truman Administration little choice but to withhold recognition from the new Communist government.

In 1949, U.S. officials from President Harry Truman down had repeatedly stated that the U.S. would not interfere with China's Civil War. However, Truman suddenly reversed himself and sent the U.S. Seventh Fleet to "neutralize" the Taiwan Strait in 27 June 1950, two days after the outbreak of the Korean War, thereby, preventing the Communists from carrying out their impending invasion of Taiwan. Peking perceived the U.S. intervention as fresh evidence of American aggression and mounted a nation-wide Hate America campaign in China.

As Japan had used Korea as the gateway to invading China in the past, Chinese leaders apparently viewed with apprehension U.S. entry into the Korean War as a prelude to extending the war into China. The fear that the U.S. forces crossed the 38th Parallel in the first week of October, 1950 and headed for the Sino-Korean border, and Peking issued stern warnings that China would enter the war to repel U.S. aggression. In mid-October, the Chinese "volunteers" began to cross the Yalu and, in a large-scale surprise assault in late November, they smashed U.S. lines along the entire Korean front, forcing the U.S. units to beat a hasty and humiliating retreat south to the 38th Parallel.

China's intervention into the Korean War and the direct armed clash with the U.S. in the winter of 1950 was to usher in a new, bitter phase in the Sino-U.S. relations. Thereafter and for almost two decades, as is well known by now, much of the relationship between the two nations was consumed by mutual recrimination, reciprocal hostility, and political as well as military confrontation. The U.S. not only renewed support for the Nationalist regime in Taiwan and set up an economic embargo against China, but also enforced a policy of containment to isolate China and block Peking's entrance to the United Nations, and constructed a network of bilateral and multi-lateral alliances with non-Communist states in Asia to contain the expansion of Chinese Communist influence.

These developments in turn strengthened Peking's phobia and hatred for Washington, and probably increased Peking's dependence on Moscow's support to counterbalance the threat of the U.S. On the other hand, however, Chinese leaders' obsession with the reunification of Taiwan and their advocacy of a militant policy against the U.S. ironically strained the Sino-Soviet alliance, as Peking was to find in later years Moscow's support wanting, and the USSR an unworthy ally.

Breaking up of the Sino-Soviet Alliance

Since 1949, national security has been Chinese leaders' overriding foreign policy concern. The major shifts in China's overall foreign policy strategy can be better understood from changes in Chinese leaders' perception of external threats and in their efforts to deter such threat. Initially, as noted before, Peking sought to play the "Russian Card" by relying on the USSR as a counterweight to the U.S. The Sino-Soviet alliance was designed to enhance China's national security in the face of perceived American threat and to obtain Soviet material and technical assistance for China's economic and defense modernization.

The alliance did pay considerable dividends. Soviet military assistance provided modern weapons and equipment to Chinese forces during the Korean War and was crucial in sustaining China's war efforts. Most probably the alliance also deterred the U.S. from escalating the war into the Chinese mainland from Korea. Seeing itself as a member of the Communist camp headed by Moscow, Peking adopted a highly militant posture against the entire non-Communist world, called for world revolution and provided active support to Communist insurgents in many Asian states.

However, the national interests of the two allies were not identical; even before the first decade of the alliance drew to a close, Peking had become disillusioned. In the economic sphere, to Peking's chagrin, the generosity of the "Russian big brother" was quite limited—during the Sino-Soviet honeymoon in the 1950s, Moscow only provided two loans (a five-year $300 million loan in 1950 and another credit of $130 million in 1954) and was unwilling or unable to extend further assistance for China's economic development. Refuting Moscow's subsequent claim of "disinterested assistance" to China, Peking pointed out that "far from being gratis, Soviet aid to China was rendered mainly in the form of trade, and it was certainly not a one-way traffic."[7] Peking also asserted that the price of many of the Soviet goods were much higher than those on the world market.

Yet the most acute conflict between the two allies centered around a host of issues which related directly to China's national security. Their differences prompted Peking to question the value and reliability of the USSR as an ally and subsequently led to the collapse of the alliance. These issues included Moscow's failure to back Peking more positively during the 1958 Quemoy Crisis in the face of U.S. nuclear threat against China, Soviet unilateral termination in 1959 of a 1957 agreement to assist China's development of atomic weapons, and Moscow's pursuit of detente with China's archenemy, the U.S. (as manifested in Khrushchev's meeting with President Eisenhower at Camp David in September 1959). Peking's increasingly vociferous demands for Communist militancy against the U.S. and the West erupted into open polemics with Moscow in 1960.

Their conflict was further exacerbated in 1963 as the Soviet leadership, in spite of Peking's repeated protest, went ahead to sign the limited nuclear testban treaty with the U.S. The treaty was apparently perceived by Peking as a U.S.-Soviet collusion against China and, to quote the words of an authority on Chinese foreign policy, probably constituted a "point of no return" symbolizing the end, for all practical purposes, of the Sino-Soviet pact as an operative alliance.[8] From then on, Chinese policy moved rapidly toward an open political and ideological break with the USSR, finally consummated by the Chinese charges of the "capitalist degeneration" of the Soviet system and denunciations of Khrushchev and, after 1964, his successors as traitors to the cause of Communist world revolution.

China's militant anti-imperialist policy, support for wars of national liberation in the Third World, and her bitter attack against the Soviet leadership were not decided without debate in her leadership councils. Premier Chou En-lai's (Zhou Enlai's) accusation in the Government Report to National People's Congress in December 1964 that some misguided comrades had advocated a capitalationist line of "three reconciliations and one reduction" (i.e., reconciliation with reactionaries, with revisionists and imperialists; and reduction of assistance to foreign revolutionaries) strongly suggested that the militant foreign policy line was not supported by every segment of the leadership. The Cultural Revolution materials subsequently accused Chinese Communist Party officials, such as Liu Shao-ch'i (Liu Shaoqi), Ch'en Yun (Chen Yun), Teng Hsiao-P'ing (Deng Xiaoping), Wang Chia-hsiang (Wang Jiaxiang), and several others of advocating such a policy in the early 1960s.

These leaders were by no means pro-Soviet. It is just that they thought it unwise and even harmful to China's national security to break up with the USSR when China was faced with a hostile U.S. They felt China was highly vulnerable in the early 1960s, in the wake of an immense economic and social crisis caused by Mao's Great Leap and commune programs. Thus Liu Shao-ch'i (Liu Shaoqi) reportedly said in 1962: "Since we are preoccupied with our own cares, how can we afford to simultaneously provoke U.S. imperialism and Soviet revisionism, and aid the struggle of the revolutionary people's of the world?"

On the other hand, Mao was vehemently opposed to the Russians. Moscow's failure or unwillingness to support Peking in the areas where China's major national interests were involved was undoubtedly a major factor underlying Mao's bitterness toward the Soviet leadership and particularly Khrushchev personally. Khrushchev's diatribe against Mao's Great Leap and commune adventure, his alleged liaison with Mao's critic Defense Minister P'eng Teh-huai (Peng Dehuai), and his defense of P'eng's challenge to Mao in the 1959 Lushan meeting, to cite only a few incidents, were taken by Mao as a personal attack; thus, differences in ideology and policy between the two nations also became intertwined with personal conflicts between two individual leaders.

Throughout most of the first half of the 1960s, most top Chinese leaders, including those who were known to harbor misgivings about the conflict in two fraternal parties, did display public support for Mao's anti-Soviet policy, possibly out of consideration of national solidarity. The ouster of Khrushchev in October 1964, and the escalation of the Vietnamese War after February 1965, in which quite a few Chinese leaders saw the likelihood of direct Sino-U.S. armed confrontation, were occasions for new decisions, and some of the Chinese leaders apparently seized the opportunity to press their case for a rapprochement with Moscow. Indeed, a heated debate in the Chinese leadership took place in private and in public during 1965 and 1966.

It is generally known that a group of People's Liberation Army (PLA) leaders led by Chief of Staff Lo Jui-ch'ing (Luo Ruiqing) advocated a larger and more active Chinese role in the Vietnamese War and pressed for a reconciliation with Moscow in order to bolster China's national defense, coupled with a policy of Sino-Soviet "unity of action" to forestall an American victory in Vietnam. In opposition to the Lo proposal were Mao, Lin Piao (Lin Biao), Chou En-lai, P'eng Chen (Peng Chen—Party leader and Mayor of Peking) and others. Their position was presented by Lin Piao in the celebrated essay "Long Live the Victory of People's War" in September 1965 which rejected both the demand for a hard line in Vietnam and the demand for reconciliation with Moscow.[9]

Although Lo Jui-ch'ing was removed from power in December, 1965, the strategic debate in Peking continued, as other leaders such as Liu,

Teng, and P'eng came to the fore to support a united front with Moscow and urged a tough line against the U.S. in the Indochina conflict.

As this foreign policy controversy was in progress, a political storm subsequently known as the Great Proletarian Cultural Revolution (GPCR) was gathering momentum inside the Chinese political system. Realizing that they were targets of Mao's GPCR purge, Liu, Teng and P'eng appeared to be using the foreign policy issue to rally support and to ward off Mao's political offensive. By championing a militant policy to aid Hanoi and to stop imperialist aggression in Vietnam through unity of action with the Soviets, they sought to captivate the revolutionaries in the CCP and the professionals in the PLA and to win the support of these elements in their forthcoming showdown with Mao and his supporters but their endeavor was to no avail.

The foreign policy debate eventually came to an end in the summer of 1966 when these dissident Party leaders were removed from power. Registering the victorious Maoist position, the Communique of the 11th CC Plenum in August, 1966 ruled out a united front with Moscow in the fight against U.S. imperialism and its lackeys, assailed the Soviet leadership for practicing "Khrushchev revisionism without Khrushchev," for its "sham support but real betrayal" on Vietnam's resistance to the U.S., and termed the Soviet revisionism as an even greater and more dangerous enemy that U.S. imperialism.[10] In addition to rejecting united actions with Moscow in the anti-U.S. struggle, most significant of all, the Chinese leadership now officially proclaimed a "dual adversary strategy," thereby casting the Soviet Union, hitherto a socialist state and China's ally, as China's enemy in the same plane with U.S. imperialism

The "Dual Adversary Strategy"

Pursuing the dual adversary strategy in opposition to both American imperialism and Soviet revisionism, Peking displayed a highly militant international posture throughout the 1960s. Perceived to be encircled and threatened by U.S. military bases, Chinese leaders apparently rediscovered the utility of Lenin's teachings on world revolution. For Peking stressed the forging of an anti-imperialist alliance, sought a leading role in it, and pressed the war of "national liberation" in Asia, Africa, and Latin America. In 1966-69, to help Hanoi defeat the U.S., China dispatched some 50-60,000 Chinese to North Vietnam to repair roads, bridges and perform other services. However, Peking's dogmatic concept of the anti-imperialist solidarity of the developing nations often blinded them to the national interests of the countries and government they sought to influence. Moreover, Peking's professions of friendship for the national regimes of Third World countries were belied by an opportunistic policy of fomenting local Communist subversion against some of the very governments it was seeking to line up in the united front against imperialism. Were even most Third World nations to follow China's lead, they would not be much of a help to China in a military security sense and would affect little the prevailing world power balance. In any case, the bankruptcy of China's revolutionary strategy was sharply underscored by the political demise of some of Peking's best friends—leaders like Ben Bella in Algeria, Sukarno in Indonesia, and Nkrumah in Ghana.

With the advent of the GPCR in 1966 and its attendant political and ideological excesses, Peking succeeded not only in offending virtually every non-Communist nation in Asia and the Third World it sought to cultivate, but also in alienating two Asian Communist states, North Vietnam and North Korea, which had hitherto been on good terms with China. By the end of 1967, virtually all of China's ambassadors abroad had been recalled to undergo ideological rectification, as Red Guard mobs sacked the British Embassy in Peking and harassed the diplomats of many other countries, while Chinese diplomatic personnel rioted in several foreign capitals. China was in total isolation.

The damage inflicted by the GPCR on Peking's international position was substantial, to say the least. As the moderate political forces prevailed in China's policy-making councils after mid-1968, however, Peking began to restore some semblance of order in its foreign relations and resume more normal diplomatic ties with foreign nations. Moreover a series of external events compelled the Chinese leadership to review its overall foreign policy strategy: the Soviet invasion of Czechoslovakia in September 1968, the enunciation of the Brezhnev Doctrine (which justifies Soviet intervention in other socialist states), the massive buildup of Soviet forces along the Sino-Russian border, and the bloody Sino-Soviet armed clashes along the Ussuri in March 1969, and in Sinkiang later that summer. As the Chinese leadership perceived a genuine danger of large-scale Soviet military action against China (and there were indeed veiled Soviet threats of nuclear attack against China in 1969 and 1970), most Chinese leaders reached a consensus that drastic adjustments in relations with the Western world would be necessary. The overwhelming concern for national survival forced the Chinese leadership to give up the dual adversary strategy and adopt a new foreign policy strategy to combat the USSR, China's principal enemy.

The most important element in China's new policy is, without doubt, her dramatic reconciliation with the U.S. and Japan, so as to deter Soviet aggression and redress the balance of power. The initial improvement of relations with these two former enemies was dramatized by the state visits made by President Richard Nixon and Prime Minister Kakuei Tanaka in February and September 1972, respectively. Since then, China's relationships with these two nations have been consolidated and substantially expanded, resulting in, among others, a Treaty of Peace and Friendship with Japan in August 1978, and the full normalization of diplomatic ties with the U.S. in January 1979

The Washington "Connection"

The drastic turnabout in China's relations with the U.S.—long regarded as China's main enemy—was not supported unanimously within the leadership circles. In the summer of 1971, Mao's heir-apparent, Marshall Lin Piao apparently opposed the Sino-U.S. rapprochement. Judging from the esoteric criticism in some Chinese sources that Lin advocated "isolationism" and capitulation to the revisionists, Lin probably opposed "opening" to the U.S. as a means to defuse the danger of Soviet attack, and instead may have favored certain measures to seek rapprochement with the Soviets.

In defense of Peking's new international alignment, its proponents spelled out the strategic rationale of the Sino-U.S. detente in an article in *Hongqi* (Red Flag), the Party's theoretical journal.[11] Ostensibly devoted to a study of Chairman Mao's 1940 treaties "On Policy," the article stressed the importance of clearly distinguishing "Who is the principal enemy, who is the secondary enemy, and who is the temporary ally or indirect ally." The implication is, instead of fighting the U.S. and the USSR at the same time, China ought to manipulate all conflicts and contradictions in the enemy camp and use the U.S. (be it a secondary enemy or temporary ally) against the USSR (today's principal enemy.)

Despite the demise of Lin Piao in September 1971, opposition among cadres to Peking's detente with Washington continued. Not a few were highly critical of China's "collusion" with the U.S. and Peking's seemingly betrayal of world revolution. A classified army document refuted these criticisms and justified China's "tilt" toward the U.S. in these words:

> The present situation is: U.S. imperialism's counter-revolutionary global strategy has met with repeated setbacks; its aggressive power has been

weakened; and hence, it has had to make some retraction and adjustment of its strategy. Soviet revisionism, on the other hand, is stretching its arms in all directions and is expanding desperately. It is more crazy, adventurist, and deceptive. That is why Soviet revisionism has become our country's most dangerous and most important enemy.[12]

The Chinese leadership, in response to the charges of "collusion" with the United States, was at great pains to reaffirm China's committment to opposing U.S. imperialism. Thus, the same army document stated:

The two principal enemies facing us are U.S. imperialism and Soviet revisionism. We are to fight for the overthrow of these two enemies. This has already been written into the new Party constitution. Nevertheless, are we to fight these two enemies simultaneously, using the same might? No. Are we to ally ourselves with one against the other? Definitely not.[13]

The document also detailed a number of considerations underlying China's improvement of relations with the U.S. Chief among them are: (1) an attempt to foil Moscow's design to generate and exploit Sino-U.S. antagonism; (2) a desire to create and exploit "contradictions" between Moscow and Washington and to prevent the collusion of the two superpowers; (3) to weaken ties between the U.S. and the Nationalist China, and to facilitate Taiwan's liberation.

If we take literally a pronouncement of the late Premier Chou En-lai, the main architect of China's foreign policy in the early 1970s, we cannot avoid the impression that the motivation behind China's "compromise" with the U.S. was rather cunning and baleful. To quote, for example, Chou's Political Report to the Tenth Congress of the Party in August 1973:

We should point out here that necessary compromise between revolutionary countries must be distinguished from collusion and compromise between Soviet revisionism and U.S. imperialism. Lenin put it well: "There are compromises and compromises. One must be able to analyze the situation and the concrete conditions of each compromise, or of each variety of compromises. One must learn to distinguish between a man who gave the bandits money and firearms in order to lessen the damage they can do and facilitate their capture and execution, and a man who gives bandits money and fire-arms in order to share in the loot." *("Left-Wing" Communism, an Infantile Disorder)* The Brest-Litvosk Treaty concluded by Lenin with German imperialism comes under the former category; and the doings of Krushchev and Brezhnev, both betrayers of Lenin, fall under the latter.[14]

The language of Chou used to describe Chin's "compromise" with the U.S. was guarded, because he was making a public speech. When Foreign Minister Chiao Kuan-hua spoke on camera to a group of selected high-ranking cadres in Tientsin on 20 May 1975 on the same subject in a closed session, his remarks were more candid and revealing.[15] In the talk, Chiao reaffirmed China's opposition to the "common enemies, namely the two superpowers," but emphasized that for tactical reasons China had to distinguish between the two hegemonic powers, deal with each differently so as to "divide the principal enemy from the secondary enemy and defeat them one by one." He explicitly stated that it was because of necessity and expediency that China had to make a temporary alliance with the U.S., a declining superpower, in order to checkmate the USSR, the superpower on the ascendency.

To succeed in its maneuver to use the U.S. to check and balance the Soviet Union, China needs a strong America which must be willing and able to hold firm against Soviets in Asia and elsewhere in the world. A weak, isolationist America would be of little use to China. For this reason, the Chinese leaders have become ardent champions of American military preparedness, a strong NATO alliance and continuing U.S. military presence in Asia.

Thus, not surprisingly, China has frequently criticized the American policy of detente with the Soviet Union. In December 1975, when President Gerald Ford visited Peking, he was sternly lectured by the Chinese leaders on the danger of detente with Moscow.[16] When the Carter Administration sought a more cooperative relationship with Moscow in the SALT negotiations in 1977, the Chinese leadership was displeased, and Party Chairman Hua Kuo-feng (Hua Guofeng) referred to the U.S. as a "temporary, vacillating, unstable, unreliable and conditional" ally.[17] Repeatedly, Peking warned the Carter Administration against following the paths of appeasing the Soviets.[18]

The establishment of full diplomatic relations between the PRC and the U.S. which took place in early 1979, considerably boosted Peking's international status and strengthened its diplomatic position. Apparently, Chinese leaders see the U.S. as a countervailing force to the USSR. For example, without normalization of relations, Peking might not have felt confident enough to launch the punitive war against Vietnam, a Soviet ally, in February 1979.

Likewise, Peking perceives the U.S. as the main source of capital, expertise and technology to be used to step up China's modernization drive. Various Chinese leaders have expressed admiration for the advancement of U.S. technology and pressed the U.S. hard on the transfer of technology in a variety of areas.[19] Since the fall of 1983, the Reagan Administration has relaxed controls on U.S. exports and has put the PRC in the category of nonaligned but friendly nations, in response to Peking's pressure. Currently, more than 13,000 students and researchers from the mainland are in U.S. universities and research institutions, to engage in study and research mostly in science and technical fields. The acquisition of foreign capital and technology is designed to accelerate the growth of Chinese economy and, eventually, military capability.

Moscow's Quest for Global Domination and U.S.-Soviet Conflict

In Peking's view, the USSR has been pursuing a global offensive strategy for world domination. According to Chinese press, Moscow has been engaged in a massive military buildup of offensive capabilities of all military forces to achieve an overall superiority over the U.S. and has been using its military might for expansion in various regions in the world.[20] Peking has warned repeatedly that the Kremlin would start a larger flanking move to encircle Western Europe and to cut off strategic material vital to the west and control major sea routes linking Western Europe and the U.S. and those linking the two with Africa and Asia.[21]

The Soviet invasion of Afghanistan was seen by Peking as such a move to outflank Western Europe. An "observer" of the *People's Daily* predicted that the next Soviet objective would be the expansion into Pakistan and Iran as a springboard to advance on the Middle East and the Persian Gulf, break through the "soft belly" and obtain access to the Indian Ocean.[22] Moreover, Peking also perceived Vietnam's occupation of Kampuchea as supported and instigated by the Kremlin and as an important part of Moscow's global strategy to achieve world hegemony. According to the *People's Daily* article cited above, "Moscow is taking advantage of Hanoi's domination of Indochina to subject China to pincers attack from north and south, to threaten Southeast Asia and to contain U.S. influence in the area." Peking also pointed out that Moscow had strengthened its Pacific fleet and increased its naval movements through the Sea of Japan southward to menace Japan's security and challenge U.S. naval presence in the

Western Pacific. In what was termed as Moscow's "dumb-bell" strategy, Peking warned that the Soviets intended to seize control of the Strait of Malacca, which joins the Pacific and Indian Oceans, so as to cut off the route for oil shipments which are vital to Japan and other countries.[23]

Peking warned that, despite Moscow's lip service to "peace," "disarmament," and "negotiation," it continued to increase its military capacity with the hope of "gaining a quantitative and qualitative edge" on the U.S., and that it used economic enticements as well as military threats to drive a wedge between the West European nations and the U.S. and to scuttle U.S. plans to deploy Pershing II and cruise missiles in Western Europe.[24] The Chinese noted the expansion of Soviet military forces in the East, the deployment of more SS-20's, backfire bombers, D-class submarines, and other surface ships in the Far East, so as to "deal with the U.S. armed forces in the Pacific and to threaten Japan and China."[25] Meanwhile, the Chinese also accused Moscow of attempts to "poison Japanese-American, Sino-American, and Sino-Japanese relations."

Moreover, in a lengthy essay on Soviet detente strategy, a pair of Chinese writers portrayed the policy as a ploy to tip the world balance in Moscow's favor and to sow dissension in the West. In their view, Moscow's skillful maneuver in the past decade has bought time for the Soviet Union and enabled the Soviets to quickly narrow the gap between the two superpowers in the way of economic and military strength. According to these two Chinese analysts, Soviet "detente" policy is also designed "to split the West, particularly to drive a wedge in the alliance between the U.S. and Western Europe, avoid a head-on conflict with the U.S., press hard its so called 'southward thrust' and realize its strategic outflanking encirclement of Western Europe."[26]

On the other hand, because of its detente policy, the Soviet Union is said to have suffered from "strategic isolation" and provided the West with an opportunity to infiltrate Eastern Europe and influence the internal life of the Soviet Union. As the Chinese pointed out, the Soviet military buildup put the West on guard and spurred the U.S. and its West European allies and Japan to catch up. Soviet maneuvers to step up its expansion southward under the cover of relaxation, according to the Chinese, had aroused the suspicions of third world countries, and "heightened their understanding of the need to drive the tiger away from the front door and resist the wolf at the back."[27]

Meanwhile, the West is said to have exploited East-West relaxation to infiltrate Eastern Europe so as to drive a wedge in the Soviet-Eastern European alliance and to promote political changes within Eastern Europe. The Polish crisis was attributed at least partly to the West's infiltration.[28]

East-West relaxation is also seen as providing an opportunity for the West to exert influence on the Soviet people, particularly the younger generation. Many of them become obsessed with so-called Western democracy, and unsatisfied with what they have to eat and wear, adopt a nihilist attitude toward the Soviet Union, "thus giving rise to social problems of every description."[29]

But these are not the only woes that the Soviets have to cope with. The huge Soviet expenditures on arms expansion and war preparations have further slowed down its economy in the early 1980's. In addition, Soviet outlays on overseas expansions in Afghanistan, and aids to Cuba and Vietnam amount to nearly $10,000 million dollars annually. All this obviously has put a crushing burden on the Soviet economy. Moreover, as the West has seen through what Moscow is up to, the Chinese feel that the Soviet Union "will find it more difficult than before to push detente in the 1980s."[30]

Implications for Chinese Foreign Policy

As the preceding sections have shown, Peking's perception of the world, of the external threats and of the U.S.-Soviet relations do undergo several major shifts over time, and such changes have also affected Chinese foreign policy. Indeed, since the early 1980s, Chinese policy has been changing once again.

Until the early 1980s, Peking used to urge a broad international united front against Soviet hegemonism. China's most authoritative spokesman, Teng Hsiao-p'ing is quoted in a *Time* magazine interview in early 1979 as calling for China, the U.S., Japan, and Western Europe to "further develop the relationship in a deepening way" and "to unite" in order to "place curbs on the polar bear."[31] Teng was explicit—"we proceed from the establishment of a united front against hegemonism and for the defense of world peace, security and stability, and this united front includes the U.S."

But since 1982, Peking has deemphasized the strategic cooperation with the U.S. Instead, China has put great stress on an independent policy and on ties with the Third World. Teng stated in his opening speech to the CCP Congress in September, 1982 that "Independence and self-reliance have always been and will forever be our basic stand . . . No foreign country can expect China to be its vassal, nor can it expect China to swallow any bitter fruit harmful to China's interests." In explaining China's policy not to form an alliance with any superpower, CCP General Secretary Hu Yao-bang said,

> "For us, an alliance with the big powers has two disadvantages. First, it would probably hinder or at least affect our efforts to make more friends. China stands for contacts with various countries on the basis of five principles of peaceful coexistence. Second, it may also hinder China's resistance to impermissible actions on the part of its allies, and our partners may possibly make use of the alignment to oppose other friendly countries."[32]

Why has Peking deemphasized or abandoned a "strategic partnership" with the U.S. and opted for an independent policy? If one can trust Peking, then the U.S. support for Taiwan is the main reason. However, the truth seems much more complex, and the Taiwan issue is only one among many causes. The most crucial factor may be attributed to Peking's redefinition of China's national priorities in the early 1980s. Once the PRC improved relations with the U.S. and Japan, Peking apparently felt strengthened and soon undertook a series of policy reviews to capitalize on its newly acquired "position of strength."

The first clear sign of change was underlined by a major speech by Teng on 16 January 1980 to ranking cadres in which he singled out containment of hegemonism, reunification of China, and modernization as the three top leadership priorities for the 1980s, but placed the emphasis on the third as the key to the fulfillment of the other two objectives. To facilitate China's modernization efforts, according to Teng, the PRC would need a peaceful international environment. Thus, the policy to "normalize" relations with the Soviets was put in place. With a shift in leadership priority, Peking has no urgency nor strong incentives to forge an alliance with the U.S., which could provoke extreme Soviet counter-moves.

Teng and other Chinese leaders appeared also to have been bothered by what they saw as the absence of a coherent U.S. global strategy and Asian policy. President Carter's unwillingness or inability to project U.S. power to rescue U.S. hostages in Tehran, his weak reactions to Soviet invasion of Afghanistan in 1980, and President Reagan's decision to lift the grain embargo against the Soviets in 1981, despite the new President's tough anti-Soviet rhetoric, served to further undermine Peking's confidence on U.S. ability to stand up to the Soviets.

Meanwhile, Peking has taken a less alarmist view of the Soviet threat.

Up to the end of 1984, the PRC and the USSR have conducted five rounds of talks and exchanged high-level visits seeking to "normalize" their relations. In so doing, Peking is undoubtedly aiming at enjoying greater leverage and flexibility with both superpowers.

Thus, unlike the 1970s when Peking spokesmen used to highlight world tensions and conflict in their pronouncements, they now emphasize positive aspects of the international balance of power and they now see hope for global peace. For example, in a meeting with an American visitor on 7 November 1984, Teng asserted that "there is hope for peace" as neither of the two superpowers "dare to act rashly because each could destroy the other and the world," and that "all the people in the world want peace . . . The factor for peace is increasing."[33]

Peking's comments on the U.S.-Soviet arms control efforts now also reflect such optimism. Thus while Peking used to disparage the arms control talks in the 1970s, now Chinese media report approvingly of the efforts by the two superpowers to halt the arms race and to ease tensions.[34] In September 1984, Huan Hsiang (Huan Xiang), a noted foreign policy advisor to Chinese leaders, asserted that peaceful coexistence is the choice of the times and stressed the necessity for international friendly cooperation.[35]

In a year-end review of China's relations with the two superpowers, General Wu Hsiu-chuan (Wu Xiuquan) asserted that "China sincerely wishes to improve its relations with both the United States and the Soviet Union. Although there will be twists and turns along the way, China still embraces a bright and positive view for the future of Sino-U.S. and Sino-Soviet relations."[36] Such optimism reflects Peking's new assessment of the "coalition of international forces" and new confidence as well as a new sense of security.[37]

Notes

1. See Chung Chen-hsien, *Mei Ti-kuo Chu-yi Shih Wo-men Ti Shu-ti* (U.S. Imperialism is Our Dead Enemy), (Peking: China Youth Publishing House, 1962).
2. Mao Tse-tung, *Selected Work of Mao Tse-tung,* vol. 1 (Peking: Foreign Languages Press, 1967), p. 14.
3. *Ibid.,* vol. 3, p. 364.
4. *Ibid.,* vol. 3, p. 355.

5. *Ibid.*, vol. 4, p. 417.

6. K'o P'ai-nien, "China's New Democratic Foreign Policy," *Hsueh Hsi* (study), I, no. 2, 2 October 1949, pp. 13-14.

7. *Peking Review*, No. 19, 8 May 1964, p. 14.

8. A Doak Bornett, "Peking and the Asian Power Balance," *Problems of Communism*, July-August, 1976, p. 38.

9. Lin Piao, *Long Live the Victory of the People's War* (Peking: Foreign Languages Press, 1965).

10. *Communique of the Eleventh Plenary Session of the Eighth Central Committee of the Communist Party of China*, adopted on August 12, 1966 (Peking: Foreign Languages Press, 1966).

11. Writing Group of the Hupei Provincial Committee of the Chinese Communist Party, "A Powerful Weapon to Unite People and Defeat Enemies," *Red Flag*, 2 August 1971, pp. 12-13.

12. The document, entitled "Reference Materials Concerning Education on the Situation," was compiled and distributed by the Political Department of Kuming Military Region to be used for "educating cadres" and soldiers. A copy of the document has found its way out of China and is available in English translation. The quotation is taken from *Issues and Studies* (Taipei), June, 1974, p. 98.

13. *Ibid.*, p. 104.

14. *Peking Review*, 7 September 1973, p. 23.

15. A full text of Chiao's speech, entitled "Current World Situation and (China's) Foreign Policy," is reproduced in *Studies on Chinese Communism* (Taipei), October, 1975, pp. 109-118. In the speech, Chiao dealt with a wide range of topics, including China's views on the Korean problem and Southeast Asia.

16. See Teng Hsiao-p'ing's speech at the welcoming banquet on December 1, 1975, *Peking Review*, 5 December 1975, p. 8.

17. Hua Kuo-feng, "Political Report to the 11th National Congress of the Communist Party of China," *Peking Review*, 26 August 1977, p. 41.

18. *Ibid.*, pp. 40-41, and Jen Ku-ping, "The Munich Tragedy and Contemporary Appeasement," *Peking Review*, 9 December 1977, pp. 6-11.

19. See Teng Hsiao-p'ing's remarks in *Time*, 5 February 1979, p. 34; also see the remarks of Premier Chao Chu-yang (Zhao Ziyang) in July, 1984, *Beijing Review*, no. 32 (August, 1984), p. 10.

20. "Soviet Military Strategy for World Domination," *Beijing Review*, no. 4, January, 1980, pp. 15-19.

21. "Social-Imperialist Strategy in Asia," *Beijing Review*, no. 3, January 19, 1979, pp. 13-16.

22. *People's Daily*, 27 March 1980.

23. Xinhua Commentator, "Moscow's Dumb-Bell Strategy," *Beijing Review*, no. 8, 25 February 1980, pp. 8-9.

24. Tang Tianri, "The Recent Soviet Strategic Trend," *Beijing Review*, vol. 25, no. 8 (22 Feb. 1982), p. 10.

25. *Ibid.*
26. Zhang Zhen and Rong Zhi, "Some Observations on Soviet Detente," *Journal of International Studies,* no. 4, 1982, as translated in *Beijing Review,* vol. 25, no. 42 (October 18, 1982), p. 19.
27. *Ibid.,* p. 20.
28. *Ibid.,* p. 21.
29. *Ibid.*
30. *Ibid.,* p. 22.
31. *Time,* 5 February 1979, p. 34.
32. Quoted in Zheng Weizhi (President of the Beijing Institute of International Studies), "China's Foreign Policy of Peace and Independence," *Journal of International Studies,* no. 4, 13 October 1984, as translated in *JPRS*-CPS-84-90, 20 December 1984, p. 5.
33. *Beijing Review,* vol. 27, no. 47 (19 November 1984), pp. 10-11.
34. *Loc. cit.,* vol. 27, no. 48 (26 November 1984), p. 15.
35. Huan Xiang, "International Conflicts and Our Choices," *ibid.,* pp. 16-17.
36. Wu Xiuquan (President of the Beijing International Strategic Studies Society), "Relations with U.S., Soviets on Track," *Beijing Review,* vol. 28, no. 2 (21 January 1985), pp. 14-15.
37. Shi Wuqing, "Superpowers Reach Military Balance," *Beijing Review,* vol. 28, no. 3 (21 January 1985), pp. 14-15.

Japanese Perceptions:

China, the United States, and the Soviet Union

DONALD W. KLEIN

Japan's elites, plus the proverbial man-on-the-street, have a consuming interest in the United States, China, and the Soviet Union. Partly because of its geographic location, Japan is almost certainly the only major country that so intensely monitors events in the combination of the two superpowers *and* China.[1]

Japan is well known for its homogeneity, but even granting that point there is plainly no single perspective on the United States, China, and the Soviet Union (the Big Three). For example, the opposition parties and intellectuals are often at odds with the ruling Liberal Democratic Party. However, for the purposes of this chapter, Japanese perceptions are principally meant to portray those of the ruling elites and majority public opinion (where polling data are available).

In some ways, Japan's intense interest in the Big Three translates into an equally intense involvement. The massive U.S.-Japan economic relationship is a case in point. But the reverse is also true: Japan is keenly interested in the strategic maneuverings of the Big Three, yet in many respects Japanese elites, with plenty of public support, have attempted to be as uninvolved as possible.

After a brief look at Japan's historical relations with the Big Three, this chapter focuses on Japan's economic, strategic, and normative links with this threesome.

The Background

At the outset, it's useful to recall some background about Japan's relations with the Big Three. Like any people, the Japanese approach these countries with a large amount of historical and emotional baggage. For example, in the half-century from 1894 to 1945, Japan fought two wars with China, two with Russia, and one with the United States. In addition, with both China and Russia, it had a number of other "skirmishes" or "incidents." During that same span, of course, Japan sought to become *the* paramount imperialist power in East Asia. Not surprisingly, it was the Big Three that stood in Japan's path.

Another part of the historic legacy is that Japan was central to the attempted strangulation of the communist revolutions in both Russia and China. Japan's Imperial Army occupied the Maritime Province in Siberia as late as 1922, and from the 1920s to the 1940s it tried to suppress the Chinese Communist Party. To be sure, this is not now uppermost in the minds of the average Japanese, but the foreign policy elites realize how little it takes for Japan's *past* militarism to resurface in *today's* world. As recently as 1982, the Chinese were deeply upset over Japan's seeming callous attempt to soft-pedal (in school textbooks) the Japanese invasion of China in the 1930s. Beijing's reactions were not confined to propaganda blasts, but were instead raised to the level of formal government protests.[2]

Not only did Japan try to kill the Russian and Chinese revolutions at birth, but even after the revolutionaries took formal power the Japanese denied their very legitimacy. In the case of the Soviet Union, Tokyo and Moscow did not resume diplomatic relations until 1925. Japan's official nonrecognition of China lasted far longer—and was all the more repugnant to Beijing because Japan recognized Taiwan. It is true that active, semi-official Tokyo-Beijing relations existed from the mid-1950s (although marked by many ups and downs), but owing in large measure to U.S. pressure on Tokyo, the Japanese did not establish formal diplomatic relations with Beijing until 1972.

Moreover, Japan added injury to insult in denying Beijing's legitimacy by voting to exclude the PRC from the United Nations through all those years. (The other side of the U.N. diplomatic coin is that the Japanese resent the fact that the Russians voted to exclude them from the U.N. until 1956.)

Geography, of course, figures into Japan's perceptions of the Big Three. China is relatively close (about 400 miles), but even at the darkest hours of the Korean War the Japanese never seemed to think of China as a nearby and threatening neighbor. The Soviet Union, in contrast, is seen as vastly more threatening.[3] In the first place, it is very close by—so near that Russian islands are within sight. The aggravating part of this fact is that the Japanese—from political right to political left—all agree that these islands so close to Japan (the "Northern Territories") were stolen by the Russians at the end of World War II. The Northern Territories represent the only real territorial dispute between Japan and any other nation.[4]

Apart from purely historical and geographical facts, Japan also perceives China, the United States, and the Soviet Union through a very different cultural lens. Japan's cultural ties to China need no elaboration, and all Japanese pay at least lip service to Japan's "cultural debts" to China. This is especially apparent in terms of language—Japan borrowed its written (but not spoken) language almost directly from Chinese. Yet at the popular level in Japan, the Chinese language is not taught as a required course in public schools, but English is. Moreover, all Japanese are fully familiar with the Latin alphabet and regularly see English-language signs as part of their everyday lives. In striking contrast, the Russian Cyrillic alphabet is totally unknown to the average Japanese.

Chinese culture may be the most admired at the "elite culture" level in Japan, but few would doubt the dominance of the U.S. at the "pop culture" level. American sports, dietary habits, music, movies, TV shows, and clothes, for example, have had an enormous impact since World War II. Even at what might be called the "middle-brow" level, most Japanese are quite familiar with best-selling American authors. Apart from an admiration for Russian ballet and some Russian classical music, there is little Japanese interest in modern Russian culture any later than Tolstoy. Nor has the barren cultural landscape of Mao's China attracted much attention in Japan.

Ultimately, of course, all of these background factors—geography, history, and culture—blend into those elements that shape Japanese attitudes toward the outside world. It is not seen as a friendly world. On the contrary, it is a high-risk, Hobbesian world. Japanese are fond of characterizing their country as being "isolated," or an "orphan" nation that is "different" and "separate." They will note that the United States has a friendly Canada to the north, plus two vast oceans on its flanks. The Common Market countries have each other as friends and allies. Japan, in contrast, stands alone in Asia. The word that best captures all these ideas and images (and is often used by Japanese) is vulnerable. With this powerful sense of vulnerability in mind, let us turn to three major subjects: the quest for markets and resources; the search for strategic safety in a dangerous world; and some normative considerations.

Resources and Markets

Much of Japan's foreign policy is, of necessity, defined by its endless quest for resources and markets. This is understood at both elite and popular levels. And because the quest is so vital to Japan's well-being, it tends to override such other important issues as ideology (it is no accident that the slogan of "separating politics from economics" has been so widely accepted in Japan for the past thirty years). China, the Soviet Union and the United States would be crucially important to Japan even if they were not at the center of world politics. All three are geographically enormous, and thus, presumptively, have vast resources that Japan might be able to buy. All three have huge populations (ranking first, third, and fourth in the world—totaling about a billion and a half people), and are thus great markets for Japan. The U.S. and China are, in fact, central to Japanese trade patterns—the U.S. is Japan's top trading partner (by a wide margin), and China ranks fourth. The USSR ranks 16th, but there is a rich potential for much greater trade.[5]

When Japan surveys the Big Three for resources, three in particular stand out: food, fuel, and all other natural resources needed for industry.

Food

Japan sees the U.S. as the boundless supplier of food, and in large measure this perception is matched by reality. The Japanese are by far the best customers for American food. Still, the Japanese recall that when there was a high demand in 1973 for soybeans in the U.S., the Nixon administration slapped on a sudden embargo—which to this day is referred to in Japan as the "soybean shock."[6]

From time to time there have been minor U.S.-Japan squabbles over Japan's whaling industry, but this has been more than balanced (at least at elite levels) by the normally generous American position in terms of Japanese fishing in U.S. coastal waters.

Ironically, the other side of the food coin is that Japan increasingly feels an unwelcome pressure from the U.S. to buy even more food. Despite Japan's rank as the top buyer of American food, in recent years Washington has pressured Japan to buy more beef and citrus fruits. Tokyo's response is twofold: first, it already buys the lion's share of American exports of both commodities (in 1981, over 62% of all U.S. beef exports went to Japan, and over 44% of its citrus exports); secondly, the U.S. is often perceived as insensitive to Japan's domestic political considerations, particularly the fact that the Liberal Democratic Party, Japan's pro-American ruling party, is heavily dependent upon the farm vote.

Little needs to be said about food from the Soviet Union and China. There is no hope now, nor in the future, for large imports by Japan. China's one billion people consume all that their farmers can grow, and the well-known Soviet agricultural incompetence needs no elaboration. What is less commonly known is that Japan and the Soviet Union are the number one and number two fishing nations in the world. From Japan's viewpoint, the Soviets have been niggardly and unfair in hampering Japanese fishermen from fishing in Soviet or Soviet-controlled waters. Moreover, the Soviets have for years arrested and detained thousands of Japanese fishermen for alleged poaching in Russian waters. With minor exceptions, Japan has had no problems about fishing in the seas off China.

In brief, when Japan surveys the Big Three for food supplies, the United States comes up quite positively, the Chinese are in a kind of neutral position, and the Russians (typically) come up with a negative rating. Further, it is hard to think of circumstances under which the huge sales of American food to Japan would be shut off.

FUEL

Unlike the relatively invulnerable food supply, the Japanese feel extremely vulnerable in terms of fuel. And with good reason. Fully half of Japan's imports (measured by value) consist of mineral fuels (mainly petroleum), and most of this (71% in 1983) comes from the volatile Middle East. The United States, the Soviet Union, and China are all major fuel producers, and thus, of course, of interest to Japan. The Japanese buy large quantities of fuel from the U.S. (about 13% of all Japanese imports from the U.S.), but this still amounts to only a tiny proportion of Japan's fuel needs.

The purchase of Chinese and Soviet fuel resources has been under discussion for years, but from Japan's viewpoint the results are generally disappointing. The Japanese business community would like to plunge into the vast Siberian fuel resources, yet it is deeply ambivalent because of the pervasive distrust of the Russians and also because the Soviets have a long record of being difficult and unpredictable in coming to concrete terms.[7] In addition, the Japanese government is uneasy about such deals for fear of provoking Washington or (in recent years) Beijing. The Chinese in particular have strategic reasons for not wanting Japan to develop Siberia in any way, and beyond that they would obviously prefer that Japan aid the PRC to develop the latter's enormous coal resources and its offshore oil. In terms of coal, the disparity between the United States and China and the Soviet Union is striking. In 1983, Japan imported 25% of its coal needs from the U.S.; it got only 4.4% of its coal needs from China, and 2.3% from the USSR.[8]

A decade ago there were embarrassingly erroneous predictions that China was about to blossom forth as the Saudi Arabia of Asia. And, as a corollary, Japan was widely seen as the obvious recipient of this new oil flow. Unfortunately, this did not pan out, but Japan does get some oil (about 5% of its needs) from China, and is working with the Chinese to develop offshore fields. Perhaps within a decade China will export a really significant volume of oil to Japan, but for now that's problematic.[9] Possibly more important are Japan's efforts to help China develop its massive coal reserves. Interestingly, the Soviets do not appear to have registered any objections to these joint Sino-Japanese projects to develop fuel resources.

OTHER RESOURCES

If half of all Japan's imports are mineral fuels, and 10% are foodstuffs, then another 20% consist of a variety of other resources (iron ore, timber, copper, etc.). Here again, the U.S. is a very major supplier—selling Japan about as much non-fuel resources as it does food. In the case of both the Soviet Union and China, it is more a matter of potential than reality. In any event, there does not seem to be any particular problem among the Big Three in terms of their sales of these resources to Japan.

MARKETS

All Japan knows, of course, the importance of the American market. Well over a quarter of Japan's total exports are sold in the United States, or twice the amount that is sold to the entire Common Market, and a figure (in 1983) almost six times greater than Japan's *combined* exports to China and the Soviet Union! Japan's exports to the United States consist overwhelmingly (about 75%) of manufactured goods, notwithstanding various quotas on such items as cars and steel.

The massive American market is in many ways a Japanese dream come true. Yet Japan's very success in penetrating and even saturating this market is also a major problem between Tokyo and Washington. The problem hit an all-time peak in the spring of 1985 when U.S.-Japan trade issues rapidly shifted from the financial pages to alarming front-page headlines. The background was a 1984 American trade deficit with Japan of a staggering $37 billion. Then, when President Reagan announced an end to a quota on Japanese car exports to the U.S., Japan announced that car exports to the U.S. would jump by nearly 25%. An angry and protectionist-minded Congress quickly moved into action. The Senate, by an eye-catching 92-0 vote, passed a resolution urging the president to retaliate, and this was quickly followed by an almost equally impressive 394-19 vote in the House on a similar resolution. Both President Reagan and Prime Minister Nakasone stepped in to counsel restraint, but the Congressional votes could leave few with any doubts about the seriousness of the trade issue.

In any case, because both nations have capitalist economic systems, it is not easy for either government to exercise tight control of the situation. Senior officials in the United States are constantly badgered by various American businesses or labor unions who see, respectively, bankruptcy and unemployment in their future if the Japanese flood of goods does not end. This in turn has led American business, labor, and government figures to issue many "warnings" to Japan about the possible rise of protectionism in the United States. Apart from protectionist threats, Americans have pressed Japan very hard to open up its markets further—especially for manufactured goods. The typical OECD country imports better than half of its goods in the form of manufactured products; less than a quarter of Japan's imports are manufactured goods.

In recent years, the Japanese have shown an increasing distaste for the many American "warnings." They are seen by many—officials and laymen alike—as unfair and often rude. The Japanese claim (and many American analysts agree) that the United States should get its own fiscal house in order. Unfortunately, as of the middle 1980s, the situation is something of an unpleasant standoff.

Japan's marketing problems with the United States have little bearing on the former's markets in China and the USSR. Both markets are so small in comparison to the American market that neither is capable of cashing in on U.S.-Japan trade problems—at least in the sense of offering a huge, rich, and diversified market. The following table illustrates the vast differences.

Table 6-1

Japan's Exports to the U.S.,
China, and the Soviet Union[10]
(US $ billions, rounded)

	U.S.	China	U.S.S.R.
1978	$24.9	$3.0	$2.5
1979	26.4	3.7	2.5
1980	31.4	5.1	2.8
1981	38.6	5.1	3.3
1982	36.2	3.5	3.4
1983	42.8	4.9	2.8
1984	59.9	7.2	2.5

[10] These figures are taken from the 1980 through 1985 editions of *Japan: An International Comparison* (Tokyo: Japan Institute for Social and Economic Affairs).

In summarizing Japan's quest for resources and markets among the superpowers (and China), it seems fair to conclude that Japan has been largely successful in its three-decade long endeavor to "separate politics from economics." During that thirty-year span there have been fundamental changes in Sino-Soviet, Soviet-American, and Sino-American relations, but for the most part Japan has benefited. Whatever the Japanese may think about Big Three maneuverings, it seems evident that they have learned to handle these changes with adroitness—at least insofar as economics are concerned.

Japan's Strategic Perceptions

An analysis of Japan's strategic perceptions of China, the United States, and the Soviet Union should begin with some hard facts that inevitably shape Japanese thinking and attitudes. First, all of the Big Three are nuclear powers. All three are U.N. Security Council members, and thus armed with the veto. Japan sits astride one of the most heavily armed corners of the earth—with the Big Three providing virtually all of the firepower, or supplying it to their North and South Korean allies. Japan has a security treaty with the United States; it has a peace treaty with both the U.S. and China; but it has no peace treaty with Moscow.

It is at this strategic level that the sense of vulnerability especially grips

Japanese statesmen. They claim—and with much justice—that Japan's options are strongly conditioned by this vulnerability. This in large measure accounts for Japan's now familiar policy of reacting to situations, rather than initiating policies. Its foreign policy is generally "passive," "seldom active," or, to use another favorite Japanese expression, "low posture." It is probably no exaggeration to say that Japan's statesmen see that their main role is to prevent "bad" things from happening, rather than to make "good" things happen.

It is doubtless true, as Chalmers Johnson has written, that the military security of the northeast Asian non-communist nations is one of the "most boringly repetitious subjects in international politics."[11] But, alas, that does not diminish the signal importance of Japan's security links to the United States. If one adds the period of the American occupation of Japan (1945-52), this means that Japan has served as a military logistics base for the United States for the past 40 years. In essence, these bases were directed against China from the late 1940s to the early 1970s, and against the Soviet Union from the 1940s to the present.

It is easy enough to trot out the above objective facts. Yet facts and perceptions are not always in accord. And here we find that the Japanese have gone to rather extraordinary lengths to create a kind of strategic equivalency to the idea of "separating politics from economics." The United States and China may and do perceive the Soviets to be enemies, and the Russians return the favor. But the Japanese make a concerted effort to act as though they don't really have any enemies. At a more operational level, they can point to their "no-war" (article 9) constitution, and to their refusal to send troops abroad (even on U.N. peace-keeping missions). They can also note their adherence to the nuclear non-proliferation treaty, to their "three non-nuclear principles" (not to make, not to store, and not to let others introduce nuclear weapons), and to their persistent calls for nuclear agreements between the superpowers. In more normative terms, Japan's opposition parties are clearly identified as devoted adherents to neutralism. A combination of operational and normative considerations are involved in Japan's self-imposed adherence (since 1976) to keep the defense budget below 1 percent of GNP.

Realists may dismiss Japan's efforts to avoid having enemies. China did just that until the early 1970s. Yet, when Beijing decided to change its policy (c. 1971), Japan was fully prepared to deal with the Chinese on quite positive terms. The Soviets, unfortunately, are another matter. Apart from the above-mentioned Northern Territories dispute, the geographic nearness of the Soviet Union is felt in other ways. Soviet overflights are commonplace, as is the passage of Russian warships through the three straits that lead from the Sea of Japan to the Pacific Ocean. The decade-long Soviet naval build-up has been so significant that one Japanese wag suggested that the "Sea of Japan" be renamed the "Sea of the Soviet Union." This proximity has an uncomfortable way of creating crises for Japan. For instance, the defection of a Soviet MIG pilot to Hokkaido in 1976 led to frosty relations for several months, as did the Soviet shooting down of the Korean civilian airliner very near Japan's territorial waters in 1983.

The combination of the Soviet military buildup near Japan and American financial problems has meant that Washington has increasingly prodded Japan to hasten its own military buildup. In one fashion or another, this has been Washington's position for thirty-odd years, but it has become more insistent in recent years. There are conservatives in Japan who essentially agree with the United States, but, in general, public opinion polls support the current size of Japan's armed forces[12] and the amount of money spent for them. Many Japanese observers (not only from the political left) argue that American pressures on Japan are counterproductive.[13] In any event, the security issue is a delicate problem between Tokyo and Washington, and most signs suggest that it will be on the agenda well into the future.

Robert Barnett has raised still another complication concerning Japan's perceptions of other powers:

> Japan assesses military danger within a frame made up of nearby neighbors, whose capabilities and supposed intentions *regionally* [emphasis added] are subjected to scrupulous analysis, but without noticeable overattention to presumed ideological compulsions of Moscow, Pyong-yang, Hanoi, and Peking.

In contrast, continues Barnett:

> The American frame for assessing military threat . . . is global and is deeply influenced by Washington's proclaimed ideological presupposi-tions with respect to Soviet intention in every troubled corner of the world. Perhaps perversely, Japan seems often to fear Russian adventur-ism nearby less than do Americans from a distance.[14]

Barnett also paraphrases former Japanese Prime Minister Miki Takeo to the effect that "a recurring Japanese difficulty in discussing strategic questions with Americans was Washington's stress on its global responsibilities. Japan's concerns, in contrast, were limited to Japan and its neighborhood."[15]

Japan's Normative Perspectives

A discussion of normative perspectives inevitably lacks the precision that one can bring to some economic issues. Still, a few points are in order. In many ways, the United States has the major advantage in this sphere. Japan and the United States share very similar political and economic systems. The U.S. has had a great advantage over both China and the Soviet Union in terms of contacts among top-level leaders. Back in the 1940s and 1950s, Yoshida and MacArthur clearly had a deep respect for one another. Richard Nixon's study of foreign leaders also displays a great admiration for Yoshida.[16] In more recent times, it appears that both Carter and Ohira and Reagan and Nakasone have had great rapport. From the 1950s to the present, American presidents and Japanese prime ministers have met with great regularity. In the 31-year span from 1954 to 1985, there have been no less than 22 U.S.-Japan "summit" meetings between the Japanese prime minister and the American president, and this figure does not include the many multilateral meetings that have brought these leaders together (such as the economic summits held every year since 1975). Every Japanese prime minister since Yoshida has been to the United States, and the last three American presidents have paid state visits to Japan. Moreover, Japanese foreign ministers and American secretaries of state have met even more often, and, indeed, American and Japanese cabinet members in each other's capital is a common sight.

Since Prime Minister Tanaka's visit to China in 1972, senior Chinese and Japanese officials have met with some regularity. Four of Japan's last six prime ministers have visited Peking. On the Chinese side, since Mao Zedong's death in 1976, the four most senior Chinese leaders (Deng Xiaoping, Hua Guofeng, Hu Yaobang, and Zhao Ziyang) have visited Tokyo. Still, top-level visits between Beijing and Tokyo don't match those between Tokyo and Washington. In this sense, the Soviet Union is not even in the running. Only two Japanese Prime Ministers have made official visits to Moscow (Hatoyama in 1956 and Tanaka in 1973). Tokyo still awaits the first Soviet premier or CPSU general secretary. However, when the Soviet Foreign Minister visited Tokyo in January 1986, an official invitation was extended to Soviet leader Mikhail Gorbachev to visit Japan, and it seems likely that the visit will in fact be made.

What is true of the most senior governmental leaders is even more true of middle-echelon diplomatic figures. American middle-level government officials have been dealing with their Japanese counterparts for four decades; indeed, many are close personal friends. Beyond these government contacts, of course, are countless business and academic links (not to mention such other ties as tourism). Similar contacts with China only date from the late 1970s. Russo-Japanese middle-level government contacts have been few and far between in the entire postwar period.

For years Japanese pollsters have been inquiring into attitudes toward foreign nations. At the most unrefined level, the results are plain enough. Except for a few years in the late 1960s and early 1970s (coinciding with the Vietnam War), the United States has consistently scored high in the "liked" or "feel-friendly-toward" categories. Attitudes toward China were largely negative through the 1960s, and reached a very low point during the Cultural Revolution (late 1960s). However, attitudes turned much more positive in the 1970s, so that by the late 1970s and early 1980s the United States and China are "liked" to approximately the same degree. The Russians have always scored quite badly in these polls. In the early 1970s, the situation improved a bit, but then (related to the Soviet military build-up and the Northern Territories) it turned decidedly sour by the late 1970s, and remains in that situation today.[17]

It is perhaps fitting to close with a few lines from an authoritative source—the latest issue of the Foreign Ministry's "Diplomatic Bluebook." The language is almost surprisingly blunt. "Japan shares the basic values of freedom and democracy with the other industrialized countries. . . . Friendly and cooperative relationship with the United States, based on the Japan-U.S. Security Treaty, is the cornerstone of Japan's foreign policy. The United States is Japan's most important partner in a broad spectrum of areas including politics, economy, and defense."[18]

The tone about China is almost equally positive: "Since the normalization of relations with China in 1972, Japan has made it a main pillar of its foreign policy to maintain and develop the friendly and stable relations with that country. . . . Japan intends to continue its positive cooperation for China's modernization policy."[19]

Not surprisingly, the Diplomatic Bluebook speaks of the Soviet Union in language that is diplomatically correct but nonetheless bluntly pessimistic. "Relations with the Soviet Union, our important neighbor to the north, are regrettably in a difficult phase, reflecting the severe East-West relations and also the Soviet military buildup in the Far East including the Northern Territories which are inherent Japanese territory."[20] In other passages, "difficulties" are described as having arisen from "factors solely attributable to the Soviet side, such as the . . . armed intervention in Afghanistan, the situation in Poland and the problem of transferring Soviet intermediate range nuclear forces (INF) from Europe to the Far East."[21] With only a few changes for specific events, the essence of these sentences could have been written in almost any year since 1945.

Conclusion

It is relatively easy to characterize Japanese perceptions of the United States, China, and the Soviet Union. They have been generally positive *vis-à-vis* the U.S. There have been many ups and downs toward China, but since the early 1970s the record has been mainly positive. Toward the Soviet Union, the situation has been an unbroken record of negativism.

Will these trends continue? Recalling that Japan's foreign policy is essentially reactive, an estimate of future trends might rest on a three-part analysis of Japanese perceptions: How will Japan see the Big Three powers in terms of their economic, strategic (coercive), and normative policies? On this basis, it seems safe to assume that Japan's perceptions will remain very poor toward the USSR. Moscow gives few indications of any serious intent to engage in a long-range economic partnership with Japan. To the degree that the Russians continue their military buildup in East Asia, and continue to hold the Northern Territories (and refuse to discuss their return to Japan), Japan's perceptions of the USSR will remain very negative, and may well grow even more so.

At the opposite pole, U.S.-Japan interdependence is so massive that short-term fluctuations (which are certain to take place) tend to be overridden by long-term benefits. That is especially true in the economic realm. In terms of strategic considerations, Japan's long-held concern that the U.S. might drag Japan into an unwanted war is mitigated by Soviet military pressures. It is these very same Russian pressures that have allowed for a rational discussion in recent years of the U.S.-Japan military alliance. Perhaps the strongest links are the normative ones that tend to tie all the industrial democracies together.

In terms of China and Japan, a previous artificial isolation from each other has given way to rapid moves toward interdependence—especially economic interdependence. The Japanese simply do not see China as a strategic threat, and so long as China's massive modernization program allows for Japan's participation (which it plainly does), the Japanese are largely indifferent to China's ideology. Therefore, it seems reasonable to expect a continuation of Japan's favorable perception of China, and very possibly the growth of an even more positive one.

Notes

I would like to thank Richard K. Winslow, Jr. of the Japanese Consulate General in Boston for supplying some useful materials, and I am also very grateful for the helpful comments of Michael Blaker on the contents of this chapter.

1. As of the end of 1982, Japan had 118 foreign correspondents in the United States. Britain and France were next, with 34 and 31 correspondents, respectively. Then came China (20) and the Soviet Union (19). The number of foreign correspondents is obviously not the only barometer of the intensity of Japan's interest in foreign affairs, but it is certainly one of the better indicators.
2. For a sophisticated treatment of the textbook controversy, see Chong-sik Lee, "History and Politics in Japanese-Korean Relations: The Textbook Controversy and Beyond," *Journal of Northeast Asian Studies,* vol. II, no. 4, Dec. 1983, pp. 69-93.
3. As might be expected, the intensity of the Soviet threat rises and falls with the tide of events. For example, in the wake of the 1983 shooting down of the Korean airliner by the Russians, one poll showed that nearly 92% of the populace felt that the Soviet military forces were a threat to Japan. See Chalmers Johnson, "East Asia: Another Year of Living Dangerously," *Foreign Affairs,* vol. 62, no. 3, 1984, p. 726.
4. Japan does have disagreements regarding the Senkaku Islands (near Taiwan) and Tsushima Island (between Japan and South Korea), but in contrast to the Northern Territories they are minor matters.
5. The rankings are for 1984.
6. Frank Langdon, "Japan and North America," in Robert S. Ozaki and Walter Arnold, eds., *Japan's Foreign Relations: A Global Search for Economic Security* (Boulder, CO: Westview Press, 1985), p. 24.
7. See, for example, Gerald L. Curtis, "The Tyumen Oil Development Project and Japanese Foreign Policy Decision-Making," in Robert A. Scalapino, ed., *The Foreign Policy of Modern Japan* (Berkeley: University of California Press, 1977), pp. 147-73.
8. *White Paper on International Trade, Japan 1984: Summary* (Tokyo: Japan External Trade Organization, 1985), p. 171.

9.   See Chae-Jin Lee, *China and Japan: New Economic Diplomacy* (Stanford: Hoover Institution Press, 1984), chapter 3. It is worth noting that 20 years ago, in 1965, the USSR supplied 3.3% of Japan's oil needs. By 1983 this had fallen to an incredible 0.1%!

10. These figures are taken from the 1980 through 1985 editions of *Japan: An International Comparison* (Tokyo: Japan Institute for Social and Economic Affairs).

11. Chalmers Johnson, *op. cit.*, p. 723.

12. An *Asahi* (newspaper) poll in December 1983 found that 60% of the respondents wanted to maintain Japan's Self-Defense Forces at their present size; 10% said they should be increased; 19% said they should be decreased; and 5% said they should be abolished. Kiyofuku Chuma, "Japanese Security Policy: Changing Perspectives from Renewed U.S.-Soviet Tensions," Center for International Studies, MIT, June 1984, p. 21. See also Shinkichi Eto, "Japanese Perceptions of National Threats," in Charles E. Morrison, ed., *Threats to Security in East Asia-Pacific: National and Regional Perspectives* (Lexington, MA: Lexington Books, 1983), pp. 53-64.

13. For a recent example, see Maeda Hisao, "A Perilous Plan for Japan's Security," *Japan Quarterly*, vol. 31, no. 4, October-December 1984, pp. 395-9. A completely orthodox view from the political left is found in Japan Socialist Party Chairman Ishibashi Masashi's "The Road to Unarmed Neutrality," ibid., vol. 31, no. 2, April-June 1984, pp. 142-4.

14. Robert W. Barnett, *Beyond War: Japan's Concept of Comprehensive National Security* (New York: Pergamon-Brassey's, 1984), pp. 124-5. Barnett's book is a gold mine of highly informed opinion on Japan from both Japanese and American sources interviewed by Barnett.

15. *Ibid.*, p. 110.

16. Richard Nixon, *Leaders* (New York: Warner Books, 1982), Chapter 4, "Douglas MacArthur and Shigeru Yoshida."

17. See Akio Watanabe, "Japanese Public Opinion and Foreign Affairs: 1964-1973," in Scalapino, op. cit., pp. 105-45; and the poll taken by the Prime Minister's Office and published by the Foreign Press Center in Tokyo in September 1983 under the title "Public Opinion Survey on Diplomacy." See also Fumio Uda, "Policy and Public Image in Japanese-Soviet Relations: Diplomatic Strains and Declining Popularity," in *Journal of Northeast Asian Studies,* Summer 1984, vol. III, no. 2, pp. 43-65.

18. Ministry of Foreign Affairs (Tokyo), *Diplomatic Bluebook: 1983 Edition* (Tokyo: Foreign Press Center, 1983), pp. 10-11.

19. *Ibid.*, p. 11.

20. *Ibid.*, p. 16.

21. *Ibid.*, p. 63.

7

Soviet Perceptions of Japan:

Foreign and Defense Policies, and Relations with the Strategic Triad

PETER BERTON

"U kogo chto bolit, tot o tom i govorit"
(One's pain is the topic of one's conversation)

Russian proverb

Japan is likely to play an increasing role in the calculations of its ally, the United States, its important trading partner, China, and its antagonist, the Soviet Union. This is particularly true in East Asia where the interests of the strategic triangle, or the U.S.-USSR-China triad, intersect most directly. Thus, mutual perceptions of the four powers are at the root of understanding the dynamics of international relations in Asia and the Pacific.

Strictly speaking, the strategic triangle is of limited value as a key to understanding the dynamics of *world* politics. At the present stage of the strategic nuclear balance, at least, the international system is still bipolar, as the on-and-off Soviet-American negotiations in Geneva and in other venues attest. To be sure, the Chinese nuclear arsenal (and the British and

French ones, for that matter) does figure in the calculations of the two protagonist superpowers, but as yet the negotiations have not been expanded to include China (or the two West European nuclear powers). Nevertheless, in a limited sense, U.S. policy toward China is influenced by consideration of probable or possible Soviet reaction, and U.S. policy toward the Soviet Union takes into account the probable or possible effect of a particular action on China. In the sense that Tokyo must calculate the costs and benefits of moving closer toward either Beijing or Moscow, Japan's policy toward the two Communist superpowers is similarly inhibited.

Another way of illustrating the limited value of the strategic triangle concept is to look at the various world conflict areas. In the European theater, there is a confrontation between the forces of NATO and the Warsaw Pact alliance systems. The Soviet Union, of course, has to worry about the security of its border with China, but certainly this is in no way comparable to the threat of a two-front war which the Soviet Union experienced in the 1930s when a simultaneous assault by Germany and Japan from the West and the East was a very real possibility.[1] And at present, no threat exists from the Japanese Self-Defense Forces. Thus, there is no triangularity in the European context, except perhaps if, some time in the future, the European NATO allies are sufficiently strong and motivated to play an independent role with the two superpowers.

Likewise, there is no substantial role that China plays in the Middle Eastern, African, and Latin American contexts to justify careful calculations by the United States or the Soviet Union of Chinese presence or policy. Asia east of Iran, however, is another matter. Here, whether in South Asia, Southeast Asia, or Northeast Asia, it *does matter* to the two superpowers what China's interests are and what Chinese policy is likely to be. But once we admit the importance of China in the Asian context, it becomes necessary to look outside the strategic triangle to see what other important factors influence the dynamics of international relations in this region. Here we must consider the role of Japan, and to a lesser extent India, in the calculations of each of the actors in the strategic triad.

As some scholars (including myself) have argued, the strategic triangle in East Asia is rapidly becoming a quadrangle. But even if one assigns a lesser role to Japan than to the other three powers (in his 1975 book Hinton treated Japan as a half power[2]), it is important to examine Japan's perceptions of the strategic triangle and its policies (discussed by Klein in Chapter 6) as well as to look at the three powers' perceptions of Japan and its role. Of these, the most important is the perspective of the chief antagonist, the Soviet Union. My task is to present and analyze the Soviet perspective on Japan, its economic potential, its foreign and defense policies, and its relations with the United States, China, and the Soviet Union.

Japan as a World Economic Power

The Twenty-fourth Congress of the CPSU in 1971 formally designated Japan as "a new center of imperialist rivalry," along with the United States and Western Europe. A recent (1984) survey, "Present-Day Imperialism," likewise identifies Japan as one of its three centers, although the cover shows a cluster of skyscrapers for the United States, a massive multiwing, multistory headquarters building for the European Economic Community, and, incongruously, a dainty Torii gate of a Shinto shrine for industrial Japan.[3] The survey itself, however, gives the Japanese economy and its industrial and financial performance their due. For example, the average annual rates of increase of industrial production and the GNP for 1970-1973, 1974-1979, and annually for 1980 through 1983 clearly show Japan in first place, except for 1983, where its performance is second to the United States.[4] In exports of machinery and industrial equipment by the seven leading capitalist countries (members of the economic summits) for 1980 and 1983, Japan is in third place behind West Germany and the United States in 1980, but first in 1983.[5]

Japan is also shown to be the top steel producer in both years[6] and number one (followed by the United States, West Germany, and Sweden) among the twenty-two leading "developed capitalist countries" in terms of the competitive capacity of their output.[7] (Conveniently, the Soviet publication does not advertise the competitive capacity of the "developed socialist countries.")

In the list of the largest forty-six multinational corporations, only six are Japanese, and their volume of sales places them only in 24th to 43rd positions.[8]

One of the articles in this survey stresses the economic, industrial, and financial competition between the three centers, and its relationship to armaments:

> The Big Business of the West European centre, and in recent years also the Japanese industrial and financial tycoons covet the multibillion [dollar] profits of their American rivals and clearly want to grab a bigger slice of the militarist pie from it. It is the avarice of Big Business that prompts the European Atlanticists and the Japanese conservatives to clamour ever

more persistently for a further swelling of military budgets, inflated as they already are.[9]

Of course, in the case of Japan, one can hardly speak of a "swelling of military budgets," considering the modest increases and the ridiculously low share (1-1.5%) that military expenditure represents in the trillion dollar plus Japanese economy. The article ends with a scare tactic that makes good propaganda, especially in nuclear-allergic Japan:

> The pursuit of superprofits by the transnational oligarchs and barons of the military business brings the world dangerously close to the threshold of a nuclear Apocalypse.[10]

Soviet scholars divide postwar Japanese economic history into three periods: (1) the era of the economic "miracle," (2) the prolonged crisis of the 1970s, and (3) the present period of far-reaching structural change.[11] Curiously, "miracle" appears in quotation marks, implying that the Japanese economic miracle is not a true one. As for Japan's future economic growth, Soviet prognoses are probably the opposite of Kahn's optimistic projections. A Soviet reviewer invited the Japanese to read a 1983 Soviet work on Japan "to stimulate thoughts about the past and present and *the thorny roads* of the future.[12] Soviet writers on Japan report its economic accomplishments, but hasten to point out and exaggerate its weaknesses, vulnerabilities, and contradictions.

Japanese Foreign Policy

A noted Soviet scholar Dmitry Petrov astutely characterized Japanese foreign policy as having developed from an emphasis on bilateral Japanese-American relations in the 1950s to regional Asian ties in the 1960s and to "active participation in the solution of global problems common to all imperialist countries" in the 1970s and the 1980s.[13] He also claims that roughly until the mid-1970s, "the Japanese ruling circles" tried to limit their participation in the "world imperialist system" to discussions of *economic* problems, citing the unique position of Japan as a strong economic power without a considerable military potential. More recently, however, Japan is showing a tendency to combine economic problems with *military* and *political* ones.[14]

S. I. Verbitskii agrees with Petrov that the main task of Japanese foreign policy in the late 1950s and during the first half of the 1960s was "economic diplomacy": to conquer new markets and sources of raw materials for the rapidly developing Japanese industry. But he argues that it was already during the second half of the 1960s that as Japanese monopolies went global, Japanese leaders began to emphasize the need to promote in international affairs Japan's political influence commensurate with its economic power. And from the beginning of the 1970s, in view of the weakening of the American position in Asia, the strengthening of the position of the socialist countries, and the deep economic depression which affected the entire capitalist world, Japan's conservative leaders began to propagandize the concept of "omnidirectional diplomacy" and a more active foreign policy.[15]

In another publication Petrov finds characteristic features of Japan's foreign policy during the 1970s to include: (1) drastic growth of the economic factor (to assure the expansion of Japanese monopolies); (2) steadfast efforts to stabilize the imperialist system as a whole; (3) deepening and strengthening of the global characteristics of Japan's foreign policy by active participation in joint actions of the imperialist powers; (4) maintenance and development of close ties with the United States, accompanied by a significant increase in Japan's role and function within the American military-strategic system in Asia; and (5) deepening of the contradictions between the officially proclaimed policy of peace and nonuse of military force and the real policy of remilitarization and buildup of military potential.[16]

At the same time, Soviet authors feel obligated to maintain that for Japan's ruling circles foreign policy is an important factor in the preservation and strengthening of their class rule. They reject attempts to portray foreign policy as being above class considerations and as expressing the "interests of the entire people" as official propaganda and bourgeois historiography. A quotation from Lenin's speech at the Ninth Party Congress in 1920 legitimizes the notion that in capitalist countries matters of greatest importance, such as war, peace, and diplomatic problems, are decided by "an insignificant handful of capitalists who deceive not only the masses of people, but also often the parliament."[17] This fully applies to postwar Japanese foreign policy, whose main objectives are (1) the preservation of the foundations of the imperialist system in its historic competition with the world socialist system, (2) the assurance of stability of the capitalist structure in Japan, (3) the strengthening of Japan's position in the competitive struggle with other imperialist powers, and (4) maximum support of the expansion of Japanese monopolies in world markets.[18] Soviet writers often emphasize the first point, namely, the strengthening of positions of the "imperialist system" as a whole. They accuse the Japanese leadership of taking measures that clearly contradict the national interests of Japan. This includes nonsupport of proposals that aim at the relaxation of international tensions in various international organizations, including the United Nations.

In the final analysis, the most important aim of Japan's foreign policy is to maintain and strengthen the domination of the country's ruling circles. This policy follows class objectives and has nothing to do with the hopes and aspirations of the broad masses of the Japanese people who resolutely demand an indigenous and independent course in foreign policy, which is aimed at assuring a durable peace and security on the basis of friendly, good-neighbor relations with all countries.[19]

Japanese foreign policy, including its foreign economic policy, is determined to a great extent by the Japanese-American political alliance and by economic relations with the United States. But while in the 1970s the Japanese authorities were, at least verbally, declaring a "diplomacy of equidistance," in the 1980s they began overtly emphasizing the "solidarity of the Western camp."[20] Above all, Japan is chastised for the "clearcut discrepancy between the officially proclaimed doctrines of adherence to peace and the real policy of regular increases in military potential," which, it is claimed, is a characteristic feature of Japan's foreign policy at the beginning of the 1980s.[21]

Thus, we find in the writings of Soviet specialists on Japan a correct reflection of the widening of the scope of Japanese diplomacy from bilateral ties with the United States, to expanded relations with its Asian neighbors, to a truly global dimension; an appreciation of the evolution of Japanese diplomacy from an almost complete emphasis on economic relations to the inclusion also of political and security matters; and a recognition of the centrality of Japan's relations with the United States. They also correctly describe the growing Japanese role in international Western summits, although they prefer to characterize it as an effort "to stabilize the imperialist system" (it would have made more sense to comment on Japan's legitimate stake in the world trade system). But one would search in vain for an acknowledgment that Soviet international behavior, especially in the mid-1970s culminating with the Soviet invasion of Afghanistan, had anything to do with modest Japanese efforts to beef up its defenses. At best, Soviet writers talk of the "myth of the Soviet menace,"[22] which is used by Japanese politicians as an excuse for the "militarization of Japan." And they prefer to draw the pejorative distinction between Japan's words of peace and its action, military buildup. But where the Soviets are most deluding themselves (because repeating a line over and over will eventually result in unconscious acceptance) is in the portrayal of Japanese government as "ruling circles" quite separate from "progressive elements" among the Japanese public, not to speak of "the Japanese people."

Japanese-American Relations

Early postwar Soviet writings on Japan stressed the almost complete dependence of Japan on the United States—politically, economically, and militarily. Japan was portrayed as a colony of the American ruling circles, monopoly capital, and the military clique. Over the years, however, the Soviet view of Japanese-American relations has stressed their *changing character,* both in terms of content and relative strength. For example, Soviet scholars point out the difference between the 1951 and 1960 U.S.-Japanese security treaties: the use of American forces for the suppression of internal unrest and riots, which was sanctioned in the first agreement, is no longer included in the second.[23] The evolution of U.S.-Japanese relations is also seen as developing along the road of gradual liquidation of the elements of dependent position of the Japanese side and the establishment of the so-called equal partnership.[24]

A recent (1984) discussion of Japanese foreign policy in a work on "The Ruling Circles of Japan" nevertheless claims that the alliance with the United States has retained its significance as the most important factor for the preservation and strengthening of the power of Japan's "ruling circles." In support of this assertion, the author provides three reasons:

(1) The alliance fully corresponds to the long-range "class objectives" of Japan's financial oligarchy; (2) In spite of the absence of official agreements, if necessary, American armed forces in Japan may be used by the ruling circles and in their interest for the preservation of political power. This is reliably guaranteed by the maintenance of American bases on Japanese territory under the conditions of closest ties and agreement on the most important international questions by the leadership of the two countries; (3) The alliance with the United States opens the road for the militarization of Japan and the strengthening of the "Self-Defense Forces" as an important factor to ensure the dominance of the ruling class.[25]

One finds in Soviet writings also the notion that Japan's interest in its relations with the United States is primarily *economic,* whereas American interest in its relations with Japan is essentially *political* and *military.*[26]

After the fall of South Vietnam in 1975, however, a Soviet scholar noted that "while trade and economic relations between these two countries are retaining their significance, military-political cooperation is now moving to the forefront."[27] This does not mean that Soviet authors do not stress the ever-growing contradictions between the two countries in their economic relations.

Japan's economic objectives are said to have included the following: first and foremost, its access to the huge American domestic market for Japanese industrial goods; second, the United States as a source for the accumulation of foreign exchange (no longer as important in the 1980s and often a source of embarrassment and friction); third, the U.S. financial market as the largest source of capital and long-term credits; fourth, participation in the huge American military expenditures, including special military procurements, which were all-important during the Korean and Vietnam wars; fifth, continuation of the intensive absorption of American technology; sixth, the utilization of the financial resources of the United States; and finally, the use of U.S. economic, political, and military influence in the capitalist world in the interest of foreign economic expansion of Japanese monopolies.[28]

As for joint objectives of the two allies, Ivan Kovalenko, the Japan expert on the CPSU Central Committee apparat; in 1978 identified the following: (1) further strengthening of the military-political alliance between the United States and Japan and sharing of responsibility and spheres of influence in the region; (2) the involvement of South Korea, which is regarded by Tokyo and Washington as a key bastion against the "communist threat" in the Japanese-U.S. alliance; (3) the inclusion of Taiwan, despite the fact that Japan has broken off diplomatic relations with it, into the Japanese-U.S. system designed to maintain a balance of forces in the Far East and Asia; (4) the strengthening of political, economic, military, and other links with the ASEAN countries, giving them "aid" in credits and loans in order to tie them closer to the Washington-Tokyo-Seoul axis; and (5) stirring up Soviet-Chinese differences and using them in their imperialist interests.[29] Some of these will be discussed in greater detail in the next section dealing with Japanese defense policy.

A Soviet monograph on Japanese-American relations published in 1970 was subtitled "Partners and Competitors."[30] More recent writings stress the competitive nature of this relationship, American political pressure, Japanese defensive economic measures, and the gradual deepening of contradictions between these two economically strongest capitalist societies.

Thus, Petrov wrote in mid-1984 of drastic intensification of contradictions between Japan and the United States especially in trade and economics as a result of the growth of Japan's material capabilities, and the tendency to resolve them in a single "package" with political and military problems.[31]

Verbitskii noted that, on the one hand, Japanese-American contradictions are sharpening (especially in the economic sphere), but, on the other, the "ruling circles" of both countries are attempting to work out a unified approach to regional and global problems, above all in political and military realms.[32]

While Japan is seen as gaining in this relationship, Professor Konstantin Sarkisov brings out certain advantages that the United States has gained from its cooperation with Japan during the past several years: (1) it has achieved greater Japanese involvement in U.S. strategy in Asia; (2) it caused Japan to carry out diplomacy unfriendly to the Soviet Union; (3) Japan has been assured a greater military role in East Asia; and (4) the United States has succeeded in assuring greater Japanese economic aid to U.S. "strategic" partners in Asia, most of whom belong to the group of "frontier states."[33] At the same time, Sarkisov maintains that in addition to trying to develop its military-political alliance with the United States, Japan is also attempting "to expand its political influence."[34]

On the whole, while noting the changes in the relative power position of Japan and the United States, especially in the economic area, Soviet writers point to the continuing asymmetry in military power between the two allies. Let us, then, take a closer look at Soviet views of Japan's defense policy and what is seen as the input and impact of the United States.

Defense Policies

In the 1980s, with increasing Japanese budgets for the Self-Defense Forces, more active Japanese support of American security arrangements in the Pacific, and participation of Japanese naval forces in joint RIMPAC exercises with the American and other allied navies, the Soviets are sounding the alarm that the United States is in the process of creating a NEATO (Northeast Asia Treaty Organization) to parallel NATO. They approvingly cited the Japanese Communist Party daily *Akahata* (without identifying it as such), which stridently criticized President Reagan's speech in the Japanese National Diet.

As a first step toward a regional Pacific alliance structure, the Soviets invoke the specter of a tripartite military alliance among the United States, Japan, and South Korea in which "the U.S. exercises overall military and political direction, Japan provides the economic muscle and South Korea the cannon fodder."[35] Leaving this crude formulation aside, there is, of course, some truth to the desire on the part of military planners in all three countries to coordinate and share intelligence information and make appropriate contingency plans. In the case of Japan, however, even the existence of such plans has in the past created serious political problems for the government. But the Soviet use of propaganda is undeterred. Here is a typical Soviet comment on the Washington-Tokyo-Seoul military cooperation and wider American security goals:

> The plans for this aggressive triangle, plus wider military cooperation with China, annexation of the Micronesia islands in defiance of international law—are all manifestations of Washington's hegemonistic policy, of its attempts to establish its unlimited influence in the Pacific.[36]

Actually, Soviet alarm over the remilitarization of Japan (and also, of course, West Germany) reflects an irrational hangover from World War II and earlier when these two countries did indeed pose a mortal danger to the survival of the USSR as a state. Many Western analysts have often wondered about the constant Soviet obsession about the potential rebirth of militarism and revanchism in both Germany and Japan which does indeed sound odd given the Soviet Union's superpower status and the rather modest conventional forces in these two countries, especially in Japan.

Soviet leaders ritualistically invoke the potential threat emanating from Germany and Japan, as General Secretary Brezhnev did at the Twenty-fourth Party Congress in 1971, saying that the Japanese militarists "seek once again to push the country onto the path of expansion and aggression."[37] After the conclusion of the 1978 Sino-Japanese Treaty of Peace and Friendship, Kovalenko, the Central Committee apparatchik, identified former National Defense Agency Director and future Prime Minister Nakasone as the originator of the doctrine of "Gaullist Japan" which calls for "unlimited buildup" of Japan's armed forces.[38] In 1979 a Soviet monograph on the military-economic potential of Japan listed basic Japanese goals in this field as the development of nuclear energy, space technology, and missiles.[39] This was followed in 1982 by a monograph on the rise of militarism in Japan, which was issued by the Military Publishing

House.[40] Soviet writers have also seized upon the revision of Japanese history textbooks which sought to describe Japan's aggression in Asia as an "advance" and the subsequent protests in China and Korea.[41] They write of samurais,[42] ultra-rightists,[43] and "militarist brainwashing" of the Japanese.[44]

Although Prime Minister Suzuki was taken to task for commencing work "on a high militaristic note like none other of Japan's postwar governments,"[45] the advent of the Nakasone administration in late 1982 provided the Soviet propaganda machine with a lot of ammunition. Thus one reads about "Outlines of a New Militaristic Alliance in the Far East,"[46] "Nakasone's Military Policy,"[47] "Japan in the Nuclear Strategy of the United States,"[48] the "NATOization of Japan,"[49] and of Japan being "the cornerstone of the Asian policy of the U.S.A."[50]

The Japanese Self-Defense Forces are described in great detail, and increases in Japan's defense budgets are carefully noted. The specter of a rearmed Japan is made more ominous by picturing it as a part of a local Tokyo-Washington-Seoul triangle[51] threatening to bottle up the Soviet Pacific fleet, which is, in turn, a part of a larger, more ambitious American plan to create a Pacific counterpart to NATO, a kind of Northeast Asia Treaty Organization or NEATO. Japan is assigned a very important role in these American plans and is said to be complying in part as a result of American pressure and in part because of indigenous militarist and revanchist tendencies.

Of course, the Soviets do not pass up an opportunity to warn Japan of the dangers inherent in this course. Japan is warned that it is being dragged toward "the nuclear abyss"[52] or that the future "may repeat the past on a more horrifying scale."[53]

Sino-Japanese Relations

How is the evolution of Sino-Japanese relations since 1972 presented and explained? A recent monograph on the subject provides the following analysis.[54]

The process of Sino-Japanese rapprochement since 1972 is divided into two periods: (1) from the normalization of relations by Prime Minister Tanaka in September 1972 to Mao Zedong's death in fall 1976, and (2) the post-Mao era. The first period saw the establishment of a legal base for the relations between the two countries as well as a considerable strengthening of trade and other economic relations. But there were problems that hindered the full development of Sino-Japanese relations and slowed down the tempo of rapprochement between the two countries. As a result of changes in *China's* policy, the second period saw a growing tempo in and expanding areas of rapprochement.[55] Curiously enough, the conclusion of the Sino-Japanese Treaty of Peace and Friendship in August 1978 does not constitute a new period in the relationship between the two countries.

Japanese policy toward China is seen not as independent action, however, but as a reflection of U.S. policy toward China and the *Soviet Union*. Thus, Japan leapfrogged the United States in its 1972 agreement with China in the sense that Japan normalized its relations and recognized the People's Republic as the legitimate and only government of China, whereas full Sino-American normalization did not occur until 1979. But the "independence" of Japan's foreign policy is a fiction. Full Japanese recognition of the PRC not only did not contradict U.S. plans, it was actually approved by President Nixon in his meeting with Prime Minister Tanaka in late August-early September, prior to the latter's pilgrimage to Beijing. Of course, Japanese recognition of the PRC was not against Japanese interests. Quite to the contrary, the parallel approach of the United States and Japan toward the PRC was based on the commonality of their imperialistic interests, which reflected the growing tendency of the Japanese ruling circles toward normalization of relations with mainland China.[56]

What happened during the second period, following the death of Mao? The situation was quite different in the second half of the 1970s when the American administration attempted to saddle China with straight cooperation aimed against the Soviet Union. The Sino-Japanese Treaty of Peace and Friendship was signed in this period under extreme American pressure.[57]

The events of the late 1970s and the early 1980s showed that in formulating its policy toward China, Japan followed the United States. The more the United States attempted to enlist China in the anti-Soviet front, however, the less this policy coincided with the interests of the Japanese ruling circles. This was a period of antidetente confrontational tendencies in U.S. policy, and unconditional support of American aggressive plans did not serve Japan's interests. First, such a course transformed Japan into a definite second-rate actor in Far Eastern politics, which in turn led to the lowering of its international prestige. Second, Japan is not a world power and does not have relations with the USSR which cover the entire spectrum of world politics. It cannot hope, therefore, to neutralize the negative Soviet reaction to its unfriendly action by offering solutions to some other global problems. In other words, by supporting the United States in matters that affect Soviet interests, Japan risks worsening its relations with the Soviet Union to a greater extent than its American ally.[58]

The history of Sino-Japanese relations over a ten-year period shows that Japan was denied any initiative, generally adapting itself to American policies toward China. Needless to say, this approach did not bring Japan any laurels, nor did it increase its prestige. It is clear that unconditional support by the Japanese ruling circles of Washington's plans to use China to "contain the USSR" not only lowered Japan to the role of a second-rate power but also led to the heightening of international tensions in the Far East. This, above all, is against the interests of Japan.[59]

Of course, Soviet writers kept stressing the contradictions between Japan and China long before the conclusion of the 1978 Treaty. For example, writing in 1976, G. K. Mekler identified five such contradictions: (1) The normalization of Sino-Japanese relations is fundamentally contradictory because it is based on differing objectives and interests. The economic relationship is most asymmetrical: if in the beginning of the 1970s China's share in Japan's trade volume was only 2 percent and Japan's share in China's trade volume was about 20 percent, it was estimated that toward the end of the 1970s these figures would be 3 percent and 40 percent, respectively; (2) China's growing nuclear missile potential, along with the Maoist leadership's hegemonic aims and adventurous character of its foreign policy course, constitutes a direct threat to the peace and security of all of Asia, Japan in particular; (3) Peking's claim to the Senkaku island (it is significant that the disputed island is given in its Japanese name and not in the Chinese name of Tiao-yu-tai); (4) Taiwan is the contradiction that is the deepest and most difficult to resolve not only for Japan but also for the United States. These two countries stand for actual maintenance and expansion of their ties with Taiwan, which contradicts the interests of the PRC; (5) The strident anti-Soviet policy of the Maoist leadership is directed against Soviet-Japanese cooperation and against the friendship between the peoples of Japan and the USSR Striving to push Japan toward a conflict with the Soviet Union, the Maoists are hoping to weaken both Japan and the Soviet Union. This policy is against the national interests of the two countries, as well as against Asian security.[60]

The conclusion of the Sino-Japanese Treaty in August 1978 elicited an immediate protest from the Soviet government, as well as a host of critical commentaries.[61]

Petrov, writing at the end of 1978 on Japan's place in U.S. Asian policy, devotes his final discussion to "The Washington-Peking-Tokyo Triangle."[62]

He talks of the *"so-called* peace and amity treaty," castigates Peking's "anti-Soviet course," and warns that Japan "may well be drawn into China's aggressive, chauvinistic policy." Quoting from Japanese newspaper sources, he talks of the "unseemly role of American diplomacy," and concludes that the prospect of "a military union binding Japan, the U.S. and China . . . offers nothing of benefit to either the national interests of Japan or the objectives of strengthening peace and security in Asia."[63]

A year later, a Soviet commentator, entitling his piece "The Sino-Japanese Alliance Runs Counter to Peace Interests,"[64] promoted the Sino-Japanese relationship to an alliance status, and spoke of Peking's and Tokyo's "common reactionary chauvinistic platform of pan-Asiatism [*sic*]," of attempts to establish "Sino-Japanese *hegemony* over Asia,"[65] (a clever use of the term made famous by Peking). He further claimed that the Sino-Japanese rapprochement was "on a basis hostile to the Soviet Union and other countries of the socialist community."[66] In conclusion, the Soviet analyst deplored the dependence of the Japanese "ruling circles" on the Chinese leaders' "aggressive anti-Soviet intentions" and argued that the interests of the Japanese people "require not an arms race, not militarization and military confrontation with the USSR . . . but peaceful cooperation with its neighbors."[67] It is clear from the tone of this article that at this juncture the Soviets are blaming China more than Japan.

In 1980, in a survey of Japan during the first quarter century after the end of World War II,[68] a Soviet scholar still blames "Maoist leaders" for attempting to push Japan toward "an anti-Soviet and anti-Vietnam policy"[69] and notes the pressure of both Washington and Beijing on Japan to start economic and trade sanctions against the Soviet Union following the Soviet invasion of Afghanistan (or as it was officially called, "the internationalist assistance to the Afghan people by the Soviet Union"). Japanese leaders, however, are blamed for trying to play the "China card" and "pushing Chinese leaders . . . toward military aggression against socialist Vietnam."[70]

In 1981, on the third anniversary of the Sino-Japanese Treaty, a Soviet commentator characterized Sino-Japanese relations as a "dangerous rapprochement"[71] and blamed the process on Tokyo's considerable dependence on Washington,[72] but he noted that many contradictions between Japan and China remain. In addition to the often-cited problem of Taiwan and the Senkaku territorial claim, these contradictions deal with both Chinese and Japanese attempts to achieve *hegemony* in Asia, Japan's return to the old militaristic slogans of the "Co-Prosperity Sphere" in the Asian-Pacific region, economic frictions arising from the Chinese cancellation of joint industrial projects and the low quality of Chinese oil,

Sino-Japanese competition in Southeast Asian markets, and differences between the two countries' positions vis-a-vis the initiative of the ASEAN countries to solve the Cambodian problem.[73]

A more positive evaluation of Japan's economic ties with China was given in early 1985 by the economist and author of a work on Soviet-Japanese economic relations, M. I. Krupianko.[74] He noted that during the 1970s the emphasis in the Sino-Japanese economic relationship was on ordinary trade, whereas toward the beginning of the 1980s greater significance was given to financial credit cooperation, scientific and technical ties, and capital investments.[75] For the remainder of the 1980s he saw further Japanese efforts to assure greater dependence on the part of China in the area of foreign exchange and credit, wider penetration of Chinese industry by Japanese experts and technicians, and a certain measure of Japanese control over China's export base.[76] Finally, Krupianko emphasized the political aspects of the participation of Japanese capital in the development of Chinese economy as a "favor" to the United States in the utilization of the China factor in global anti-Soviet strategy.[77]

In summary, before the conclusion of the 1978 Sino-Japanese treaty, Soviet scholars stressed contradictions between the two countries, while after its conclusion the Soviets invoked the specter of a Sino-Japanese hegemony over Asia, hoping to stir up trouble for the two countries in Southeast Asia and Korea. Both China and the United States are blamed for pressuring Japan to sign the treaty, which is so patently against Japanese national interests since it is bound to have an adverse effect on its relations with its northern neighbor, the USSR. More recently, as Sino-Soviet relations (especially economic ties) have warmed up a little, while Soviet-Japanese relations seem to be in a freeze, the Soviets warn China that in economic relations it should not fall into the dependency trap being set up by Japan.

Soviet-Japanese Relations

Nineteen eighty-five marks the sixtieth anniversary of the establishment of Soviet-Japanese diplomatic relations. This was accomplished when Karakhan and Yoshizawa, the Soviet and Japanese ministers in Peking, signed a convention in January 1925. Since the Soviet government was forced to acknowledge the validity of the Russo-Japanese peace treaty concluded through the mediation of President Theodore Roosevelt in Portsmouth, New Hampshire, in September 1905, it is not clear why the Soviet Union chooses to commemorate the 1925 date when the correlation of forces was so much in favor of Japan rather than the 1956 Joint Soviet-Japanese Declaration, which ended the state of war and restored diplomatic relations after World War II. But in fact a symposium volume entitled "USSR-Japan: On the Occasion of the Fiftieth Anniversary of the Establishment of Soviet-Japanese Diplomatic Relations, 1925-1975" was published in Moscow in 1978 by the Institute of Oriental Studies of the USSR Academy of Sciences.[78] It was noted in the preface that the 1925 convention was an important milestone in the history of Soviet-Japanese ties,[79] and the work covers such topics as "The Struggle of the USSR for the Establishment and Development of Goodneighborly Relations with Japan," "The Struggle of the Soviet Union for a Peaceful and Democratic Development of Japan, 1945-1952," and "The Movement for Friendship Between the Peoples of the USSR and Japan." The twenty-fifth anniversary of the 1956 declaration was noted only in a journal article.[80]

From the vantage point of the sixtieth anniversary, Konstantin Chernenko, in a specially written preface to a Japanese edition of his collected speeches and articles, stressed that:

> in this nuclear age, when we all are living in an interconnected and fragile world, there is an imperative need to establish truly neighbourly, full-blooded relations between the USSR and Japan.[81]

Soviet writers usually do not like to mention that for four years, until after the restoration of diplomatic relations with Japan in November 1956, the Soviet Union vetoed Japan's application for admission to the United Nations. They generally applaud the evolution of diplomatic, economic, commercial, legal, and cultural relations with Japan until 1980, when Japan joined the United States in imposing economic and other sanctions against the Soviet Union in the wake of the Soviet invasion of Afghanistan. They did object to and protest the signing of the revised Japanese-American security treaty in 1960 and the Sino-Japanese Treaty of Peace and Friendship in 1978. The latter is depicted as a "so-called 'treaty of peace and friendship' . . . [which] has objectively nothing to do either with peace or friendship."[82] (See also the preceding section of this chapter.)

Soviet writings on Soviet-Japanese relations for the past five years reflect the deep disappointment that Japan chose to follow the United States' lead and apply economic sanctions against the USSR. Soviet scholars and journalists constantly point out that Japan slipped from second to fifth place among the USSR's capitalist trading partners[83] and that the slack was taken up by West European NATO countries. But writing for an American audience, Japan expert Igor Latyshev downplayed Japanese sanctions:

The policy of "sanctions" was often symbolic since restrictions were applied primarily to those spheres of Soviet-Japanese business relations in which the prospects were not very bright, while bilateral collaboration in more promising sectors (e.g., preparations for offshore drilling for oil and gas near Sakhalin Island) went on without any significant hindrances on the part of Japanese governmental departments.[84]

Besides economics, a favorite topic is the "unlawful claims to territories belonging to the Soviet Union"[85] and the anti-Soviet actions taken by the Japanese government in proclaiming Northern Territories Day to be observed every February 7, the anniversary of the conclusion of the 1855 treaty between Tsarist Russia and Tokugawa Japan, a treaty that significantly acknowledged the two southernmost Kurile islands, Kunashiri and Etorofu, as Japanese territory.

Yet in spite of the cool state of Soviet-Japanese relations, or perhaps because of it, Soviet leaders have used a variety of forums to appeal to the Japanese public: Chairman of the Council of Ministers Nikolai Tikhonov's response to a correspondent of the Japanese newspaper *Yomiuri*,[86] Foreign Minister Andrei Gromyko's address to the readers of the *Asahi* newspaper,[87] and Chernenko's (above-mentioned) special preface.[88]

During the second half of 1984 there was also a good deal of diplomatic activity: Gromyko met with Foreign Minister Abe at the United Nations in New York in September, Tikhonov had a talk with Prime Minister Nakasone during the funeral of Indira Gandhi in New Delhi in November, and a delegation from the Supreme Soviet headed by Politburo member D. Kunaev visited Japan in October-November. In addition, there were several meetings of Soviet and Japanese delegations and joint meetings of the Soviet-Japanese and Japanese-Soviet committees on economic cooperation.

A veteran Japanese observer of Soviet affairs characterized all this activity as "a thaw in chilly Soviet-Japanese relations."[89] Will all this activity bring concrete results to the state of Soviet-Japanese relations? This remains to be seen.

Concluding Remarks

Recent Soviet policy toward Japan is a disaster for the Soviet Union and a blessing for China and the United States. Soviet diplomatic intransigence combined with military pressure not only pushes Japan toward the United States but also simplifies the Japanese government's attempts to influence public opinion concerning the need for a military alliance with the United States and the maintenance of the Self-Defense Forces with a gradually increasing defense budget.

What are the reasons for the dismal failure of Soviet policy toward Japan? Is it the result of the Soviet leadership's tendency to simply apply more pressure if a policy does not work? Or is it the result of erroneous perceptions of Japan's economic potential, political stability, and growing popular support for security arrangements with the United States and the need for a defense establishment. It appears that Soviet leaders do not fully appreciate Japan's phoenixlike rise from the ashes of defeat in World War II, the dynamism of its present-day economy, and its bid for equality, if not supremacy, in high technology. Perhaps the Soviets are also overestimating current pacifist and neutralist sentiments (exemplified best by the Japanese Socialist Party), which were quite prevalent among opposition parties and a sizable segment of the Japanese public during the 1950s and 1960s. But with Chinese support of the Japanese-American alliance and of Japanese rearmament, public sentiment as well as the policies of several opposition parties have changed. Do the Soviets believe there are actually "ruling circles" in democratic Japan, when fully 90 percent of the population considers itself part of the middle class? Do they believe in the exploitation of the Japanese "working class," which made possible the economic growth and progress in Japan? Would a less doctrinaire approach to Japan help formulate more effective policies toward its neighbor?

I believe that faulty Soviet perceptions of Japan, its political system, its economic and technological potential, and its activities in the international arena, particularly its relations with the United States and China, lie at the root of Soviet policy toward Japan, which was described by a noted Japanese scholar as "inept," "counterproductive," "very unimaginative, if not stupid," "almost a total disaster," and "diplomatic failure."[90] In turn, Soviet failure in its policy toward Japan has a profound effect on the dynamics of its relations with the other two members of the strategic triad—China and the United States.

Notes

I wish to thank Michael Frost of the School of International Relations, University of Southern California, for timely research assistance.

1. In 1936 Japan and Germany concluded that Anti-Comintern Pact; in 1940 Japan, Germany, and Italy signed the Tripartite Pact; and in early July 1941, following Hitler's attack on the Soviet Union, Japan made plans to attack its northern neighbor as soon as it was sufficiently softened by the German armed forces. See Chihiro Hosoya, "The Soviet-Japanese Neutrality Pact" (translated, with an introduction, by Peter A. Berton), Part I of James William Morley, ed., *The Fateful Choice: Japan's Advance into Southeast Asia, 1939–1941* (New York: Columbia University Press, 1980), pp. 3–114.

2. Harold C. Hinton, *Three and a Half Powers: The New Balance in Asia* (Bloomington: Indiana University Press, 1975)

3. "The Three Centres of Present-Day Imperialism: U.S.A., E.E.C., Japan: A Survey, *New Times,* supplement, 1984.

4. Felix Goryunov, "Measured by Economic and Financial Muscle," in *ibid.,* p. 7.

5. *Ibid.,* p. 9.

6. *Ibid.,* p. 10.

7. *Ibid.,* p. 13.

8. *Ibid.,* p. 15.

9. *Ibid.,* p. 16.

10. *Ibid.*

11. V. B. Ramzes, "Sovremennaia Iaponiia/Contemporary Japan/," *Problemy Dal'nego Vostoka* /Far Eastern Problems/, No. 3 (1984), p. 178.

12. Emphasis added. Review of I. I. Kovalenko, ed., *Iaponiia nashikh dnei* /Present-day Japan/ (Moscow: Izdatel 'stvo "Nauka," 1983), 256 pp. in *ibid.*

13. D. V. Petrov, "Vneshniaia politika v sisteme sredstv obespecheniia gospodstva praviashchikh krugov Iaponii" /Foreign Policy Within the System of Methods to Assure the Domination of Japan's Ruling Circles/ in I. A. Latyshev and V. A. Popov, eds., *Praviashchie krugi Iaponii: Mekhanizm gospodstva—Sbornik statei* /Japan's Ruling Circles: The Mechanics of Government—A Collection of Articles/ (Moscow: Izdatel 'stvo "Nauka," 1984), p. 203.

14. *Ibid.* Emphasis added.

15. S. I. Verbitskii, "Formirovanie poslevoennogo vneshne-politicheskogo kursa Iaponii v otnoshenii SSSR" /The Formation of Japan's Postwar Foreign Policy Toward the U.S.S.R./ in S. I. Verbitskii and I. I. Kovalenko, eds., *SSSR-Iaponiia: K 50-letiiu ustanovleniia sovetsko-iaponskikh diplomaticheskikh otnoshenii (1925–1975)* /USSR-Japan: On the Occasion of the Establishment of Soviet-Japanese Diplomatic Relations, 1925–1975/ (Moscow: Izdatel 'stvo "Nauka," 1978), p. 97.

16. Petrov's chapter on foreign policy in Ia. A. Pevzner, D. V. Petrov, and V. B. Ramzes, *Iaponiia* /Japan/ (Moscow: "Mysl'," 1981).

17. Cited in Petrov, "Vneshniaia politika," p. 202.

18. *Ibid.*

19. *Ibid.,* p. 215.

20. Stanislav Modenov, "USSR-Japan: Who is Obstructing Goodneighbourly Relations?" *Asia and Africa Today*, no. 2 (1983), p. 19.
21. Prof. D. Petrov, "Militarisation of Japan Is a Threat to Peace in Asia," *Far Eastern Affairs*, no. 2 (1981), p. 49.
22. The Soviets seize upon the publication of Japanese books that take a pro-Soviet and anti-American line, such as Takeo Iwashita's *Soren Kyoiron no kyoko* /The Fiction of the Soviet Menace/ (Tokyo: Shakai Tsushin Sha, 1983), 196 pp. This book was reviewed by V. Zatsepin, who approvingly quoted at length from the book and referred to the author as "the well-known Japanese publicist." Sample quotation: "If there is a threat to peace, it comes from the USA." V. Zatsepin, "A Myth Debunked," *International Affairs*, no. 2 (February 1985), pp. 145–146.
23. See note 13, p. 207.
24. Iu. V. Georgiev, "Ezhegodnik 'Iaponiia'" /The Annual "Japan"/, *Narody Azii i Afriki* /The Peoples of Asia and Africa/, no. 3 (1979), p. 196.
25. See note 13, p. 207.
26. S. K. Ignatushenko, *Iaponiia i SShA: Partnery i Konkurenty* /Japan and the USA: Partners and Competitors/ (Moscow: Izdatel 'stvo "Nauka," 1970), p. 277.
27. D. Petrov, "The US-Japanese Alliance and the New Situation in Asia," *Far Eastern Affairs*, no. 4 (1976)—no. 1 (1977), p. 57.
28. Ignatushenko, *Iaponiia i SShA*, p. 8.
29. I. Ivkov (pseud.), "Japanese Militarism Rears Its Head," *Far Eastern Affairs*, no. 4 (1978), p. 50.
30. See note 26.
31. Professor D. Petrov, "Japan and the USA: Their 'Special' Relations," *International Affairs*, no. 5 (May 1984), p. 43.
32. S. I. Verbitskii, "Os' Tokio-Vashington: istoki odnogo soiuza" /The Tokyo-Washington Axis: The Sources of One Alliance/, *Problemy Dal'nego Vostoka*, no. 3 (1984), p. 136.
33. Konstantin O. Sarkisov, "Japan and the U.S. in Asia: Cooperation and Contradictions," *Asian Survey*, vol. XXIV, no. 11 (November 1984), p. 1174.
34. *Ibid.*
35. Sergei Zinchuk, "From Political to Military Alliance," *New Times*, no. 15 (April 1982), p. 27. Zinchuk used this formula again in "The Threat to the Pacific: Washington's Chain of Blocs," *New Times*, no. 25 (June 1984), p. 18.
36. Zinchuk, "From Political to Military Alliance," p. 27.
37. Cited in Ivkov, "Japanese Militarism Rears Its Head," pp. 43–55 at p. 43.
38. *Ibid.*, p. 48.
39. S. T. Mazhorov, *Voenno-ekonomicheskii potentsial sovremennoi Iaponii* /The Military-Economic Potential of Contemporary Japan/ (Moscow: "Nauka," 1979).
40. M. I. Ivanov, *Rost militarizma v Iaponii* /The Growth of Militarism in Japan/ (Moscow: Voenizadat, 1982), 159 pp. In 1978 Ivanov published an eyewitness

account of Japan during World War II, *Iaponiia v gody voiny* /Japan During the War Years/. Mention should also be made of a historical survey of Japanese militarism published in Moscow in 1972, *Iaponskii militarizm: voenno-istoricheskoe issledovanie* /Japanese Militarism: A Military-Historical Study/.

41. Yuri Tavrovsky, "Japan: Falsified Textbooks and Lying Films," *New Times*, no. 43 (October 1982), pp. 26–27.

42. Vyacheslav Bunin, "Japan: Samurai Silhouettes," *New Times*, no. 47 (November 1981), pp. 20–23.

43. Y. Tavrovsky, "Japan: Sinister Spawn—The Ultra-Rights /sic/ and Their Paymasters," *New Times*, no. 5 (January 1984), pp. 24–27.

44. V. Bunin, "Tokyo: A Course Toward Militarisation," *Far Eastern Affairs*, no. 2 (1983), pp. 69–70.

45. S. Modenov, "Tokyo: Following Washington's Lead," *International Affairs*, no. 5 (May 1981), pp. 64–71 at p. 64.

46. S. Chugrov, "Outlines of a New Militaristic Alliance in the Far East," *International Affairs*, no. 7 (July 1983), pp. 102–108.

47. V. Bunin, "Nakasone's Military Policy," *Far Eastern Affairs*, no. 2 (1984), pp. 64–74.

48. Prof. D. Petrov, "Japan in the Nuclear Strategy of the United States," *Far Eastern Affairs*, no. 3 (1984), pp. 52–62.

49. Valentin Petukhov, "The US-Japan-South Korea: NATO's Double in the Pacific?" *Asia and Africa Today*, no. 2 (1984), p. 11.

50. Editorial "Ugroza miru i bezopasnosti na Dal'nem Vostoke" /The Threat to Peace and Security in the Far East/, *Problemy Dal'nego Vostoka*, no. 4 (52) (1984), pp. 3–15 at pp. 5–8.

51. See also my paper "Soviet Perceptions of the Republic of Korea and Its Relations with the United States and Japan" prepared for the conference on "Changing U.S.-Soviet Relations and the Emerging New Order in Asia: Continuity or Change?", Center for American and Soviet Studies, Dankook University, Seoul, August 1985.

52. Y. Tavrovsky, "Japan: Another Millstone Round Their Necks—That's What the American F-16s Being Sited at Misawa Mean for the Japanese," *New Times*, no. 18 (April 1985), p. 13.

53. Leonid Mlechin, "Japan: In the Shadow of the Yasukuni Temple," *New Times*, no. 35 (August 1982), p. 23.

54. G. F. Kunadze, *Iapono-kitaiskie otnosheniia na sovremennom etape, 1972–1982* /Contemporary Sino-Japanese Relations, 1972–1982/ (Moscow: Izdatel 'stvo "Nauka," 1983), 184 pp.

55. *Ibid.*, p. 5.

56. *Ibid.*, pp. 165–166.

57. *Ibid.*, p. 167.

58. *Ibid.*

59. *Ibid.*, p. 169.

60. G. K. Mekler, "K voprosu o iapono-kitaiskikh otnosheniiakh" /On Sino-Japanese Relations/, *Narody Azii i Afriki,* no. 1 (1976), pp. 32–46 at pp. 45–46.

61. For a detailed analysis of Soviet reaction to the treaty, see Hiroshi Kimura, "The Conclusion of the Sino-Japanese Peace Treaty (1978): Soviet Coersive Strategy and Its Limits," *Studies in Comparative Communism,* Vol. XVIII, nos. 3 & 4 (Autumn/Winter 1985).

62. D. Petrov, "Japan's Place in US Asian Policy," *International Affairs,* no. 10 (October 1978), pp. 52–59.

63. *Ibid.,* pp. 58–59. Emphasis added.

64. Y. Bandura, "The Sino-Japanese Alliance Runs Counter to Peace Interests," *International Affairs,* no. 8 (August 1979), pp. 70–77.

65. *Ibid.,* p. 75. Emphasis added.

66. *Ibid.,* p. 77.

67. *Ibid.*

68. B. G. Sapozhnikov, "Iaponiia mezhdu 1945 i 1980 godami: itogi i uroki" /Japan Between 1945 and 1980: Results and Lessons/, *Narody Azii i Afriki,* no. 5 (1980), pp. 29–39.

69. *Ibid.,* p. 38.

70. *Ibid.,* p. 39.

71. V. Kulikov, "Pekin i Tokio: Opasnoe sblizhenie" /Peking and Tokyo: Dangerous Rapprochement/, *Aziia i Afrika Segodnia* /Asia and Africa Today/, no. 8 (290) (August 1981), pp. 16–19.

72. *Ibid.,* p. 16.

73. *Ibid.,* pp. 18–19. Emphasis added.

74 M. I. Krupianko, "Ekonomicheskie sviazi Iaponii s Kitaem" /Japan's Economic Ties with China/, *Problemy Dal'nego Vostoka,* no. 1 (53) (1985), pp. 52–60.

75. *Ibid.,* p. 52.

76. *Ibid.,* p. 60.

77. *Ibid.,* p. 59. Quotation marks in the original.

78. Verbitskii and Kovalenko, *SSSR-Iaponiia.*

79. *Ibid.,* p. 3.

80. N. Nikolayev, "Tokyo's Political Zigzags," *International Affairs,* no. 11 (November 1981), pp. 37–43.

81. S. Modenov, "USSR-Japan: Looking Ahead," *International Affairs,* no. 3 (March 1985), p. 80.

82. Ivkov, "Japanese Militarism Rears Its Head," p. 53.

83. N. N. Nikolaev and V. N. Arsen'ev, "K 60-letiiu ustanovleniia diplomaticheskikh otnoshenii SSSR s Iaponiei" /On the Occasion of the Sixtieth Anniversary of the Establishment of Diplomatic Relations Between the USSR and Japan/, *Problemy Dal'nego Vostoka,* no. 1 (53) (1985), p. 48.

84. Igor A. Latyshev, "Soviet - U.S. Differences in Their Approaches to Japan," *Asian Survey,* Vol. XXIV, no. 11 (November 1984), p. 1168.

85. Modenov, "USSR-Japan: Looking Ahead," p. 81.
86. *Pravda,* 2 January 1984.
87. *Pravda,* 2 January 1985.
88. *Pravda,* 5 September 1984.
89. Col. Etsuo Kohtani in *K.D.K. Information* (Tokyo), no. 11/84 (1 November 1984), p. 4.
90. Hiroshi Kimura, *Soviet Policy Toward Japan* (Providence, RI: Brown University, The Center for Foreign Policy Development, August 1983) (Working Paper no. 6), p. 33.

Indochina:

Still The Cockpit

BERNARD K. GORDON

Familiar as it is to say it again, there is no area of the world where the roles and security interests of the U.S., China, and the USSR so clearly overlap as in East Asia—and within that region there is no place where this is more evident than in Indochina and Southeast Asia. Indochina, which comprises much of the "continental" portion of Southeast Asia, remains today one of the two or three regions of the world with genuine potential to lead to major world conflict, and the reasons it continues in that cockpit category can be placed under two main headings.

The first derives from the fact that two of the three major external powers–China and the United States—have long-standing historical interests either directly in Indochina itself, or in immediately-adjacent states. The third—the USSR—is a relative newcomer to the region, but its East Asian goals have led it to adopt policies pertaining to Indochina that may be functionally equivalent to the level of the Chinese and American interests involved.

The second main reason for Indochina's continuing and dangerous prominence stems from a quality of uncertainty. The region is characterized by an absence of agreement on the limits of great-power influence, and in some cases on borders, that is probably akin only to the Middle East in world politics. Unlike the condition in Europe, or for that matter even on the Korean peninsula, where there are formal or at least implicit understandings on demarcations and on the roles of the great powers, no such tacit agreements are in place in Southeast Asia and Indochina.

The convergence of these two factors gives to Southeast Asia—and especially to Indochina—a quality of great-power ambition, mixed with uncertainty, that is the classic formula for explosive international politics. Equally classic is the region's status as a "subordinate" international system. Its most essential political and economic features are often more the result of the actions of external states than of these within. This means that to understand the tensions that characterize Indochina today, the region needs to be examined within the context of the behavior of the great powers involved there, and in this discussion we will begin with China.

China's Relationship to Indochina

Because of its obvious geographic proximity, and the long-standing nature of its historical connections with Indochina, it is useful to consider first China's concerns with the region. Its relationships with Vietnam, and in particular its thousand-year dominance in what is sometimes called "the lesser dragon" have been described often, and only the broad outlines need to be recounted. What is essential to recall is that China was enormously, though not completely influential in at least two of the historically differentiated portions of what is now "Vietnam." In Tonkin, i.e., the northernmost portion centering on Hanoi, and in Annam, the coastal portion centering on Hue, China's influence on culture and on government organization was massive. In Vietnam's south, or what was historically referred to as "Cochinchina," the evidences of China's long rule are somewhat less clear.[1]

Yet however strong was its role in parts of Vietnam (and among the upper classes in particular), China's dominance was never complete. The reason was that the Vietnamese, North and South, retained their language and consequently their identity. As one of the most eminent historians of the region has put it: "Every time a person spoke, Vietnamese identity was reaffirmed. Thousands of loan words and the writing system borrowed from China did not destroy the non-Sinitic foundation of Vietnamese."[2] The result is that despite the thousand-year period of Chinese rule (from roughly 111 B.C. to 939 A.D.), a solid sense of Vietnamese identity and nationalism survived, and prevails to this day. Indeed from a Vietnamese perspective—as we will see again later—it has never been much in doubt that the long-term and continuing challenge to Vietnam's independence emanates from Beijing.

From a Chinese perspective, on the other hand, it has been important to retain influence in this region. Among other considerations, we should not forget that it was from these southern lands that the French undertook their colonial expansion in ways that affected China. Accordingly, China recognized its potential vulnerability in the area, and particularly as a result of the arrival in East Asia of the Europeans, it has continued to concern itself with the region it first called An-Nam ("the Pacified South") and that eventually came to be called Vietnam.

It is important, however, to distinguish carefully between *control* and *influence*. During the period of the American war in Vietnam, it was sometimes argued that Hanoi was China's agent—and that a Vietnamese victory would mean an expansion of Chinese influence. That was never the case, and this was recognized and stressed at the time by the few close students of Sino-Vietnamese history—though not with wide success. China of course "endorsed" Hanoi's struggle against the US, as it had supported the Vietnamese in their war for independence from the French. But in both cases, China's support was less than complete, and it was never a matter of Chinese "control" over the Vietnamese. What was involved instead was a Chinese concern with Vietnam that can be characterized as negative.

To put this another way, China knows what it does *not* want in Indochina, and from that root stems much of its behavior toward Vietnam. Its support for Ho Chi-minh, in his war against the French, should not lead us to forget how short-lived was that support—nor how clearly it was cast off at the time of the Geneva conference in 1954.[3] Quite aside from the fact that Hanoi has since made of China's behavior at Geneva a centerpiece of modern Vietnamese mythology, the events are worth recounting here.

The issue involved at Geneva in 1954, following the defeat of the French at Dienbienphu, was how much of French Indochina should come under Hanoi's rule. The Vietnamese, convinced that their forces and *their* political leadership had brought about the defeat and humiliation of France, believed that in one form or other they should fall heir to France's former colonies. They meant, in other words, to resuscitate their old plan for an "Indochina Federation." It would of course be led by Vietnam, and it would include not only South Vietnam, but Laos and Cambodia as well.

The French, however, insisted that their defeat on the battlefield should lead to the loss of not much more than Tonkin, or Northern Vietnam. They were especially concerned not to lose influence over southern Vietnam, or "Cochinchina," and they asked that the international community accept the independence that France had so recently extended to its other Indochina colonies. Cambodia, for example, had been granted "independence" as recently as 1953.

In a story that is now well known, the U.S. endorsed that position, and Moscow—hoping to enlist French support against German rearmament —also supported Paris. Molotov in effect argued to the Vietnamese that they should accept the proverbial "half a loaf." Zhou Enlai, representing China, supported the Soviet position, and Hanoi—faced with the united opposition of China and the Soviet Union (to say nothing of the position of the Western states)—had no choice except to bend.

Thus after terrible losses and years of struggle against the French in Indochina, in which the Vietnamese had taken the lead, Ho Chi-minh's party had to settle for only some of the fruits of victory. The Vietnamese had expected to succeed to all of French Indochina, just as Sukarno and the Indonesian nationalists had fallen heir to all that Holland had ruled in the Dutch East Indies. When they were denied that at Geneva, the Vietnamese negotiators were perhaps understandably livid, and from those events stems Hanoi's conviction to this day that it was "betrayed" at Geneva—principally by its ostensible Chinese ally.

This was the principal theme of the famous "White Paper" that Hanoi published in 1979.[4] Vietnam argued there that far from being as close as "lips and teeth" (as Lin Biao had once put it), the truth is that China, both under Mao Zedong and afterward, has consistently and repeatedly "betrayed" Vietnam's national interests. Aside from the tendentiousness and exaggerations in Vietnam's argument, there is evidence that both in 1954, at the conclusion of the first Indochina conflict, and in 1975–76, at the end of the second, China's behavior was deeply disappointing to Hanoi.

The common element in both cases is what was referred to earlier as China's *negative* goals: Beijing consistently has been opposed to a unified Indochina, particularly under Vietnamese auspices. It has instead strongly endorsed the concept of separate Indochina states, and the legitimacy given to Cambodia's independence in 1954 (as Prince Sihanouk knew at the time), as well as that accorded to Laos, owed much to China's support at Geneva.

In the ensuing years—particularly in the 1960s as the Vietnamese war against the Americans widened, and Hanoi's forces made very free use of Cambodian territory[5]—Sihanouk repeatedly turned to China in his efforts to seek Vietnamese restraint. It is not by accident that the Prince was in Moscow, literally on his way to China, when he heard the news of the *coup* that overthrew him in 1970. And it was likewise not by accident that China warmly welcomed him, and made available for his use a comfortable residence on the outskirts of Beijing. China continues to this day to provide generously for Prince Sihanouk's material needs, both in China and when he travels abroad.

The same pattern of Chinese support for a plural Indochina lies at the heart of the present conflict in Indochina. It has been evident throughout the 1970s and continues today. The clarity of China's goals, and their effectiveness, has been most evident in connection with Cambodia, whereas its efforts on behalf of Laos have been much less successful. The reason lies in large part in the fact that with regard to Laos, the Vietnamese struck quickly, though peaceably, in 1977. Hanoi's method was a formal "Friendship Treaty" with Laos, but its effect was virtual annexation.

In Cambodia, on the other hand, a much more nationally identifiable and armed Khmer group was in place to bring about the defeat of the Long Nol government in 1975. Indeed the fall of Phnom Penh slightly preceded the collapse of Saigon. This allowed the Cambodians to argue that their military victory was not dependent on Hanoi's nearly-simultaneous conquest of the South, and the concomitant final withdrawal of the Americans from Indochina. Nevertheless, the new government included many so-called "Khmer Rouge" who had for years been trained and supported in Vietnam. Through this group of "Hanoi Khmers" Vietnam evidently hoped both to assure generally friendly and close ties with Phnom Penh, and to exercise some degree of influence there.

The new Khmer government, however, the now infamous Pol Pot regime, had its own views about the nature of the new "Kampuchea" it would create, and from the outset it had considerable Chinese support. The result was an incendiary mixture, and while many specific events of that period, i.e., late 1975–76, are shrouded in mystery and vengeance, some main points are clear. Among them are that the Pol Pot group quickly began to purge the Vietnam-trained cadres; commenced border hostilities with Vietnam; and worst of all, undertook to establish particularly close links with China.

Tensions between the Hanoi leadership and the so-called "Khmer Rouge" (the label is a Sihanouk original, dating to the early 1960s), were evident well before the decisive military outcomes of 1975. Pol Pot (known then by his apparently genuine name of Saloth Sar) had purged Hanoi elements in the early '70s, and as William Duiker writes: "Vietnamese leaders allegedly gave serious consideration to a proposal to overthrow Pol Pot and replace him with a leader more sympathetic to Hanoi."[6] From Vietnam's perspective, that would have been a prudent step, because once

Pol Pot was in power in 1975, he resumed the purges. As he said later on, referring to "internal enemies," (their) secret agent network lying low in our country was very massive and complicated . . . (they) are still planted among us to carry out subversive activities against our revolution."[7]

In the same period, Cambodian forces sought to rectify some long-standing border disputes with Vietnam. Initially, in the Spring of 1975, the focus was on contested islands in the Gulf of Siam. Later, the clashes concerned interior borders—well-known from Vietnam War reporting as the regions of the "Parrot's Beak," and the "Fish Hook." All of these events were reminiscent of border tensions that had erupted in the 1950s and early '60s between Cambodia and the South Vietnamese government in Saigon. They reflected, of course, the deep-seated animosities between the Khmer and the Vietnamese, and grew especially from the recognition among Cambodians that their territory has historically been subject to Vietnamese pressure and expansion.

From a Vietnamese perspective, however, these developments were the actions of an ungrateful upstart. Among the most serious of the Cambodian provocations were the purges—for in these exterminations many of the Vietnamese leaders saw the decimation of revolutionary comrades with whom they had spent much time, and in whose training Vietnam had made a major investment.[8] No doubt Cambodia's behavior also rekindled Hanoi's long-standing interest in an "Indochina Federation" led of course by Vietnam.

But perhaps the most serious of Cambodia's actions in 1976–77 was its turning, just as Sihanouk had done years before, toward China. To Vietnam, linked now more closely than ever with the Soviet Union, this was ultimately the most unacceptable provocation. Hanoi had become quite dependent on the Soviet Union as a result of its military and material needs in the late stages of the war, and its isolation in international affairs after the war reinforced that Moscow connection. By 1977-78, Vietnam was clearly in the Soviet camp, and in this context it was the last straw for Vietnam's upstart Cambodian neighbor to seek and receive Chinese support. As Duiker writes, "Hanoi lost patience and began to prepare for the overthrow of the Pol Pot regime."[9]

This of course was accomplished by Vietnam's armed forces in a quick strike that began in December, 1978. The Vietnamese routed the Cambodians, and installed in Phnom Penh a Khmer government led by Heng Samrin much more to Hanoi's liking. That remains the situation to this day, and Hanoi insists that it will neither leave Cambodia, nor accept the installation of any new Cambodian government, until it receives ironclad assurances from China on two points: (1) non-interference in Cambodia, and (2) assurances that China will no longer support the remaining Pol Pot forces.

None of these audacious Vietnamese steps were undertaken, however, before Hanoi profoundly cemented its relations with the Soviet Union in 1978. Important Soviet guarantees were extended to Vietnam, and other significant connections were put in place between Moscow and Hanoi that year. Indeed 1978 was an uncommonly important year for Soviet policy generally in East Asia, and it is appropriate that at this point we turn our attention to the USSR.

The Soviet Union

Soviet perspectives on Asia, as other chapters in this volume make clear, are overwhelmingly concerned with China. Close Chinese ties with either Japan or the U.S. represent a special spectre, and this anxiety is reinforced in the case of Japan because of Tokyo's close security relationship with the U.S. Thus it is not surprising that in the mid-70s, a period when China was seeking improved relations with Japan, Moscow reacted negatively, and took steps that had important implications for Indochina.

The background for this development lies in China's desire in the late 1970s to enlist economic help from the Japanese, and to finally complete the long-delayed Peace Treaty with Japan. In December, 1977, a major first step was taken: Tokyo and Beijing announced a five-year $20 billion "long-term trade agreement." This was the first time in which China was prepared to accept the equivalent of foreign aid. During the same period, pressures began to build in Tokyo to conclude the long-sought "peace treaty." This effort had foundered in part because of China's insistence that it include the "anti-hegemony" clause that Moscow regards as an anti-Soviet code word.

The Soviet reaction to these developments was clearly negative, and Moscow particularly cautioned the Japanese on the wording of any new treaty with China. Nevertheless, and for reasons deriving largely from Japan's domestic politics, Tokyo decided to move ahead. In August, 1978, even in the face of this evident Soviet opposition, China and Japan signed the treaty—with the Japanese explaining that the "anti-hegemony" clause was not incorporated in the "main" text. It was difficult to believe that the Soviet Union would *not* see the Treaty as a new Chinese provocation, but the then Japanese Foreign Minister Sonoda insisted that "I am now convinced that there will be no Soviet retaliation."

He was wrong. Only weeks before this, Moscow had made clear it would not ignore a pattern of tightening Sino-Japanese ties which, by implication, linked Beijing closer to the U.S. as well. In July, in a very major step, the USSR announced that Vietnam would join the Soviet-run Council for Mutual Economic Assistance (COMECON). Aside from the questionably independent Mongolia, this made Vietnam the first Asian member of the COMECON, and indeed the first new member since Cuba had joined in 1962. This was of course a significant development, and one that made quite clear where, in the world communist firmament, the Socialist Republic of Vietnam is located.

Any remaining doubts were entirely removed on 3 November 1978. At an impressive meeting in Moscow that day, Party Secretary Brezhnev hugged Le Duan, his counterpart from Vietnam. Also present, as I had occasion to note several years ago, were such notables as Kosygin, party theoretician Suslov, military leader Ustinov, and for the Vietnamese, Pham Van Dong and chief of staff Van Tien Dung. The occasion was "the signing of the Soviet-Vietnam Treaty of Friendship and Cooperation."[10]

Without question, this treaty represents a major Soviet accomplishment, in part because for more than twenty years the USSR had sought a direct presence in Southeast Asia. It had made early efforts in Indonesia in the 1950s, and again later in Cambodia in the early 60s. All had failed for one reason or another. Thus it was with great satisfaction that not long before the signing of this treaty, Brezhnev noted the developing pattern of close relations between Moscow and Hanoi. They meant, he said, that the USSR had achieved "an important outpost for peace and socialism in Southeast Asia."[11]

There have been considerable benefits to the USSR as a result of the treaty. The effects on Vietnam and Indochina—though hardly beneficial in many cases—have been no less clear. For Hanoi, as already suggested, an immediate major consequence was its decision to invade Cambodia and oust Pol Pot. While we cannot know with certainty whether Vietnam would have moved without the treaty (and its implied Soviet guarantees), it is clear that only weeks later, Vietnamese forces were in Phnom Penh and had removed from power a leadership strongly supported by the Chinese.

There were prices to be paid. China, in order to "teach Vietnam a lesson" undertook a quick and brutal invasion of Vietnam's northern provinces in early 1979. The USSR did not intervene militarily, but this may have been because no help was needed. There is some reason to think, in other words, that the Chinese encountered more than they bargained for when they entered Vietnam.[12] Nevertheless, Beijing has continued to threaten that it will "teach Vietnam another lesson," and perhaps the fact that Moscow did not intervene at the time of the first lesson will embolden Beijing. Yet Vietnam retains its authority over Cambodia (and over Laos as well), and this means that Hanoi has achieved the long-sought "Indochina Federation."

There have been other prices for the Vietnamese. The Cambodia takeover rekindled fears of Vietnamese aggression and expansionism (especially in Thailand), and this has reinforced Hanoi's already nearly-total dependence on the Soviet Union. The limited aid that Vietnam was receiving after its victory in 1975 for example from France, Japan, Sweden and a few others, ended almost completely after its Cambodian conquest and Hanoi has experienced nearly-total isolation in world affairs. Indeed, whatever hopes realistically might have been entertained for an early economic recovery came to an end at the same time.

The USSR stepped into that breach. It has undertaken scores of construction and technical assistance projects (and assigned large numbers of Soviet and East European specialists) to help the Vietnamese in their reconstruction and development tasks. The cost for all this has been considerable: most estimates suggest that along with several of the East European members of COMECON, Moscow has supplied aid and assistance to Vietnam in amounts widely thought to be in the range of $3 million daily. For the period 1979–82, for example, Hanoi was to receive about $3 *billion* in Soviet and East European assistance,[13] and the most recent reporting indicates that even these amounts may have been exceeded.[14]

In order to understand what the USSR has received in return for all this largesse, one need only refer again to Brezhnev's already-noted remark about Vietnam . . . "an important outpost for peace and socialism in Southeast Asia." From a Soviet perspective, its generous support for Hanoi has brought both general political benefits, and direct national security advantages.

The political accomplishment was in connection with China. Beijing hoped to prevent Vietnam from incorporating all of Indochina, and particularly Cambodia, within its sphere.[15] It has failed in that goal, and the USSR was quick to note that Pol Pot's ouster also meant a setback for the Chinese. Within hours of the fall of Phnom Penh, on 7 January 1979, *Tass* exultantly described the ousted Pol Pot government as "a tool of the expansionist policy of the ruling circle of Peking."[16]

The national security and military aspect of the Soviet connection with Vietnam is that the USSR now has direct access to, and presence within, the South China Sea. As already suggested, this is a goal to which Moscow has fallen heir to the famous and excellent anchorage at Camh Ranh Bay—which Russian naval officers first visited en route to their ill-fated naval engagement with Japan in the war of 1904–05. In the present period, and especially in the years since Admiral Gorschkov launched the USSR on its program to become a genuine world-class naval power, Moscow's need for a warm-water port in Asian waters has been underlined.

It needs to be recalled that except for Petropavlovsk, the Soviet Union's naval facilities in the Pacific, including its main base at Vladivostok, border the ocean on the Sea of Japan, and the Sea of Okhotsk. In all cases they involve severe limitations on egress to the open sea—either because of winter ice, or because navel units must pass through straits adjacent to Japanese territory. In those cases, access to the safer operational environment of the Pacific Ocean is subject to monitoring and interdiction by the U.S. navy (and increasingly by Japanese units) *before* those ocean expanses are reached.

It is in this context that Cam Ranh Bay is so attractive to Russian naval considerations: it is an outstanding safe anchorage for vessels of every size, on an all-year basis, and during the American effort in Vietnam, Cam Ranh was the site of an extensive naval facility built by the U.S. With the departure of the U.S. from South Vietnam in 1975, the Soviet Union was quickly able to make use of the site, and within months of the collapse of Saigon, i.e., since 1976, the USSR began a regular pattern of calling-in at Cam Ranh. Despite Hanoi's frequent protestations to this day that no "Soviet base" has been acquired on Vietnamese territory, the scale and regularity of Moscow's operations at Cam Ranh Bay clearly have intensified.

Up to 1980, for example, it seemed still the case that only a handful of Soviet naval vessels was using the Vietnamese facility on a regular basis. By 1982, however, the U.S. navy was reporting that the number had increased to perhaps 10–15, and that this included one cruise-missile armed submarine; one major and two minor ships; and a variety of support and intelligence-gathering craft. By the end of 1983, according to the Commander of all U.S. forces in the Pacific (CINCPAC), there were "up to 22 Soviet warships . . . at Vietnam's American-built Cam Ranh Bay on any given day."[17] And as a very recent report indicates, "At the last count, twenty to twenty-six Soviet surface ships and four to six submarines were operating out of Cam Ranh Bay."[18]

These developments are clearly part of what is generally referred to as the Soviet naval and military "build-up" in the Pacific. At Cam Ranh itself, an 8500 ton floating dry-dock was installed in 1982, and in late 1983 the USSR took the unprecedented step of deploying Tu-16 (Badger) aircraft to the airfield at Cam Ranh. A well-informed source reported that "they are the only Russian strike aircraft deployed anywhere in the world beyond Soviet borders."[19] These units provide the USSR for the first time with interdiction capacity in the immediate vicinity of U.S. bases in the Philippines. Beyond that, by keeping ships on station at Cam Ranh, the USSR is able to deploy units to the Indian Ocean in ten days less time than would be required from the main Soviet Pacific base at Vladivostok.

In the North Pacific itself, the Japanese have reported both intensified Soviet naval activity in that region, as well as an increasingly-regular pattern of voyages between Soviet facilities in the North and the Vietnamese facilities on the coast of the South China Sea. This provides the USSR with previously unavailable opportunities for familiarization generally in the Pacific, and certainly calls into question the traditional notion of the South China Sea area as an "American lake." It must not be forgotten, after all, that the largest U.S. naval installation outside of the continental United States is at Subic Bay in the Philippines, and that this overridingly-important American installation is only 700 miles due East of Cam Ranh Bay.

It is equally clear that Vietnam, by enabling the USSR to make use of its territory in these respects, has heightened the distaste in which it is held by several of its neighbors. The Chinese repeatedly refer to the Vietnamese as Moscow's "Cuba in the Pacific," and the ASEAN nations have watched with considerable worry these signs of new great-power involvement in Southeast Asia. In response, Hanoi stresses that it has not sacrificed its sovereignty to the Soviets, and that Moscow's use of Cam Ranh (and the nearby air facilities at Da Nangh) is temporary. After all, the Vietnamese argue, they did not joust the French, defeat the Americans, and then take on the Chinese in order to lose their independence to the USSR.

The argument is not entirely false. Even American officials concede that Moscow evidently has not built permanent installations on the coast of Vietnam. As no less than a U.S. Assistant Secretary of Defense has pointed out, most of the Soviet assets at Cam Ranh are still moveable: "(They) have built their own installations . . . and have not taken over any large compounds that we built there. They have their own little sections. They still have a sandbag-type appearance."[20]

Nevertheless, the new Soviet presence in the region, and the extent to which Vietnam has facilitated that role, continues to cause considerable anxiety. Vietnam retains very large armed forces in Cambodia, and in early 1985 Hanoi demonstrated its willingness again to use those forces. In a series of punishing attacks that militarily decimated its opponents, Vietnamese forces destroyed the remaining base-camps of the Pol Pot forces still remaining in Cambodia, and routed the much smaller armed resistance groups associated with the non-communist opposition as well.

This most recent dry-season offensive, the most complete to date, has significantly changed at least the military dimension of the Indochina conflict. It has left Cambodia, at least for the present, largely free of an effective military opposition to the Vietnam-installed Heng Samrin regime, and it has further heightened the view among many Thai that their nation is the "front-line" state now confronting Vietnamese aggression.

Among other considerations, it has also resulted in an even greater presence within Thai territory—very close to the border with Cambodia —of large numbers of Khmer who are unable to return to Cambodia, and at the same time are largely unwelcome and much suspected by the Thai. Another result has been to cause Thailand to request the purchase of F-16 aircraft from the U.S. (a considerable upgrading from the F-5 aircraft on which most ASEAN forces now depend), and to ask that other suppliers of U.S. military equipment be hastened. Finally, it has led the ASEAN nations (in mid-February 1985) to appeal to the world community for greater assistance—especially military help—to the anti-Vietnamese Cambodian forces, and by March and April it was evident that at least some in the United States were prepared to respond.

Specifically, in a move led by Congressman Steven Solarz of New York, the House Foreign Affairs Committee voted to spend $5 million in assistance, including military help, for the Son Sann and Sihanouk forces in the anti-Vietnam coalition. The Reagan administration had to that point been opposed to any direct U.S. military assistance for any of the Khmer groups, but in April, 1985, Secretary of State Shultz met with Son Sann. While no decision to provide direct help was announced, it was nevertheless clear that requests of this kind, along with the joint appeals of ASEAN and the unilateral appeals of the Thai, were again causing American policy-makers to re-examine the nature of the American role in Indochina in the 1980s, and it is to that issue that we turn now.

The United States in Indochina

American policy in Indochina is dominated by one overriding fact: in modern times, this is the only region in world politics where U.S. military forces have not prevailed, and where the political will of the United States was clearly defeated. Americans recall with anguish the humiliating sight of the flag being lifted from the Embassy building in Saigon, and even today the long U.S. effort in Indochina brings to mind painful memories. As a result, some of the issues already discussed here, including the implications of the Soviet presence in Vietnam, and the character of China's interests in Indochina, are overshadowed in the U.S. by the nature of that recent and war-dominated experience. The consequence is that despite several troubling developments in the region in the period since that war, its legacy has constrained the U.S. from a more prudent policy today.

Nowhere is this more clear than in connection with the controversy over Vietnam's occupation of Cambodia ("Kampuchea"). Despite the abhorrence with which Americans (and the U.S. government) regard the Khmer Rouge, the U.S. has given its support in the UN to a Cambodian government-in-exile that includes Pol Pot. Similarly, and despite its knowledge that China's goals in Indochina and Southeast Asia are probably inconsistent with long-term American hopes, Washington has been silent while China has quietly used Thai territory to send military supplies to Pol Pot's forces. It has in that respect closed its eyes to an expansion of China's role in the region. Finally, although the U.S. has staked much of its hopes for Southeast Asia's continued stability on the cohesion of ASEAN, it has seen the Kampuchea issue bring some division there as well.

These circumstances have developed in good part because it has been difficult for the United States to come to grips with the meaning, in particular the political meaning, of Hanoi's victory in 1975. In contrast, and as indicated by the important speech of Defense Secretary Weinberger on 28 November 1984, the *military* lessons of the conflict have begun to be integrated. For example, in an obvious reference to the Vietnam experience, Mr. Weinberger argued that without popular and Congressional support, armed efforts by the United States are not likely to succeed, and in any case no U.S. military efforts should be undertaken unless to protect clearly vital American national security interests. And in what seemed to be a recognition that no initially-vital U.S. interest was involved in Vietnam, Mr. Weinberger warned against the sort of "incremental" decisions that led finally to America's massive effort there.[21]

The broader and political lessons of the Vietnam conflict, however, have been much more difficult for Americans to digest. It has been particularly troubling to accept the conclusion that Hanoi's aims for Vietnam, and even for Indochina, did not threaten the security interests of the U.S. Instead, and precisely because the U.S. had lost more than 55,000 men in Vietnam, and made such a massive effort in every other way, there was a great need in the U.S., both intellectual and political, to affirm that as a result of Hanoi's victory, frightful consequences must unfold.

For example, and while no effort will be made here to minimize the repression and "re-education" camps to which Hanoi subjected many Southerners after Saigon fell, the "blood bath" that many Americans had been led to expect did not materialize. Similarly, as the case of the *Mayaquez* will call to mind, the U.S. was at pains to demonstrate that it had not lost its willingness to use armed force. Otherwise, it was asserted, adversaries might conclude that U.S. interests could be attacked with impunity. Thus when the *Mayaquez* was seized—only weeks after the end of the war—it was argued that the merchant ship and its crew were prisoners of the same forces that had brought about the defeat in Vietnam. Washington launched a "rescue" operation and in the effort lost a larger number in Marine casualties than there were members of the ship's crew. Yet as seemed likely at the time (and as Phnom Penh said later),[22] the vessel appeared in the first instance not to have been taken prisoner by an act of the Cambodian or the Vietnamese governments, nor did its crew seem to have been in danger.

The *Mayaquez* incident was of course portrayed as a U.S. victory, hard on the heels of the Vietnam defeat. After that, both the American government and its people sought as thoroughly and as quickly as possible to put Indochina out of their minds. From 1976–78, to the extent that the U.S. did not ignore Indochina and that was its main posture in that period, it still sought to punish and isolate the victors. Washington was concerned, for example, to assure that no aid from Western nations, or from such international agencies as the World Bank, would reach either Vietnam or Cambodia.

Despite occasional reports from Cambodia suggesting the horrors brought about by Pol Pot, it was not until quite late in the Carter Administration, in 1979, that the U.S. began to show concern. This came in the wake of the Vietnamese invasion, thereby allowing the U.S. to argue that Cambodia's travail was the result of internecine warfare among Communists. Likewise, the U.S. seized upon Vietnam's ejection of many of its Chinese population, the so-called "boat people." This was seen as yet another indication that the communist regimes against whom the U.S. had fought were indeed barbaric and inhumane.

In all of this, the American posture can best be summarized as one of the *shadenfreude,* or the pleasure that one takes in another's misery. Thus, despite the fact that in 1976–77 Washington had largely ignored the mass killings then taking place in Kampuchea, it was able to summon up great humanitarian concern for the Khmer people in 1979. The difference was that Vietnam had invaded Cambodia, and the U.S. was now anxious to point to this violation of another state's boundaries, and to Vietnam's "aggression," as its cause for concern. In this posture, it was readily joined by Thailand, and reflecting the Thai concern, by some of the others in ASEAN as well.

The question must be asked, however, what have been the results of this American posture toward Indochina, and what issues does the U.S. face today in the region. Any attempt to answer must first recognize three features that now characterize the region, and that bear on American concerns: (1) the heightened Soviet presence, especially its military role at Cam Ranh Bay; (2) the status of Vietnam's continuing occupation of Cambodia; and (3) the level of tension stemming from that issue, between the Soviet-backed Vietnam and the U.S. and China-backed ASEAN.

Any long-term analysis of Soviet behavior in Asia, beginning indeed with Yalta in 1945, makes clear that what Moscow has now accomplished in Vietnam represents the successful culmination of enduring goals. It will be recalled, for example, that what Stalin sought at Yalta, and obtained from Chiang Kai-shek's government in the summer of 1945, was an arrangement by which the USSR could use Chinese maritime facilities at Dairen and Port Arthur. When it was evident that Chiang would fall, the USSR simply transferred that request to Mao Zedong. Stalin achieved approval in the famous and difficult negotiations in Moscow during the winter of 1950. As Mao later pointed out, it was only with considerable difficulty that the Russians were finally induced, years later, to leave those "extra-territorial" facilities.

As already pointed out, the USSR then turned its continuing desire for Pacific warm-water ports to Indonesia, and in the early 1960s to Cambodia under Prince Sihanouk. The longevity and consistency of that record should underline the significance the USSR attaches to the matter. From the perspective of the United States, it should clarify the extent to which the new Soviet naval presence in the Pacific, strongly aided by its Vietnam presence, has fundamentally altered the strategic environment.

For one thing, the U.S. is more than ever before concerned with trans-Pacific trade and access: since at least 1981 and for the first time in history, more of America's trade has been across the Pacific than the Atlantic. For another, the keystone of its naval access in East Asia (at the Subic Bay facilities in the Philippines) is under greater political uncertainties than ever before. Whatever the future of the Marcos regime in Manila, the United States must anticipate increasingly difficult negotiations to retain its base-rights there. Against that background, the Soviet Union's achievement in Vietnam, of both air and naval access directly in Southeast Asia, should be understood as a strategic accomplishment of the first order.

It will *not* be argued here that the West or the United States, "forced" Hanoi into its relationship with Moscow. That decision was taken by Vietnamese for their own reasons, and derives in good part both from historically long-standing connections between the communist leaderships in Moscow and Hanoi, and from the even longer-standing antipathy between Vietnam and China. It will, however be argued that in the years since the end of the American war in Vietnam, the U.S. has done less than it might have to reduce the opportunities for an extension of Soviet influence in this region. It has aligned itself with China in Beijing's campaign to "bleed Vietnam" (sometimes even to the discomfiture of the ASEAN group), and championed the cause of Khmer independence in ways that lay the U.S. open to charges of hypocrisy.

Yet even were Washington's sympathy for Khmer well-being and Cambodia's juridicial independence unimpeachably genuine, those goals would have to be weighed, in the scale of American national interests, against the significance of an enhanced Soviet naval capacity in the South China Sea. In that perspective, an American policy that has not been more effective in reducing the opportunities for this new Russian presence cannot be called a success.

The second question that must be asked concerns the political role the Vietnamese have taken in Cambodia, and in particular the prospects for a removal of their large armed forces. The most recent estimates suggest that between 160,000–180,000 Vietnam troops remain in Cambodian territory. Hanoi justifies this by pointing readily to the 40,000–50,000 Khmer guerrillas (largely Pol Pot remnants) who remain active in the Northern and Western border areas.[23] They are supplied by China, and to some extent by one or more ASEAN members.

In addition to Vietnam's large military presence in Cambodia, there is also a very large Vietnamese administrative infrastructure (and an increasing technical-assistance contingent from the USSR and East Europe). In the earliest stages after the ouster of Pol Pot, the Vietnamese could argue plausibly that their takeover of Cambodia's government functions was necessary simply because the Pol Pot terror had left the country almost devoid of trained people. Even today, that remains a not entirely unreasonable assertion, and the question for the long term is whether Hanoi plans in any sense to "leave" Kampuchea.

That issue is largely dependent on external developments; Hanoi has made it clear there can be no returning to a Cambodia aligned with China, or that undertakes the sort of provocations that helped bring on its invasion in the first place. China, of course, argues that its support for Pol Pot is justified by Hanoi's 1978 invasion; so long as Vietnamese forces remain there, Beijing will continue to help the resistance.

In these two diammetrically opposing positions lies the crux of the dilemma about Cambodia. Nobody doubts the patience of the Chinese: Beijing's threat to "bleed Vietnam" has been followed by the phrase, "for years, if necessary." By the same token, Hanoi's leadership long ago impressed on the world a principal characteristic: an enduring will, and in order to achieve its national interests, the ability to exact great sufferings and trials from its own people.

Some ASEAN members, recognizing the depth of commitment on each side, and fearing that the conflict will erupt again and embroil other states, have sought to find room for accommodation. The main element lies in what is sometimes termed a "negative solution" for Cambodia, by which is meant a government in Phnom Penh that will not again pose a threat to Vietnam, nor to Thailand. Implicit in this suggestion is a recognition that Hanoi had some basis for its invasion in 1978–79, and it is worth noting that the United States now incorporates this perspective in its own statements. For example, in late 1984 the Assistant Secretary of State for Asian and Pacific affairs affirmed a U.S. willingness to endorse a "political settlement that promises Vietnam and all the nations of the region a Cambodian government that is not dominated by the Khmer Rouge (and) is free of outside interference."[24]

As that statement indicates, the U.S. is clearly discomfited by the suggestion that it is in any way associated with the Pol Pot group despite the fact that the government-in-exile "coalition" recognized by the West includes the Khmer Rouge. Thus Washington was careful to point out, in the same State Department policy statement, that "The United States gives diplomatic and political support to the noncommunist elements in the (Cambodian) coalition, under Prince Sihanouk and Son Sann, which represent the genuine alternative to the Khmer Rouge under Pol Pot and those under Vietnam." A similar strong distaste for the Khmer Rouge was evident in the Congress, when Committee action approved the $5 million in military assistance to the Cambodian resistance that we have mentioned. In that case, it was stipulated that none of this aid was to fall into the hands of the Pol Pot forces, and partly for this reason this U.S. aid, if it does materialize, will be channeled through Thai hands first.

Nevertheless, the U.S. has been constrained from taking any initiatives toward a settlement of the Kampuchea issue because it has chosen a policy mainly to "support ASEAN." Since ASEAN itself, however, has been loathe to break ranks with Thailand, the policy of the group has been limited to what Thailand has been willing to endorse. Bangkok, reflecting its long-standing distrust and fear of Vietnam, as well as its hope to restore Cambodia as a "buffer-state" has given little evidence of flexibility. It has instead stressed Vietnam's historic "expansionism"; insisted that Hanoi remove its troops from at least Western Cambodia (while continuing to support the anti-Vietnam Khmers operating there); and obtained added levels of military aid from the U.S.

Thus the United States, despite both the potential for escalation inherent in this conflict, as well as the enhanced role Moscow now plays in politically-isolated Vietnam, has in effect limited its own national security choices to parameters set by Thailand. In this case as in others, it is seldom a prudent policy for a great-power to mortgage its own national interests to the narrower perspectives of a weaker ally.

Conclusion: An Acted-upon Region

At the beginning of this essay, we pointed to Indochina's status as a "subordinate international system." By that we meant that its states have had less influence on their political and economic fortunes than has the behavior of the exogenous great powers who are so involved in the region. The people of Indochina have certainly been deeply affected by the great-power conflicts which still characterize the region, but it is very evident that in many respects they have hardly benefited.

For example, the destruction that Cambodia has experienced is well-known, and need not be recapitulated here in detail. It owes much to the initial failure of Prince Sihanouk, in the 1960s, to take more effective action to protect his nation's sovereignty and particularly its borders against the incursions of Hanoi's forces. Thus in a harsh but not entirely misplaced judgement, the Foreign Minister of the present Vietnam supported Cambodian government recently remarked that "Of all the Khmer kings in the past 20 centuries, Sihanouk was the weakest."[25] Later, when General Lon Nol took power after Sihanouk was deposed, he sought (as he had wanted to do for years) to eject the Vietnamese, but by then it was much too late. His already weak forces were quickly defeated by the Vietnamese, and this paved the way for the arrival of Pol Pot.

That brought untold horrors to Cambodia, which ended only with the arrival of the Vietnamese. The genocide brought on by the Khmer Rouge resulted in the murder of perhaps a million Khmers, and certainly not fewer than 300,000. The country was decimated, and its administrative structure destroyed. While Khmers today certainly do not welcome the Vietnamese occupation, the present Vietnam-ensconced regime is preferable to any return of Pol Pot. Indeed it is said that the most potent factor operating on behalf of Cambodia's quiet acceptance of the Vietnamese is precisely that fear of Pol Pot's resuscitation. With Hanoi's representatives in place, the country has begun again to function at moderate levels, though it will be many years before genuine reconstruction will have been completed.

In Vietnam itself, the nation still shows the signs of 35 years of almost continual warfare. Clearly, the heavy destruction brought about by the Americans had major consequences, but ten years after Saigon's collapse there is still little evidence of recovery in Vietnam. As William Duiker wrote recently, "Abroad Vietnam is surrounded by enemies; within, it suffers from a deep sense of malaise."[26] As I wrote in 1980, after a visit to Vietnam and Hanoi, "An American visiting Hanoi is left with one strong impression: five years after its famous victory, Vietnam seems to have won the battle but lost the war. There are signs everywhere of a strong ambivalence . . . heroic posturing on the one hand, and a pervasive sense of political and economic isolation on the other. Hanoi itself is a city of shortages and worker lethargy."[27]

Other independent observers come to much the same conclusion. Paul Kattenburg, a former Foreign Service Officer who had known Hanoi in the early 1950s, and returned there in 1983, was as struck as I had been three years earlier to observe a city that seemed still so backward and redolent of another era. As he recently wrote, "the North has just gone on living much as it had ever since 1954: levels of want and poverty are just so high that a lack of amelioration is barely noticed; outright starvation has thus far been avoided, and in fact a slight improvement in agricultural production (if in nothing else) has taken place."[28]

But however uniformly depressing is every observer's report of present-day conditions in Hanoi, none has suggested that its economic difficulties will bring about a change in Vietnam's Cambodia posture. The Vietnamese leadership consciously regards itself as having taken on and bested any challenge, and looks upon its ability to have withstood French, American and Chinese pressure as firm evidence of its peoples' endurance. Indeed Hanoi's leaders frankly concede that Vietnam's political isolation is a severe economic hardship, and they do not hide evidence of discomfort with Hanoi's nearly total reliance on the Soviet Union.

For their part, the Russians themselves are known to be sometimes irritated with what they find as the "stiff-necked" Vietnamese. Tales circulate of Russian anger over Vietnamese "pilfering" of Soviet aid items, and these are certainly credible. There is probably very little love lost among the two groups, and in Hanoi, for example, the many Soviet aid technicians keep very much to themselves. Nevertheless, and as already stressed here, what Vietnam provides to Moscow at Cam Ranh Bay is invaluable, and it must be assumed that the Soviet Union is prepared to pay very high financial and other costs in order to maintain its presence there. Although the USSR has shown some interest in developing other maritime facilities in Cambodia (and maintains a technical assistance presence in the country of about 1000 East European and Soviet personnel), the present marriage of convenience between Moscow and Hanoi has a very wide, if not very deep, base of mutual interest.

Indochina accordingly presents to us an environment of seemingly irreconcilable conflict between the goals of China and the Soviet Union. Both of these states, moreover, in contrast to the United States appear to have a clear sense of what they want in the region. The U.S., the years since the war's end, has allowed itself to drift, and seemingly to be pulled along by the changing tides.

Its most recent and somewhat erratic behavior, in the Spring of 1985 was again illustrative of that tendency: despite a several-year insistence that the U.S. would *not* provide military aid to the Khmer resistance, at the first sign of a change in Congressional sentiment the Administration began to shift its view. By April 1985, State Department spokesmen were saying that although the U.S. still "preferred" that others make military aid available to Sihanouk-Son Sann forces, it might after all become necessary for the U.S. to join in that role.

How to explain such irresolution on the part of a great power like the U.S.? One explanation is that policy on Indochina is again being made incrementally, in a manner reminiscent of the decision-style that led the U.S. to such travail in Indochina two decades before. It is evident, for example, that former Cambodian Prime Minister Son Sann is an appealing figure, and that his dedication to an independent Cambodia, free of Vietnamese dominance, has impressed many in Washington and especially in the Congress. But to say that is to recall how Ngo Dinh Diem, another appealing figure then heralded as the "George Washington of Vietnam" impressed so many Americans precisely thirty years ago.

Another explanation, already intimated here, is that the U.S. is extremely reluctant to appear in the eyes of its important ASEAN partners lacking in will and commitment to *their* concerns. That is certainly a laudable goal, but it has to be questioned whether $5 million in U.S. assistance can be of more than symbolic meaning, and whether the symbols conveyed are those the U.S. wishes in fact to convey. The amount is too small to be militarily meaningful, and if it comes to be regarded as simply the first downpayment on more that will follow, there are many reasons to question whether the American people or the Congress are prepared for that sort of venture against the Vietnamese yet again.

There is another possible explanation, one that is altogether too likely to be ignored. The Reagan Administration, after all, is far more concerned with events in Central America than with the struggle in Indochina. It is entirely possible that it recognizes that in this latest evidence of Congressional sympathy for the cause of a free and non-communist Cambodia, the President's advisors see an opportunity to hoist the Congress on its own petard. How, after all, can Congress support the cause of the free Khmer without lending similar support to the no-less-worthy and much closer to home "contras" in Nicaragua?

Whichever explanation or combination of them is accurate, it seems most likely that events in Indochina, and their implications for long-term U.S. interests, have not been as fully thought out in Washington as in Moscow or Beijing. In an earlier era, U.S. policy toward Indochina and Vietnam was grounded in attitudes, later largely discarded, about China's role in the region. Today it is possible that a new generation of American policy is being made without sufficient thought as to long-term Soviet roles in the region, and even worse, that U.S. policy in Indochina is liable to be shaped on an anvil that has more to do with contemporary developments in Latin America.

None of these is a satisfactory basis for American policy. The U.S., both as the world's leading trading power, and as a state whose values and interests are best promoted by peaceful conditions, has much to gain by a peaceful resolution of the Indochina conflict. That may mean coming to grips, finally, with the need to bring a genuine end to the long American conflict with Hanoi. In turn, that is likely to mean recognizing, in one form or another, the fact of Vietnam's *fait accompli* in Cambodia.

While that is distasteful, and will certainly in the short run be disappointing to Thailand in particular, it is the task of a great power to prioritize its interests correctly. It should not be beyond the capacities of American statesmanship to participate in the shaping of a new regime in Indochina that provides the necessary guarantees to the Thai, and at the same time begins to make it possible for the Vietnamese to loosen their present too-close connection to the Soviet Union. It is *that* development, which has brought Moscow's presence to the South China Sea in a manner never before realized, that needs to occupy the attention of the U.S. government and the American people more than it has to date.

Notes

1. This may derive from the fact that the south, as the historically most agricultural region (centering on the Mekong Delta) was less "developed" than were Annam and Tonkin, and also from the different ethnological composition of Cochinchina. It has been home to many of the Khmer people, the so-called Khmer Krom, who are themselves the vestiges of an era when the Cambodian empire ruled much of what is now Indochina.
2. Lea E. Williams, *Southeast Asia: A History* (New York: Oxford University Press, 1976), p. 41.
3. China could hardly have *not* supported Ho Chi Minh. There was no love for French imperialism among any Chinese leadership, nationalist or communist, and it was certainly easier for a Chinese Communist government to endorse Ho than it might have been for a KMT regime.
4. Socialist Republic of Vietnam, Ministry of Foreign Affairs, *The Truth: Vietnam-China Relations Over the Last Thirty Years* (Hanoi, 1979), 87pp. The tenor of the document is captured in this excerpt: "China was the main supplier of arms to Vietnam by the end of the resistance war against the French colonialists. It took advantage of this situation to act as the principal negotiator with the French imperialists, and colluding with the latter, to work out a solution advantageous to China and France, but not to the peoples of Vietnam, Laos and Kampuchea. They sacrified the interests of the Indo-chinese peoples to ensure China's security in the South, to carry out the design of controlling Vietnam and Indochina, and at the same time to secure the role of a great power in settling international affairs, particularly in Asia"(p.5).
5. Note the following by Milton Osborne: "And the ultimate success of the Vietnamese Communists was greatly aided by the way in which their armed forces were able to use Kampuchean and Laotion (sic) territory for a broad range of strategic purposes" ("Kampuchea: The Politics of Recognition," in *World Review,* Australian Institute of International Affairs, vol. 20, no. 2 June 1981, p.5. American officials, during the controversy over Cambodia's "neutrality" in 1969-70, would have welcomed this analysis by a leading historian of Indochina.
6. William J. Duiker, *The Communist Road to Power in Vietnam* (Boulder, CO: Westview Press, 1981), p.336.
7. Quoted by William Shawcross, "Cambodia: Nightmare Without End," *Far*

Eastern Economic Review, 14 April 1978. This article and the longer one in the *New York Review of Books* from which it is excerpted, is one of the best analyses of Cambodian-Vietnamese relations in that period.

8. This point was made to me strongly and emotionally by Nguyen Co. Thach, Vietnam's Foreign Minister, and others with whom I spoke in Hanoi in 1980. As other analysts have also noted, Vietnamese leaders continue to resent bitterly Pol Pot's bloody purges of the Vietnam-trained Khmer cadres.

9. Duiker, *ibid.*

10. See Bernard K. Gordon, "Southeast Asia" in K.L. London (ed.) *The Soviet Union in World Politics* (Boulder, CO: Westview Press, 1980), p. 175. I have also discussed some of the background leading to the Treaty in my chapter, "Normalization and Southeast Asia," in J.B. Starr, ed., *The Future of US-China Relations* (New York: New York University Press, 1981).

11. *Radio Moscow*, 25 June 1978, in FBIS, 25 June 1978.

12. See, for example, reports in *The Far Eastern Economic Review* of 18 December 1981, and 11 June 1982, where it is suggested that "the 1979 invasion of Vietnam . . . nearly failed in the first few days," and that "the PLA's overall performance at a tactical level was mixed to dismal."

13. Early Soviet reporting on the number of Russian projects was contained in *Novosti Daily Review* (Moscow), 9 November 1978. An early Western estimate of the costs of Soviet aid is contained in *The Christian Science Monitor*, 27 October 1978, which noted that Soviet oil shipments alone to Vietnam were valued at $300 million.

14. *Far Eastern Economic Review*, 8 November 1984. This very recent report concludes that "according to the best estimates (the USSR) is still providing something in excess of U.S. $1 billion a year in non military aid."

15. We can dismiss the possibility that China was motivated by a concern for the welfare of the Khmer people. It should not be forgotten that China turned a blind eye to Pol Pot's reign of terror committed against the Khmers. The same must be said for the Vietnamese themselves—Hanoi, after all turned against Pol Pot for reasons having to do with direct Vietnamese interests; whatever empathy Hanoi may have felt for the Khmer peasantry was safely repressed until Pol Pot's political extremism stepped on Vietnam's security toes.

16. As quoted in *The Christian Science Monitor*, 9 January 1979.

17. *Far Eastern Economic Review*, 29 December 1983.

18. *Far Eastern Economic Review*, 8 November 1984.

19. *Armed Forces Journal*, April 1984, pp. 38-40.

20. Quoted in *The Far Eastern Economic Review*, 6 September 1984.

21. This was precisely the point I addressed at the height of the Vietnam war, in a book published in 1969. I wrote there that the U.S. "by its own actions had escalated the level of national interests involved. Yet that is precisely what occurred in the Vietnam instance . . . particularly when the interest derives not from a tangible resource, but from incremental and separately small specific commitments." See Bernard K. Gordon, *Toward Disengagement in*

      Asia: A Strategy for American Foreign Policy (Englewood Cliffs, NJ: Prentice-Hall, 1969), p. 25, and Chaps. 1-2.

22. *New York Times,* 9 September 1975.
23. For an excellent discussion of contemporary Vietnam-Cambodia issues, see "The Long Road Back," in *The Far Eastern Economic Review,* 29 November 1984.
24. U.S. Department of State, "Cambodia: The Search for Peace," *Current Policy* no. 613, 11 September 1984.
25. Hun Sen, quoted in *The Far Eastern Economic Review,* 29 November, 1984.
26. William J. Duiker, "The Legacy of History in Vietnam," *Current History,* December 1984, p. 409.
27. Bernard K. Gordon, "Hanoi, Part One: Signs of Ambivalence, *"Asian Wall Street Journal,"* 22 May 1980.
28. Paul M. Kattenburg, "Reflections on Vietnam," *Parameters,* Autumn 1984.

The Superpowers and Korea

DONALD S. ZAGORIA

Since the 19th century, when Tsarist Russia established a common border with Korea at the Tumen River, Russia's main interest in Korea has been determined by geopolitical considerations. Korea borders on Russia's Maritime Province and is close to Russia's principal Far Eastern naval base at Vladivostok. Korea also borders on China and only a narrow body of water separates it from Japan. The Korea Straits, strategically located between Korea and Japan, block one of the exits from the Sea of Japan to the Pacific Ocean.

In view of these strategic considerations, Russia's minimal goal has been to ensure that Korea does not become a base for a hostile foreign power. At the most, Russia has sought to bring Korea into her sphere of influence. In the 19th century, Japan and Great Britain were the main rivals and Russia's refusal to cede Korea to Japan was one of the causes of the Russo-Japanese war of 1904-05. Since the end of the Second World War, and particularly since 1950, the United States has been the main antagonist. Since the development of the Sino-Soviet split in the 1960s, China also looms as another serious long range rival in the Korean peninsula.

In more recent years, the growing strategic rivalry between the United States and the Soviet Union in Northeast Asia has given Korea an even greater importance.

Since 1978, the Soviets have established a Far Eastern unified command;

171

they have begun to deploy SS-20 medium range nuclear missiles in Siberia; they have deployed ground forces in the northern territories disputed with Japan; there has been a continuing buildup of the Soviet Pacific Fleet and a modernization of ground and air forces stationed in Siberia; and there has been the development of the Sea of Okhotsk-Sea of Japan-Maritime Province complex into a new core area.

Even more recently, as a result of Kim Il Sung's trip to Moscow in May 1984, the Russians have begun to sell North Korea some of their most advanced fighter planes, the MIG-23s, presumably in an effort to counter the F-16s that the United States has sold to South Korea. The Soviet Union has already made a port call at Wonsau in North Korea.

The United States, for its part, has begun to increase the quantity and quality of the American Seventh Fleet; to provide that fleet with nuclear-capable Tomahawk missiles; to station F-16 fighter airplanes in Japan; and to increase military assistance to South Korea. The United States has also been trying to develop an informal security coalition among the Pacific nations with the aim of containing Soviet expansion. U.S. security ties with both Japan and South Korea have been increasing at the same time that a U.S.-China security dialogue is underway. The United States has also been paying more attention to the non-communist countries of Southeast Asia (ASEAN).

According to the Soviets, the United States is trying to turn the Asia-Pacific region into a new arena of confrontation with the Soviet Union, using Japan as a "key link" in its new anti-Soviet "eastern front," and involving Tokyo, Seoul, ANZUS, and ASEAN in its plans.[1]

The burgeoning strategic rivalry between the Soviet Union and the United States in the Western Pacific is bound to give both superpowers an increased stake in the Korean peninsula. As a result, the Soviet Union is already in the process of strengthening its ties to North Korea while the United States seeks to draw South Korea closer.

How this increased strategic rivalry between the superpowers is likely to impact on the Korean peninsula is the subject of this essay.

Let me begin with a discussion of Soviet-North Korean relations which now seem to be entering a new phase. A great deal has been written on the relations between Moscow and Pyongyang and it is not my intention here to duplicate this literature in any detail.[2] Rather, I should like to make what seems to be the most important generalizations that emerge from it.

I think there is general agreement among the specialists that the Russians do not trust or like Kim Il Sung. To begin with, North Korea under Kim has during the past three decades generally been much closer to China than to Russia. Second, Kim has, at least until quite recently, opposed Soviet policy in both Afghanistan and Cambodia. He continues to provide a residence in Pyongyang for Prince Norodom Sihanouk, the nominal leader of the anti-Vietnamese resistance in Cambodia, a man whom Russian media routinely describe as a "hireling of the imperialists." Third, Kim has in the past publicly accused Russia of "dominationism" and of efforts to exploit the North Korean economy. Fourth, during the past several decades, Kim has developed into something of a state religion his philosophy of *chu'che,* or self-reliance, and although he has not been able to live up to this philosophy to the extent that he has preached it, it symbolizes his determination not to become dependent on the Russians. Finally, Kim has conducted a thoroughly independent foreign policy and has on various occasions involved the Russians in risks of confrontation with the United States, risks that the Russians would have preferred not to take.

Moscow's suspicion of North Korea is reciprocated. Kim's distrust of the Russians stems from a number of considerations. First, he remembers how close the Russians came to incorporating North Korea into the Soviet Union during the period from 1945 to 1950. Kim knows only too well how the Russians use their military and economic advisors, their troops, and their KGB agents to infiltrate governments which they intend to dominate. That is why he has allowed only a few such Russian advisors in North Korea during the past thirty years. It can be assumed that all of these still remaining are under strict surveillance. Moreover, Kim has seen the fate of a number of Russia's neighbors from Eastern Europe to Outer Mongolia to Afghanistan. And he knows about the "Brezhnev Doctrine" by which the Russians have arrogated to themselves the right to intervene in the internal affairs of any "socialist state" which defies Moscow. For such reasons alone, he would keep his distance from Russia.

Second, Kim saw for himself during the Korean War that Russia would not risk war with the United States in order to save the North Korean regime. Even at a time when American troops were marching towards North Korea's Tumen River border with Russia, the Russians gave no indication that they were prepared to intervene in the war. It was only the Chinese intervention that saved Kim Il Sung's government from being toppled by the Americans. To this day, North Korean media celebrate the anniversary of the Korean War with reminders of the common blood bond that North Korea shares with China.

But if both Moscow and Pyongyang look upon each other with suspicion, there is another side to this unusual relationship that is often lost sight of—one of mutual dependence and of geopolitical convergence. The fact is that both sides have a strong interest in good relations with the other.

North Korea is dependent upon the Soviet Union for deterrence of the United States and South Korea and it has maintained a treaty with the Soviet Union for this purpose since 1961. North Korea also wants continuing Soviet support for its unification policy and although the Soviets may in fact be ambivalent or even negative about Korean reunification, they do support Pyongyang's proposals in a variety of international meetings. Pyongyang also relies on the Soviets for much of its oil supplies and for somewhere around 25 percent of its total trade turnover. Finally, and not least important, the Soviets have from time to time supplied North Korea with a variety of weapons. Although Moscow has in the past been rather tightfisted with its most advanced weapons, this policy seems to be changing since Kim Il Sung's visit to Moscow in May 1984, his first in 17 years. North Korea has already purchased several MIG-23 advanced fighter planes from the Russians and is expected to buy an additional 35 to 45 later.

The Soviets, for their part, also have a substantial stake in North Korea. First, North Korea borders on Russian territory and is close to Vladivostok. Russia has a long-standing interest in Korea for this reason alone. Second, because of the growing strategic rivalry with the United States throughout the Asia-Pacific region, the Korean peninsula is becoming an increasingly important arena for Russia. The Soviets assert that the United States is now in the process of creating an "Eastern NATO" and that South Korea and Japan play an important role in this process.

The Soviets also have an interest in keeping North Korea from moving too close to China or to the West. In recent years, North Korea has improved its relations with China, tried to expand its economic relations with Japan, and sought—without much success so far—an opening to the United States. In the meantime, there are some signs that North Korea —under China's influence—may be trying to resolve its economic problems by opening up its economy to the West. At a time when Russia's worst fear in the Pacific is that it may be "odd man out", and that an anti-Soviet coalition comprised of the United States, Japan, South Korea, China and ASEAN is developing, the very last thing that Russia wants to see is a North Korea gravitating in the direction of its adversaries.

The Soviets and the North Koreans also share an important long-term geopolitical objective—the removal of American troops from South Korea and, eventually, the separation of Seoul from Washington.

Although the Soviets and North Koreans thus share some important objectives and have a stake in improving relations, there are risks for both sides in courting the other. The North Koreans do not want to move too close to the Soviets for fear of alienating China. Nor do they want to be dominated by Moscow. The Soviets, for their part, do not want inadvertently to encourage North Korea to take actions that could risk a new Korean war. Moscow has consistently been much more prudent in regions close to its borders than it has been in regions much further away. Quite apart from this important factor, the Russians could not afford to let Pyongyang win or lose a new Korean war. A North Korean loss in a new war would have profound political and psychological consequences among the Soviet Union's other allies and treaty partners. A North Korean victory would run the risk of a Soviet-American military confrontation on Soviet borders; end whatever chances there are for improving Soviet-American relations; carry the risk of Chinese intervention; and lead to great pressure within Japan for Japanese remilitarization—all of which would be severely detrimental to Soviet interests.

But there is no reason why these risks cannot be managed by both sides. During recent years, Pyongyang has been improving relations with both China and Russia at the same time. Given its desire to increase its leverage on both its allies, this is doubtless the most sensible course for it to pursue. And, in the process of improving relations with Moscow, the North is not likely to take actions that would jeopardize its independence.

The Soviets, for their part, have probably warned Kim Il Sung privately that the price of increased military and economic assistance is greater obeisance to Soviet foreign policy positions. It is instructive to note that in all the Soviet commentary on North Korea since Kim Il Sung's visit to Moscow in 1984, one theme has predominated—the importance of "proletarian internationalism," i.e. Moscow's code word for loyalty to Soviet foreign policy. As recently as April 1985, in commenting on the visit to Moscow of the North Korean Foreign Minister, the Soviets again stressed that cooperation with North Korea could only take place on the basis of the principles of "proletarian internationalism."[3]

Moreover, these warnings seem to have had some effect. The North Koreans have in the past year or so toned down their opposition to Soviet policy in Afghanistan and Cambodia and Pyongyang has sent its ambassador back to Hanoi. Also, North Korean media have gone out of their way to express Pyongyang's approval for a variety of recent Soviet foreign policy initiatives.

At the same time, there has been increasing diplomatic contact between the Russians and North Korea. Since Kim Il Sung's visit to Moscow in 1984, Deputy Foreign Minister Kapitsa has visited North Korea in November 1984 and the North Korean Foreign Minister, Kim Young-nam visited Moscow in April 1985. There are also signs of increased Soviet-North Korean trade.

It seems, then, as if Kim Il Sung's visit to Moscow in the spring of 1984 has ushered in a new phase of Soviet-North Korean relations. In the past, Soviet-North Korean relations have been erratic and Pyongyang has tilted more to China than to Russia. In the future, Pyongyang may seek to preserve a more even balance. The improvement in Sino-Soviet relations that has been taking place in the past few years will facilitate such a North Korean policy.

What does this new phase of Soviet-North Korean relations portend for South Korea and the West more generally? North Korea seems at the moment to be engaged in a two track policy.

On the one hand, North Korea is introducing a series of newly improved weapons; in the past ten years, it has increased ground strength to 750,000 men and doubled the numbers of main equipment, including tanks and guns; it has more than twenty special attack brigades and 100,000 commandos capable of surprise attack against the ROK; and its air force is striving for modernization via the purchase of advanced fighter planes from the Soviet Union. According to American military estimates, North Korea has a stockpile of war material sufficient for sixty days of fierce fighting.[4]

On the other hand, North Korea is also engaging in the most sustained dialogue with South Korea it has had since the early 1970s. There have been economic and Red Cross talks and proposals for an inter-parliamentary dialogue. Some North Korean spokesmen have even held out the possibility of a summit meeting between the leaders of the two Koreas.

This two track policy seems intended to increase pressure on both Seoul and Washington and to help Pyongyang attain its diplomatic goals. There is no reason to suppose that Pyongyang has abandoned its ultimate goal of dominating South Korea in a reunified communist Korea but, for the moment, it is engaging in more flexible tactics.

The two key variables in the Korean problem remain the American commitment to South Korea and political stability in the South. If the United States were to withdraw its troops from South Korea, as President Carter ill-advisedly tried to do, an entirely new and unstable situation could be created on the peninsula. If the Russians and North Koreans were to come to the conclusion that the American commitment to Korea is not credible, one or the other party might well be inclined to take much greater risks in order to dominate the southern part of the peninsula.

A protracted period of political instability in South Korea might also encourage the North towards adventurism.

On the other hand, if the American commitment remains credible, and if South Korea remains relatively stable during the next few years, the pressure will be on the North to move towards accommodation. The North is losing the economic and diplomatic race with South Korea and if present economic trends continue, there will also come a time when it will fall behind in the military competition as well. Neither of its two principal allies—the Soviet Union and China—want a new Korean war. Thus, there will be increasing pressure on Pyongyang from both internal and external sources to reach a *modus vivendi* with Seoul.

The Russians will not oppose a North-South accommodation provided they are part of the process that helps bring it about. In the past, the Soviets have been uneasy about the easing of tensions between the two Koreas because it was the Chinese who were acting as intermediaries between Pyongyang and Washington, thus increasing Soviet fears that they might be isolated from the negotiations to follow. But the recent warming up of the Soviet-North Korean relations must have helped allay these fears.

The Russians are well aware that any accommodation between North and South Korea is at best likely to be a long and protracted process. Even if this process was ultimately to yield the fruit of "cross-recognition" of the two Koreas by the major powers, the Soviets could expect to profit from such an arrangement. A long period of better relations between North and South Korea leading to cross-recognition could help lay the groundwork for the removal of American troops from South Korea, Moscow's principal objective. Over the longer run, the Soviets would hope to weaken American-ROK ties by exploiting their own massive military presence near the Korean peninsula and South Korea's uncertainty about American staying power in the region.

On the other hand, the Russians can also live with a continuation of the present stalemate between North and South Korea. A true detente between North and South Korea might make Pyongyang less dependent upon Soviet military assistance. Also, if Pyongyang makes peace with the South and goes on to concentrate on economic development like the Chinese, it is the West that can be most helpful in furnishing the capital and the aid that is required. Thus, a modest level of tension short of actual conflict may best suit Soviet interests.

But if there is an easing of tension between the two Koreas, Moscow will seek to insert itself into the process. Over the longer run, the Soviets intend to increase their influence in both North and South Korea, to prevent North Korea from moving too close to China or the West, and to inhibit South Korea from assuming a more active role in what Moscow sees as a new American-Japanese-South Korean triangle in Northeast Asia.

It remains to say a few words about the Soviet policy towards South

Korea. There have been a few basic themes in the Soviet writing on South Korea in recent years. South Korea has been identified as a "base of American imperialism in the Far East"; as "an arena of the struggle between the two world systems"; as a "chariot of the Pentagon directed against the USSR"; as "a springboard for various provocations and military adventurism"; as "a country of oppressive military-bureaucratic dictatorship"; as "an appendix of American and Japanese imperialistic monopolies"; as "the last American outpost on the continent of Asia"; as "a backbone of the American defense treaty system in the Pacific"; and as "a little American partner in the Far East."[5]

Whether the Soviets actually believe what they write about South Korea is, however, another matter. Much of their commentary simply reflects an awareness that South Korea is heavily dependent on the United States for its security and that there is, at least for the moment, very little that the Soviets can do to shake Seoul loose from its alignment with Washington.

Probably the principal Soviet concerns about South Korea are that its economy is one of the most dynamic in the world, that its military power is growing and that its ties with the United States and Japan are proceeding apace. Informal connections with China are also developing. It is this gnawing fear that a new anti-Soviet power complex is developing in Northeast Asia—a Seoul-Toyko-Washington axis—that is most alarming to the Russians. Recent Soviet commentary stresses both some real and some fictional signs of such a development. But the theme is unmistakable. South Korea, Japan and the United States are stepping up their military cooperation against the socialist camp.[6]

Until the shooting down of KAL 007 in 1983, there were some signs of a slight thaw in Soviet-South Korean relations.[7] Beginning in the early 1970s, a major shift in South Korean policy towards the Soviet Union took place and Seoul abandoned its previously uncompromising anti-communist posture. South Korea changed its policy for a number of reasons: growing doubts about American credibility; anxiety to avoid diplomatic isolation; recognition that the Soviets did not support Kim Il Sung's belligerent approach towards unification; and at least some American encouragement of an ROK "Nordpolitik."[8] Seoul was also concerned about the increasing naval activities by the Soviet Union in and near the Sea of Japan. The Soviets responded to the South Korean overtures with a certain flexibility of their own. In 1973, the Soviets allowed visits to the Soviet Union by a South Korean dramatist and two leading businessmen and this was followed by South Korean participation in the Universiad games held in Moscow. Since 1973, South Korean visitors have been allowed into the Soviet Union as participants in international events.

The Soviet attitude towards Seoul has displayed certain patterns.[9] First, it seems as if the Soviets increased their attention to South Korea largely as a means of constraining Pyongyang. Their "South Korea card" gave the Soviets useful leverage over North Korea. The occasional appearance of Soviet "friendliness" to South Korea was intended to warn Pyongyang against moving too close towards Beijing.

A second aspect of Soviet behavior towards South Korea was its passivity. The Soviets were flexible enough to cause some degree of expectation among South Korea and its allies, but not positive enough to undermine the Soviet Union's basic pro-North Korean stance. Clearly, for the Soviets, their position in North Korea was too important for them to undermine by appearing too friendly towards South Korea.

Third, although the Soviets did not actively seek a political settlement of the Korean question, there were many signs that they did not want a new Korean war.

From this overview, a few general conclusions may now be drawn. First, since the end of the 19th century, it has been a rather consistent Russian objective to have a sphere of influence in the strategically located Korean peninsula bordering on Russia's Maritime Province.

Second, Russia's historic interest in Korea—that it should not be used as a base by a hostile power—is probably stronger today than it has been at any time during the past century. As the Russians see it, the United States is trying to create a new "eastern front" in which Japan and South Korea play key roles. The Russians thus have a very powerful interest in removing American forces from South Korea and in driving a wedge between Washington and Seoul. This is a goal they share with North Korea.

Third, the Soviets are handicapped in the pursuit of their interests in the Korean peninsula by the fact that their present opportunities are limited because they do not trust Kim Il Sung, because China continues to offset Soviet power in North Korea, and because South Korea is, at the moment, firmly aligned with the United States.

But if history teaches us anything, it is that Russian foreign policy is extraordinarily patient and persistent. We can thus assume that the Russians will, over a long period of time, continue to pursue their ultimate goal of dominating the Korean peninsula. The United States and South Korea therefore need to be wary and need to ensure that an effective balance of power on the peninsula continues to deter the North.

There are several requirements for a peaceful solution to the Korean issue. First, North Korea must come to the realization that it cannot unify Korea by force or incite an armed rebellion or instability in the south. This requires the continued economic prosperity and political stability of South

Korea and continued close relations between the United States and the ROK and between Japan and the ROK. Also, further improvement of Chinese-South Korean relations could enhance this process.

Second, the two Koreas need to conduct a series of high level meetings leading to a long period of "confidence building measures" that will help reduce the high levels of mutual mistrust between them. There is considerable room for constructive actions by the United States, Japan, China and the Soviet Union that will help facilitate this process.

The United States, Japan and China should communicate to the Soviet Union that Soviet cooperation in bringing about a peaceful solution to the Korean problem is desirable. Indeed, if the Soviet Union truly desires to relax international tensions and to improve relations with the United States, its conduct in Korea could be one indication of such an intention.

Over the longer run, if some kind of *modus vivendi* is eventually worked out between the two Koreas, it may be desirable to convene a conference including all the major powers to ratify such an agreement. The Soviet Union should be included in such a conference.

Notes

1. Pravda, 22 June 1985, "Set About it Together," in FBIS (Soviet Union, 26 June 1985), pp. CC 7-10.
2. See Thomas P. Bernstein and Andrew J. Nathan, "The Soviet Union, China and Korea," Summer 1981; Harry Gelman and Norman D. Levin, "The Future of Soviet-North Korean Relations," Rand, October 1984.
3. FBIS, Soviet Union, 22 April 1985, p. CC7.
4. *Asian Security,* 1984, pp. 123-124.
5. See Basil Dmytryshyn, "Soviet Perceptions of South Korea" in Jae Kyu Park and Joseph M. Ha, *The Soviet Union and East Asia in the 1980s* (Boulder, CO: Westview, June 1983).
6. For a recent example, which includes the charge that South Korea is planning for the development of medium range Pershing II missiles, see FBIS (Soviet Union, 12 April 1985), p. C2.
7. Sung-joo Han, "South Korean Policy Toward the Soviet Union," Conference on Soviet Policy in Asia, Seoul, 10-12 April 1980.
8. Han, *op cit.*
9. Han, *op cit.*

The Implications of the Triangular Relations for Taiwan:

An Emerging Target of Opportunity

MICHAEL Y. M. KAU *

Despite Beijing's repeated claim that the Taiwan issue is "entirely China's own internal affair" in which no foreign powers are permitted to interfere, the realities surrounding the Taiwan issue over the last thirty-five years are far more complex.[1] Taiwan has in fact emerged since 1950 as a major issue of international concern and controversy, which at times has brought even the superpowers and China to the brink of military confrontation. Ever since President Truman's statement of 27 June 1950 regarding Taiwan's future, Taiwan's status and security have become inseparable from political and security strategies of the Sino-Soviet-U.S. triangular competition in the Asia-Pacific region.

The international security system of East Asia underwent a most dramatic transformation in the 1960s, triggered by a number of crucial developments, such as the intensification of the Sino-Soviet dispute, the

*Much of the research for this chapter was done by David A. Reynolds, who at the time was a graduate research assistant of the East Asian Security Project, also at Brown University.

181

Soviet military buildup and global expansion, and the relative decline of U.S. power in the world. As China broke away from the Soviet camp and emerged as an independent actor in the world arena, the rigid bi-polarized system of the Cold War era of the 1950s began to evolve into a triangular pattern of power play in the 1970s. This great transformation is generally viewed in the West as a positive development, because it reduced the danger of stiff two camp confrontation and allowed more room for flexible accommodations and tension-relaxation. To the U.S., more importantly, it means a golden opportunity to cultivate strategic cooperation with and economic access to China at the expense of its arch adversary, the Soviet Union.

The positive benefits of this increasing global strategic flexibility notwithstanding, some of the negative and potentially dangerous effects of the emergence of an unstable strategic triangle operating in Asia, however, are often overlooked. The shifting flexibility and fluidity of international interactions provided by the new system, it should be noted, also creates a fertile ground for stimulating exploitation, opportunism and miscalculation. The triangular strategic game played in a multipolar world, by nature, easily multiplies the complexity of power configurations in managing political competitions and controlling security conflicts. The political gains achieved by the Soviet Union in Indochina and Afghanistan in the last decade demonstrate clearly the potential dangers that exist in the triangular competition for power and influence in Asia today.

From the perspective of the Republic of China (ROC) on Taiwan, the development and intensification of the triangular power game in the Western Pacific since the early 1970s have already created a very disturbing and destabilizing impact on its security arrangement. The long-term future of its security and stability could become even more unpredictable and threatening. This article attempts to assess the dynamics and impact of the triangular strategic game on Taiwan's security in recent years and highlight one of the worst possible scenarios of development in the context of the power competition of the Sino-Soviet-U.S. triad.[2]

The Evolution of Taiwan's Security Environments

When World War II was drawing to an end, there is no doubt that the creation of a new regional system for the peace and stability of East Asia was a major concern of the U.S. However, the postwar confusion and withdrawal syndrome in the 1940s hindered the quick articulation of a well-formulated strategy. This was clearly reflected, for example, in the rather incoherent and haphazard actions taken by Washington in dealing with the collapse of the Japanese empire and the reassertion of Russian interests in Northeast Asia: while maintaining a firm "activist" occupation policy in Japan and the Philippines, U.S. posture and strategy in both Korea and China were highly ambiguous and ill-prepared to meet the challenges of the postwar years.

The dramatic Communist victory in China in the fall of 1949 and the outbreak of the Korean War in the summer of 1950, however, shocked the U.S. into examining its passive policy posture, and prompted Washington to assert in earnest a stronger and different role in East Asia. A militant strategy of forward "containment" was instituted in response to the crises brought on by Communist revolutions and expansions. American fire power was employed to repel the North Koreans and their allies, and a series of political alliances and military bases were established to encircle the People's Republic of China (PRC). As the containment strategy developed, so did U.S. security commitments to the ROC on Taiwan. The first overt U.S. military commitment to Taiwan's defense came on 27 June 1950, when President Truman ordered the Seventh Fleet to patrol the Taiwan Strait. In declaring this dramatic policy shift, Truman stressed that henceforth any use of force against the island would be taken as a "direct threat to the security of the Pacific area and to the U.S. forces."[3] Washington even went so far as to declare that "the determination of the future status of Formosa [Taiwan] must await the restoration of security in the Pacific, a peace settlement with Japan, or consideration by the United Nations."[4]

June 1950, therefore, marked an absolutely critical transition, as far as Taiwan's external security was concerned. The great uncertainties and confusion experienced by the Nationalists in the late 1940s were quickly alleviated by the strong signal of security support sent by Washington. In May 1951, a U.S. Military Assistance and Advisory Group (MAAG) was established on Taiwan to channel military aid to the island and to assist in the training and equipping of the island's armed forces. The inauguration of the Eisenhower Administration in 1953 further speeded up the process of U.S.-ROC military cooperation started earlier in the wake of the outbreak of the Korean War. Under the energetic and bold stewardship of Secretary of State John Foster Dulles, Taiwan was fully integrated into the U.S. defense perimeter in the Western Pacific, which extended from Japan and South Korea in the north to the Philippines and Indochina in the south. The close military and political ties between the ROC and the U.S. were officially sealed by a Mutual Defense Treaty, signed in December 1954. In January of the following year, Congress was even persuaded to authorize the President "to employ the Armed Forces of the U.S. as he deems necessary for the specific purpose of securing and protecting Formosa [Taiwan] and the Pescadores [Penghu] against armed attack."[5]

It was not until the second Taiwan strait crisis of 1958, however, that the U.S. actively and unequivocally demonstrated its military commitment to Taiwan's security. On 23 August, the PRC initiated one of the largest shellings of the Nationalist-held island of Quemoy. In response, President Eisenhower declared that the U.S. would not "desert our responsibilities or the statements we have already made."[6] Subsequently, he ordered the dispatching of six aircraft carriers to the region, the deploying of U.S.-escorted convoys to support and reinforce Quemoy, and the shipping of eight-inch howitzers capable of firing tactical atomic shells from the besieged garrison. As the conflict escalated, Secretary of State John Foster Dulles issued a stern warning that the U.S. would not "hesitate to use armed force," if necessary, in ensuring Taiwan's security.[7] The strong resolve of the U.S. to protect Taiwan's security, which was explicitly communicated to the PRC through such concrete deeds, eventually forced Peking to back down from its military adventurism.

The escalation of the war in Indochina in the 1960s greatly enhanced the strategic value of Taiwan to America's war efforts. Taiwan was used as a staging and logistic base for U.S. forces operating in Southeast Asia. During the peak of the Vietnam War, over 10,000 U.S. troops and advisors were stationed in Taiwan. In the two decades since 1950, the U.S. had poured over $2.5 billion in military aid into the island to strengthen Taiwan's armed forces, and made the island an integral part of the American security perimeter in the Pacific region.[8] There is no question that such extensive military cooperation between the two countries and the conspicuous U.S. military presence on the island helped consolidate Taiwan's security position. More importantly, U.S. intentions with regard to Taiwan were made unequivocal and were explicitly demonstrated through concrete actions. There was a clear consistency in rhetoric and action as far as U.S. policy and resolve to defend Taiwan was concerned.

Emerging Uncertainties of U.S. Commitments

Major developments in the world arena in the late 1960s, particularly the worsening of the dispute between Beijing and Moscow; the growing challenge of Soviet military power and expansionism; and the worsening U.S. burden of war in Vietnam began to generate pressure on Washington to reexamine its Cold War strategy of rigid containment against China and strong alliance with Taiwan. In February 1969, President Nixon ordered a major reevaluation of U.S. foreign policy in Asia. In a briefing to reporters on 25 July 1969, the President, in discussing what would later become known as the Nixon Doctrine, declared that the U.S. should no longer act as a "global policeman" and should reduce its military presence on the Asian continent. Washington signaled that while continuing to provide friendly nations in Asia with the necessary means to defend themselves, the U.S. was contemplating a move away from an activist and direct containment of the PRC.

The implications of such a major policy change for Taiwan were immediately evident. In 1969, the U.S. quietly ended the nineteen-year presence of the Seventh Fleet in the Taiwan Strait. Starting in 1971, steps were taken by the Administration to urge Congress to repeal the "Formosa Resolution," one of the most important symbols of the strong American security commitment to Taiwan. It was under this new mood of searching for a new strategy that President Nixon undertook his historic trip to Beijing in February 1972, and opened up a new era of accommodation and cooperation with the PRC. In the Shanghai Communique, signed jointly by Premier Zhou Enlai and the President, both sides formally declared their desires to normalize relations. While acknowledging that "all Chinese on either side of the Taiwan Strait maintain there is but one China and that Taiwan is a part of China," the U.S. also reaffirmed "its interest in a peaceful settlement of the Taiwan question." To placate Chinese senti-ments on the Taiwan issue, however, the U.S. promised that "with this prospect in mind, it affirms the ultimate objective of the withdrawal of all U.S. forces and military installations from Taiwan."[9] The immediate result of the Communique for Taiwan was a stepping up in the withdrawal of U.S. troops stationed on the island. Less obvious, however, was its importance as the first step in a long process leading to the eventual decouplement of the U.S. defense and political commitments to Taiwan.

While both President Nixon and his successor, President Ford, were clearly interested in keeping the process and momentum of "normaliza-tion" going, it was equally evident that they were not quite prepared to push "normalization" at an expense too costly to Taiwan's security. They were unwilling to accept Beijing's demand for abrogating the 1954 Mutual Defense Treaty and severing formal diplomatic ties with the ROC without getting in return Peking's explicit promise to renounce the use of force in settling the Taiwan issue. Moreover, Washington also sought Peking's agreement to allow a unilateral U.S. commitment to the island's security, continued arms sales to Taiwan, and the maintenance of a semi-official relationship with the ROC at a "Liaison Office" level. The stalemate in negotiations for establishing full diplomatic relations throughout the Nixon and Ford Administrations between 1972 and 1977 reflected in part the seriousness of the U.S. in trying to persuade the PRC to accept a compromise formula which could, in the judgment of Washington, still provide Taiwan a reasonable assurance of security and stability. Recalling the tough negotiations with the Chinese, Richard Nixon wrote in retrospect:

> In our negotiations with China we refused to renounce our treaty commitment to Taiwan, and we stated clearly in the communique our firm position that the Taiwan question should be settled peacefully. . . . Even on the intensely emotional issue of Taiwan, China, while not retreating from its own position, had to accept the fact that we would not accede to the demand that we abandon our commitment to Taiwan.[10]

It was during the Carter Administration that U.S. commitments to Taiwan began to seriously deteriorate as Taiwan emerged clearly as a "pawn" in the triangular power game among the U.S., and PRC and the Soviet Union. To begin with, the relative decline of U.S. military strength and world leadership in the 1970s created an impetus for Washington to further exploit the Sino-Soviet conflict to counter the expanding Soviet military might and global activism. It was assumed that improved relations with the PRC would not only place pressure on the USSR's eastern flank, thereby restraining its ability to cause trouble elsewhere, but also force the Soviets to come to terms on such critical issues as the overdue SALT II treaty.[11]

The emergence of Deng Xiaoping as the dominant leader in China in the post-Mao years and his emphasis on the pragmatic goals of modernization and stability were an added incentive for Washington to pursue normalization. The PRC's new moderate economic and foreign policy became more amenable to the establishment of strategic and trade links with the West. Moreover, the progressively worsening international crises stretching from Iran and Afghanistan to Vietnam all brought enormous pressure on President Carter to score quick victories on the foreign policy front in order to bolster his sagging political image at home and abroad.

Normalization and Its Impact on Taiwan's Security Arrangement

As political pressure mounted on President Carter and time grew short, the White House became ever more willing to compromise on the Taiwan issue in order to achieve a breakthrough in normalization with China. Hence, during the negotiations with Beijing in 1978, Washington not only dropped its long-standing demand for a non-use-of-force pledge but also acquiesced to a downgrading of its relations with Taiwan to an unofficial, non-governmental level. Furthermore, the U.S. accepted all of China's "three conditions" that demanded Washington to remove all U.S. troops from Taiwan, sever diplomatic relations, and terminate the 1954 defense treaty. In the Joint Communique on the Establishment of Diplomatic Relations signed 15 December 1978, the Carter Administration went beyond the promise made by President Nixon in the Shanghai Communique of 1972 by "recognizing the Government of the People's Republic of China as the *sole* legal Government of China" and "*acknowledging* the Chinese position that there is but one China and [that] Taiwan is part of China [emphasis added]." The Joint Communique on normalization further stated that it was "within this context the people of the United States will maintain cultural, commercial and other unofficial relations with the people of Taiwan."[12]

Serious confusions ensued immediately with reference to the meaning of U.S. "*acknowledgment*" of "the Chinese position that there is but one China and [that] Taiwan is part of China." While Washington interpreted the word "acknowledge" to mean "understand" or "take note of," Peking translated the term "acknowledge" as "*chengren*" to signify "recognize" or "give legitimacy to." Hence, the PRC insisted that the U.S. had "*recognized*" the Chinese position. Worse still, the American position was further distorted by truncating and omitting the passage that it was the "Chinese position" that was being addressed. This resulted in the Chinese claim that "the U.S. *recognizes (chengren)* that there is one China and that Taiwan is a part of China."[13]

Concession to China's "three conditions" and the implicit acknowledgment of the PRC's sovereignty over Taiwan notwithstanding, the Carter Administration asserted that the security of Taiwan and the well-being of its people would not be jeopardized. First, it was explained, the U.S. Government had made clear to the Chinese that "we have an *interest* in the peaceful resolution of the Taiwan issue and that we *expect* this issue to be settled peacefully by the Chinese themselves [emphasis added]."[14] In the context of China's ambitious and energetic pursuit of the "four modernizations" and its fundamental turn to the West and Japan for their supply of advanced technology and capital, it was extremely unlikely that China would use force on Taiwan at the risk of disrupting its newly cultivated ties with the U.S. and Japan. More importantly, China was under serious military pressure from the Soviets in the North and from the Vietnamese in the South. Under these circumstances, according to the Carter Administration, it was virtually impossible that China would seriously contemplate a reunification of Taiwan by force. The PRC simply could not afford to ignore the fifty divisions of Soviet troops deployed along the 4,500-miles of its northern border.

The Carter Administration apparently concluded that Taiwan's security could be adequately protected by relying on the "expectation" and "interest" unilaterally expressed by the U.S. on the one hand, and on both internal and external constraints limiting the range of China's policy choices and military options, on the other. This low-key approach was also clearly reflected in the President's approach to the Taiwan Omnibus Bill proposed to Congress on 26 January 1979. In the Bill, the Administration deliberately and cautiously avoided including any words which explicitly addressed the issue of Taiwan's security. Nowhere in the bill did the Carter Administration mention U.S. concern over a military threat to or economic harassment of Taiwan by external forces. Nor did the bill say anything about U.S. interest in continuing to provide arms sales to Taiwan to maintain the island's capabilities of self-defense.[15]

The Congress and public opinion, however, disagreed strongly with the Carter Administration's ambiguous and informal approach to the protection of Taiwan's security. Congressional leaders were quick to point out the inadequacies and dangers of such a low-profile approach. They contended that unless American resolve and commitment were stated formally and explicitly, U.S. credibility would be subject to needless doubts and speculations in the eyes of adversaries and friends as well. Worse still, the ambiguity and implicity of U.S. stance might even create a dangerous ground for misinterpretations and miscalculations. Hence, the Congress deemed it essential to rewrite the Administration's proposal by stating in unequivocal terms America's concern and commitment to the safeguards for the security of Taiwan. The Taiwan Relations Act (TRA), adopted by Congress in the spring of 1979, declares openly:

> It is the policy of the United States—
> (1) To preserve and promote extensive, close, and friendly commercial, cultural, and other relations between the people of the U.S. and the people of Taiwan . . .;
> (2) To declare that peace and stability in the area are in the political, security, and economic interests of the U.S., and are matters of international concern;

(3) To make clear that the U.S. decision to establish diplomatic relations with the People's Republic of China rests upon the expectation that the future of Taiwan will be determined by peaceful means;

(4) To consider any effort to determine the future of Taiwan by other than peaceful means, including by boycotts or embargoes, a threat to the peace and security of the Western Pacific area and of grave concern to the U.S.;

(5) To provide Taiwan with arms of a defensive character; and

(6) To maintain the capacity of the U.S. to resist any resort to force or other form of coercion that would jeopardize the security, or the social or economic system, of the people on Taiwan.[16]

According to Congress, the TRA was meant to be a functional replacement for the Mutual Defense Treaty of 1954 which the Administration agreed to terminate by the end of 1979. By making its stand and commitment to Taiwan's security crystal clear in advance, Congress hoped to achieve the effect of dissuading potential adversaries from needless speculations or miscalculations with the potential of escalating into action and violence. The utility of the TRA as an instrument of deterrence, however, ultimately depends upon its active implementation by the executive branch of the U.S. government. For any security deterrence to be credible, deed is needed to back up rhetoric.

Beijing's Continuing Pressure on the Taiwan Issue

During the 1980 presidential campaign, candidate Ronald Reagan, reflecting his long-held strong commitment to Taiwan, criticized President Carter for paying "too high a price" in normalizing relations with Beijing and for failing to implement the TRA as faithfully and rigorously as required by the law.[17] In a major statement on his policy toward Asia issued on 25 August 1980, Reagan condemned the concessions President Carter had made to the Chinese as "not necessary and not in the national interest."[18] The expectation, then, was that once Reagan was elected the political indifference and stringent restrictions on arms sales to Taiwan imposed by the Carter Administration would be lifted. Reagan would act to assure Taiwan politically and to protect the qualitative edge of the island's deterrence capabilities.

After the election, however, President Reagan did not rush to fulfill his campaign promises given on the Taiwan issue. The long-standing request by Taiwan to purchase sophisticated U.S. aircraft (F-5G, F-16, and/or F-20) and other advanced arms were declined. Of particular significance was the conclusion of the U.S.-China Communique on Taiwan on 17 August 1982 which addressed the key issues of American arms sales to Taiwan and the ROC's sovereign status. On the question of arms sale, contrary to the spirit and the letter of the TRA, the Reagan Administration was pressured by Beijing into agreeing: (1) "it does not seek to carry out a long-term policy of arms sales to Taiwan," and "it intends to reduce gradually its sales of arms to Taiwan, leading over a period of time to a final resolution"; and (2) "its arms sales to Taiwan will not exceed, either in qualitative or in quantitative terms, the level of those supplied in recent years since the establishment of diplomatic relations."[19] It should be recalled that the TRA clearly provided for arms transfers at such a level that Taiwan could maintain a "sufficient self-defense capability," which implied a periodic upgrading for quantitative and qualitative improvement. Although no specific date for an ultimate termination of arms sales to Taiwan was mentioned in the Communique, the negative impact of the Communique on Taiwan was obvious: Washington has formally pledged to reduce arms sales over time. The issue is no longer whether or not arms sales should be limited under Chinese pressure, but rather how fast and how much they will be limited in the years ahead.

On the issue of Taiwan's sovereignty and independence, Beijing continued to argue that, according to the Chinese text of the Communique, the U.S. "*recognizes* [*chengren* instead of '*acknowledges*'] the Chinese position that there is but one China and [that] Taiwan is a part of China." It should be noted that this time the wording in favor of the PRC was specifically written into the Communique under Beijing's pressure and Washington's acquiescence:

> The Chinese Government reiterates that the question of Taiwan is China's internal affair. . . . The U.S. Government attached great importance to its relations with China, and reiterates that it has no intention of infringing on Chinese sovereignty and territorial integrity, or interfering in China's internal affairs, or pursuing a policy of "Two Chinas" or "one China, one Taiwan."[20]

An official statement such as this naturally raised tremendous doubts and anxieties in the minds of the people of Taiwan over the value of the TRA and the credibility of the U.S. as an "informal ally" and "old friend."

The Eroding Edge of Taiwan's Security Deterrence

The infusion of large quantities of U.S. military aid worth over $2.5 billion during the 1950s and 1960s enabled the Nationalist Armed Forces on Taiwan to transform themselves into a respectable fighting force with modern defense capabilities. Qualitatively, they became superior to their counterpart on the mainland in many respects, especially in such important areas as jet fighters, missiles, and radar systems. This slight but crucial qualitative edge helped the Nationalists maintain a reasonable air and naval superiority over the Taiwan Strait.[21]

Quantitatively, however, Taiwan is clearly no match for the mainland. The PRC enjoys an approximately ten-to-one superiority over Taiwan in personnel and in almost all categories of equipment.

Crucially, the People's Liberation Army (PLA) Air Force has 5-6,000 fighter aircraft versus Taiwan's 340. Estimates by military specialists indicate that Taiwan's Air Force could be neutralized by the overwhelming numbers of PRC fighter aircraft in two to three weeks. Following the establishment of air superiority, the PRC could easily transport eighteen infantry divisions to Taiwan at one time by mobilizing its limited and dated sea-lift capabilities. The only viable deterrent to such an attack or a more feasible blockade of the Taiwan coast is the enormous toll that Taiwan's forces could inflict on PRC equipment. Using the 1958 Quemoy conflict as a basis, in which Taiwan's jet fighters established a fifteen-to-one kill ratio, military specialists project a loss of as much as one third of the PLA Air and Naval Forces in a full-scale invasion.[22]

It is abundantly clear, therefore, that the credibility of Taiwan's military deterrence rests ultimately on the qualitative superiority of its arms over the PRC's, on the one hand, and on the availability of arms replenishment on a continuing basis from reliable sources, on the other. Taiwan's current arsenal of F-5As/Es/Fs and F-104s may still be capable to dissuade an attack when compared with the PLA's online MiGs. However, the series of developments regarding arms transfers to Taiwan since normalization —ranging from the 1979 moratorium and the 1982 Communique to the continued restraint and selectivity exercised by Washington—have indeed raised serious questions as to how long the qualitative edge of Taiwan's defense capabilities can remain credible *vis-à-vis* the far greater numerical strengths of the PRC's.

Moreover, the increasing military cooperation between the U.S. and the PRC has further compounded Taiwan's anxieties over the tenuous military balance between the two Chinas. In recent years, Washington has progressively conceded its restrictions regarding the PRC's access to U.S. military technology and hardware. The Soviet military buildup in Vietnam and the invasion of Afghanistan in 1979 provided the U.S. further impetus to speed up strategic cooperation with the PRC. In January 1980, U.S. offers of military transfers expanded greatly from the "dual-use" technology to military equipment, such as air-defense radar, advanced computers, navigation equipment, helicopters, transport aircraft, and underwater search radar.[23] A decision in 1981 extended this "open" list to include selected defensive weapons, including anti-tank and anti-aircraft missiles. In May 1983, Washington formally reclassified the status of PRC on the "export control categories" from "P" (for Communist countries) to "V" (for friendly nations) in order to permit Peking to have an easier access to a wide variety of advanced technology normally banned against the Soviet bloc countries. Secretary of Defense Caspar Weinberger, on a trip to the PRC in September 1983, made it clear that he "expected greatly expanded cooperation in the future" in military areas. New export guidelines disclosed during his trip permitted the PRC to purchase 75% of the high technology items it previously had difficulty purchasing because of Pentagon restrictions.[24]

The friendly exchange of state visits between top leaders of the two countries also ushered in an even better political climate for strategic cooperation. In 1984, Zhao Ziyang's state visit to Washington in January was reciprocated by President Reagan's grand trip to Beijing in April. In 1985, PRC President Li Xiannian and U.S. Vice President exchanged state visits in July and October, respectively. In January 1985, General John Vessey, Chairman of the U.S. Joint Chiefs of Staff, was welcomed in Beijing. Aside from arranging for expanded exchanges of military missions, the general also offered the Chinese new weapon transfer packages, including such items as the Phalanx ship-defense system and torpedoes.[25] In the past two years, Beijing has sent eleven high-level military delegations and procurement missions to the U.S. to shop for weapons and military equipment. Negotiations on a variety of arms and dual-use technologies estimated at over $5.6 billion were reported to have been completed. The purchases included twenty-four Black Hawk combat helicopters, guidance systems and avionics to equip fifty Chinese F-8 intercepters, technology and equipment for a modern ammunition plant, and dual-use nuclear technology.[26]

From Taiwan's perspective, the implications of the PRC's expanding access to U.S. military technology and weapons, coupled with Beijing's drive for "military modernization" signal disasters. It is granted that the PRC has limited capital resources available for arms acquisition; however, given the enormous quantitative disparities between Taiwan and the PRC, only relatively small qualitative changes are needed to tip the scale of deterrence and place Taiwan's security in a precarious position. This explains precisely why Taiwan shows such great agonies and frustrations over the issue of reducing and restricting Taiwan's access to U.S. arms.

Beijing's Intensified Campaigns for Unification

Throughout the last three-and-a-half decades, the PRC has been absolutely consistent in asserting its ultimate national goal of incorporating Taiwan into the motherland. What has varied from time to time are strategies and tactics employed for achieving such a goal. Beijing's unification campaigns show a clear pattern of alternating between periods of "militant liberation" and periods of "peaceful unification."

Following the conclusion of normalization, Beijing entered a phase of rigorous peace campaigns. The PRC's recent peace offensive was greatly dramatized by such appeals as the "Message to Compatriots on Taiwan" issued on 1 January 1979 and the "Nine-point Unification Proposal" made on 30 September 1981.[27] While the former invited the Taiwan authorities to open up for "three exchanges" in postal service, trade and tourism between the two sides of the Taiwan Strait, the latter offered to the Nationalist Government that Taiwan would be allowed to keep a high degree of political and economic autonomy, and even its own armed forces and secret police so long as it was willing to surrender its sovereignty and independence.

It should be noted that this is by no means the first time that such generous peace offers were made by Beijing. During the period of political moderation in the mid-1950s, peace overtures made by Premier Zhou Enlai were essentially the same in substance. Nevertheless, Zhou's offers were reversed many times during the radical campaigns of the Great Leap Forward in the late 1950s and the Cultural Revolution of the 1960s. During the violent Quemoy Crisis of 1958, more than half a million artillery shells fell on the tiny offshore island. The bitter experience of Tibet's "peaceful liberation" is another chilling lesson of which the people on Taiwan often remind themselves. Beijing's peace offer to Taiwan today, in fact, bears a great similarity to the generous offer that the Tibetans had accepted in good faith in 1951. However, the PLA invaded Tibet in 1959, and tore up the legally guaranteed "peaceful liberation" and "regional autonomy" through a bloodbath of military suppression.[28]

Since the conclusion of the Beijing-London Agreement on the future of

Hong Kong in September 1984, the PRC has been trying very hard to convince Taiwan of the great attraction of the "Hong Kong model." Under the principle of "one nation, two systems," articulated by Deng Xiaoping himself, Beijing pledged to allow Hong Kong, as a "Special Administrative Region" of China, to maintain a separate and autonomous political and economic system for fifty years after the restoration of Hong Kong's sovereignty to China in 1997. Stepping up its appeal for "peaceful unification" to Taiwan, Beijing promises to give the island "even better terms."[29] However, the campaigns have so far achieved little positive response from the Nationalist Government and the people on the island.

Even amidst the most conciliatory moods of the 1970s and 1980s Beijing continued to refuse to renounce the possible use of force against Taiwan. For example, Deng Xiaoping declared publicly on numerous occasions: "We cannot commit ourselves to use no other than peaceful means to achieve the reunification of the motherland. We cannot tie our hands on this matter."[30] A blunt statement made by Wu Xiuquan, Deputy Chief-of-Staff of the PLA General Staff, in a talk with Japanese military experts was even more revealing. "A seizure of Taiwan by means of force would be carried out if two conditions were met—suitable international circumstances and military preparations to a point where PLA forces would be able to secure command of the air and sea in the Taiwan Strait in order to stage an amphibious assault."[31] In a widely publicized interview given by Party General Secretary Hu Yaobang on 25 May 1985, the leader elaborated at length on the same strategy of unification. While admitting openly that Peking lacked sufficient military capabilities to take Taiwan at the present time, Hu stressed that when China's military modernization bore fruit in the future, means of "coercive nature" could be employed.[32]

Evidence seems to be clear that Beijing's unification campaigns in recent years have yielded little positive response from Taiwan. The island's leadership as well as the general public remain highly skeptical of the sincerity of the PRC's basic motives and strategy. Ironically, the urgency and magnitude of the peace campaigns by Beijing may have served only to further heighten Taiwan's fear of the growing urgency of the aging PRC leadership to take control of Taiwan.

The Sino-Soviet Conflict and Taiwan

The official policy of the Soviet Union with regard to the Taiwan issue has always been support for the PRC's "unification policy" and "one China" position.[33] Evidence shows, however, that Moscow has done so only half-heartedly and rhetorically. In fact, the Soviet Union has never actively promoted or supported by concrete deeds the PRC's reunification attempts. This seems to have been particularly true since the eruption of the Sino-Soviet dispute in the late 1950s.

A dramatic case in point may be found in the self-serving Soviet rhetorical backing for the PRC's militant action for unification during the 1958 Taiwan Strait crisis. Not only did the Soviet Union deliberately withhold its material aid to China's war efforts, but its declaratory support came only after Beijing had made the crucial decision, under U.S. pressure, to stop escalating the armed confrontation.[34] Furthermore, ever since 1960, when the Sino-Soviet dispute turned into open conflict, and especially after the onset of the Cultural Revolution in 1966, evidence has demonstrated that the Soviet Union did not really perceive an incorporation of Taiwan by the PRC to be in its own strategic interest. It has been clear all along to Soviet strategists that an independent and strong Taiwan helps to reduce the PRC's political and military pressure on the Soviet Union. China's behavioral pattern during the border clashes with the Soviet forces in the spring of 1969 demonstrated without any doubt that Beijing was deeply concerned over the possibility of a two-front conflict. The rumors of contacts between Taiwan and Soviet military leaders in Tokyo in the spring and a commando raid conducted by Taiwan on the PRC naval base at Dinghaiwan, Fujian in July of the same year were reported to have gravely aggravated the PRC's anxieties. Any liaisons between the Nationalists and the Russians would naturally have a serious effect of constraining the PRC's military options in dealing with the Soviet Union.

Active Soviet interests in Taiwan have been revealed on many different occasions as well. In October 1968, Soviet "journalist" Victor Louis (Vitali Yevgenevitch), a recognized semi-official representative of the Soviet government and suspected KGB officer, visited Taiwan.[35] He reportedly met with the then Defense Minister, Chiang Ching-kuo, who is now the ROC President. He also extended an "unofficial" invitation for Taiwan's journalists to visit the Soviet Union. The exchange was followed by a trip to Moscow in May 1969 by Ku Yu-hsiu, former ROC Minister of Education. Then, in 1973, there were unconfirmed reports that Louis made a return visit to the island. It was also rumored that Moscow requested access for Soviet merchant ships to supplies and maintenance in the Pescadores. Of equal interest is that, since 1973, Soviet warships have been making frequent trips into the Taiwan Strait and have circumnavigated the island. In February 1984, the ROC government publicly acknowledged that Soviet reconnaissance aircraft had repeatedly ventured into Taiwan's air defense identification zone.[36]

The Soviet press has also engaged in what could be termed as the signaling of an interest in Taiwan. Between 1965 and 1970, various implicit indications of Soviet recognition of the ROC appeared in the national press of the Soviet Union. In 1965, the magazine *For the People of the World* published a conspicuous picture of the Nationalist flag, an act which the PRC considered a sinister demonstration of Soviet flirtation with the Nationalists. In 1966, Taiwan was referred to as a "state" in the Soviet magazine *Abroad* on several occasions, which were followed by a similar use of terminology by the official TASS news agency in 1967, calling Taiwan a "country." Furthermore, in March 1972, *New Times* presented a favorable news article on Chiang Kai-shek's nomination for a fifth term as President of the ROC, which the PRC interpreted as an outright manifestation of "support of a two-China policy."[37]

Aside from Soviet press reports, the Soviet Union even hinted in the 1960s that it might support the dual membership of both the PRC and the ROC in the United Nations. During the 1967 session of the UN General Assembly, for example, the Soviet representative raised first the question of admitting the PRC into the UN and then talked about the admission of the two German states, which implied a commonality between the Chinese and German situations. It should also be noted that ROC delegations were invited to international conferences in the Soviet bloc on a number of occasions in the second half of the 1960s. Most notable was the May 1969 World Inter-Governmental Conference on Tourism held in Sofia, Bulgaria.[38]

Beyond the overt signalings of a Soviet interest in Taiwan, Moscow's efforts to obtain and analyze information about Taiwan have expanded significantly in recent years. Major Soviet research organizations, such as the Institute of the Far East and the Institute of World Economy and International Relations, have extended invitations to many Taiwan specialists from America and Japan to visit the Soviet Union. Extensive seminars were organized with these foreign experts to discuss a wide range of Taiwan's domestic and external developments. Selected Soviet libraries have also built up impressive collections of publications and documents on Taiwan. In recent years, Soviet agents are always present at professional conferences and U.S. Congressional hearings dealing with major developments in Taiwan and the problem of China's unification.

It should be further noted that in the past several years the Soviet bloc's economic relationship with Taiwan has been significantly upgraded. Since 1979, East European members of the Council for Mutual Economic Assistance (CMEA) have engaged in direct-trading relations with Taiwan, instead of going through intermediaries in Singapore and Hong Kong as was done previously. Of particular interest in the area of economic connections are the intermittent rumors implying that in the early 1970s the Soviet Union contributed funds, via Switzerland, for the construction of a modern shipyard at Kaohsiung.

Soviet designs and interests in Taiwan may well go beyond the short-term attempts to ensure Taiwan's separation and continued hostility towards the PRC. Indeed, it is conceivable that if Sino-Soviet relations fail to improve, Soviet interests in Taiwan may constitute a significant component in the Soviet grand strategy of the encirclement of China. The strategic and geopolitical value of Taiwan is clearly of particular interest to the Soviet Union. Taiwan is situated at the approximate mid point between the major Soviet naval base of Vladivostok in the Far East and the new Soviet anchorage at Cam Ranh Bay in Vietnam. Taiwan is also centrally located between the East and South China Seas, and is just 100 miles off the PRC coast. Soviet military access to Taiwan would greatly facilitate communication between the two most important Soviet naval bases in the western rim of the Pacific, thus strengthening its force projection to the Indian Ocean and along the full length of the international shipping lanes between the Middle East and the Western Pacific region.[39]

Strategically, a Soviet relationship with Taiwan would practically finalize a containment structure around the PRC. The rim of this encirclement already extends from Soviet Siberia and Outer Mongolia in the north through Afghanistan and India in the west, to Vietnam and Kampuchea in the south (see map, Figure 10.1). Operating out of Taiwan, Soviet naval and air forces can easily institute a formidable blockade of the PRC, prevent the PRC's East China Sea and South China Sea Fleets from joint operation and mutual reenforcement, and make China's entire newly-developed off-shore oil fields extremely vulnerable. There is no question that Soviet entry into Taiwan and the Pescadores would greatly enhance Moscow's ability to coerce Beijing, if and when the Sino-Soviet conflict deteriorates in the future.

From Taiwan's perspective, to foster a political liaison of some sort with the Soviet Union in the context of the Sino-Soviet conflict carries the strategic benefits of security protection against PRC threat. The leadership, however, is keenly aware of the high costs and risks involved in pursuing such a policy. In view of Taiwan's existing arms dependency and profitable economic ties with the West, especially the U.S., there is little reason why Taiwan would choose to actively seek a "Russian connection" to alienate Washington. Nevertheless, if and when Taiwan's leadership perceives that continued U.S. concessions to the PRC have gone far enough to endanger the minimum requirements for the security of the

THE SOVIET ENCIRCLEMENT OF CHINA

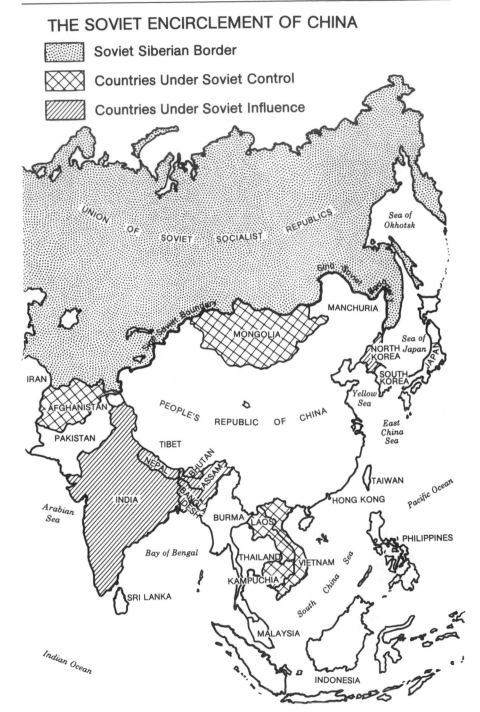

Soviet Siberian Border

Countries Under Soviet Control

Countries Under Soviet Influence

island and that Taiwan's ability to cope with Beijing's mounting pressure for unification all on its own is no longer tenable, the logic of strategic calculus is bound to dictate Taiwan's leadership to reorient its political and security alignments for the compelling reason of national survival.

When people on Taiwan are convinced that they are politically deserted by the U.S. and militarily threatened by the PRC, a loose security relationship with the Soviet Union may emerge as the only viable option left open to them. Taiwan could, for example, expand and upgrade its current trade and other contacts with various CMEA nations to include the Soviet Union itself. It will not be difficult for Taiwan to respond to Soviet strategic interests favorably by cultivating a level of "friendly cooperation" comparable to that of Soviet-Indian interactions. Like India, Taiwan can continue to keep, simultaneously, its extensive economic ties with the West. Such a connection with the Soviets would be judged to be more tolerable and manageable than a complete takeover and subjugation by Beijing. If and when Taiwan takes up the option of playing the "Russia card," one can be sure, such a move will not be Taiwan's early choice by preference, but rather its last resort by necessity.

Taiwan: An Emerging Target of Opportunity?

From the Cold War of the 1950s through the "hot peace" of the 1980's, Taiwan has played a strangely conspicuous and critical role in the triangular game of strategic calculus. Despite all the frustrating experiences, which have seriously complicated its security arrangements since the Shanghai Communique of 1972, Taiwan today still considers the U.S., on balance, to be the most indispensable ally for its security and prosperity. To Taiwan, there is no other arms supplier and trade partner more important than the U.S.

However, Taiwan is also deeply troubled by Washington's susceptibility to PRC pressure. Both the leadership and people on Taiwan have been trying to believe that Washington wishes to continue to maintain its long-standing political and moral commitments to the 16 million people on Taiwan, but events of the past decade have demonstrated clearly that Washington, for its own security interests, is strongly driven by a desire to deepen strategic relations with the PRC in order to constrain Soviet expansionism. Being fully aware of Washington's dilemma, the PRC leadership is obviously convinced that it can skillfully exploit it to its own advantage. Indeed, the development of major events—such as President Nixon's visit to the PRC in February 1972, the normalization of Sino-

American relations in January 1979, and the issuance of the August 1982 Joint Communique with China—illustrates well Beijing's remarkable success in this regard. Over the years, the U.S. has acquiesced, step by step, to the PRC's mounting demands to downgrade formal ties with Taiwan and disengage itself politically from the island. The weakness of Washington to concede under pressure in recent years seems to have encouraged Beijing to believe that they can, with skills and patience, isolate Taiwan gradually first, and then integrate it under Peking's control without provoking strong U.S. reactions and interventions. In this respect, 1972 marked the beginning of the making of a security vacuum in and around Taiwan.

Alarmed by the threatening deterioration of its security position, Taiwan has been trying desperately in recent years to buttress its amputated security system. It has explored, with some success, such measures as developing its own defense industry and technology, broadening the sources of arms supplies, and expanding substantive political and economic ties with all nations which are willing to develop friendly contacts. Taiwan was reported to have been actively engaged in the research and development of advanced technology and weapons applicable to the chemical, biological and nuclear warfare in order to create its own independent security deterrence. Two years ago, Taiwan succeeded in placing an order for two modern attack submarines from Holland. Press reports also suggest that Taiwan has been in touch with Israel and South Africa for advanced aircraft and missiles.[40] Since 1979 Taiwan has established direct trade contacts with the Communist countries of Eastern Europe. However, it remains to be seen how meaningful these measures would be in coping with the disproportionately greater power of the PRC without the active and reliable support of allies like the U.S. or the Soviet Union powerful enough to counterbalance the enormous weight of the PRC.

Both the logic of strategic reasoning as well as the evidence of political trends are pointing to a dangerous possibility that if Beijing continues to step up its unification campaigns and that if U.S. commitments to the island's security continues to erode, Taiwan is likely to emerge as an attractive *"target of opportunity"* uniquely tailored to Soviet exploitation. For the Soviet Union, the geo-strategic values of Taiwan are just too great and timely to overlook. After having pursued for so many years a strategy of encirclement and containment around the PRC and the projection of its power to the Western Pacific and the Indian Ocean, there is no doubt that Moscow can detect a good target of opportunity when it emerges. For Taiwan, when its very survival is at stake, adjusting the security alignment to survive must by necessity override all other considerations.

It is unfortunate that the U.S. policy approach to the Taiwan issue is often based on a mistaken assumption: so long as Beijing insists that Taiwan is the principal obstacle to the deepening of U.S.-PRC relations, no constructive relations with the PRC can be achieved without making concessions on U.S. security and political commitments to Taiwan. This need not be the case. It should be emphasized that the PRC has a clear and urgent economic and security interest in maintaining a viable relationship with the U.S. Beijing needs support from the West not only to counterbalance Soviet pressure but also to help fulfill its ambitious modernization goals. Above all, both Washington and Beijing now share a common strategic interest in preventing further expansion of Soviet influence anywhere in the Asia-Pacific region, especially the area in and around Taiwan. It would be extremely ironic that if the triangular "card game," so masterfully devised and played out by both Beijing and Washington, would result in, inadvertantly, forcing the desperate Taiwan "pawn"—by default or miscalculation—into the Soviet orbit. Should this be allowed to happen, it would clearly be a tragic loss to both the PRC and the U.S. in the balancing game of the triangular competition.[41]

Notes

1. For the historical background of the emergence of the Taiwan issue, see Ralph N. Clough, *Island China* (Cambridge, MA: Harvard University Press, 1978); and Hungdah Chiu, ed., *China and the Taiwan Issue* (New York: Praegor, 1979).
2. Portions of the analysis contained in this paper are drawn from the author's previous works, "The Changing Power Configuration and Its Implications for Taiwan," a paper prepared for the Conference on Changing International Relations in Asia, St. John's University, 26-27 October 1984; and "The Security of Taiwan: An Evaluation of the Carter Approach." In Senate Foreign Relations Committee & Congressional Research Service, *Taiwan: One Year After U.S.-China Normalization* (Washington, D.C.: U.S. Government Printing Office, 1980), pp. 129-135.
3. Harry S. Truman, *Years of Trial and Hope*, II (Garden City, NY: Doubleday, 1956), p. 339.
4. *American Foreign Policy, 1950-1955: Basic Documents*, II (Washington, D.C.: U.S. Government Printing Office, 1957), p. 2467.
5. *U.S. Statutes at Large*, LXLX (Washington, D.C.: U.S. Government Printing Office, 1955), p. 7. For the details of the U.S.-ROC alliance and defense

cooperation, see the author's work, "Security and Defense Capabilities," in James C. Hsiung, ed., *The Taiwan Experience, 1950-1980* (New York: Preager, 1981), pp. 419-494.

6. *China: U.S. Policy Since 1945* (Washington, D.C.: Congressional Quarterly, 1980), p. 116.
7. *Ibid.*, p. 107. For a detailed analysis of the Quemoy Crisis, see J. H. Kalicki, *The Pattern of Sino-American Crises: Political Military Interactions in the 1950s* (London: Cambridge University Press, 1975).
8. See the author's work cited in note 5 above.
9. For detailed studies of the normalization process with the PRC and collections of relevant official documents quoted in this discussion, see Robert L. Downen, *The Taiwan Pawn in the China Game* (Washington, D.C.: Center for Strategic and International Studies, 1979); and *Normalizing Relations with the People's Republic of China* (Occasional Papers/Reprints Series in Contemporary Asian Studies, School of Law, University of Maryland), no. 2 (1978).
10. Richard M. Nixon, *The Real War* (New York: Warner Books, 1980), pp. 138-140. In his State of the World Address on 9 February 1972, President Nixon declared for example, "Our new dialogue with the PRC would not be at the expense of friends. Nevertheless we recognize that this process cannot help but be painful for our old friend on Taiwan, the Republic of China . . . With the ROC we shall maintain our friendship, our diplomatic ties and our defense commitment." *The New York Times*, 10 February 1972.
11. For more details of the Carter Administration's foreign policy problems and its playing of the "China Card," see sources cited in note 9 above. Also, Robert L. Downen, *The Tattered China Card* (Washington, D.C.: Council for Social & Economic Studies, 1984).
12. All the texts of the documents discussed in this section may be found in sources cited in notes 5 and 9 above.
13. *Beyond Normalization: Report of the UNA-USA National Policy Panel to Study U.S.-China Relations* (New York: United Nations Association of the USA, 1979), p. 29; "Chinese Foreign Ministry Spokesman's Statement on China-U.S. Joint Communique," *Beijing Review* (23 August 1982), p. 16.
14. For more elaboration, see the author's work cited in note 2 above.
15. For a detailed study of the legislative politics of the TRA and related document, see Lester L. Wolff and David L. Simon, eds., *Legislative History of the Taiwan Relations Act* (Jamaica, NY: American Association for Chinese Studies, 1982). Also Michael S. Frost, *Taiwan's Security and United States Policy: Executive and Congressional Strategies in 1978-79* (Occasional Papers/Reprints Series in Contemporary Asian Studies, School of Law, University of Maryland), no. 4 (1982).
16. *Ibid.*, p.288 of the first work cited.
17. Ronald Reagan "Decency for Taiwan," *The New York Times*, 28 January 1979.
18. *Reagan Campaign Press Release*, 25 August 1980; and "Excerpts from

Reagan's Statement on Ties to China and Taiwan," *The New York Times,* 26 August 1980.

19. For the full texts and related documents, see Wolff and Simon, *op. cit.,* pp. 312-330.

20. *Ibid.;* also *New York Times,* 18 August 1982; "China Issues New Warning to U.S.," *Providence Journal,* 31 March 1982.

21. For a more detailed analysis of Taiwan's military capabilities, see Edwin K. Snyder, et al., *The Taiwan Relations Act and the Defense of the Republic of China* (Berkeley, CA: Institute of International Studies, University of California, 1980). Also, the author's work cited in note 5 above.

22. *Ibid.*

23. See, for example, "The Arming of Red China," *Current Analysis,* II: 9 (November 1980); Harry Harding, "China Arms Sales Could Brew New Troubles for U.S.," *Los Angeles Times,* 3 July 1981; "Should We Arm the Chinese?" *Chicago Tribune,* 4 April 1981; "Rebuilding China's Army," *U.S. News and World Report,* 9 November 1981.

24. "U.S. and China Warm Relations," *U.S. News and World Report,* 10 October 1983. Also, *The New York Times,* 16 October 1981; 30 September, 23 December 1983; and 20 March, 18 October 1984.

25. *The New York Times,* 12-15 January 1985.

26. See, for example, *The New York Times,* 3 and 15 January, 7 April, 1 and 10 October, 16 December 1985; 13 and 15 January 1986. Also, William T. Tow, "Arms Sales to China," in Gerald Segal and William T. Tow, eds., *Chinese Defence Policy* (Urbana, IL: University of Illinois Press, 1984), pp. 149-166.

27. For the texts, see *Beijing Review,* no. 1 (5 January 1979), pp. 16-17; and *Renmin Ribao* [The People's Daily, Peking], 1 October 1979.

28. Important documents related to Peking's "United front" strategy may be found in the author's work cited in note 5 above.

29. See, for instance, "Hu Yaobang Fangwenji" [An Interview with Hu Yaobang by Lu Keng], *Baixing* [Hong Kong], no. 87 (1 June 1985), pp. 3-16.

30. *Beijing Review,* no. 2 (12 January 1978), p. 17.

31. *Korean Herald,* 30 April 1978, cited in Karl-Gottfried Kindermann, "Washington Between Beijing and Taipei: The Restructured Triangle, 1978-1980," *Asian Survey* (May 1980), p. 467.

32. See note 29 above.

33. See, for example, V. Baryshnikov, "The Soviet Stands on the Taiwan Issue," *Far Eastern Affairs* [Moscow], no. 4 (1982), pp. 45-54.

34. Kalicki, *op. cit.* (note 7 above).

35. The developments of the events discussed in this section are largely based on John W. Garver, "Taiwan's Russian Option," *Asian Survey,* XVIII: 7 (July 1978); John F. Copper, "Taiwan's Options," *Asian Affairs,* VI: 5 (May-June 1979), pp. 282-294; and Frederic A. Moritz, "Soviet Eyeing of Taiwan Worries China," *The Christian Science Monitor* 21 July 1978.

36. *The Free China Journal* [Taipei], 2 February 1984, p. 2.

37. See note 35 above.

38. *Ibid.*

39. For an excellent collection of essays analyzing Soviet strategy in the Western Pacific, see Donald S. Zagoria, ed., *Soviet Policy in East Asia* (New Haven, CT: Yale University Press, 1982).

40. See, for example, "Taiwan zhizhao di wuqi" [Arms Produced in Taiwan], *Zhongbao* (Centre Daily, New York), 25-26 June 1985.

41. An elaboration of this argument may be found in the author's essay, "Taiwan as Challenge to Reagan-Zhao Summitry," *The Washington Times,* 12 January 1984.

11

Leadership and Policy-Making

JANE SHAPIRO ZACEK

The thirteen years between 1969 and 1982 witnessed vast changes in the relationships among the United States, the Soviet Union, and the People's Republic of China (PRC). Within that period, each country experienced unprecedented political changes at the apex of power. An American President resigned from office; the Soviet leader who served longer than any other save Josef Stalin died; and the architect of the Chinese Communist revolution, who had remained in power for almost thirty years, also died. Some leaders within these countries had staked a substantial portion of their foreign policy strategy on improved relations with one or the other (or both) countries, while others sought to bolster their reputations domestically by promoting a less conciliatory line abroad. In retrospect, policies evolved rather consistently during the period under review, although it is clear that individuals with a substantial impact on policy-making could hasten or retard the policy process.

This paper seeks to ascertain the impact of identified leaders on policy adoption and implementation. Would policies have been substantially different had other leaders been in power? Can policy changes be linked directly to leadership changes at the highest levels? Are linkages substantially different in democratic and authoritarian political systems? Because of both space limitations and lack of hard data availability, the policy formation process, which includes internal debates and disagreements, has not been examined. In using the term "leadership," we do not mean to imply that policymakers were united in their determination of which policy options to select. It is likely that this was rarely, if ever, the case. Rather, we are interested in reviewing those policies that were adopted and, in so doing, trying to determine what the political leadership sought to achieve.

U.S. Policies: The First Phase

Because of the unusually large turnover in chief executives (four served within the time period under review), U.S. policy toward the USSR and the PRC can be related rather closely to particular presidential administrations. Despite the efforts of Presidents, Secretaries of State, and Assistants to the President for National Security Affairs to carefully delineate the substantial and overarching policy differences between their administration and the one that preceded it, the evidence demonstrates that most policy shifts took shape within administrations rather than between them. While one administration may have adopted a more conciliatory line than another, the trends were usually quite clear before the power transition occurred. But there are also identifiable instances in which particular leaders undertook bold policy initiatives that unmistakably hastened or retarded a trend. This is particularly evident with respect to U.S. relations with China.

The possibility of building a new relationship with China emerged out of the deterioration of relations between that country and the Soviet Union, the need to enlist Chinese support to help end U.S. involvement "honorably" in Vietnam, and a recognition that, as China emerged from the ravages of the Cultural Revolution, it sought to establish a firm position for itself in the international arena through exchange of diplomatic relations. The Nixon administration, which came into office in January 1969, was determined to introduce and implement major foreign policy initiatives. With some quiet encouragement from China in late 1968, the newly elected President and his Assistant for National Security Affairs, Henry L. Kissinger, sought to broaden the base of unofficial contacts with Beijing. Sporadic contact had been made during the 1960s within diplomatic circles in Warsaw; they were soon to be expanded by utilizing Romanian and Pakistani officials as intermediaries. During his visit to both Pakistan and Romania in August 1969, Nixon reportedly enlisted agreement from both Pakistani President Aya Khan and Romanian President (and General Secretary of the Romanian Communist Party) Nicolae Ceausescu for this role. The Chinese initially were reluctant to accept the latter's role, perhaps fearing Soviet infiltration.[1] Pakistan, which both China and the U.S. had supported in various disagreements with India, proved to be a more viable intermediary, although contacts and responses tended to occur slowly.

Once the opening through Pakistan began to develop, the Warsaw talks between ambassadors became more substantial and were based upon more careful preparations.[2] In January 1970, the U.S. proposed through Ambassador Walter Stoessel that more direct contacts be made in Washington or Beijing to discuss issues of substance between the two states at a higher level. Events moved swiftly. In April, the U.S. eased travel restrictions to the PRC and approved the sale of parts for nonstrategic goods. In July, the Chinese released Bishop James Walsh, who was serving a twenty-year sentence (due to end in 1980) for anti-Chinese activities. Nixon sought to alert the Chinese through various channels of contact of his interest in rapprochement. That December, Mao Zedong told Edgar Snow that he would be happy to receive Nixon in China, and in January, Zhou Enlai proposed (through Romania) that Nixon visit China.[3] Arrangements for Kissinger's secret visit in July 1971, were prepared primarily through Pakistan, and it was while formally visiting that country that the venture to Beijing was undertaken. On 15 July, Nixon publicly announced that he had been invited to visit China and would accept. The visit was planned for February 1972. Preparations for the joint communique that would result from the historic trip were conducted by Kissinger and a National Security Council/State Department team in October, at the very time that China was voted membership in the United Nations and Taiwan was excluded.

Nixon's visit resulted in the signing of the Shanghai Communique, which served as a guide for relations between the two states during the 1970s. It provided the impetus for substantial and rapid expansion of trade, economic, and cultural exchanges, while leaving diplomatic exchanges to be worked out in the future. Both sides understood that the Taiwan issue, which needed to be settled before diplomatic relations could be established, would be troublesome and would take time to resolve. China insisted that diplomatic relations could not be achieved until the U.S. recognized Beijing as the sole legitimate government of China, agreed that Taiwan was part of China, ended diplomatic relations with Taiwan, abrogated the 1954 Mutual Defense Treaty with that country, and withdrew all U.S. forces from the island.[4]

Trade and various economic and cultural exchanges expanded rapidly after Nixon's visit. China was put into a less restrictive category than the U.S.S.R. and the East European countries regarding purchase of U.S. goods, and the possibility of offering most favored nation (MFN) status with regard to import duties and restrictions was considered seriously by both the White House and the Congress. As the Vietnam war began to wind down, relations with China improved further.

In February 1973, during a visit to Beijing, Kissinger proposed to Zhou that liaison offices be established in each other's capital and that diplomatic privileges and immunities be conferred upon those offices and staffs. The Chinese leader accepted. After Nixon's visit, the two countries had maintained communications primarily through their respective embassies in Paris and through the Chinese mission to the U.N. in New York. Establishment of liaison offices turned out to be the high point in cooperative relations between the two states for several years; further substantive negotiations on issues of mutual interest stalled.[5] Watergate and the growing influence of the Gang of Four contributed substantially to this turn of events.

Nixon's increasing preoccupation with Watergate and its impact on his ability to function effectively as chief executive, Mao's frail health, and, more importantly, Zhou's ill health and apparent political decline, contributed in a major way to the stagnation. For, just as Nixon had played a critical role in seeking to improve relations, so had Zhou, who understood well the advantages of a rapprochement with the U.S. Indeed, as discussed below, Zhou had faced earlier opposition to the policy of an opening to the U.S., which at least partially accounts for the sporadic communications in Warsaw and the intervals of no contact during 1969 and 1970. Gerald R. Ford's accession to the presidency in August, 1974, did not have a substantial impact on U.S.-Chinese relations, and his visit to China in December 1975, produced no tangible results. While both countries affirmed the principles enunciated in the Shanghai Communique, there was no movement on the Taiwan issue. It remained for successor policy makers to promote improved relations after 1974.

As has become commonplace knowledge, the U.S. initially sought to use the new relationship with China to encourage greater cooperation from the Soviet Union. U.S.-Chinese and U.S.-Chinese-Japanese collaboration in the Far East coupled with NATO revitalization in the West was a potential security nightmare for the Soviets, one that they would seek assiduously to avoid. Indeed, the initial Soviet reaction to the announcement of Nixon's planned visit to China was to invite the President to a Moscow Summit, which had been discussed early in the Nixon administration but had not been finalized. Moscow had not been able to settle on a precise date. Nixon had signalled the Soviets that he was seriously interested in a summit conference in the fall of 1970, but the Soviets had delayed in their response. When the invitation finally came, Nixon agreed to go to the

Soviet capital in May 1972, at what was hoped would be the conclusion of the Strategic Arms Limitation Talks (SALT) negotiations, which had dragged on for several years.

Announcement of the U.S.-Chinese breakthrough was the precipitating event for setting a Moscow summit date, but it also seems clear that the Soviet leadership recognized the positive consequences of a meeting of heads of state in which issues of trade and economic cooperation as well as arms control would be the main items for discussion and possible agreement. Kissinger traveled to Moscow several weeks before the summit was scheduled to "try to remove Vietnam as an obstacle"[6] in summit negotiations, for the U.S. was taking a harder line in Vietnam to try to get the Paris talks moving toward a final settlement. Despite American mining of the Haiphong harbor to disrupt supply routes, and heavy bombing of both Haiphong and Hanoi, the Soviets indicated their continued interest in meeting with Nixon. The latter, according to Kissinger, was worried that the summit might be aborted as it was in 1960, after the Soviets shot down an American U-2 reconnaissance plane. Nevertheless, he agreed to press the bombing offensive on Hanoi in an effort to bring the war to an end at last.

The Soviets apparently chose not to cancel the summit, for clearly they saw that there was more to gain than the embarrassment they were obliged to suffer as a result of the U.S. offensive. They even agreed to try to pressure North Vietnam (DRV) into serious negotiations in Paris, despite the fact that several Soviet ships were damaged and a number of naval personnel killed as a result of the mining operations.

What did the U.S. hope to achieve from the summit? One of the primary foreign policy objectives of Nixon's first term (which continued into the second as well) was to end American involvement in Vietnam and to enlist Soviet support in doing so. To this end, the administration sought to establish the policy of linkage as a guiding principle in U.S.-Soviet relations. If the Soviets wanted better and more cooperative relations with the U.S., they would need to act more responsibly in international affairs, especially with regard to Vietnam and the Middle East. As Kissinger has described it, he and the President set forth three overriding principles for dealing with the Soviets: strict reciprocity, mutual restraint in international affairs, and coherence of policy worldwide rather than dealing with separate issues in a piecemeal fashion.[7] The SALT Treaty, which was concluded in time for signing at the summit, would permit the U.S. to catch up with what had been a continual Soviet nuclear buildup for more than a decade. Expanded economic and trade relations would facilitate sale of goods to the Soviet Union by American companies as well as investment in

Soviet economic development. Finally, by engaging the Soviets in a continuing relationship, it was anticipated that they would behave in a more responsible and cooperative manner. U.S. policy sought to provide incentives for Soviet restraint and penalties for adventurism. How well it succeeded is still a matter of controversy.

Results of the May summit included the signing of the SALT accords, the Anti-Ballistic Missile Treaty, and agreements on joint cooperation on the environment, medicine, technology, and space. A joint commission was created to work out details of a comprehensive trade agreement, and was scheduled to meet in July. The leaders agreed to begin working toward a SALT II Treaty that would be more encompassing, and to hold annual summits, the next of which would take place in the United States in 1973.

General Secretary of the Communist Party of the Soviet Union Central Committee (CPSU CC) and Chairman of the Presidium of the Supreme Soviet, Leonid Brezhnev, arrived in the U.S. for his first (and only) visit in mid-June 1973. The Agreement on the Prevention of Nuclear War, which included the renunciation by each signatory of the use of nuclear weapons against the other as well as a determination to prevent the use of nuclear weapons by a third party, was signed, as was the commitment to undertake SALT II negotiations in earnest. Discussion on SALT II had begun soon after the 1972 Summit, but the Soviets had not indicated much interest in moving the talks along. Nixon had not focused on it nor encouraged serious negotiations. The Soviets took several opportunities at the summit to warn their hosts of Chinese treachery and belligerence. While they had "no objections" to the U.S. and the PRC improving their state to state relations with one another, they were clearly very concerned about any kind of military arrangement that might be concluded between the two. The U.S., for its part, reiterated the position that it could not "remain indifferent" in the event of a Soviet attack on China.[8]

Indeed, the Soviets had expressed concern from the time they learned in 1971 that vast changes in U.S.-Chinese relations were likely to be forthcoming. They had tried unsuccessfully to enlist U.S. support for the idea of "controlling" the accidental launching of nuclear weapons by other nuclear powers (namely China), and there had been numerous reports of a serious Soviet interest in preempting Chinese nuclear weapons' development.[9] The Chinese, for their part, expressed continual concern that the U.S. and the Soviets would attempt to establish themselves as the arbiters of all international conflicts, and settlements would be reached at Chinese expense. After each U.S.-Soviet summit, the U.S. took special care to assure the Chinese that no agreements designed to be directly detrimental to China had been concluded. (The U.S. did not take similar precautions with regard to the Soviets.)

The third Nixon-Brezhnev summit, held in Moscow in June, 1974, achieved nothing of substance. Congress made its determination clear that it would not give the President any negotiating leeway in the event that he might seek to bolster his position at home by concluding significant agreements with the Soviets. For their part, the Soviets well understood that Nixon's political power had eroded, impeachment hearings were imminent, and the President was not in a position to make any long-term commitments. Within two months, Nixon had resigned and his successor, with very limited foreign policy experience, sought to move the SALT negotiations forward, but does not appear to have looked to develop a personal working relationship with his Soviet counterpart, as Nixon had. Nor did he see the need for a continuous dialogue with the Soviets that would entail annual summit meetings. A cooling of relations that began during the Ford administration was to be accelerated in the Carter years. To be sure, this shift was shaped in no small measure by the Congressional role in U.S.-Soviet relations through the Jackson-Vanik and Stevenson amendments to the 1973 trade bill, which made the bill as finally passed into law unacceptable to the Soviets. Senator Henry Jackson persevered in linking the granting of MFN with a more liberal policy toward emigration of Soviet Jews. Senator Adlai Stevenson's limitation of a $300 million ceiling in loans to be provided by the Export/Import (Ex/Im) Bank indicated the extent to which the U.S. was willing to invest in Soviet economic development. The Soviet rejection of the trade legislation's terms unavoidably included rejection of MFN as well.

Soviet Policy During the Nixon-Ford Years

The Soviets had a number of objectives in seeking to improve relations with the U.S., perhaps most important of which were trade and economic investment. They were especially eager to open up and develop Siberian oil and gas resources both for domestic consumption and for sale abroad. They were also anxious to try to narrow the technological gap by buying from the West rather than devoting considerable internal resources on research and development. They also recognized that in order to effect these purchases, whether from the U.S. or Western Europe, they would need substantial Western credits. The signing of an arms limitation treaty that established Moscow as a military equal to the U.S. was of major importance, as was the reestablishment of MFN treatment (cancelled during the Korean War), and the acceptance of a continuing Soviet role in the Middle East. Soviet leaders were also interested in broadening exchanges in a variety of technical, scientific, and cultural areas. With the collapse of the trade treaty in 1974-75, the Soviets became less willing to cooperate in other areas, and renewed their interest in working more closely with Western Europe, as they had done in the initial stages of detente, before improved relations with the U.S. became the major priority. Negotiations on strategic arms limitations continued, as did those on the possibility of a reduction of conventional forces in Europe through continuing NATO and Warsaw Pact discussions in Vienna. The latter, Mutual and Balanced Force Reduction (MBFR) Talks, continued with sporadic progress through the 1970s. Brezhnev seems to have had considerable support within the Politbureau for the policy of improved relations with the U.S. Indeed, one of the few Politbureau members who reportedly was not in favor of the policy, Petr Shelest, was removed from that body in late April 1973, and from his position as Vice Chairman of the Council of Ministers soon thereafter.[10] Brezhnev's failure to establish better trade and credit relations with the U.S. undoubtedly had some impact on his own position of authority and probably contributed to the less conciliatory relationship that emerged between the Soviet leaders and Ford and with the Carter administration.

The Soviet search for better relations with the U.S. resulted from two significant developments of the 1960s. One was the more cooperative relationship that was constructed with the major West European states, especially France and the Federal Republic of Germany (FRG). With the emergence of Willy Brandt as FRG Chancellor in October, 1969, a new policy of reconciliation with the East European states and with the Soviet Union was enunciated. Recognition of the postwar territorial changes, of the boundary between Poland and East Germany as well as the reality of "two German states within one German nation,"[11] were cardinal features of that policy, which came to be known as Ostpolitik. Moscow pressed for an all-European security conference to recognize the postwar boundaries. Britain, France, and the U.S. insisted upon a satisfactory agreement on Western access to Berlin before either the FRG treaties with the Soviet Union and Poland were ratified or an all-European conference was called. After months of negotiation, the Quadripartite Agreement on Berlin was signed. Improved relations with the U.S. were a natural extension of Soviet-West European relations, particularly in light of U.S. reluctance to support the idea of the all-European conference. The Soviets also recognized the advantages that would accrue to greater trade and economic cooperation with the U.S.

The second and immediate impetus for working to improve relations with the U.S. was that country's relationship with the PRC. A cooperative relationship with the U.S. would hopefully give the latter a stake in at least remaining neutral in any Soviet confrontation with China. A situation in which the U.S. saw it as advantageous to assist China in some material way against the Soviets would be needlessly threatening.

Despite the failure of the trade bill and Moscow's inability to gain back MFN status, bilateral economic relations flourished. In 1972, trade between the two countries amounted to $638 million, while in 1973 it more than doubled that amount. By 1975, it had reached $2.08 billion.[12] The joint U.S.-Soviet Commercial Commission, established in May 1972, had called for a tripling of bilateral trade between 1972-75, and this goal was achieved. U.S. corporate investment in the Soviet Union was another matter, however, for the Ex/Im Bank was not authorized to consider applications for credits in support of U.S. exports to the Soviet Union.

Sino-Soviet Relations, 1969-75

Relations between the Soviet Union and China had deteriorated extensively during the decade of the 1960s. Differences between the two Communist-ruled states ranged from interpretations of Marxist-Leninist ideology to the personality of each country's leader. Ambassadors had been recalled, embassy staffs vastly reduced, and trade and economic relations virtually halted. Each side attacked the other vociferously and continuously in the open press. The Soviets sought unsuccessfully to expel the Chinese from the international communist movement, and Beijing and Moscow frequently found themselves on opposing sides of third world confrontations (e.g., India and Pakistan). Sporadic efforts to improve relations, at least on a state to state basis, after Khrushchev's ouster in October 1964, had failed. Relations reached an unprecedented low when, in March 1969, both states engaged in armed clashes along the Ussuri River border. Clashes in which both sides sustained losses continued during the spring and summer of 1969 and spread to the Central Asian border of Sin-Xiang and Kirgizia.[13]

Both sides sought to contain the clashes through establishment of bilateral discussions on various issues (the border, navigational rights, reestablishment of a workable relationship) and at various levels (ambassadorial, special commission, deputy Foreign Ministerial, etc.). Even a meeting between Soviet Chairman of the Council of Ministers Aleksei Kosygin and Zhou Enlai in Beijing in September 1969, upon the former's return journey to Moscow from Ho Chi-minh's funeral in Hanoi, failed to produce results. Reportedly, the Soviets had sought the meeting and learned only at the last minute that Zhou would receive Kosygin. Sporadic clashes continued; more ominously, the Soviets had expanded their military reinforcements along the border substantially. In the early 1960s, they had stationed about fifteen divisions; by 1969, the number had more than doubled, and had reached forty-four by the early 1970s. Although it is not known whether all divisions were up to strength, it is estimated that during the '60s (especially after the buildup began in late 1964), there were approximately 450,000 soldiers stationed in the military districts bordering China. By 1972, this figure had risen to approximately 750,000.[14] CIA estimates in the late 1970s were that the Soviets had been spending 12-15 percent of their defense budget to support the military effort on the Sino-Soviet border.[15] The tying down of so vast a number of men under arms in Asia contributed heavily to Soviet determination to improve relations with the West, as well as avoid a military confrontation with China.

Relations between the two states did not improve notably during the Nixon-Ford years. Indeed, as China sought to improve relations with Japan and the U.S., the Soviets felt increasingly threatened, although not sufficiently so to seek a measurable breakthrough in the border talks or to agree to withdraw a substantial number of troops from the border areas. In mid-June 1973, the Soviets offered to conclude a nonaggression treaty with the PRC, which would prohibit the use of force in settling boundary disputes and prohibit the threat of attack. In September, Brezhnev declared that the Soviet Union had no territorial designs on China and wanted to develop better relations based on the principles of peaceful coexistence.[16] The Chinese did not respond for more than a year. When they apparently were prepared to be more flexible, the Soviets had lost interest.[17] Concurrently, the Soviets continued to promote their proposal for a collective security arrangement in Asia. First enunciated at the June, 1969, meeting of international communist parties in Budapest (which the Chinese did not attend), the arrangement was described as anti-imperialist, but was interpreted by China as anti-Chinese, for it sought to build a friendly (to the Soviets) ring of states around China. Although reiterated on various occasions during the 1970s, the proposal never got off the ground. China denounced it vehemently, and most Asian states were opposed to any scheme that would facilitate Soviet hegemony in the region.

China's Policy Shifts, 1969-75

China emerged from the Cultural Revolution and diplomatic isolation confronted by increasing Soviet hostility at the very time that its level of military preparedness was especially low. The decision to begin to build a working relationship with the U.S. stemmed from the official determination that the Soviet Union had become the main enemy and posed a real military threat; that threat could be countered only by improving relations with Japan, the U.S., Eastern and Western Europe. As Zhou remarked at the X Chinese Communist Party (CPC) Congress in August, 1973, it was "necessary to compromise" with the U.S. in order to enhance Chinese security *vis-à-vis* the Soviet Union. It was not unlikely, the Chinese apparently believed, that the Soviets would undertake a surprise attack, for which China had to be prepared,[18] although militarily it was scarcely the Soviets' equal.

There had been some interest on both the Chinese and American parts in 1964 and 1965 to improve relations, but lack of support from the Secretary of State, Dean Rusk, and the focus of American attention on Vietnam to the exclusion of virtually everything else Asian after 1966 put a damper on whatever might have developed from the initial probings.[19] China then became preoccupied with the Cultural Revolution and seems to have recognized the utility of building a cooperative relationship with Japan and with the U.S. only toward the end of 1968.

Mao's then chosen successor, Minister of Defense and CPC Politbureau Standing Committee member Lin Biao, was reportedly opposed to building a better relationship with the U.S. while, as noted earlier, Zhou Enlai favored it. Mao's position is unclear, although he probably supported Lin's opposition, at least until the fall of 1970. Late that year, Lin appears to have been overruled, and secret communications between China and the U.S. took on a new life. In fact, during 1970, China continued to label the U.S. as its main opponent, while relations with the Soviet Union eased somewhat. New ambassadors were exchanged (the Soviet ambassador had left Beijing in 1967 and a new one had not been designated). 1971 was a critical year domestically and diplomatically for China. A major purge within the Politbureau occurred: nine out of 21 members were ousted or

demoted by October of that year.[20] Lin Biao's authority was badly eroded
and his desperate effort to rebuild support ended with his unexpected
death in September, 1971. Additionally, the radical elements of the
Cultural Revolution had lost much of their influence for the time being.
Zhou reemerged as the leading policy making figure and he strongly
favored improved relations with the U.S. for tactical purposes. Mao's role
in China's policy shift remains obscure. According to one report, Mao
became interested in the U.S. "in his seventies, read about it, and this
resulted in the invitation to Nixon to visit China."[21]

There is no evidence to suggest that the Chinese expected any U.S.
military support in the event of a Soviet attack or an escalation of the
border events. Rather, Beijing sought to at least neutralize the U.S. and
may have hoped to enlist American support to dissuade the Soviets from
undertaking a major military effort against China. China certainly hoped
to restrain American opposition on the U.N. representation issue. While
U.S. support could not be expected, at least avoidance of the need to get a
two-third's vote in the General Assembly because Chinese representation
was deemed an "important issue" might be replaced by a simple majority
vote. Despite U.S. opposition, the General Assembly voted in October,
1971, to seat the PRC and to exclude Taiwan.

What did China seek from a rapprochement with the U.S.? Perhaps,
most importantly, as noted earlier, it sought security. Further, the Chinese
must have recognized that they had a stake in the triangular relationship
with the U.S. and the USSR. Improved relations with the U.S. would
inevitably worry the Soviets and perhaps prompt them to act more
responsibly. Similarly, improved relations with the Soviets might render
the Americans more conciliatory on such issues as relations with Taiwan.
Prevention of superpower codominion internationally, from which China
would be excluded but would be affected by, was of continuing concern.
Further, China saw U.S. recognition of the PRC's position as a major
world power as important, although formal diplomatic recognition would
have to await resolution of the Taiwan issue. The Chinese also sought
economic advantages that would accrue from a better relationship: trade,
credits, perhaps joint exploitation of natural resources such as offshore oil
deposits in the Gulf of Bohai and the South China Sea.

The Chinese received more than they expected. On the eve of Nixon's
visit to Beijing, he announced that it was the U.S. intention to treat China
and the Soviet Union "evenhandedly" with respect to trade issues. While
U.S.-Soviet trade legislation floundered because of the emigration and
limits on credit issues, it did not do so with respect to China. Rather, while

the U.S. was anxious to improve trade conditions, the Chinese internal situation changed substantially; Zhou's illness coupled with the increasing influence of Mao's wife, Chiang Ching, and her associates (who later became known as the Gang of Four), radicalized Chinese policy *vis-à-vis* the U.S. and helped to account substantially for the increased stagnation in relations after 1973.

Meanwhile, there was sporadic improvement in relations with the Soviets. While both sides of the border for long stretches remained an armed camp, border negotiations continued. Verbal attacks did not abate, but physical damage was no longer inflicted on each other's embassy or on embassy personnel. Relations had plummeted the preceding year as Sino-Japanese rapprochement flourished. The emphasis on opposing Soviet hegemony in Asia and Chinese support for Japanese demands that the Kurile Islands be returned were hardly to Soviet liking. Japanese and U.S. rapprochement with China at Soviet expense was scarcely pleasing to Moscow. By 1975, relations had worsened again. Ideological polemics were stepped up. The Soviets augmented the number of troops along the border and increased naval patrol activities. Supplies that had been used during autumn maneuvers were retained by the border forces, including tactical missiles, tanks, and armored personnel carriers.[22] The Chinese failed to respond to Soviet overtures, and it was widely believed that relations between the two countries would not improve until the Chinese leadership changed.[23]

Still, China clearly was worried about increased Soviet influence in Southeast Asia after the U.S. completed its withdrawal.[24] In a conciliatory gesture to the Soviets late in the year, Beijing released the crew of three who had been captured when their helicopter had strayed into Chinese air space and was downed, almost two years earlier.[25]

During 1976, with Zhou's death in January, Deng Xiaoping's ouster in April (as a consequence of the Tien An Men demonstrations), Mao's death in September, and the Gang of Four's removal from positions of authority by the end of that year, the rapidly changing top leadership was in no position to adopt and implement major foreign policy shifts *vis-à-vis* the USSR or the U.S. There was some effort to put a cap on deteriorating relations with the Soviets by revitalization of border talks, which had not been convened for 18 months, but no concrete results were produced from the latest round of negotiations. Relations with the U.S. remained stable; President Ford's late 1975 visit seemed to have been designed to balance the summit talks with Brezhnev in Vladivostok the previous November, and to assure the Chinese of policy continuity after Nixon. The U.S.

commitment to normalization, based on the principles enunciated in the Shanghai Communique, remained firm, but neither side seemed prepared to negotiate the hard details.

U.S. Policy During the Carter Years

U.S. China policy in the Carter administration initially appears to have been assessed within the context of the triangular relationship, although administration officials denied it.[26] Both Secretary of State Cyrus Vance and Assistant for National Security Affairs Zbigniew Brzezinski concentrated on the U.S.-Soviet relationship and sought to differentiate the new administration's policy from that of its predecessors. But, by the fall of 1977, Brzezinski began to press Carter for renewed attention to relations with China. He saw the achievement of normalization as a "key strategic goal" for the new administration: not only would it enhance political stability in the Far East, but it would also provide important global competition for the Soviets.[27] Vance, who had visited China in August, agreed that relations were stagnant, but worried that increased rapprochement with China might have adverse effects on the SALT II negotiations that had taken on new life with the advent of the Carter presidency. According to the Secretary, normalization with China was a goal from the outset of the administration, although it was not one of the first priorities.[28] Brzezinski had some difficulty in getting the President to focus on China, to consider whether the timing was appropriate to proceed to a new stage in the normalization process and, if so, what the composition of an American delegation to China should be. Vance was opposed to such a trip in general and one that Brzezinski would head in particular. Nonetheless, Brzezinski prevailed; the President approved the trip as well as Brzezinski's determination to "transform the U.S.-Chinese relationship into an increasingly enduring one."[29]

Brzezinski's visit resulted in both sides calling for normalization, satisfactory settlement of the Taiwan issue, and greater bilateral scientific and technical cooperation. Brzezinski called for the possibility of selling military equipment to China and engaging the latter in some Western military briefings through NATO. The de facto leader of China (restored to membership in the CPC Politbureau Standing Committee and as Vice Premier in 1977), Deng Xiaoping, was invited to visit the U.S. to work out the details of normalization.

Events moved swiftly. Normalization was agreed to prior to Deng's visit. It is possible that the Chinese wanted to conclude normalization as a reaction to the Soviet-Vietnamese Treaty of Friendship and Mutual Assistance, signed in November, which enhanced the Soviet position in Southeast Asia, to China's discomfort. Normalization details were worked out between Leonard Woodcock, head of the U.S. liaison office in Beijing, and Deng. A joint communique announced that the U.S. and the PRC officially would establish diplomatic relations on 1 January 1979. Both sides had compromised on the Taiwan issue. The U.S. agreed to abrogate its 1954 Mutual Defense Treaty with Taiwan, "acknowledged" that there was only one China and Taiwan was part of it, and declared its "expectation" that the Taiwan issue would be "settled peacefully by the Chinese themselves."[30] The U.S. was to maintain commercial, cultural, and other relations with Taiwan, including the sale of defensive military equipment. It agreed to withdraw all remaining U.S. personnel from Taiwan by mid-1979. For its part, China objected to continued U.S. arms sales to the island but, as Premier Hua Guofeng expressed it, "our two sides had differences on this point. Nonetheless, we reached an agreement on the joint communique."[31]

Deng's formal visit to Washington, 28 January - 5 February 1979, was the first by a Chinese Communist leader, for all had refused to reciprocate the Nixon and Ford visits because of the presence of the Taiwan embassy in the U.S. capital. Deng and Carter signed agreements on cultural, scientific, and technical cooperation, and emphasized mutual interest in concluding further trade, economic, aviation, and other agreements in the near future.[32]

In December, Congress approved granting China MFN status, and the U.S. announced at about the same time that up to $2 billion in credits through the Ex/Im Bank would be made available through the mid-1980s.[33] Vice President Walter Mondale's visit to China in late August emphasized the renewed U.S. interest in building a closer relationship with China. The earlier U.S. concern with "evenhandedness" in dealing with the Soviets and the Chinese was largely abandoned, although Secretary Vance consistently sought to retain at least some semblance of it.[34]

The tilt toward China became even more obvious with Secretary of Defense Harold Brown's visit to Beijing in January, 1980 (just after the Soviet invasion of Afghanistan). Discussions with the Chinese included the sale of aircraft with sophisticated navigational equipment and the possibility of selling technical equipment that could be used for military purposes, so-called "dual use technology." (Vance argued against the sale of any equipment to China that would not have been sold to the Soviet Union.[35]) In April, China was transferred from the Y category of countries to which goods could not be sold to a less restrictive one, category P, and a number of defense-related materials were now permitted to be sold to the Chinese.[36] But, despite the rapid improvement in relations between the two countries, the President did not pay a return visit to China, probably because of the continuing crisis after the U.S. embassy in Teheran was occupied and embassy personnel held hostage from 4 November 1979 through the end of the Carter presidency. In September, the U.S.-China Joint Economic Committee reached agreement on a variety of issues of mutual concern, including civil aviation and textile trade; in October, a major grain agreement was signed, whereby China could purchase up to eight million tons of grain annually for four years.[37]

U.S.-Soviet relations took on a different character during the Carter years. Rather than continue a bilateral policy that served as the cornerstone of U.S. foreign policy, as Kissinger was perceived to have done, the new administration sought to downplay the Soviet relationship and emphasize the reality of multipolarity, with China, Japan, and Western Europe playing increasingly important roles in international affairs. Although there were substantial public differences between Vance's and Brzezinski's perceptions of how the relationship with Moscow should evolve, both believed that Kissinger had oversold the virtues of detente and had failed to insist upon more restrained and responsible Soviet behavior as an element of detente; if the Soviets wanted to maintain or develop better economic and trade relations with the U.S., they would have to reciprocate by providing at least some of what the U.S. wanted, namely less active involvement in the Third World and a more restrained arms control policy. At the same time, though, the Carter administration sought to increase U.S.-Soviet cooperation in such areas as demilitarization of the Indian Ocean, limitation of arms transfers to Third World countries, substantive agreement in the MBFR talks, and renewed efforts to reach a SALT II agreement.[38] Brzezinski championed the principle of linkage in assessing Soviet behavior, and argued that the U.S. should deliberately reduce cooperation in areas that the Soviets were especially concerned about should Soviet behavior so warrant it. Thus, trade and economic agreements should be directly tied to Soviet Third World behavior and even progress or the lack of it in the SALT negotiations. For their part, the Soviets felt unceremoniously left out of the Middle East settlement when the Camp David accords were reached between Egypt and Israel, with the U.S. as mediator and the Soviets not even invited to participate.[39]

The SALT II Treaty was signed by Brezhnev and Carter in Vienna in June, 1979, but the administration faced a difficult time as the Senate sought to use ratification as a vehicle for reviewing the main thrust of Carter's foreign policy since the President had taken office. With the Soviet invasion of Afghanistan in December, it was clear that SALT would not be ratified and, in early January 1980, the President announced that the treaty was being withdrawn from further consideration by the Senate. In retaliation to the invasion, Carter put renewed restrictions on the sale of technological goods to the USSR, banned further grain sales, curtailed Soviet fishing privileges in U.S. waters, and prohibited participation of U.S. athletes in the forthcoming Moscow Olympics. The administration also sought, with limited success, to gain West European acquiescence in these policy decisions. Indeed, in assessing Carter's Soviet policy, some Western observers saw it as a return to "containment without confrontation."[40]

Soviet Policies

While the U.S.-Soviet relationship took a decided downturn in the Carter years, the arms limitation treaty had finally been signed. The Soviets were not deterred from substantial and continual forays into Third World internal strife, at least in part because the U.S. Congress sought to limit American involvement even in counteracting Soviet or Soviet-Cuban intervention (a consequence of the determination not to get involved in another Vietnam). In May 1977, Nikolai Podgorny, Politbureau member and Chairman of the Presidium of the Supreme Soviet, resigned from the Politbureau,[41] and in mid-June, Brezhnev was named to succeed him in the Supreme Soviet position.[42] Despite his strengthened position domestically, Brezhnev no longer attempted to build a special relationship with the American President, and appears not to have set much store in annual summit meetings. Early in his administration, Carter had proposed to the Soviet leader that a summit meeting would be welcome. The President even considered useful an informal annual dialogue with Brezhnev. But the Soviets were determined to have an arms agreement before any summit, so the idea was shelved.

When it became obvious that detente without strings attached was not possible, especially with Congress active in U.S.-Soviet relations, Brezhnev's personal stake in continued detente declined. Its design had sought to serve Soviet interests; U.S. limits on trade and credits, and an unprecedented emphasis on human rights' violations in the Soviet Union, curtailed its utility for the Soviets. In general, Moscow seemed to have decided that it could capitalize on policy divisions in Washington and did not need to exercise undue restraint as a quid pro quo for continued conciliatory relations with the U.S. The invasion of Afghanistan was surely undertaken as part of this policy determination and there is evidence that the Soviets were taken aback by the scope and intensity of the U.S. reaction. Still, they did not withdraw from Afghanistan.

1978-79 was also a period in which Sino-Soviet relations improved, after a year of sharp decline following Mao's death. Agreement was reached on Amur-Ussuri River traffic in October 1977, although the boundary dispute remained unsettled.[43] A 1 April 1978 *Pravda* editorial hailed the return of ambassadors in each other's capital, called for substantive negotiations on the border issue, and cited the need to avoid further armed conflict. But Brezhnev's visit to the border area in the Far East at the same time and his review of military maneuvers near Khabarovsk seemed to underline Soviet intentions to maintain troop readiness.[44] The Afghan invasion also impacted heavily on Sino-Soviet relations. Even as the Chinese announced that the thirty-year Treaty of Friendship, Cooperation, and Mutual Assistance signed in early 1950 would not be renewed, they called for talks to try to end the border dispute and to establish the principles upon which relations between the two states could be built. Talks were conducted in Moscow from September-December 1979, at the Vice Foreign Ministerial level; they were adjourned without agreement having been reached. In fact, an agenda could not even be agreed upon. Talks were to be reconvened in early 1980, but the Afghan events interfered. Henceforth, as one of the regular demands put forth by China before bilateral negotiations could be resumed was Soviet withdrawal from that border state. Another was that the Soviets compel Vietnam to withdraw from Kampuchea; and the third was that the Soviets withdraw all military equipment and personnel from Mongolia as well as withdraw troops and equipment from the border areas. Despite Chinese emphasis on the need for reduced Soviet support in Vietnam as a precondition for improved relations, the Soviets have made it clear that they have no intention of giving up their position in Southeast Asia.[45]

For their part, the Chinese seemed concerned that the increasingly cooperative relationship with the U.S. might cause the Soviets to overreact. After the January 1980 announcement on U.S. military sales to China, the Soviets stepped up the combat readiness of the 45 divisions stationed in military districts bordering on China as well as the SS-20's deployed near the border.[46]

Once the Gang of Four, apparently opposed to improved relations with either the Soviet Union or the U.S., was removed from power in October 1976, the more moderate leadership that gained control of foreign policy-making seems to have favored a policy of both reducing tensions with the Soviets and improving relations with the U.S. Less attention was paid to foreign policy while the post-Mao power struggle went on; after Deng had reasserted his authority and engineered the "election" of supporters into the Politbureau and Standing Committee, substantial efforts were undertaken to improve relations with both superpowers. Normalization with the U.S. became of high priority, because of the economic and trade benefits that would result as well as the international prestige the formal exchange of diplomatic relations would bring. In fact, it is more difficult to trace a consistent policy *vis à vis* the Soviets than with the U.S., which suggests a continuing Chinese dilemma as to how best to manage Sino-Soviet relations to greatest advantage. Indeed, Chinese policy seems quite contradictory. For example, while rejecting a February 1978 Soviet proposal to collaborate on a joint statement of principles that would govern state relations, the Chinese sought to promote trade relations. While ambassadors were exchanged, polemics, especially on the Chinese side, became more vitriolic. From the Soviet vantage point, expectations that relations might improve substantially after Mao's death did not materialize.

Policy Shifts with the Reagan Administration?

Nor was there an abrupt shift in Soviet-American relations with the installation of a conservative Republican administration in 1981. Rather, the new administration inherited a deteriorating relationship as well as a renewed determination to increase military expenditures. Reagan's policy was to expand the already established trend that had been set by 1979 and confirmed after the Afghan events. The rapidity with which relations worsened may be attributed to the new administration, but there was scarcely a fullscale policy reversal. One aspect of the U.S. policy toward the Soviets that was quickly reversed was the grain sales embargo. In April, the embargo was lifted for, the President argued, the only group to be hurt by it had been the American farmers. The Soviets had managed to buy sufficient grain elsewhere and would continue to do so. Reagan's unwillingness to negotiate an arms reduction agreement until the U.S. had "caught up" with the Soviets militarily was certainly a departure from previous policy as was the flat unwillingness of the President to consider seriously any summit meeting with his Soviet counterpart. There was a decided return to the Dulles era of containment rhetoric, including a publicly stated belief that the Soviet regime was unlikely to retain power indefinitely. Reagan also sought to reconstitute an international anti-Soviet coalition through arms sales with "cooperative" Third World countries and through a tightly coordinated NATO policy toward Moscow, which could not be achieved. U.S. restrictions imposed on trade and economic relations in late 1981, in reaction to the imposition of martial law in Poland, included a ban on further high technology, oil, and gas equipment sales, closing of the Soviet Purchasing Agency in the U.S., and nonrenewal of exchange agreements.[47] Most West European states did not agree to these restrictions. (Carter had faced similar difficulties with the European allies several years earlier.)

U.S. relations with China followed a similar pattern. During the campaign, Reagan had said he would try to reestablish diplomatic relations with Taiwan if elected,[48] and called for turning the liaison office in Taipei into an operation of the U.S. government rather than continue its support through a private foundation. Such official contact would not be the same as diplomatic relations, he declared,[49] but, when a newsman asked him to "answer yes or no" as to whether he still favored official relations with Taiwan, the candidate responded, "I guess it's a yes."[50] Further, the Republican Party platform called for giving "priority consideration to Taiwan's defense requirements."[51] Soon after Reagan assumed office, the administration announced the sale of F-16 advanced jet fighters to Taiwan. Beijing's reaction came swiftly, despite Secretary of State Alexander Haig's offer to sell the PRC dual-use technology and defense support equipment. During the latter part of the year, the PRC indicated a serious interest in restricting diplomatic relations with the U.S. over the Taiwan issue. Domestic opposition to the F-16 sale mounted and, by early 1982, the administration announced that a co-production arrangement of F-5E jets with Taiwan had been reached. In August, the U.S. and China issued a joint communique regarding the limitation of arms sales to Taiwan. The U.S. pledged not to exceed current sales levels and China agreed to continue to seek reunification with Taiwan through peaceful means.[52] The U.S. continued to offer China the possibility of buying military equipment, but the Chinese have been restrained in their purchases. Foreign capital for economic development clearly has been more crucial for them.

The rapid freeze in relations with the U.S. seems to have prompted the Soviets to try to achieve better relations with China, although not at the expense of troop withdrawals or a reduction of support for Vietnamese efforts in Southeast Asia. Ideologist Mikhail Suslov's death in January, 1982, may have had some impact on the decision to improve relations. Suslov reportedly had maintained a staunch, consistently anti-Chinese position and, as a Politbureau member for more than twenty-five years, had played an important and sometimes critical role in major policy decisions during the Khrushchev and Brezhnev eras. Trade between the two countries rose substantially in 1982, and the Soviets have provided some goods that will help China renovate heavy industrial plants that were built in the 1950s with Soviet assistance. Both sides ceased reporting border incidents in 1980, and local trade across some of the borders reportedly resumed after 1981. Negotiations on reducing military forces along both sides of the border resumed with the promise of more fruitful results in 1982.[53] Earlier Chinese recalcitrance in responding to Soviet negotiation overtures softened, and some possibility for improved state relations became evident.

Concerned with the Reagan administration's apparent interest in modifying the terms and underlying principles of normalization seems to have prompted the Chinese to consider more serious negotiations with the Soviets. Thus, Beijing seems to have deliberately decided to play its Soviet card. The fear of a Soviet military invasion or preemptive strike has receded, although Soviet troops and missiles remain stationed near the border. China's overriding priority of economic development has also contributed to what appears to be a more conciliatory attitude toward the Soviets. And, with Brezhnev's death in November 1982, the Soviets renewed their efforts to seek a satisfactory solution to the continued Sino-Soviet conflict.

Conclusions: Political Leaders and Policy Shifts

In reviewing policies over a twelve-year period, it is clear that leaders and their supporters make a difference in policy formulation, adoption, and implementation. Without Nixon's determination to achieve substantial foreign policy breakthroughs, rapprochement with China would have occurred later and might not have received the same welcome reception. Without Brezhnev's personal predelictions, annual summits probably would not have been convened, although there is doubt as to their continued utility. Once the Americans, Soviets, and Chinese all recognized the utility of the triangular relationship in playing one state off against another, particular leaders seemed to play a lesser role in broad policy changes. The relationship seems to have been a central force in guiding policies among the three states during most of the period under review (after U.S.-Chinese rapprochement was established). No one of the three handled the two competitors equally. The U.S. was very aware of the

China card *vis-à-vis* the Soviets but does not appear to have used a Soviet card to try to influence Chinese behavior. The Soviets used their American card to enhance their global position and minimize the offensive danger from China. Only the Chinese seem to have tried to use both their American card to put the Soviets on notice that a military confrontation would be unwise, and their Soviet card when there was particular concern about U.S. interests and intentions regarding Taiwan.

Policy shifts tended to occur within administrations, not between one and the next. In the case of the USSR, one leader remained preeminent during the entire period, although there were some changes in the top leadership (CPSU CC Politbureau) that might have impacted on foreign policy decision making. Most of the personnel shifts resulted from death or illness rather than expulsion for political reasons. There is little hard evidence that these personnel changes had a significant impact on foreign policy determination and execution. Leadership changes in China were much more farreaching and seem to have been more directly linked to foreign policy. In the early period following the Cultural Revolution, Lin Biao's opposition to a consideration of improved relations with the U.S. stalled that process; in the mid-'70s, the Gang of Four's influence seems to have done the same. Deng's pragmatism and continued authority since 1978 have aided careful rapprochement with the U.S. What impact the replacement of Hua Guofeng by Hu Yaobang as Chairman of the CPC and the emergence of Zhao Ziyang as Premier have had on Sino-American or Sino-Soviet relations has not been determined.

With respect to the U.S., policy shifts clearly occurred within administrations, although particular leaders hastened or retarded them. Thus, the plateau that Sino-American relations had reached by late 1973 was not changed notably until the spring of 1978. Ford appeared unwilling to seriously consider negotiating an agreement on normalization, and the Carter administration did not seek to attempt it soon after assuming office. Relations with the Soviets had already cooled during the Ford years and were not to improve substantially during the Carter administration. Reagan inherited a deteriorating relationship with the Soviets, and his own biases sought to hasten that process. Similarly, with respect to China, the 1979 Taiwan Relations Act that followed abrogation of the U.S.-Taiwan Mutual Defense Treaty, provided for the sale or co-production of substantial defensive military equipment. Reagan's announcement of the plan to sell advanced technology jets to Taipei could be construed as an extension of the Act, although the plan was quickly modified. Despite the rhetoric of having sold Taiwan down the river, and the need to revive a two-Chinas policy, the Reagan administration in fact has offered to sell Beijing a wider array of dual-use technology and equipment than had the previous administration.

The expectation that top leadership changes would have a pronounced effect on the course of Sino-Soviet relations proved incorrect. Evidence suggests that the Soviets sought to improve relations after Khrushchev's ouster and Brezhnev's death, but were not successful at either time. (A more consistent policy of rapprochement on the state level seems to have been undertaken after Brezhnev's death, but that goes beyond the parameters of this essay.) Soviet efforts during the Brezhnev era stemmed from a position of strength, which the Chinese did not appreciate. Moreover, the Chinese, having stipulated the circumstances under which they would negotiate meaningfully with Moscow (circumstances that the Soviets have demonstrated they have no intention of complying with), will need to find face-saving mechanisms before substantive negotiations can be concluded. Meanwhile, the pragmatic leadership has favored enhanced bilateral trade and economic relations.

Substantive policy changes, then, result from a variety of factors, including specific leadership concerns, timing, the difficulties encountered in determining policy shifts, and adequate means to effect those shifts. While the predeliction of particular leaders in power has some influence on policy determination, it is by no means preponderant, either in democratic regimes or in bureaucratic authoritarian ones in which there are fewer institutional and popular restraints.

Notes

1. Henry Kissinger, *White House Years* (Boston, MA: Little, Brown, 1979), p. 181.
2. *Ibid.*, p. 193.
3. See the details of these and other related events in Charles W. Freeman, Jr., "The Process of Rapprochement: Achievements and Problems," in Gene T. Hsiao and Michael Witunski, eds., *Sino-American Normalization and its Policy Implications* (New York: Praeger, 1983), pp. 2-4.
4. *Ibid.*, p. 10.
5. *Ibid.*, p. 11.
6. Kissinger, *White House Years*, p. 1226.
7. *Ibid.*, p. 128.
8. Henry Kissinger, *Years of Upheaval* (Boston, MA: Little, Brown, 1982), pp. 294-95.
9. Kissinger, *White House Years*, p. 547.

10. *Pravda,* 28 April 1973. At the same Central Committee Plenum, KGB Chairman Yuri Andropov, Minister of Defense Andrei Grechko, and Foreign Minister Andrei Gromyko were named to full membership in the Politbureau.

11. *The New York Times,* 29 October 1969.

12. Hertha W. Heiss, et al., "United States-Soviet Commercial Relations since 1972," U.S. Congress. Joint Economic Committee. *Soviet Economy in a Time of Change.* Vol. 2 (Washington: G.P.O., 1979), p. 191.

13. John W. Garver, "The Sino-Soviet Territorial Dispute in the Pamir Mountains Region," *The China Quarterly,* no. 85 (March, 1981).

14. Thomas W. Robinson, "Soviet Policy in East Asia," *Problems of Communism,* XXII 6 (November/December 1973), p. 46 n.

15. Allen S. Whiting, "Sino-Soviet Relations in the 1980s," in Richard A. Melanson, ed., *Neither Cold War nor Detente?* (Charlottesville, VA: University Press of Virginia, 1982), p. 94.

16. *Pravda,* September 25, 1973.

17. See Harry Harding, "The Domestic Politics of China's Global Posture," in Thomas Fingar, et al., *China's Quest for Independence: Policy Evolution in the 1970s* (Boulder, CO: Westview, 1980), pp. 105-08.

19. James C. Thompson, Jr., "On the Making of U.S. China Policy, 1961-9," *The China Quarterly,* no. 50 (April-June, 1972).

20. Harry Harding, Jr., "China: The Fragmentation of Power," *Asian Survey,* XII, 1 (Jan., 1972), espec. pp. 1-7.

21. Fox Butterfield, *China: Alive in the Bitter Sea* (New York: Times Books, 1982), p. 303, quoting a "member of Mao's family" with whom he met in 1981, whose identity he agreed not to reveal. For a general discussion on policy shifts and the utilization of issues to enhance one's personal political position, see Parris H. Chang, *Power and Policy in China,* 2d ed. (University Park: Penn State Univ. Press, 1978); and Lucian Pye, *The Dynamics of Chinese Politics* (Cambridge: Oelgeschlager, Gunn and Hain, 1981), espec. chap. 7.

22. "Documentation," *The China Quarterly,* no. 65 (January 1976), p. 197.

23. *London Times,* 4 November 1975.

24. "Documentation," *The China Quarterly,* no. 64 (December 1975), pp. 505-08.

25. *Ibid.,* no. 65 (January 1976), p. 197. See also the discussion in John Bryan Starr, "From the 10th Party Congress to the Premiership of Hua Kuo-feng," *ibid.,* no. 67 (September 1976).

26. Cyrus Vance, *Hard Choices* (New York: Simon and Schuster, 1983), p. 75.

27. Zbigniew Brzezinski, *Power and Principle* (New York: Farrar, Straus, Giroux, 1983), p. 196.

28. Vance, *op. cit.,* p. 75.

29. Brzezinski, *op. cit.,* p. 209.

30. U.S. Government Statement, 15 December 1978, published in Hsiao and Witunski, *op. cit.,* p. 243.

31. *Ibid.*, p. 245.
32. Freeman, *op. cit.*, p. 18.
33. *Ibid.*, p. 19.
34. Brzezinski, *op. cit.*, p. 421.
35. *Ibid.*
36. *Ibid.*, p. 424.
37. Fred Greene, "The United States and Asia in 1980," *Asian Survey,* XXI, 1 (January 1981), pp. 2-4.
38. Brzezinski, *op. cit.*, pp. 165-175.
39. See the discussion of changing Soviet attitudes toward detente in Dmitri K. Simes, "Soviet Policy toward the United States," in Joseph Nye, Jr., ed., *The Making of America's Soviet Policy* (New Haven, CT: Yale, 1984).
40. See the discussion in Alexander L. George, "Political Crises," in Nye, *op. cit.*
41. *Pravda,* 25 May 1977.
42. *Pravda,* 17 June 1977.
43. Harry Gelman, "Outlook for Sino-Soviet Relations," *Problems of Communism,* XXVIII, 5-6 (September/December 1979), p. 59.
44. *Pravda,* 1 April 1978.
45. Gerald Segal, "Sino-Soviet Realities: The Road to Detente," *The World Today,* 40, 5 (May 1984). See also Steven I. Levine, "The Unending Sino-Soviet Conflict," *Current History,* 79 (459), (October 1980).
46. "Documentation," *The China Quarterly,* no. 83 (September 1980). According to the Chinese in July 1980, the Soviets retained 54 divisions along the Sino-Soviet border. See *The New York Times,* 27 July 1980.
47. *The New York Times,* 31 December 1981.
48. *Ibid.*, 21 August 1980.
49. *Ibid.*, 17 August 1980.
50. *Ibid.*, 24 August 1980.
51. *Ibid.*, 12 July 1980.
52. *Ibid.*, 18 August 1982.
53. See the discussion in Edmund Lee (pseud.), "Beijing's Balancing Act," *Foreign Policy,* 51 (Summer 1983); and Segal, *op. cit.*

Internal Dynamics in the
Sino-Soviet-U.S. Triad

JAMES C. HSIUNG

I propose to examine Sino-U.S.-Soviet relations in their triadic context, drawing upon some of the theoretical insights made available from studies of three-person games by sociologists and social psychologists. In doing so, I am guided by the conviction that we should not indulge in ad hoc explanations, but should bring theory to bear, in this as in other studies of international politics. Theories are generalizations from prior empirical studies that should help explain new situations, ceteris paribus.

I shall also examine the players' calculations of their respective gains and losses from existing alignments as a relevant variable for future alignment shifts. In using this rational-choice approach, I am guided by an underlying assumption that nations, like individuals, do learn lessons from their past mistakes and correct them periodically.

I am extrapolating data from a much larger study, some preliminary findings from which are included in a book I edited.[1] I hope that in the course of the discussions below it will become clear that the three-person-game (i.e., triadic) paradigm used here is distinct from that of the habitual "triangle." The latter perspective often evokes the imagery of the prover-bial "romantic triangle," which blinds one to other possible alignment patterns that are equally available within a triad. It also tends to focus primarily on domestic attributes, as distinct from intra-triadic dynamics, as a variable for alignment shifts.

N-Person Game and the Triad

Although the "n" in the n-person game should be any number, differentiation between dyads and triads, according to Georg Simmel, is much sharper than between triads and tetrads or higher-numbered groups. Indeed, higher-numbered groups can be reduced to triadic forms. Thus, analyses of triadic interactions (or 3-person games) can be a very fruitful enterprise, and can form the basis for an expansion to higher-numbered groups (n-person). Because the use of three-person games in the analysis of Sino-U.S.-Soviet relations is relatively new, it is necessary to mention some of the key characteristics associated with triadic behavior that are relevant to our concerns here.[2]

(1)   One is the relative fluidity in alignment patterns in a triad. Although Georg Simmel and others such as Von Neumann and Morgenstern have noted a tendency toward segregation into a pair and an other,[3] this specific line of segregation is only one of the many possible alignments in a triad. Furthermore, in triadic game experiments, the third player is found to fare better when facing a conflict than facing a solidary bond between the other two.[4] According to Simmel and others, the weak man (tertius) in a triad that includes two strong players is found to profit, far out of proportion to his real power, by aligning himself with one of the two more powerful members. The weak tertius is found to profit even more handsomely when the two more powerful players are in a lockjam of contention.[5]

(2)   If the relative strength or power of the three members is known, it is possible to predict the appearance of particular coalitions. On the basis of the relative strengths of the three, Theodore Caplow has constructed eight basic types of triads having different coalitional relations.[6]

(3)   There is the basic distinction between "continuous" triadic situations and two short-lived variations. The two variations are: "episodic" situations, which are like one-shot deals such as voting episodes; and "terminal" situations, in which the players are trying to get rid of one another.[7] In a "continuous" situation—of which the Sino-U.S.-Soviet triad is an example—coalitions are formed for a variety of purposes. Although

one coalition may be dominant most of the time, the other coalitions are expected to form when appropriate.

(4)   Relations within a triad are not merely calculated on the basis of gains for one's own coalition and losses for the adversary, but equally on the basis of which of the two partners gains more. These calculations eventually account for coalitional shifts.

In our study below, we are using games as analogies, to illustrate the dynamics of coalition making and remaking in a triad. We are not using game theory per se, which is a sophisticated science using mathematic (deductive) reasoning. Game theorists focus on optimal strategies based on the calculation of possible outcomes (winning the game), rather than the initial power ratios among the players. The work by Anatol Rapaport, Thomas Schelling, Steven J. Brams, etc., is representative of this approach.[8] The study of how the interactions of participants correspond to their expectations stemming from perceptions (of power ratios) and motives, on the other hand, is the concern of social psychologists. It is sometimes called "perception theory," to distinguish it from game theory, although both study relations within a group.

Whereas game theory under the initial influence of economics is concerned with what purports to be a player's rational strategy if he is to win the game, perception theory developed by social psychologists and sociologists examines what actually occurs in a group consisting of members confronted with a variety of seeming power relationships to each other. In this study, I shall rely more on the works of Georg Simmel, Theodore Caplow, W. Edgar Vinacke and Abe Arkoff, and Sheldon Stryker and George Psathas than on those of the game theorists.[9]

The Vinacke-Arkoff Series

We shall first make use of findings from the Vinacke-Arkoff pachisi experiment.[10] In this game involving three players, each player was given a "weight" to reflect an uneven power distribution. The game board of pachisi has sixty-seven spaces numbered consecutively; a single die is cast instead of a pair; and at each move the player advances his marker a number of spaces equal to the number thrown times his assigned weight. The game is an instrument for studying the effect of any initial power distribution on the formation of coalitions in triads. The Vinacke-Arkoff game is unusual in that every player moves on every throw of the die. The predictions to be tested in the Vinacke-Arkoff experiment were drawn from a formulation made by Theodore Caplow. Under certain conditions, according to Caplow, the formation of particular coalitions depends upon the initial distribution of power in the triad and may be predicted to some extent when the initial distribution of power is known.[11]

All together six types of coalitions were predicted on the basis of the assigned weights, as are seen in Figure 12.1.

In the experiment, each group of subjects played 18 games, repeating six power distributions in random sequence. Table 12-1 shows the results obtained by Vinacke and Arkoff when their student subjects played 99 games of each type. In general the results conformed to the theoretical expectations.[12]

Table 12-1

Coalitions Formed in the Six Types of Power Patterns in Triads

Allies	Type 1 (1-1-1)	Type 2 (3-2-2)	Type 3 (1-2-2)	Type 4 (3-1-1)	Type 5 (4-3-2)	Type 6 (4-2-1)
AB	33	13	24	11	9	9
AC	17	12	40	10	20	13
BC	30	64	15	7	59	8
Total	80	89	79	28	88	30
(No Coalition)	10	1	11	62	2	60
P	>.05	<.10	<.01	<.70	<.01	<.50

SOURCE: W. Edgar Vinacke and Abe Arkoff, "An Experimental Study of Coalitions in the Triad," *American Sociological Review*, Vol. 22, No. 4 (August 1957), p. 409.

Type 2, 3, and 5 are of particular interest to us in that they seem to help explain the patterns of alignment that have existed in the evolution of Sino-U.S.-Soviet relations. Before we proceed any further, however, a few words of clarification are in order. First, it should be noted that there were exceptions to the predicted outcomes in the Vinacke-Arkoff experiment. In the Type 2 game, for example, with a 3:2:2 ratio, the predicted outcome is a BC coalition. In the experiment, this was borne out in 64 of the 89 games actually played. Although the conformity rate was nearly 72 percent, there was still a 28 percent deviation (including both the 13 AB and 12 AC bonds as well as 1 no coalition), as is shown in Table 12.1.

The Vinacke-Arkoff Game	Assigned Weights	Predicted Coalition
Type 1	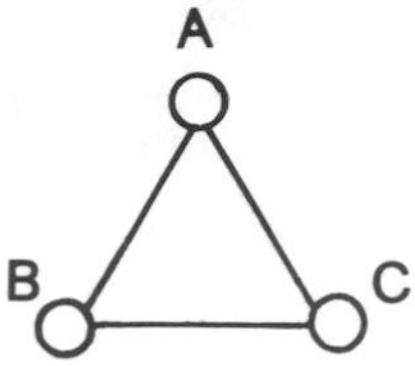 A=1 B=1 C=1	Any
Type 2	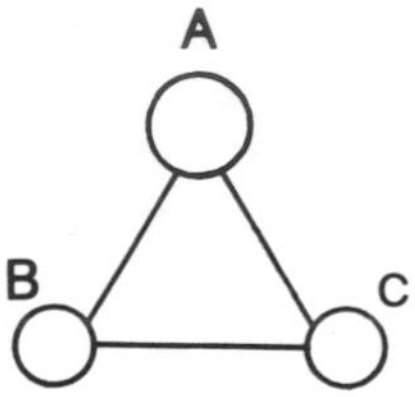 A=3 B=2 C=2	BC
Type 3	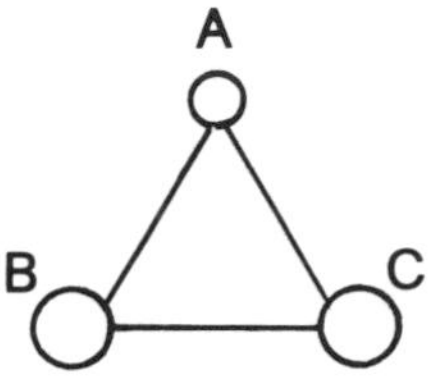 A=1 B=2 C=2	AB or AC
Type 4	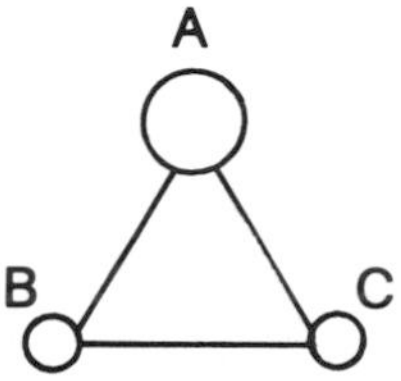 A=3 B=1 C=1	None
Type 5	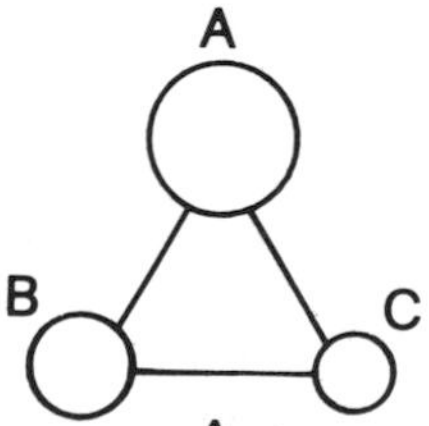 A=4 B=3 C=2	AC or BC
Type 6	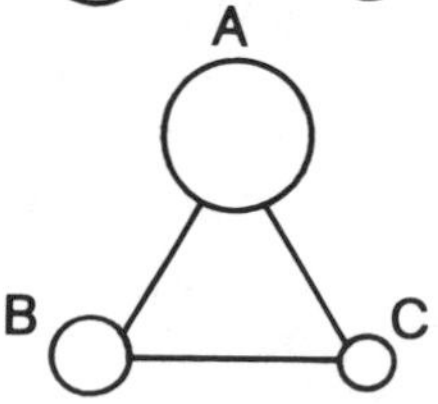 A=4 B=2 C=1	None

Figure 12-1

In the real world of international politics, exceptions to the predicted outcomes can also be frequently found. For example, although the balance-of-power rules may call for a weak state to align with the lesser of the two powerful members of a triad,[13] actual behavior may be different at times. I do wish to point out, however, that exceptions are exceptions. The Vinacke-Arkoff findings do establish high rates of conformity to the predicted outcomes. That should give us some confidence that these findings do have some significant inferential value when applied to the real world, if necessary adjustments are made to allow for extraneous circumstances.

Second, in our attempt to apply these and other findings from perception-theorists' studies of triadic coalitions, we are only dealing with "undirected" dyads within the Sino-Soviet triad. Strictly speaking, because of asymmetry and non-reciprocity, there are more than three dyads in a triad. As Steven J. Brams noted, for a triad constructed from three linked dyads, there are twenty-seven (3 x 3 x 3) possible ways of combining them.[14] In an AB dyad, besides, A might be much warmer toward B and much more anxious to keep the dyad than B is. To indicate these differences, one would have to use directed dyads. However, since we are looking at past coalition patterns and possible future trends, rather than at the symmetry or reciprocity in the relations between any two actors in our triad, we have chosen to use undirected dyads, just to keep things simple.

Third, although the Vinacke-Arkoff games used assigned weights, the purpose of the exercise was to see the effects of perception, i.e., how actors behaved in reaction to their perceived relative strengths in the triad. In trying to apply their findings to our own triad under study, we are also relying on perception, or the perceived strengths of the triadic members. We are highly aware of the problems of defining perceived power (and often one may rely on one's own perception of the actors' perceptions). However, these problems are not any more or less serious than attempts to measure power by any "objective" criteria, as have been done by some more quantitative analysts, or to plot a rational winning strategy on the basis of outcomes defined (i.e., perceived to be rational) by game theorists.

Now back to the Vinacke-Arkoff experiment. We shall now see if its findings can help illuminate the coalition shifts in the Sino-U.S.-Soviet triad. In the 1950s and early 1960s, when there were clearly perceived discrepancies in power distribution, approximating 4:3:2 (for the U.S. qua A; the USSR qua B; and China qua C), a Type 5 alignment would be most probable. This would mean either an AC or BC coalition. However, the strong ideological division at the time made an AC (U.S.-China) coalition out of the question, leaving BC (a Sino-Soviet bond) the only feasible alternative.

In fact, the AC (U.S.-China) alignment was not as improbable as one might assume, now that we know that Mao Zedong and Zhou Enlai had, indeed, in the spring of 1949, approached Washington in an attempt to establish a *modus vivendi* in anticipation of the establishment of the PRC later that year. It was only after the State Department had rebuffed the offer that the Chinese Communist leaders were left with no other choice than to "lean upon" the Soviet side.

Even if we put aside the ideological factor, the power distribution can explain why adding China's 2 to the Soviet Union's 3 would be more desirable than adding China's 2 to the United States's 4. In a U.S.-China alignment with an aggregate weight of 6, China could easily be engulfed by the United States if the coalition had served its purpose of trouncing the Soviet Union. On the other hand, at a 3:2 ratio, the Soviet Union would treasure the Chinese connection more than the United States would. While the United States could cope with the Soviet Union unaided, given the 4:3 ratio, the Soviet Union would need the Chinese ally to increase the combined weight to 5, just a little over the 4 weight of the United States.[15]

In the late 1960s, however, the United States was saddled with the Vietnam debacle and suffered a decline in power, more especially in the perception of the world. In nuclear weapons, the Soviets probably did not reach a parity with the United States until some time later. If conventional power and perception are added to the equation of power, the Soviet Union was clearly gaining, while U.S. power was on the wane. Domestic protests and reactions including Congressional moves to block another Vietnam-type foreign involvement cast further doubts on U.S. ability to project its power abroad. In these relative terms, the power ratio in the triad approached that in the Type 2 of the Vinacke-Arkoff game, that is, 3:2:2 (USSR = A; U.S. = B; and China = C). As the predicted coalition in Type 2 is BC, the "normalization" of relations between the United States and China (BC) was therefore not surprising.

In the 1970s and early 1980s, however, there has been a parity between the two superpowers, with China lagging behind, approximating the power distribution in Type 3. In the 1:2:2 ratio (China = A; U.S. = B; and USSR = C), the predicted coalition patterns are either AB or AC. When applied to our actual situation, an AB (Sino-U.S.) coalition dominated much of the 1970s; and in view of the expanding dialogue between the PRC and the Soviet Union since 1982, an AC coalition is not a too far-fetched development. Many analysts are now beginning to speak about a possible

AC (Sino-Soviet) bond, although nobody expects a return to the kind of Sino-Soviet alliance of the 1950s.

The Stryker-Psathas Series

The dynamics of the Type 3 triads is obviously of enormous interest to those concerned about future developments in Sino-U.S.-Soviet relations in the years ahead, as long as the power ratio approximates 1:2:2.

Stryker and Psathas experimented with a pachisi game involving only Type 3 triads.[16] Among the rules in this game variation is that no ties are permitted. Players who tie are forced to replay the game until the tie is broken. The rule is to make coalitions compulsory. For that reason, the findings from the experiment would be more relevant to our attempts to forecast what is likely to happen to relations in the Sino-U.S.-Soviet triad, given the power ratio noted above.

As shown in Figure 12.2, certain restrictions on coalitions were imposed. In the first series, all coalitions were allowed. In the second series, player A enjoyed an absolute choice between partners B and C, as the BC coalition was prohibited. In the third series, C was the chooser, as the AB coalition was prohibited. In the fourth series, the AC coalition was compulsory.[17]

If we translate this game into our real-world triadic situation and consider A to be the U.S., B to be the Soviet Union, and C to be China, then, we can see the following results:

(1) The Fourth Series seems to be the situation that actually existed during the latter part of the 1970's, when no AB (U.S.-Soviet) or BC (Sino-Soviet) alignment was possible.

(2) The United States will be the winner in a situation similar to the Second Series, as it has the freedom to choose either the Soviet Union or the People's Republic, while a Soviet-Chinese coalition is blocked. This seems to have actually existed during the years of the Nixingerian detente (1969-1974).

(3) The Soviet Union, on the other hand, will be the winner in an obverse version of the Second Series, switching roles with the U.S. (although this is not shown in Figure 2), where no AC (U.S.-China) coalition is possible. This was the situation during the 1950s, when a Sino-Soviet alliance existed.

(4) China will be the winner in the Third Series, which rules out an AB (U.S.-Soviet) coalition and which makes China the only player that can freely align itself with either of the other two players.

(5) In view of the above, the only situation in which all players will

The Stryker-Psathas Game

First Series

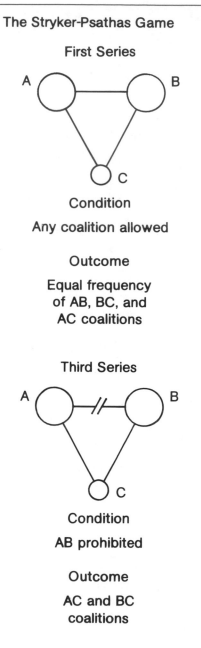

Condition

Any coalition allowed

Outcome

Equal frequency
of AB, BC, and
AC coalitions

Second Series

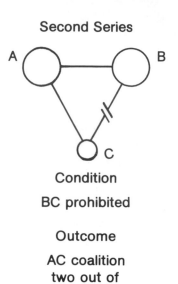

Condition

BC prohibited

Outcome

AC coalition
two out of
three times

Third Series

Condition

AB prohibited

Outcome

AC and BC
coalitions

Fourth Series

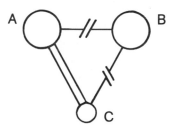

Condition

AB and BC prohibited

Outcome

AC coalition
in every game

Figure 12-2

have an equal freedom to make coalitions and benefit from triad-wide stability is the First Series. This situation approaches what Lowell Dittmer calls *ménage à trois,* though it is not exactly the same.[18] In a menage a trois (harmony among the three), any improved relations between any two players is good for the entire triad and, hence, stabilizing to it. While this is ideal, it is the most difficult to realize because of mutual suspicions and the urge of players to increase their margin of security at the expense of the others. In all the other series (including both variations of the Third Series), as is typical of nation-state behavior in the real world, each player is trying to benefit from blocking the coalition between the other two players and making either of them its own sole coalition partner. As long as this syndrome continues, no *ménage à trois* is possible. What all this suggests is, nevertheless, that the player that maintains all channels open and retains the freedom of aligning itself with one or the other player in the triad has an edge over one that does not do the same.

Let's now see the results in the Stryker-Psathas experiment. In the first series, the two strong players (A and B) chose the weak player (C) twice as often as they chose each other, but only on the basis of the weak player's willingness to accept a lesser share of the prize. In the second series, in which A alone was the chooser, C was again chosen two out of three times on the same terms. C's average share of the prize was 34% in the first series and 35% in the second series.

In the third series, C was in the strongest position, enjoying an uncontrolled choice of coalition partners. His average share of the prize was 53%. In the fourth series, when the coalition AC was in effect made compulsory, most of the C's in the experiment, which included 144 games, negotiated an approximately even division with A.[19]

The results from the Stryker-Psathas experiment suggest an advantage for C, the weakest of the three, that is disproportionate to its power weight in the triad.[20] This merely confirms similar findings by George Simmel and by Vinacke and Arkoff.[21] We shall see in the section below whether this is true in the real world of Sino-U.S.-Soviet relations. If it is true, China will have shown to be in the same advantageous position that the weak C enjoyed in the Stryker-Psathas experiment.

Correlations in Shifts Within the Triad

In my on-going project mentioned earlier, I have been attempting to establish some correlations in the changing dyadic relations within the

Sino-U.S.-Soviet triad. When completed, the project will have examined all major shifts in the alignments between each two of the three powers since 1949 and the possible correlations between these dyadic changes. For example, if there was a significant improvement in Sino-U.S. relations in a particular period, was it followed or preceded by a decline in U.S.-Soviet relations, and vice versa?

Although correlations, even if established, do not demonstrate causality, they may indicate some trends and patterns, especially if they are found to be frequent and consistent. Thus far, the project has covered the years between 1969 (the inception of the Nixon Doctrine) and 1980. What I have done is, first, to establish three sets of chronologies, one for each dyad: Sino-U.S., U.S.-Soviet, and Soviet-Chinese. Then the chronologies, after having been verified, were turned over to two coders, each of whom was asked to evaluate them and to see whether there were any correlations in the ups and downs between any two of the three sets of data. Neither coder knew the work of the other beforehand. One coder did an eye-ball evaluation. The other used a scheme for defining and scaling the ups and downs. The scheme was patterned after but considerably refined from the categories of foreign-policy behavior used in the World Events Interaction Survey (WEIS) established by Charles McClelland.[22]

The scheme divides dyadic interactions into cooperative and conflictual acts, and defines them on a scale of 0 to 10 (cooperation) and 0 to -10 (conflict), thus making it possible to make comparisons and, by adding up the scores, to "measure" the extent of changes.

It may appear desirable to break down the ups and downs of dyadic relations by issue area, since the degrees of conflict and cooperation may vary across issue areas. However, for two reasons we are not doing that. First, each player's strategic concerns still dominate over all others, and mutual adversity has made each cooperative move an adjunct to the larger competitive or conflictual relationship. The U.S.'s opening to the PRC, for example, was a means of keeping the Soviet adversary at bay. In cooperating with the PRC, each U.S. administration was concerned that the assistance Beijing received would not be used against the United States. Secondly, our primary interest is to chart the volatility (ups and downs) within the entire triad as a function of the reciprocal interactions among all three players, not just the changing relations between any two of them per se. The patterns we find below are the results of triad-wide interactions.

Without going into great detail of data analyzing, I shall merely state that the activities in the triad, seem to suggest four subperiods for analysis: 1969-1971, 1972-1974, 1975-1977, and 1978-1980.[23] Some conclusions can

Dimensions of Foreign Policy Behavior

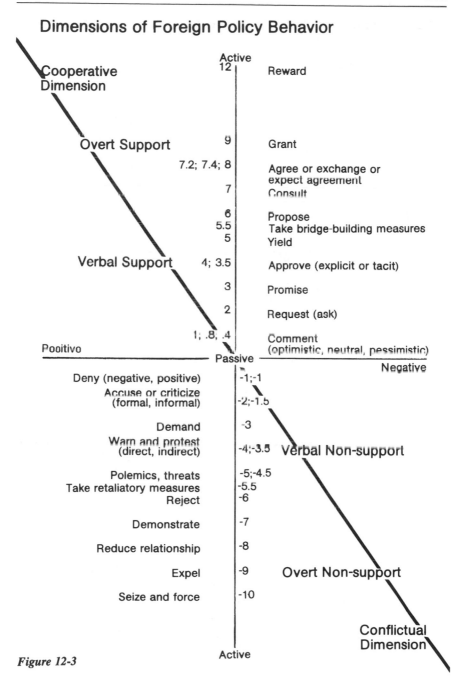

Figure 12-3

be drawn from an analysis of the apparent correlations between the three subsets of data:

(1)   First, the Nixongerian tilt in 1969-1974 seems to have accomplished what it purported to do, namely, to get the Soviets to cooperate by manipulating the prospect (as opposed to the reality) of China-card playing. The peaks in U.S.-Soviet detente, reaching sixty-four in 1971, eighty-seven in 1972, and sixty-eight in 1973, are probably unprecedented. Certainly, they have never been duplicated since, as the China-card playing was no longer a prospect but an on-going game for real, only to pick up momentum as time went on.

(2)   In 1975/mid-1978, the China tilt resulted in a general record of steady cooperation between China and the United States (in the 0-22 range). Simultaneously, however, consistent U.S.-Soviet conflictual oscillations ensued, until an all-time low of -33.5 was reached in late 1975 through early 1976. The original intent of getting the Soviets in line was not achieved as during 1972-1974.

(3)   From mid-1978 to 1981, the same trend deepened. While Sino-U.S. relations went from moderate peaks to higher peaks between late 1978 and early 1980—although dropping off somewhat after mid-1980—the China-card playing seems to have precipitated greater U.S.-Soviet confrontation. In view of the growing Soviet military presence in Indochina, which was in part a result of the U.S. China-card playing, the policy of using a U.S.-China coalition to constrain the Soviets seems to have failed to achieve its original purpose.

(4)   Despite the usual impressions to the contrary, Sino-Soviet relations have witnessed far fewer and less dramatic shifts than have U.S.-Soviet relations. Although they were at an all-time low of -30 in the first half of 1969, Sino-Soviet relations never again went down below -22. By contrast, U.S.-Soviet relations registered both higher climbs in cooperative interactions (peaking to 87 in mid-1972) and more frequent and deeper declines in conflictual interactions (reaching -33.5 in 1976; -24 in 1977; and -22.5 in 1980).

Viewed together, these findings indicate that (a) U.S.-Soviet relations were more adversely affected than were Sino-Soviet relations by the improved relations between the United States and China; (b) The Soviet Union did not gain enough from improvements in their relations with China to offset their losses from the deteriorating U.S.-Soviet relations; and (c) China gained considerably from improvements in Sino-U.S. relations, without much definable adverse effects in Chinese-Soviet relations.

The most obvious conclusion to draw is that China is the weak player in the triad that has benefited more than either of the other two from the coalitional shifts since 1969. Earlier in discussing the Stryker-Psathas experiment, it was noted that in a 2:2:1 power distribution among players A, B, and C (a Type 3 game in the original Vinacke-Arkoff taxonomy), the weak C is found to have an advantage disproportionate to its power. In the U.S.-Soviet-Chinese triad, which since the late 1970's approximates a 2:2:1 ratio, China seems to enjoy a similar advantage.

However, the C-type advantage which China has been able to enjoy is not necessarily permanent. A number of variables may change that.

In the first place, the power ratio in the triad may change. Second, the two superpowers may learn from past mistakes. If they realize that their disadvantages *vis-à-vis* China and that their losses were not compensated by their gains, they may act to correct them by not blocking out the possibility of an AB (U.S.-Soviet) coalition or, as in the U.S. case, by not relying too heavily on a coalition with C (China).

Third, although China has been the tertius gaudens (the laughing third) and thus far the gains China has scored from the AC (Sino-U.S.) coalition may surpass the gains by either of the other two players, there are "hidden" costs for China—"hidden" because they are largely outside the triadic relations. We shall address this question in our next discussion on gains and losses as a factor in coalition shifts.

Gains and Losses within the Romantic Triangle

The separation of the U.S.-China pair and the Soviet Union on two opposing sides in the triad is the ideal promoted by the China-card players as most conducive to the containment of the Soviet threat. It is usually called a "romantic triangle." Contrary to what our China card players may wish, however, neither is this the only coalition pattern within the triad, nor are the gains and losses symmetrically distributed even between the stable-marriage partners. There are gains for both; but, there are also costs. The costs include the third player's reactions calculated to offset or frustrate what the "stable marriage" attempts to do. The weight of these costs, and each partner's calculation of which of the two partners have gained more than the other, will determine the duration of any "stable marriage" within a triad.

I am not suggesting that our triadic players are locked in a zero-sum game in which each gain is canceled out by a loss, or each player's gain is offset by another's loss. Nor am I suggesting that there are no goals that can be shared noncompetitively, such as peace, stability, environmental control, nuclear deterrence, and other "collective goods," whose benefits are not divisible. What I am suggesting is that (1) there are costs, sometimes even high costs, not offset by the gains in the competition-predominate triad; (2) the costs may not be proportionately distributed across the triad; and (3) the high costs cannot be reduced to "normal" proportions without a prior reduction in the intensity of intra-triadic competition.

If nations do learn lessons from their past mistakes, then the lessons inherent in the dynamics of the triad, i.e., the way the triadic game has been played thus far, may offer a clue to the shape of things in the future.

The formal beginnings of the U.S.-Chinese coalition were marked by President Carter's acceptance of the anti-hegemony (code word for anti-Soviet) clause, at the insistence of Deputy Premier Deng Xiaoping, in the joint communique signed in Washington, on 2 February 1979. If Carter's endorsement was partial and half-hearted then, the Soviet invasion of Afghanistan at the end of the year probably made it complete. The U.S. acceptance of anti-hegemonism has since been reaffirmed many times, including under the Reagan administration. The reason is simple: Constraining global Soviet expansionism (hegemonism in the Chinese parlance) is the identical strategic goal professed by both nations, and constitutes therefore the cornerstone of the Sino-U.S. coalition.

There are, nevertheless, both gains and costs for both partners; and the common Soviet adversary is not necessarily the only loser. Let's enumerate the gains and losses on the Chinese side first.

Advantages to China

The U.S.-China tilt, begun in the summer of 1979, has obviously brought many advantages to the Chinese. The PRC has been receiving special treatment denied to the Soviets, such as Most-Favored-Nation (MFN) status granted to Chinese imports, Ex/Im Bank credits, availability of insurance by the Overseas Private Investment Corporation (OPIC) for U.S. investors in China, increasing instances of technology transfers even in quite sensitive areas (involving possible military use), etc.

The U.S. connection has obviously provided the Chinese with an added leverage in dealing with Moscow, as they can play the "American card." The cautious inaction by the Soviets during Beijing's "pedagogical war" against their Vietnamese ally in the spring of 1979, following on the heels of Deng's U.S. visit, was a good, early indication that Moscow did not take

China's American connection lightly. The relaxation of Soviet rigidity toward China, beginning with the Tashkent speech by President Brezhnev in March 1982, was a further indication that the Soviets do worry about China's American factor. Since then, five new rounds of talks have taken place, alternately in Beijing and Moscow. Soviet congeniality has increased since Brezhnev's death in November 1982. Exchanges have increased between the two countries, including visits by high-level officials and scholars. In December 1984, First Deputy Premier Ivan Arkhipov, the highest Soviet official ever to visit China since Premier Kosygin met with Premier Zhou Enlai in 1969, concluded four important agreements on further cooperation in trade, science and technology, and economic matters. China has reasons to expect more concessions from the apparent Soviet willingness to be conciliatory.

Costs to China

All this is fine for China. However, there are costs to Beijing's playing of the American card:

(1) In the first place, to play the American card requires the continuation of the Sino-Soviet discord without regard to changing circumstances. Continuation of the Sino-Soviet feud would mean the continuing presence of the 50 Soviet divisions, or one quarter of the total Soviet army and air force, along the border. An armed stalemate would place considerable burdens on Beijing's defense budget. The continuing feud with Moscow can only encourage Vietnamese intransigence in their dealings with Beijing. Increasing dependency by the Vietnamese on Moscow will only fortify that intransigence, which is bad for the Chinese. A reversal in China's anti-Soviet stand could pave the way for a possible reduction of hostility between Beijing and Hanoi, a reduction in Vietnam-Kampuchea conflict, and, above all, a reduction in Vietnamese dependence on the Soviets.[24]

(2) As long as Beijing is known to be unbending on the question of Sino-Soviet rapprochement, North Korea would have a better chance of holding Beijing "hostage" to its own radical positions, which may not complement China's interests.

(3) Increasing Chinese alignment with the industrial North, more especially the United States, runs the risk of alienating Beijing from the rest of the Third World, in which there is clear evidence of a decline of Chinese influence in more recent years.[25] To arrest the decline, China has

had to distance itself from Washington, starting from late 1981.[26] Although the Taiwan issue has been a very convenient device for doing that, it remains true that Beijing's relations with Washington belong to a totally different genre from those of the Maoist era. The American connection cannot but affect Beijing's standing in the Third World.

(4)   Continuation of the discord with Moscow has one other disadvantage for the Chinese. As Washington is negotiating in earnest with Moscow regarding the removal from the European theatre of the Soviet intermediate missiles, including the SS-20's, any agreement cannot but have a fall-out in Asia. What assurance is there that an agreed removal of these missiles to the Soviet Far East will not result in their being retargeted against China? In the absence of a dialogue with Moscow, the Chinese would be at a total disadvantage. Beijing's recent inclination toward a rapprochement with Moscow, therefore, cannot but be, in part at least, associated with this Chinese concern for its own security in the nuclear balance of terror.[27]

Advantages to the U.S.

The first and foremost strategic gain for the United States is the return of China to its original place on the U.S.'s strategic map. After a three-decade "loss," China is once again back in the eastern "rimland" which, along with Western Europe (as the western rimland), will play a critical role in the common defense against the threat of the "Heartland power" (i.e., Russia). The United States can now fully operationalize this rimland strategy without going through detours, as during the years between 1949 and 1979, and in a manner as anticipated by its original author, Nicholas Spkyman back in the early 1940s.[28]

Another significant advantage for the United States is the tying down of fifty divisions of Soviet troops along the Sino-Soviet and Sino-Mongolian borders, alleviating Soviet troop pressures in Europe.

Still another advantage for the United States is the counterweight that China can provide against the Soviet-Vietnamese coalition and in the search for an eventual settlement of the Kampuchea conflict. In the United Nations, an anti-Soviet China could help combat Soviet influence among Third World members. This is still relatively true despite the decline of Beijing's standing in the Third World in recent years and the disappointing Chinese abstention on the crucial Security Council vote condemning the Soviet downing of the Korean Airline plane in September 1983.

Costs to the U.S.

Against these gains, there are also costs for the United States in its pro-Beijing tilt.

(1)   The resultant termination of U.S. even-handedness toward Moscow and the death of U.S. Soviet detente has had a tendency of abetting Soviet belligerency. The Afghanistan incident may just have been a result of this heightened belligerency as much as a cause for further U.S. hostility.[29]

(2)   Another cost is the deterioration of the situation in Indochina, where Soviet military presence has been expanding. The suspension of the process of normalizing U.S. relations with Hanoi and the continuing U.S. nonchalance has driven the Vietnamese (confronted by a hostile Beijing) more and more deeply into Soviet arms. If the original intent of U.S. playing of the China card was to help contain Soviet expansionism in Asia, the increased Soviet military presence in Indochina cannot but be evidence that the U.S. goal has been relentlessly frustrated.

(3)   The U.S.-China coalition has served to undercut U.S. leverage in dealing with Moscow directly, such as in the strategic arms control negotiations. Following Deng's visit, for example, Brezhnev refused to go to Washington for the SALT summit as originally expected.[30] President Reagan's offer to supply lethal weapons to Beijing, first announced by Secretary Haig in Beijing in June 1981 (albeit not immediately picked up by Beijing), only served to deepen the chill in U.S.-Soviet relations.[31]

(4)   The China tilt, necessary to win Beijing's favor, does not tie the Chinese to a wholly antagonistic policy toward the Soviet Union, as might be expected by Washington. Indeed, the contrary may hold, as Jonathan D. Pollack laments: "By placing ourselves so unequivocally in a posture of total hostility toward the USSR, we would leave the PRC free to deal however it pleased with the USSR, secure in the knowledge that the United States and its allies had reduced their room for maneuver to dangerously low levels."[32] Mortgaging Washington's manueverability to Beijing is another cost incumbent upon the United States in its current preoccupation with the U.S.-China coalition.

Soviet Gains and Costs

Since by and large Soviet gains and losses are already reflected in those of the other two triadic players mentioned above, we need not be long in this enumeration.

The gains for Moscow in continuing the Sino-Soviet feud are that it would (1) relax NATO's vigilance, (2) alleviate U.S. fears, (3) help perpetuate Soviet influence in Indochina, etc. The losses from the Sino-Soviet split are, on the other hand: (1) the immobility of some fifty divisions of troops along the Sino-Soviet borders, (2) impediments to greater trade with China, including Soviet imports of Chinese agricultural produce to relieve pressures on the current supply-lines from the European half of the Soviet Union to Siberia; (3) enabling the United States to continue playing the China card, etc. Even for the Soviet gains in Indochina, Moscow has had to pay for them, on the order of some $5,000,000 a day at one point, as the aid was badly needed to prop up its Hanoi client so that the latter could continue the operations in Kampuchea.

Vis-à-vis the United States, Moscow has little to gain from the perpetuation of the Sino-Soviet feud, as it would only help drive the Chinese and the Americans closer to each other. With the Chinese partner on its side, the U.S. would only be more intransigent in dealing with Moscow, on matters such as the strategic and INF (intermediate nuclear force) arms-control negotiations.

Concluding Remarks

Both the teachings about the dynamics of three-person games, noted in an earlier section, and the calculations about gains and losses by each player combine to indicate at least two things:

(1)   There is no permanence in any of the coalition patterns, as all depend on the prevailing power balance and the kind of cost-gain calculations just suggested. There are no gains without costs, and, as we have seen, the costs could be formidable. The power balance, too, cannot be expected to be permanent. Shifting coalitions, therefore, should not be surprising. If one coalition happens to be in existence at the moment, it does not mean that other coalitions will not form in other times.

(2)   There is no permanent tertius gaudens (the laughing third that

benefits from the conflict between the other two) in the triad. Not only that, there are costs for the tertius gaudens, too. China, very much like the Player C in the Stryker-Psathas game, may have an advantage disproportionate to its relative power, thus approximating a tertius gauden. Nevertheless, as we have seen, China has not escaped the cost dilemma.

If all three players will learn their lessons, eventually they will probably come to the realization that *ménage à trois* (triadic harmony) will be in the best interests of them all. However, this is difficult to materialize in the foreseeable future, because of mutual distrust, the newness of the idea of triadic harmony (unlike a romantic triangle, which to most people seems to be the only logical thing to happen), and the requirement that short range interests of the players be submerged under their long-term interests.[33]

The next best thing to a *ménage à trois* is a willingness on the part of each player to adopt an even-handed policy toward the other two. In the 3-person game language used before, this means that each player should maintain the freedom of entering into coalitions with either of the other two. It is as though all three players were playing the First Series in the Stryker-Psathas game.

China seems to be doing just that in its current effort to develop a rapprochement with Moscow, without foresaking its bond with the United States. Furthermore, China has been urging the two superpowers to resume a dialogue and work out an agreement to control the arms race. These are the central ingredients of China's current "independent" foreign policy.[34] Whether the other two players will be doing the same remains to be seen. However, the advantages of playing a pivot's role, maintaining good relations with both wing players and enjoying the ability to mediate between them, are understandably great. There is a reasonable chance that the two superpowers will eventually also learn to appreciate the value of playing the pivot. When all have learned the lesson and compete for the role of the pivot, the triad will be much more stable than at any previous point.

Gerald Segal, in a study of U.S.-Soviet-Chinese relations, discovered three basic rules for the pivot in a triad.[35] (1) The pivot stands to gain from some "common ground" that exists between the two wings. There has to be certain amount of contacts between B and C before pivot A can play off one against the other. (2) The pivot's leverage depends on both wing players' concern lest a coalition (or "stable marriage") develop between the pivot and one of them.[36] (3) The pivot's leverage depends on the competition of the other two players for its friendship.

Segal's rules merely confirm the value of the Stryker-Psathas findings and the results of my own study of the triadic shifts summarized above. Those who maintain the freedom of entering into coalitions with either of the other two triadic players, as in the Stryker-Psathas First Series, have great advantages. In view of the fact that these various studies corroborate one another, I am emboldened to suggest the following likely developments within our triad: (1) The Sino-Soviet split will gradually give way to a more normal working relationship; (2) U.S.-Soviet hostility will gradually wear down, over the long haul, in favor of more pragmatic interchanges; and (3) the U.S.-China romance will eventually enter into a period of more realistic give-and-take, less tinged by the anti-Soviet emotionalism which has colored it from the very inception.

I do not expect all these to happen all at once in the next few years or so. Nor do I expect them to unfold at the same pace. But they are anticipated in the intermediate future by the "logic" that one can discover of intra-triadic dynamics as presented above. That logic, in a nutshell, suggests that each player is swayed by calculations of its own gains versus those of its adversary and coalition partner; and that alignments shift as power ratios shift and also as the players react to their own mistakes. ("Mistakes" here are defined in terms of each player's relative gains and losses from a given coalition pattern.) The ultimate lesson that all will learn, to recapitulate, is that the Stryker-Psathas First Series is the next best thing to the optimal, but nearly impossible, *ménage à trois*.

Notes

1. James C. Hsiung, ed., *Beyond China's Independent Foreign Policy* (New York: Praeger, 1985), Chapter 7. A somewhat similar, but more restricted, study is Peter Yu, "A Strategic Model of Chinese Checkers: Power and Exchange in Beijing's Foreign Policy" (dissertation completed in the Department of Politics, New York University, October 1983).
2. For a discussion of the characteristics of triadic behavior, see Theodore Caplow, *Two Against One: Coalitions in Triads* (Englewood Cliffs, N.J.: Prentice-Hall, 1968).
3. Kurt H. Wolff (trans. and ed.), *The Sociology of Georg Simmel* (Glencoe, IL: The Free Press, 1950), chaps. 2, 3, and 4; John Von Neumann and Oskar Morgenstern, *Theory of Games and Economic Behavior* (Princeton, N.J.: Princeton University Press, 1944), chap. 5; Theodore M. Mills, "Power Relations in Three-Person Groups," *American Sociological Review*, vol. 18, no. 4 (August, 1953), pp. 351ff.

4. Mills, "Power Relations," *ibid.*, p. 352.
5. Kurt H. Wolff (trans. and ed.), *ibid.*, p. 157.
6. Caplow, *ibid.*, p. 23.
7. *Ibid.*, p. 5.
8. Cf. Anatol Rapaport, *N-Person Game Theory: Concepts and Applications* (Ann Arbor, MI: University of Michigan Press, 1970); Thomas Schelling, *The Strategy of Conflict* (New York: Oxford University Press [Galaxy Books], 1963); and Steven J. Brams, *Game Theory and Politics* (New York: Free Press, 1975).
9. See works cited in nn. 5, 10, 11, and 12.
10. W. Edgar Vinacke and Abe Arkoff, "An Experimental Study of Coalitions in the Triad," *American Sociological Review,* vol. 22, no. 4 (August 1957), pp. 406-414.
11. Theodore Caplow, "A Theory of Coalitions in the Triad," *American Sociological Review,* vol. 21, no. 4 (August 1956), pp. 489-493; also idem, Two Against One, n.2 above, p. 22.
12. W. Edgar Vinacke and Abe Arkoff, n. 10 above; and Caplow, *Two Against One*, pp. 21-27.
13. Kenneth N. Waltz makes the same point ("Because power is a means and not an end, states prefer to join the weaker of two coalitions."), in *Theory of International Politics* (Reading, MA: Addison-Wesley, 1979), p. 126.
14. Steven J. Brams, "The Search for Structural Order in the International System: Some Models and Preliminary Results," *International Studies Quarterly,* vol. 13, no. 3 (September 1969), p. 256.
15. Cf. discussion above at reference for n. 13.
16. Sheldon Stryker and George Psathas, "Research on Coalitions in the Triad: Findings, Problems, and Strategy," *Sociometry,* vol. 23, no. 3 (September 1960), pp. 217-230.
17. *Ibid.*; Caplow, Two Against One, p. 27.
18. Lowell Dittmer, "The Strategic Triangle: An Elementary Game Theoretical Analysis," *World Politics,* vol. 33, no. 4 (July 1981), pp. 485-515.
19. Stryker and Psathas, "Research on Coalitions," n. 16 above, p. 229.
20. *Ibid.*, pp. 219; 229.
21. Vinacke and Arkoff, "An Experimental Study," n. 10 above, pp. 408; 413; Simmel, n. 5 above; Caplow, n. 2 above, p. 29.
22. Charles McClelland, "The Acute International Crisis," in Klaus Knorr, ed., *The International System* (Princeton, N.J.: Princeton University Press, 1961), pp. 182-204. Also C. McClelland, *Theory and the International System* (New York: Macmillan, 1966).
23. For a more detailed analysis of these subperiods, see Hsiung, n. 1 above, chapter 7.
24. Gerald Segal, "China and the Great Power Triangle," *China Quarterly,* no. 83 (September 1980), p. 501.
25. Decline in Chinese influence in the Third World can be seen (a) in Beijing's

lack of support when Castro denounced it at the 1979 Havana conference of the nonaligned nations; and (b) in China's setback in the United Nations General Assembly's debate on the resolution on controlling "hegemonism" in the fall of 1974. See Samual S. Kim, "Whither Post-Mao Chinese Global Policy?" *International Organization,* vol. 35, no. 3 (Summer 1981), p. 439.

26. Starting in late 1981, Beijing appeared to be making an effort to put distance between it and Washington. Officials from Premier Zhao Ziyang (while visiting North Korea in December 1981) to Foreign Minister Huang Hua (during visits to Nigeria and Ghana in November the same year) began to characterize the United States as being just as bad a superpower as the Soviet Union. Such unkind language was reminiscent of earlier protrayals during the reign of the Radicals before Mao's death. Christopher Wren, "China Attacks the Foreign Policy of the U.S.," *New York Times,* 28, December 1981. In an attempt to regain China's good will in the Third World, Premier Zhao Ziyang embarked upon an eleven-nation tour of Africa, December 10, 1982 through January 17, 1983. *Beijing Review,* nos. 1, 2, 3, and 4 (3, 10, 17, and 24, January 1983).

27. For the Chinese view on the question of Soviet SS-20's, see *Renmen Ribao* (People's Daily) editorial, 17, September 1983, p. 3.

28. For a fuller discussion on the rimland strategy and U.S. strategic thinking since Spykman, see James C. Hsiung, *U.S.-Asian Relations: The National Security Paradox* (New York: Praeger, 1983), chap. 1.

29. For a list of Soviet grievances against the U.S. long before Afghanistan, see Robert Legvold, "Caging the Bear: Containment Without Confrontation," *Foreign Policy* (Fall 1980), p. 78.

30. *New York Times,* 17, June 1981, p. 1.

31. Hedrick Smith, "Deepening U.S.-Soviet Chill," New York Times, 18, June 1981. See also John Bryan Starr, "U.S.-China Relations in 1980," briefing packet distributed by the China Council of the Asia Society, Washington, D.C. (March 1981).

32. Jonathan Pollack, in Douglas T. Stuart and William Tow, eds., *China, The Soviet Union, and the West* (Boulder, CO: Westview, 1982). p. 290.

33. Dittmer, "The Strategic Triangle," n. 18 above, p. 513.

34. On China's new independent foreign policy, which consists of these aspects, see my edited book, *Beyond China's Independent Foreign Policy,* cited in n. 1 above, esp. Chapter 10.

35. Segal, n. 24 above, pp. 499-505.

36. Similarly, Theodore Caplow notes that each power in the triad is restrained from attacking another by the expectation that his attack would provoke the other two powers into a winning coalition against him. The feared possibility of an opposing coalition, not its actual existence, nor a symmetric power distribution, is the most effective source of deterrent, hence stability, in triadic balance of power. Caplow, *Two Against One,* no. 2 above, pp. 5-7.

Triadic Struggle and Accommodation in Perspective

R. J. RUMMEL

From the general perspective of a theory of conflict and war, the Sino-Soviet-American relationship is but an exemplification of a general process of triadic conflict and accommodation. This process involves balancing interests, capabilities, and wills, fundamentally a balancing of powers; and establishing a structure of expectations and core status quo based on the resulting balance. So long as they are congruent with this balance of powers, these expectations define a stable relationship and enable cooperation to take place. If a gap develops between the balance of powers and the structure of expectations of any pair within the triadic relationship, conflict and possibly war within the triad is liable to occur.

I have much to define and clarify about this theoretical perspective, and a number of elements to discuss. Above all, I should make clear that I view this process as fundamentally psychological; in the minds of the participants. As such, this process entails different situations of conflict, and within each situation: the perception of each state of the other two; the differences among the states in interests, capabilities, and wills; their policy and behavioral dispositions; and their expectations of the outcome of their behavior.

253

Situation, perception, differences, dispositions, and expectations provide the conceptual framework for understanding any triadic relationship.
But to also comprehend the dynamics of this relationship, particularly the
stability of peace or the increasing or decreasing risk of violence, we must
consider power and the nature of the triadic status quo. For we will find
that in any triadic relationship this simple equation holds: the greater the
gap between those expectations defining the status quo and the balance of
powers, the greater the likelihood of violence occurring within the triad.

For example, these elements and this process can be seen in the history
of Soviet-American relations since World War II, as will be mentioned
later. The dangerous Cold War years from 1948 to the mid-1950s involved
a working out through conflict of a stable structure of expectations—a
world order of the superpowers—and an acceptable status quo based on
what each wanted, was capable of getting, and had the will to pursue.
Unfortunately, this balance of powers has changed radically since the 1960s
while the status quo has remained basically the same as that achieved in the
1950s. This has created a gap between the current status quo and the
underlying balance of powers; and thus an increased risk of Soviet-
American violence. Indeed, as most analysts will agree, the risk today of
such violence is at least as great as during the Cold War years.

Although moving at a different pace and currently in different phases,
such a process can also be seen in Sino-Soviet and Sino-American
relations. What makes the three dyadic processes particularly important
here is that each dyadic power balance and related status quo depends on
the third state.

This is the perspective to be elaborated and clarified in the following
pages.

A Conflict Helix

Although we may view the Sino-Soviet-American relationship as triadic,
fundamentally it is made up of three dyadic processes—the Soviet-
American, Sino-American, and Sino-Soviet—with each process anchored
by the third power. Accordingly, I will first focus on this dyadic process,
called a *conflict helix,* and then the role of this third power will be
subsequently illuminated. A conflict helix is a general process whereby
states establish and maintain the understandings, accommodations, and
agreements that enable them to cooperate and satisfy their interests.
Within this process conflict itself is a means through which states adjust to
their different interests, capabilities, and wills; it is a trial-and-error,

mutual learning process that achieves an accommodation of some sort between what states want, can get, and are willing to pursue. These accommodations, whether forced or negotiated, explicit or implicit, written or unwritten, constitute a *social contract:* a structure of expectations defining who owns, controls, influences, gets, or does what. And this structure of expectations is based on a balance of powers (such as the capability of states to persuade, bargain, use authority, threaten) achieved by the conflict.

The social contract that is an outcome of conflict is initially congruent with the balance of powers established between states and defines their social order: it establishes and permits cooperation between them and delineates for them an oasis of peace. Unfortunately, what states want, can, and will get changes in time and causes the balance of powers to shift away from the structure of expectations. As the balance becomes less congruent with expectations a gap is formed between the social contract and the underlying balance of powers. As the gap gets larger it becomes an increasing source of tension until some trigger event surfaces the disparity between power and expectations; conflict then erupts, and the structure of expectations—social contract—is disrupted. This new conflict establishes a more realistic balance of powers and associated social contract; a new phase of cooperation and peace is determined. And eventually, this peace will likewise breakdown into conflict as for this structure of expectations a gap between power and expectations also develops.

Although this process seems cyclic—conflict to cooperation to conflict to cooperation, and so on—and unending, conflict actually can become less intense and frequent. As the two parties learn more about each other through successive conflicts and periods of peace and cooperation, and assuming no change in the fundamental conditions of their relationship, their conflict becomes less intense and shorter, the periods of cooperation more solidary and durable. Thus the helix: an upward spiral in mutual learning as the relationship between two states cycle through conflict and cooperation.

Now, to detail some of the elements of this process specific to states, and the United States, Soviet Union and China in particular. A first principle of a conflict helix is that states relate to each other through the deliberate or unconscious signs and cues they transmit by their words and deeds and character (size, economic capability, military establishment, political system, leadership, etc.); and this mutual reading, this mutual signaling, is a continuous conversation between what each expresses as a totality, a field.

Besides communicating, states apply power to some end. They use force, they coerce, they bargain, they persuade, and the like. The most important of these powers they direct at the mental fields of the leaders and people of other states, at their beliefs, interests, and will, in order to get them to do something they want. Within a conflict helix, all these powers are dynamic; they are producing, bringing into being, causing. They are the pushing-pulling-forcing-struggling-nature of the state. Dynamic, such powers have a *direction*, a *base*, and *determination*.

Power is given direction by a state's interests. Its wants, purposes and goals, and its strength, intensity, and vitality point and energize its power; that is, it exercises power to some end. Power also has a particular base, such as threats for coercion, promises for bargaining. But all such bases utilize and depend on a state's capabilities. These are its skills, abilities, and resources, which together enable it to exercise power.

But, except for force, these powers are directed towards the minds of the leaders of other states to affect their decisions, will, interest, needs, and so on. They are primarily psychological: they depend on the operation of another leader's perceptions and expectations in his mental field. The *appearance* of power is as important, therefore, as its substance.

While a state's interests direct its power, and its capabilities, including the ability to appear powerful, give power strength, it is a state's determination that gives power reality. And determination depends on will. Exercising power—producing effects—is therefore largely an equation. It can be put simply:

$$\text{Power} = \text{Interests} \times \text{Capability} \times \text{Will}$$

If a state's interests, capability, or will are zero, then its power is zero.

Now, a state exercises power, tries to produce effects. A state persuades, threatens, promises, commands, requests, and manipulates. But these powers often confront the interests, capabilities, and will of another state. What ensues is a power struggle, a *balancing of powers*.

For a conflict helix this all means that the outcome of *conflict is a simultaneous solution to two equations of power; it is a mutually satisfactory outcome in which neither side has the further determination, purpose, or capacity to do what is necessary to further improve it. Conflict therefore achieves a new balance of powers. And this balance is the basis of a new structure of expectations determined by the conflict.*

Expectations guide behavior, they order the lives of states according to the predictions each makes about how others will respond to their behavior. These expectations divide into patterns associated with the different relationships, interests, and activities among states. Some expectations involve their economic relations, some their defensive alliances, some their giving or receipt of aid, some their scientific and cultural relations, and so on. Each pattern of expectations may be a different set of understandings, agreements, and rules that states have mutually worked out. Some are achieved through minor balancing; some through major conflicts and confrontations; some through a recognition of a common interest. Each pattern is a mutual *structure of expectations*—a structure in that the expectations fit together and usually remain relatively unchanged over months, or sometimes, years. A structure of expectations defines what states will do in a particular situation. It is an implicit and sometimes explicit *international contract* governing the behavior between states.

At the core of any structure of expectations is a *status quo* defining the mutual rights, obligations, and duties among the parties. It defines what a state owns, its property—those things it has absolute command over and at its whim can exclude other's from using. Rights, obligations, duties, and property are the most important expectations to determine between states (as will be noted, violence is caused by a breakdown in this status quo).

Cooperation, collaboration, partnership, association, mutual aid, and the like, then take place within—indeed, require—mutually reliable expectations. For a conflict helix, mutual cooperation assumes some agreement, some common basis for mutually predicting behavior. It assumes that states know when they are right or wrong, helpful or unhelpful, correct or incorrect with regard to each other. And this assumes shared expectations (a balance of powers).

States balance, develop expectations, and cooperate. But interests shift, capabilities alter, wills vary. A state may get a new revolutionary government; its leadership may change; or it may vastly increase its military capability. Unfortunately, however, such changes usually do not immediately carry over to the associated structure of expectations, which may remain largely the same. Informal expectations are like habits. Regardless of domestic changes, they stay with a state until something dramatic in its relations with other states happens to change them significantly. Of course, formal expectations, such as those defined by written agreements or treaties, do undergo subtle and incremental reinterpretation, but even then the core expectations remain much the same until the agreement expires, the treaty is abrogated, or the rule is changed.

In other words, change in the balance of powers usually creates a gap between the structure of expectations and its underlying interests, capabilities, and will. *It is a gap caused by two different rates of change: the slow evolution of expectations versus the possibly rapid change in what states want, can, and will do.*

Now, as a result of this gap, strain, friction, a pressure towards readjustment of power or expectations, builds up. Alarming tension and hostility may appear. Suddenly, some small thing, often unimportant by itself, occurs and triggers a breakdown of expectations. The trigger is simply the "final straw"; the excuse for "having it out." It is the immediate cause of conflict.

To now put together the whole process of conflict and cooperation for a conflict helix: through conflict with others states communicate and adjust, and learn to read each other's field of expression; through trial and error each establishes with others a balance of powers; and through control over a situation and opportunities and through persuasion, altruism, legitimacy, promises, and threats, states establish a mutual balance of their wants, capabilities, and determination. This supports a mutual structure of expectations—of reliable predictions about the other's responses to their behaviors. This establishes the framework for cooperation. *This enables states to cross the vast cultural, socioeconomic, political, and psychological gulf separating them.*

But change will occur, usually much faster in the balance of powers. Figure 13-1 pictures this process. At the left is a structure of expectations and its supporting balance of powers formed out of the conflict between two states. From left to right is illustrated the change in the structure and the balance of powers. Both may change at different rates and in different directions, causing a gap between what a state expects of another and their mutually supporting interests, capabilities and will. As this gap gets larger the probability increases that some trigger event will eventually occur to persuade one or the other state that things cannot go on—*to stimulate or provoke a willful decision to have it out or change the order of things.* Expectations are thus disrupted, as shown in Figure 13-1. And the resulting conflict renegotiates a new structure of expectations and supporting balance of powers.

A state's conflicts end in cooperation; but such cooperation ends in conflict. Are states caught in a vicious cycle? No, states learn from their conflict and cooperation. Each round of conflict and cooperation makes the subjective gulf between states easier to bridge. Each round requires less adjustment, and each round of peace lasts longer; harmony becomes more durable, cooperation more enduring.

A *conflict helix,* therefore, is a process of iteration towards harmony and peace. The previous conflict and expectations are input to the current conflict; this and the consequent expectations will be input to the next. And because of this learning and continual process of communication, the mutual adjustments and expectations between states come closer and closer to truly reflecting their diverse interests, capabilities, and wills.

Empirical Basis of Defense Policy

Figure 13-1

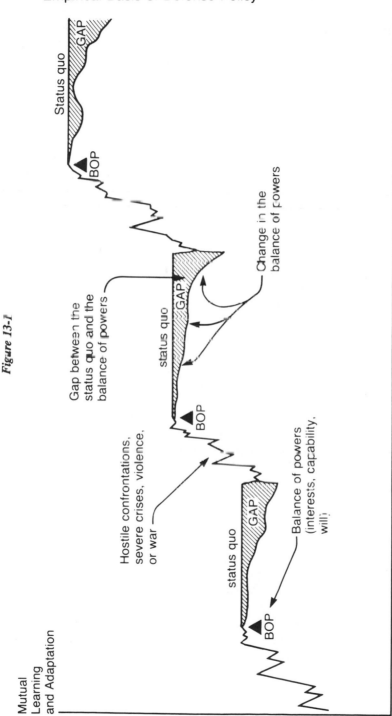

Mutual
Learning
and Adaptation

Status quo

GAP

BOP

Gap between the
status quo and the
balance of powers

status quo

GAP

BOP

Change in the
balance of powers

Hostile confrontations,
severe crises, violence,
or war

status quo

GAP

BOP

Balance of powers
(interests, capability,
will)

Time

Were the lives of states from birth to death a continuous helix, then states should have the most conflict when they are young, like Mali or Fiji, least when old, like Egypt or China. But history is not so accommodating. Why?

The helix assumes that the framework within which states interact remains fairly constant. Of course, within this framework change will always occur. But presumably, for example, the leadership remains the same in ideology and policies, alliances are supported at more or less the same level, and no major increase or reduction in defense is undertaken. Presumably there is no new revolutionary government, no reevaluation of aid commitments, no radical shift in alliances, or no withdrawal from foreign commitments. Any such dramatic changes may require a whole new series of adjustments, a new rephasing of a conflict helix. Of course, states will not have forgotten the previous conflicts and expectations, but the changed situation may stimulate a radically different set of interests and demand capabilities that were dormant before. Simply consider the Cuban-American adjustments necessary when Castro overthrew Batista, or the impact on the international relations of Southeast Asia of the American defeat in Vietnam.

Now, within all international conflict lurks the potential for violence; and when violence does occur, it is over a *status quo*. As discussed above, a status quo is the core of a structure of expectations. It delimits a state's rights, obligations, and property, and thus its most basic values and interests regarding others. For this reason a breakdown in the status quo involves bedrock values and goals most difficult to compromise, and the resulting conflict can easily escalate to a test of might. When issues are so vital, violence is the ultimate means for communicating vital interests, capability, and resolve, and deciding who prevails or what compromises will be made. By risking sovereignty, territory, or life, a state communicates a supreme interest in the outcome and a most resolute will.

As a form of violence, however, war will not occur without satisfying four conditions. The most important is the presence of a significant change in the balance of powers supporting the status quo: interests, capabilities, and will, singly or in combination, must have changed sufficiently that the status quo is now felt to be unjust, threatened, or ripe for readjustment. Such change will then create a gap, resulting in a tense, cold or hostile climate between the states. It will be obvious to informed observers that unless something is done, violence and possibly war will break out.

Second, there must be a will-to-war. That is, each potential combatant must have a will to fight either in defense of or to change the status quo. Appeasement and concessions can avoid war, at least for the short run. Such, of course, may cost, in honor, benefits, potential gain, or freedom, more than a state is willing or able to bear; and thus stimulating a subsequent will-to-war. Third, each potential combatant must expect success as its leaders define it. That is, each state believes that it can achieve its war aims (desirable slice of territory, defeat the others border encroachment, force Big Power intervention and mediation, etc.).

And fourth, there must be a disruption of the status quo, as discussed above. Some, perhaps surprising, event must communicate injustice, threat, or opportunity in a way to crystallize the conflict situation and provoke the will-to-action for one or both parties.

Aside from these four conditions, which comprise the most important necessary causes of war, there are a number of aggravating and inhibiting conditions that influence the likelihood of war once these necessary causes are present. These cannot be presented in full here, but I should note two which are most relevant to the Sino-Soviet-American triad. One is the weakness of the status-quo-power. Given the presence of the necessary causes, if the status-quo-power displays an unwillingness or inability to defend an already unstable status quo, then this makes more likely its disruption and the escalation of violence and war, once they occur. A second is power parity, or a sufficient equality of coercive power and force such that each side believes that it can successfully oppose the power of the other.

In any conflict, however, there are also conditions inhibiting its occurrence and escalation, among which only the two most relevant can be mentioned here. Especially important is the strength of the status-quo-power. If in spite of a change in the balance of powers, the supporter of the status quo appears willing and able to defend it, this tends to work against its disruption. A second important inhibitor is power disparity. While power parity worsens a war-potential situation, power disparity tends to restrain it.

These then are the most relevant causes and conditions of war within a conflict helix. They are forces of the international field that most bear upon the likelihood of war among China, the Soviet Union, and the United States.

The Sino-Soviet-American Tri-Helix

I will use the concept of tri-helix to describe any international situation where: (1) the relationships between three states fundamentally divide into three distinquishable dyadic processes each constituting a conflict helix (the three do not establish their expectations and status quo through multilateral negotiation and bargaining among themselves); (2) the dyadic process between any two of the three is basically dependent on the conflict helix each has with the third; (3) the status quo and thus the peace between any two of these states could be disrupted by a basic change in the interests, capability, or will of the third.

What needs to be made clear at this point is the precise nature of the dependency of the conflict helix between two states on the third. Recall that states establish a structure of expectations as an outcome of balancing powers. The key here is that the resulting balance is between two equations of power, each involving the state's interests, capability, and will. This dependency is created when a third state significantly influences this dyadic balance through its effect upon or relationship to these equations.

The remainder of this section will try to make the tri-helix clearer and more specific.

Now, a conflict helix is fundamentally dyadic, it is a process of conflict and cooperation between two states. And many relationships are truly dyadic in this manner, such as those between the United States and Canada, Burma and India, France and Algeria. Other states play a role, of course, and their interests and behavior may from time to time vitally influence the helix, but there is no structural linkage between their helices and a third party.

But for periods of time the helices between two states may become fundamentally coupled to a third state. Indeed, it is possible and not uncommon for the helices between a large number of states to become basically coupled to each other. This is most evident when opposing multilateral defense alliances define the major foreign and defense policies within and between the hostile coalitions. The dyadic helices become so coupled that the disruption of the status quo between any two opposing states may presage war not only between them, but between both coalitions.

But our interest here is in the Sino-Soviet-American triad and the peculiar nature of their coupling should be made clear. In what way does a third party vitally influence a conflict helix? No doubt, all helices are influenced to some degree by other parties. No two states can totally ignore others in their conflict and accommodations, and in this sense also, nations exist in a field of relationships and interest. Our concern, however, is when that influence becomes so strong that the helix now depends in some way on a third state.

This dependency acts fundamentally through the equation of power. Recall that states establish a structure of expectations congruent with the balance of powers between them. This balance is of two equations of power, where power is understood as a product of each state's interests, capability, and will. It is precisely on this equation that a third state has its greatest influence on a helix, as illustrated in Figure 13-2.

Figure 13-2
UNCOUPLED VERSUS COUPLED CONFLICT HELICES

KEY
```
        I = Interests
        C = Capability
        W = will
    Power = I × C × W
      BOP = Balance of Powers
```

Uncoupled Conflict Helix i-j

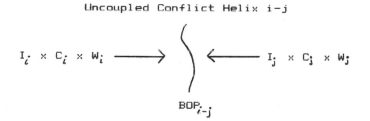

Coupled Conflict Helix

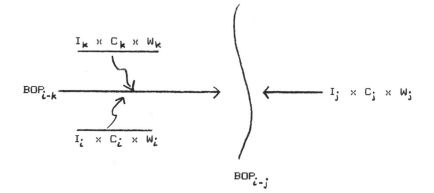

To clarify this, let a conflict helix be between states i and j, with k being the third state as in Figure 13-2. Some well known ways in which k can influence i and j's balance of powers is by supporting i's interest in maintaining or changing the status quo with j. By threats or warnings, by diplomatic moves, by military alerts, movements, or shows of force, or by sanctions, k can display support for i's interests. Moreover, k can add to i's capability by military and economic aid or by a defensive alliance that commits k to come to i's defense. Finally, through such words and deeds, k can influence j's determination to change the status quo and i's resolution to defend it. By expressing an unshakeable commitment, perhaps manifested by actually basing a division of troops or so in i, k can provide the final will necessary to maintain the status quo between i and j.

Most often such couplings are asymmetrical, in that while k strongly influences the balance of powers between i and j, i cannot have much influence on the balance between j and k, or likewise j may have little influence on the i and k balance of powers. A current example is the confrontation between El Salvador and Nicaragua. Clearly, while the United States is vitally involved in the balancing of powers between these two states, El Salvador has little influence on the Nicaragua-American balance of powers, and similarly for Nicaragua regarding the El Salvador-American balance. Such an asymmetric triad can be called *uni-coupled,* and the helix so influenced is an *uni-coupled helix,* as shown in Figure 13-3.

Another form of asymmetry is when not only can k influence the i-j helix, but i also can vitally influence the j-k one, while the i-k helix remains largely uncoupled. Such an asymmetric relationship currently obtains between Nicaragua (j), the Soviet Union (k), and the United States (i). While Nicaragua's balance with each of the others can be strongly influenced by the third party, Nicaragua has virtually no influence on the Soviet-American balance.

Then, as shown in Figure 13-3, there are two asymmetric triads. One is the *uncoupled triad* where each of the three helices are independent and the prior discussion of the conflict helix applies to each pair without important qualification by reference to the third state. Such would be, for example, the Canadian-Australian-American triad.

The other symmetrical helix is one in which all three dyadic helices are coupled to the third state through its balance of powers. This is now the most relevant triad for viewing Sino-Soviet-American relations.[1] But before dealing with this triad, one more consideration should be covered.

What, precisely, does this coupling mean for the process of conflict and cooperation that is the conflict helix? When two helices are interdependent as in the bicoupled triad, then both helices are in phase: the periods of the

Figure 13-3

TYPES OF TRIADIC COUPLINGS

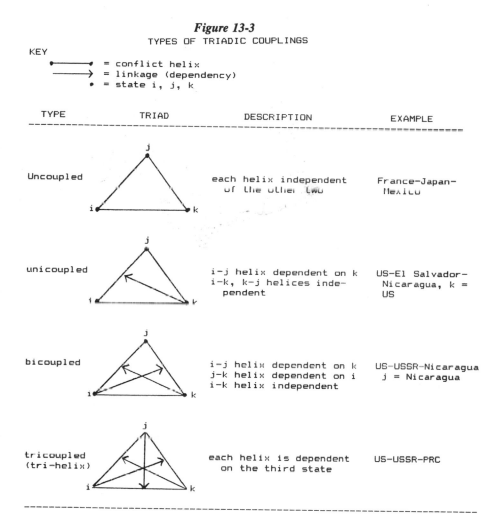

KEY

•————• = conflict helix
————→ = linkage (dependency)
• = state i, j, k

TYPE	TRIAD	DESCRIPTION	EXAMPLE
Uncoupled		each helix independent of the other two	France-Japan-Mexico
unicoupled		i-j helix dependent on k i-k, k-j helices independent	US-El Salvador-Nicaragua, k = US
bicoupled		i-j helix dependent on k j-k helix dependent on i i-k helix independent	US-USSR-Nicaragua j = Nicaragua
tricoupled (tri-helix)		each helix is dependent on the third state	US-USSR-PRC

balancing of powers, establishment of a balance, structure of expectations, and disruption of expectations would more or less co-occur. This is because the change in the fundamental interests, capabilities, and wills involved in helices i-j and j-k are linked through the common state j (see the bicoupled triad in Figure 13-3); as their interests, capabilities, and wills shift so eventually goes the coupled helices. Thus, the coupled Nicaragua-American and Soviet-Nicaragua helices are interdependent. As the balancing or balance of powers of Nicaragua with the United States (or Soviet

Union) goes, so will be determined Nicaragua's corresponding relations with the Soviet Union (or United States).

In the tricoupled triad (tri-helix, for short), all three helices are in phase. This is the situation with the Sino-Soviet-American triad. That is to say, the question of Soviet-American peace or war, hostility or détente, is no longer a matter of Moscow and Washington, but now is fundamentally coupled to decisions in Beijing; likewise for peace or war, hostility or détente, between China and the Soviet Union, or China and the United States.

The Empirical Sino-Soviet-American Tri-Helix

At this point, an empirical analysis of Sino-Soviet-American conflict and cooperation should help clarify their tri-helix. Azar and Sloan (1975) provide annual scaled conflict and cooperation event data for the PRC, USSR, and U.S., 1948–1973. There are some problems with these scales,[2] but they reasonably fit my purpose of tracking the three conflict helices by year and determining their coupling. Now, it is the dyad's net conflict that is of empirical interest. This is because the phasing of the conflict helix is manifested by changes in both conflict and cooperation: intense conflict manifests the balancing of powers phase; much less intense and routine conflict (as in frozen relations) or increased cooperation manifest the structure of expectations phase. The movement in *net conflict* (conflict minus cooperation) thereby should reflect the phasing of a conflict helix.

That the empirical data end on 1973 is unfortunate. Since it is important and interesting to view Sino-Soviet-American net conflict up through 1984, I estimated their net conflict 1974–1984 from chronologies and my knowledge of events during this period.

Figures 13-4a–13-4c present the plots of net conflict for all three dyads.[3] Actual and polynomial net conflict are shown. The latter comprises the regression estimates of a polynomial equation fitted to the actual net conflict.[4] A polynomial equation is used to define the stable points in the net conflict that reflect the balancing of powers and structure of expectations phases. These stable points are necessarily (but not sufficiently) the minima and maxima of the polynomial,[5] as we will see in interpreting them below.

Therefore, along with a chronology and sense for the history of these dyads, the polynomial curves will help discriminate the balancing of powers and structure of expectations phases of the helix. A clear local maximum or minimum of the curve is a stable region of conflict *or*

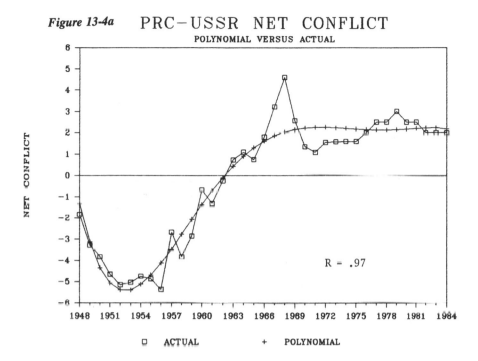

Figure 13-4a   PRC-USSR NET CONFLICT
POLYNOMIAL VERSUS ACTUAL

R = .97

□   ACTUAL   +   POLYNOMIAL

structure of expectations. A sharp upward or downward movement is a necessary condition for either the achievement of a balance of powers and consequent structure of expectations; or for the breakdown in the structure of expectations and sharp increase in conflict behavior. For comparison, Figure 13-5 therefore shows the three polynomial curves together; and Figure 13-6 overlays each curve with its probable structure of expectations (and status quo), as shown by the straight heavy line.[6]

Now, to consider each dyad in turn. Figure 13-4a shows Sino-Soviet net and polynomial conflict, Figure 13-5 compares its polynomial to the others, and Figure 13-6 pictures the underlying conflict helix. How do we now understand as history these pictures for the Sino-Soviet dyad? On 2 October 1949, the PRC was formally recognized by the Soviet Union and appropriately, the plot beginning in 1949 shows a continuation of the decline in net conflict begun under the Kuomintang regime. From late 1949 through 1950 the PRC and USSR were engaged in intensive bargaining as to the shape of their relationship; really the degree of subordination of new communist China to the transnational and ideological claims of Moscow. The major outcome of this balancing of powers was their Treaty of Friendship in 1950 and subsequent transfer to China of the Soviet Rights in

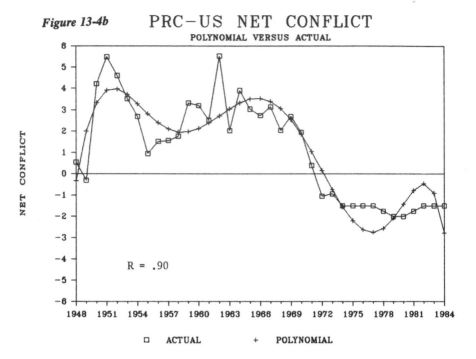

Figure 13-4b   PRC–US NET CONFLICT
POLYNOMIAL VERSUS ACTUAL

□   ACTUAL   +   POLYNOMIAL

the Manchurian Railroad (1952); establishment of joint control of Port Arthur (1952); and increased economic aid (1953). The basic framework of their relationship and their status quo was made final in this period, and thus we may take 1950 as the start of their structure of expectations phase.

This phase lasted until about 1959. Conflict had been building up, such as over the Soviet's handling of the Lebanon Crises (1958), and China's Great Leap Forward; and in 1959 the Soviet's repudiated their secret nuclear agreement and tried to remain neutral in the Sino-Indian conflict. By 1960 conflict boiled into the open and escalated, until by 1964 there was an intense hostility, a polemical war, rising border tension and military buildup, and diplomatic sanctions. Thus, the jagged increase in net conflict shown in Figure 13-4a for the 1960s reflects this balancing of powers period of intense conflict, including the border incidents of 1967–1968, Damansky Island clashes of 1969, and possibility of a Sino-Soviet war.

But through 1968 to 1970 the United States clearly communicated its opposition to any Soviet invasion of China, asserting that she could not remain neutral were the Soviets to attack China. While on their side the Soviets backed off, began intermittent border negotiations, and eventually

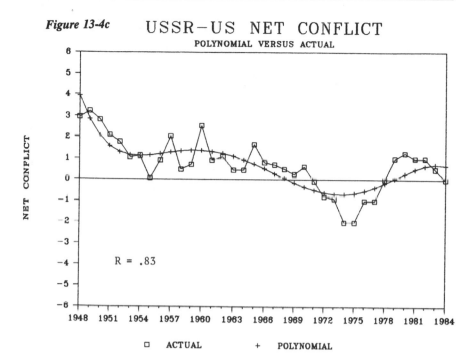

Figure 13-4c   USSR–US NET CONFLICT
POLYNOMIAL VERSUS ACTUAL

□   ACTUAL   +   POLYNOMIAL

made offers of a nonaggression pact, the Chinese also cooled their rhetoric. Most significantly, they reopened Warsaw diplomatic talks with Washington, culminating in the Nixon visit of 1972.

In substance, after skirting the edge of war in 1968–1969, both the Soviet Union and China settled into a relatively stable balance of conflict—a structure of expectations beginning about 1969 (as shown in Figure 13–6) that involved an interweaving of diplomatic visits and sanctions, warm and cool negotiations, formal offers and rejections, and conciliatory and harsh polemics. Underlying all this was a relative balance of Sino-Soviet powers that involved a massive Soviet military buildup and modernization on the Chinese border, the enormous area of China and its mass but poorly armed army, China's limited nuclear capability, and the threat of American military support for China and a possible escalation of any limited war involving China into a Soviet-American nuclear war.

In essence, and regardless of the stresses of the Sino-Vietnam War (1979) and the abrogation of the Sino-Soviet Friendship Treaty, conflict and cooperation has oscillated around the level established in 1969–1972. This can be seen in Figure 13–6, where the polynomial net conflict line is practically horizontal. In sum, then, the data suggest that about 1969–1970

Figure 13-5   POLYNOMIAL NET CONFLICT

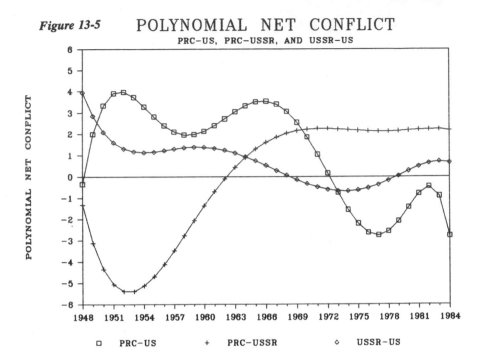

PRC–US, PRC–USSR, AND USSR–US

□   PRC–US   +   PRC–USSR   ◇   USSR–US

a new structure of expectations came into being that better reflected the reality of Sino-Soviet antagonism; and that this replaced the expectations of the 1950s that were based on Sino-Soviet amity.

Considering now the Sino-American dyad, Figure 13-4b shows their net conflict and polynomial fit; and Figure 13–6 pictures the likely underlying structure of expectations phases. Over the period 1948–1984 there has been two distinct structures of expectations. The first resulted from the Sino-American conflict and adjustments necessitated by the revolutionary new fact: a communist government in Beijing that had effective military control over the Mainland. Not until the Korean War and the American declaration of full military support for the Nationalist government's control of Taiwan, was established the extent and limits of Sino-American capabilities, interests, and will; and was forged a relatively stable structure of expectations. Therefore established about 1953–1954 and thoroughly tested in the subsequent Matsu-Quemoy crises, these mutual expectations well delimited the tacit Sino-American status quo involving the reality of the PRC, a communist North and anticommunist South Korea, and an American guaranty of the independence of the Republic of China on Taiwan.

Mutual
Learning
Adaptation

Global US-Soviet status quo

unstable status quo

GAP

BOP

Balance of powers
(interests, capabilities, will)

BOP

Hostile
confrontations
crises, violence,
wars

BOP

	1945	1950	1955	1960	1965	1970	1975	1980
WARS		Korean (U.S.)	Suez	Sino-Indian	Indo-Pakistan Arab-Israel	Vietnam Indo-Pakistan Arab-Israel	Indo-Pakistan Arab-Israel Egypt-Libya Lebanon Civil Jordon Civil	Angola Civil Ethiopia-Soma- lia N. Yemen-S. Yemen Cambodia-Viet. China-Vietnam Nicaragua Civil Lebanon Civil	Afghanistan Iran-Iraq El Salvador Civil
INTERVEN-TIONS	China Civil Greek Civil Arab-Israel	Iran (USSR) Czech. (USSR) Poland (USSR) Rumania (USSR) Bulgaria (USSR) Hungary (USSR)	Lebanon (US) Hungary (USSR)	Cuba (US)	Dom. Rep. (US) Czech. (USSR)		Angola (USSR, Cuba) Ethiopia (USSR, Cuba) Lebanon (Syria) Chad (Libya) Nicaragua (Cuba)	Poland (USSR) El Salvador (Cuba) Chad (Libya)
CRISES	Iran Greek Czech. coup Yugoslavia Berlin Blockade Turkey		Berlin Quemoy-Matsu	Congo Berlin Cuban Missile Laos	Sino-Soviet border USS Pueblo Arab-Israel N. Korea-S Korea	US-USSR dur- ing Arab-Israel War Portugal East-Pak star. OPEC	Mayaguez (US) Panmunjom Vietnam	Iran Hostages Lebanon (Israel) Afghanistan Poland
SOVIET ADVANCES	N. Vietnam	Bulgaria Hungary Poland Czechoslovakia E. Germany N. Korea Romania		Cuba Congo	S Yemen Mali	India Syria Guinea-Bissau	Angola Laos Cambodia S. Vietnam Ethiopia Mozambique Libya Afghanistan	Nicaragua El Salvador? Iran? N. Yemen?

US-USSR RELEVANT

*Satellites; strong allies & ties. ? = in contention

U.S. Status quo and Balance of Powers   *Figure 13-7*

forged that was based on an equilibrium between Soviet and American global and regional interests, military and economic strength, will and credibility. This balance held firm in the late 1950s and was reaffirmed through several crises and confrontations involving the status quo. However, the withdrawal from Vietnam that began in earnest after 1968, the subsequent Vietnam syndrome that began to block any strong American involvement elsewhere, and the consequent sharp unilateral reduction in the absolute defense effort, seriously altered the balance of powers in favor of the Soviet Union; thus leaving the status quo hanging in air, as shown in Figure 13–7. The resulting large gap, so well evidenced in the figure by the upsurge in related wars, interventions by the Soviet Union or its proxies, and crises, has destabilized the status quo. And this instability is itself manifest by the upsurge in Soviet advances since 1975. This large gap between the balance of powers and the status quo has produced the greatest risk of Soviet-American war since at least the early 1950s, if not since World War II.

Changes in Soviet-American military capability do not alone account for the gap shown in Figure 13–7, which also reflects shifts in national interests and will. However, these shifts do significantly influence American military expenditures and forces. Thus, changes in the Soviet-American military balance provide a rough empirical estimate of the overall change in the balance of powers.

The Soviets had a relatively overall military advantage in the immediate postwar period, which was overcome in the 1950s as a result of the huge American arms buildup catalyzed by the Korean War. However, with the conclusion of the war, President Eisenhower increasingly cut into American relative capability, which was overtaken in the late 1950s and early 1960s as a rapid growth in Soviet strategic forces was added to its continuing large conventional capability. However, the subsequent rearmament program of President Kennedy, later conjoined with the Vietnam War buildup, served again to rebalance military forces in favor of the United States. Then, beginning in 1969, with the gradual withdrawal from Vietnam and the Vietnam-engendered frustration and isolationism, increasingly large cuts were made in conventional forces and a decline in relative strategic capability accelerated. This relative disarmament continued until the late 1970s, when Congress and President Carter were persuaded by such events as shown in Figure 13–7 and the massive Soviet buildup, to increase real (relative to inflation) defense expenditures and upgrade conventional and strategic forces. Although still underway, the relative effect of this new buildup has probably been no more than to level off the negative trends in the Soviet-American military balance.

In total, then, the hypothetical gap in the balance of powers shown in Figure 13–7 not only correlates with an increasing instability in the status quo and growing net political advances, but also reflects the actual shift in the strategic and overall military balance of powers. All this tends to support the validity of the gap shown between the balance of powers and status quo in Figure 13–7.

Sino-Soviet-American Interdependence

Based on the previous understanding of the three dyadic relations, it is most likely that their helices have become dependent since at least 1973 and the Shanghai Communiqué, as pictured in Figure 13–6: the stability of the structure of expectations and its status quo for each dyad now depends on a balance of powers involving all three states. It is now inconceivable that the United States would remain aloof from a Soviet military attack on China; or that a Sino-Soviet rapprochement and a Hitler-Stalin like nonaggression pact would not have the most serious impact on the Soviet-American balance of powers and peace.

As a result of this triadic dependency—cophasing—the behavior within each dyad for the period 1974–1984 should be more interdependent than for the period 1948–1973. In fact, we see this is the case from Table 13.1. This table gives the squared multiple regression correlation coefficient (R^2) for the simple linear regression of the net conflict of each dyad on that of the other two.

Table 13-1

**The Squared Multiple Correlation Coefficient
of each Sino-Soviet-American Dyad Regressed
on the Other Two**

Dependent Variable	Squared Multiple Correlation Coefficients[a]			
	1948-1973		1974-1984	
	R^2	F-Test[b]	R^2	F-Test[b]
Sino-American Dyad	.20	.08	.67	.012
Sino-Soviet Dyad	.11	.25	.64	.02
Soviet-American Dyad	.26	.03	.46	.082

a. The squared multiple correlation coefficient gives the proportion of variance in the net conflict of the dependent dyad explained by the variance in net conflict of the other two dyads.

b. The values shown for the F-test are its achieved significance levels. For example, for the Sino-American Dyad and 1948-1973, its R^2 is significant at $p < .08$.

As can be seen from Table 13-1, in each case the R^2 for 1974–1984 sharply increases over that for the previous years; and even though there is less than half as many years in the later period (11 versus 26), the F-test shows the R^2 to be much more significant for the later period in two out of the three cases. For the Soviet-American dyad, the F-test is slightly less significant, indicating that the increase in R^2 from .26 to .46 may be due to the loss of degrees of freedom and not an increase in triadic dependence.

This interpretation would be a mistake, however, for it would ignore the important and substantial explanation: the structure of expectations in place during 1973–1984 also existed for about 1953–1973; and therefore net conflict varied much less between these two periods than for the other two dyads (see Figure 13-6), and this is reflected in the smaller difference in R^2. Keep in mind that this difference, almost a doubling from pre to post 1974 only looks small in comparison to the more than *tripling* of the Sino-Soviet's R^2 and *six-fold* increase in the Sino-American's.

Conclusion

To conclude, a conflict helix theory of dyadic behavior between states has been presented and extended to triads. One particular type of triad—the tri-helix—has been shown to represent the current Sino-Soviet-American triadic relationship. That is, the different status quos of the Sino-Soviet, Sino-American, and Soviet-American dyads have become interdependent, such that the change in the balance of powers for one dyad will cause a change in that of the other two dyads; a breakdown in the status quo of one will cause a breakdown in the status quos of the others. Empirical analyses of dyadic conflict and cooperation tends to support this argument.

All this raises the most serious question for American defense and foreign policy. In an independent dyad, one state can act to influence the other's decisions and thus exercise some control over their relationship; in a tri-helix, one state usually has no control over how the other two will act toward each other. Therefore, if the above theory and analysis is correct, by its implicit alliance with China the United States has conceded important control over its future, particularly over peace or war. The fate of American policy towards the Soviet Union and China now depends to an uncomfortable degree on continued deep Sino-Soviet hostility and the political and military status quo along China's borders.

Notes

1. This is also the most appropriate type of triad for applying balance theory. Balance theory tries to gauge the political stability and likely direction of political change in a triad in terms of the balance of the solidary-antagonistic relationships between the three states. Quite simply, it is an application of the understanding that "a friend of my friend is a friend, an enemy of my friend is an enemy, and a friend of my enemy is an enemy." Then a situation, for example where my "friend is a friend of my enemy," would be unstable and involve psychological and political forces pushing for a redefinition of either my friend as an enemy or my enemy as a friend.

   However, for such balance theory to apply, the triad must be tricoupled, what few applying balance theory realize. To take a common example, an uncoupled triad would be husband, wife, and postman. Whether the wife (or husband) is antagonistic or friendly to the postman would hardly matter to the husband (or wife).

2. Azar and Sloan give too much weight to minor events in forming their scale, thus overweighting it in terms of accusations and threats. For example, they accord a weight of 16 to an accusation and 102 to a war. This means that seven accusations together exceed any one war in intensity—questionable, indeed.

3. The Azar and Sloan (1975) "DI" was used for conflict and cooperation. The net conflict score for each i–j dyad was then created as follows.
   * a one was added to all raw DI scores to eliminate zeros;
   * each resulting DI was log transformed to reduce the effect of a few very large scores;
   * the net conflict score for each directed dyad i to j was then formed by subtracting the transformed cooperation DI from the transformed conflict DI;
   * the result for the directed i to j dyad was then added to that for j to i, and the sum was divided by two to get the total net conflict for the symmetrical i–j dyad; this is the score plotted in Figures 13-4a–13-4c for 1948–1973.

4. For the PRC-USSR dyad, the polynomial equation (t = year, where 1948 = 1, 1949 = 2, . . . , 1984 = 37) is:

$$\hat{y} = 1.2 - 2.9t + .4t^2 - .02t^3 + .5E{-}3t^4 - .4E{-}5t^5$$

   with R = .97. For the PRC-U.S. dyad, it is:

$$\hat{y} = -3.9 + 4.3t - .78t^2 + .05t^3 - .1E{-}3t^5 - .35E{-}5t^6 - .4E{-}7t^7$$

   with R = .9. And for the USSR-U.S. dyad, the equation is:

$$\hat{y} = 5.5 - 1.8t + .26t^2 - .016t^3 + .4E{-}3t^4 - .4E{-}5t^5$$

   with R = .83.

   Only coefficients with t-tests greater than or equal to 2.00 are given.

5. See Rummel (1983: copies available upon request) for my mathematical development of these ideas in modeling the conflict helix by Catastrophe Theory.

6. The line is horizontal because the structure of expectations and core status quo change little, until disrupted, even though the associated behavior may vary considerably (as shown by net conflict).

7. In Figures 13-6 and 13-4b the Sino-American polynomial clearly shows a new minimum and maximum around this structure of expectations, while the actual net conflict in Figure 13-4b is relatively flat. Although the actual net conflict is based on events during this period, I believe the polynomial better reflects the sense—texture—of Sino-American relations. In any case, the new maximum does not define a breakdown in the structure of expectations, but rather the oscillation of net conflict around it.

REFERENCES

Azar, E.C. and T.J. Sloan (1975) *Dimensions of Interaction: A Sourcebook for the Study of the Behavior of 31 Nations From 1948 through 1973.* Occasional Paper no. 8: International Studies Association.

Rummel, R.J. (1983) *A Catastrophe Theory Model of The Conflict Helix, With Tests.* Honolulu, Hawaii: Department of Political Science, University of Hawaii.

Conclusion

MORTON A. KAPLAN

Professor Ilpyong Kim deserves great credit for putting together this exceptionally interesting conference on the triadic relationship between the United States, the Soviet Union, and China. Although this relationship is very significant in the current era of world politics, its potentialities have often been misperceived by those who direct foreign policy in the United States as well as by the ordinary citizenry.

It has been a relatively constant feature of the democratic age that international political relationships tend to be perceived more in terms of myth than in terms of the hard, unsentimental realities perceived by the statesmen of the major states during the aristocratic periods of the eighteenth and nineteenth centuries. The American image of the Soviet Union, for instance, has undergone great shifts as Soviet and American interests have converged and drifted apart. It has shifted from the favorable image of the projected united front against Hitler, to, in Drew Pearson's phrase, the "communazi" image, to that of the wartime alliance, through postwar disillusionment and cold war images, to images of detente, and eventually of cynicism.

The American image of China has also gone through a number of significant shifts. The initial postwar, and quite unrealistic, policy of fostering a coalition government in China was replaced, after the defeat of the Nationalists, and especially after Chinese entry into the Korean War, with a period of great public hostility that lasted well into the 1960's. For many years, the modal American image of the relationship between the United States and China, at least for the near future, was expressed by Senator J. William Fulbright when he referred to China's "implacable hostility towards the United States."[1] I was dismayed that a well-informed Senator would subscribe to Khrushchev's disinformation tactic and responded, "Undoubtedly the Kremlin would like us to believe this, but why should we play into its hands? And where is the evidence for this hostility? Korea? We threatened legitimate Chinese interests when we marched to the Yalu. Our disclaimers that China should not have regarded this as a threat would have been worthless even had not our action in marching to the Yalu repudiated earlier statements by the Secretary of State that our only objective in Korea was to restore the *status quo ante.*"[2]

However, it would be a mistake to think that those who guided American policy misperceived the realities of China as much as did Senator Fulbright or the public at large. Secretary of State Acheson recognized the potential discrepancy between Chinese and Russian interests, but seemed to regard Chinese entry into the Korean war as evidence for Russia's domination of Chinese policy. Whether Acheson really believed this in the dogmatic way in which he expressed it is subject to doubt, for his lack of credibility with conservatives in the Senate at times made him posture in ways that may not have accorded with his understanding of conditions. On the other hand, there can be no significant doubt that the analysis of the relationship between Russia and China by John Foster Dulles was remarkably prescient. Unlike Senator Fulbright, who leaned upon psychiatrists such as Jerome Frank for the argument that the best way to produce independence of positions among Communist powers was to behave in friendly ways toward them, Dulles believed that a policy of overt hostility toward China would exacerbate the strains between China and the Soviet Union and would tend to produce a split between them. Although I have not seen any evidence that John Foster Dulles relied upon the Yugoslav example in reaching this conclusion, events seem to have justified his insight.

The potential conflicts of interest between China and the Soviet Union might have produced a split eventually, even in the absence of Dulles' policies, for Russia was ever wary of a potential strong China and refused, or perhaps more accurately reneged on its promise, to assist China in the development of nuclear weapons. Nonetheless, the pressure placed upon

China in 1958 in the offshore island's crisis, during which Russia refused to come to China's assistance, most likely played a significant role in exacerbating the conflict of interests between the two parties and in precipitating the split between them.

Still, the commonality of interests between China and Russia had never been as great as was believed by many. The hard bargaining between Mao and Stalin during the 1949 treaty negotiations after the accession to power of the Communists in China illustrated a less than comradely posture between the two parties.

On the other hand, it is unlikely that the pact between the two countries could have been averted by a more friendly American posture in 1949 and 1950. That Zhou Enlai would have been receptive to aid from the United States and that he offered the possibility of a more flexible Chinese foreign policy apparently is factual, but its implications should be taken with several grains of salt. China did want more economic assistance than Russia was willing to give and more than the United States, in any event, would have been willing to give. But Mao and Zhou were true believers in Communism and were determined to impose a dominant Communist regime on a potentially resisting Chinese population. They needed an enemy for that purpose, and the United States fit that role best. It is unlikely that any initial flexibility would have had more significance than Lenin's NEP or the international politics of the Rapallo period. Despite all the potential conflicts between China and the Soviet Union, in my opinion their perceived commonality of interests outweighed their conflict of interests at that stage of the Chinese revolution. It would take two generations of experience both with Communism and with relations with the Soviet Union for a major shift to become possible in Chinese foreign policy.

There were those in the 1950s and '60s who argued for the American recognition of Communist China. There seems little doubt that this is the posture towards which Acheson had been heading in 1949, when he established the commission headed by Harold Stasen to investigate the problem. In the situation arising out of the Korean War, that policy orientation had lost its credibility. Moreover, the reasons offered for the policy made little sense after the war. The usual argument was that the Communist control of China was a fact and that one had to recognize facts. However, no one, least of all the U.S. government, denied the facts; the real issue concerned the policy consequences of various courses of action. The recognition of Communist China by Britain hardly was an inspiring precedent. And it could be argued that the United States had more sustained relations with China through the Warsaw meetings than did

Britain through its embassy in Beijing. The truth is that China was insufficiently receptive to change in American policy to make it worthwhile for the United States to shift its policy gears.

It is interesting to note in this respect that even after Khrushchev aided India in the border clash of 1962, where the equities were more on the Chinese than on the Indian side, the Chinese still were not receptive to a shift toward the United States, possibly because they were still recovering from the Great Leap Forward. And shortly thereafter the Cultural Revolution was set off.

Before he took office in 1969, Richard Nixon published an article in *Foreign Affairs* that indicated his interest in an opening to Beijing. Few Americans recognized the significance of that comment, but the Chinese, with their usual acuity, did. Still, they did not act on that recognition until 1970.

During Nixon's first year in office, the Russians passed hints that they would be interested in American neutrality if they knocked out the nuclear facilities of Communist China. The U.S. rebuffed that overture, but these public Soviet threats against China did not yet suffice to provide an opening to the U.S. Although initial overtures from China began in 1970, it was not until 1971, when the Russian threats against China had virtually ceased, that Kissinger was able to make his secret trip to China. If the Chinese were not prepared to move in their year of greatest peril, and could not implement the policy both Mao and Zhou wanted in 1970, this provides some evidence for the difficulty of legitimating that major shift in Chinese foreign policy.

One important interest of the United States in arranging an American opening to China lay in putting pressure on the Russians in turn to pressure the Vietnamese in the Paris negotiations on Vietnam. It is probably correct to assert that the Shanghai Communique of 1972 sacrificed no important American interests. The differing views of China and the United States on Taiwan were expressed in the communique; and neither side conceded anything of significant substance in that communique. Both shaped a situation that was to their mutual advantage in their dealings with the Soviet Union.

The same cannot be said for President Carter's dealings with Communist China. Unlike President Nixon, who was too wise either to attempt to use China as a card against the Soviet Union or to give the appearance of doing so, President Carter succumbed to that temptation and, except for the action of the Congress in passing the Taiwan Relations Act, would have completely delegitimized the Republic of China. It was China that played the American card in this episode, for the attack on Vietnam for all practical purposes coincided with the visit of Deng Xiaoping to the United States. However, China not only paid nothing for that American concession but extracted a price.

I know that the people who conduct President Reagan's foreign policy argue that he paid no significant price—I don't think that they would argue that he paid no price at all—for the arrangement that he arrived at with China. However, even to have discussed the supply of American arms to Taiwan was an important concession, which the People's Republic can build upon. Our position should have been that there is only one China, that both the People's Republic and the Republic of China agree upon this, that China should one day have a unified government, but that in the present period it is in the same situation as Germany and Korea, with separate governments operating in particular parts of the territory of the state and with each having rights under international law, including the right of self-defense and the making of treaties.

Recently Deng Xaioping has referred to the American position on Taiwan as insufficient and has stated that it may lead to deep trouble in relations between the two states. That indeed it may do, for the experts of the State Department have really got us into trouble on this one. Not only should we have not made the concessions we have made, but we should have pressured the Republic of China to respond to the overtures of the Mainland for talks but on a different basis from that offered by the Mainland. Then we in partnership with Japan should have supported the proposals of the Republic of China. Because the situation has continued to drift, any move now by the government of the Republic of China toward talks with the Mainland runs the risk that the people in Taiwan will fear excessive concessions to the Mainland, in which case there may well be a local revolt and a second Chinese state established. If that occurs, it is likely that the United States will feel obligated to recognize and support that state. And, if that occurs, the possibility of a tragedy that neither China nor the United States wants will become prominent. Although the government of the Republic of China shares some of the blame for this, for advice has been offered to it for at least eight years to make reasonable counterproposals, blame also falls on the People's Republic and the Department of State of the United States.

Of course, our interests must be less in the history of this affair than in where we go from here. I have a number of short observations to make. In a military sense, the world is still bipolar. The chief protagonists are the United States and the Soviet Union. China does play a useful role in creating a potential threat on Russia's border, which, given the paranoia of the Russians on the subject of China, leads them to place approximately

750,000 troops on the Chinese border. But China has no significant conventional offensive capability. It demonstrated that in its attack on Vietnam. China did admit that at the present time it is unable to launch an attack against Taiwan. The truth is it would be exceptionally costly for the People's Republic even to attack the offshore islands.

In the global contest between the United States and the Soviet Union, China is simply a very large uncommitted actor which, because it fears the Soviet Union more than the United States, leans toward the American side. This has some usefulness for us. We certainly don't want a restoration of the alliance between China and the Soviet Union, for that would seriously complicate our defensive arrangements both for Europe and for Korea and Japan. However, there is little likelihood of this unless the United States becomes so weak and ineffective that China moves back into the Soviet sphere out of fear.

On the other hand, the United States has no interest in maintaining the present level of hostility between China and the Soviet Union. If the Soviet Union ever were tempted into a war with China, it would win in the short run, but at such great cost, and with such bad long-term consequences, that in desperation it might be tempted into a forced Finlandization of Western Europe in order to solve its internal problems. This might lead to the collapse of the Soviet regime, which certainly would be desirable, but it also might produce a larger war from miscalculation. Surely no one wishes to risk this result. It is true that a reduced level of hostility between China and the Soviet Union would permit China to move back toward the middle in a triangular relationship between the United States, China, and the Soviets; but this is in the Chinese interest. In any event, it is likely that China will move eventually in that direction. At the moment, the only thing preventing that shift is Soviet intransigence on the issues of Vietnam, Afghanistan, and the buildup of Soviet forces on the Chinese border. Thus, effectively the United States has little influence on this process. It can be only counterproductive to attempt to constrain something over which we have no significant control and that will be seen by the Chinese as contrary to their interests and even as unfriendly.

I see no virtue in a U.S.-China alliance against the Soviet Union or a U.S.-Soviet alliance against the Chinese. The latter, of course, would be completely senseless, for it would swing the Eurasian alignment dominantly in the favor of the Soviet Union. Even if a U.S.-China alliance, on the other hand, was not ruled out by the considerations previously expressed, such an alliance would make no sense in terms of the values that the United

States is trying to implement through its foreign policies. The significant common interests the U.S. has with China have specific reference to pressures stemming from the Soviet Union. We have few of the common interests we have with Western Europe, Israel, Japan, Korea, or the Republic of China. If, God forbid, we were in a war with the Soviet Union, China could do nothing of significance to help us apart from the fact that the Soviet Union needs to keep troops on the border of China: something that will happen regardless of whether there is an alliance between us. The Chinese have little influence in Vietnam that could help us. They do have influence in North Korea, but the competition between them and the Russians for North Korean favor reduces that influence. On the other hand, we can do little to help China, except with respect to investment and technology. In a war between China and the Soviet Union, we might ship China some military supplies, but those would be marginal at best. We can, of course, keep the Russians nervous. But that will happen in any event.

The present Soviet influence in Vietnam is not entirely contrary to American interests. I do recognize that Russian control of Cam Ranh Bay is a threat to American strategic projections. However, the Soviet presence in Vietnam takes Chinese pressure off other Southeast Asian states. In the absence of Soviet pressure, it is possible that the Chinese would be supportive of national liberation movements in those states. Moreover, the Vietnamese who dislike and are fearful of the Chinese are likely to develop an animus against the Russians the longer the Soviet Union remains in place. Perhaps the worst thing the United States could do would be to normalize relations with Vietnam and to take these pressures off the other parties.

Finally, however, it is important to recognize that the American interest lies in world order and not in conflict. American policy should be directed toward establishing stable regimes in Europe and Eastern Asia. It is in that type of stable climate that the roots of democracy and economic development can flourish. Thus, despite what I said earlier about the virtues of a continued Soviet presence in Vietnam, the general thrust of American policy should be against the intensification of conflict. Therefore, I would argue for a positive policy of reducing conflict between China and the Soviet Union. Both the reality and appearance of American policy must be directed towards this end. Only this will serve American external interests best and only this will stimulate significant domestic support for American policies directed towards the implementation of American objectives abroad. The triangular relationship will endure within the larger framework of world politics. But we should work to make it a relatively benign and reasonably cooperative triangle.

Notes

1. J. William Fulbright, *Old Myths and New Realities* (New York: Random House, 1974), p. 38.
2. Morton A. Kaplan. "Old Realities and New Myths," *World Politics,* Vol. 17, Jan. 1965, pp. 334–347.

About the Contributors

Peter Berton: Professor of International Relations at the University of Southern California.

Parris H. Chang: Professor of Political Science, Chairman of Asian Area Studies at Pennsylvania State University

Lowell Dittmer: Professor of Political Science at the University of California at Berkeley.

Bernard K. Gordon: Professor of Political Science at the University of New Hampshire.

James C. Hsiung: Professor of Political Science at New York University.

Morton A. Kaplan: Professor of Political Science at the University of Chicago; Editor and Publisher of *The World & I* Magazine.

Michael Y.M. Kau: Professor of Political Science at Brown University.

Donald W. Klein: Professor of Political Science at Tufts University.

Ilpyong J. Kim: Professor of Political Science at the University of Connecicut.

Steven I. Levine: School of International Service at American University.

Thomas W. Robinson: Professor of Political Science at Georgetown University.

R.J. Rummel: Professor of Political Science at the University of Hawaii.

Richard C. Thornton: Institute for Sino-Soviet Studies at George Washington University.

Jane Shapiro Zacek: Rockefeller Institute of Government at the State University of New York.

Donald S. Zagoria: Research Institute on International Change at Columbia University; Professor of Government at Hunter College and City University of New York, Graduate Center.

Index

The index is to proper names and major themes in the book.

The index to this volume's authors includes pages written by them.

The index uses the Pinyin spellings of Chinese names when there is more than one spelling in the text, e.g. a Wade Giles spelling is used only when it is the only one given for a name.

Notes are not indexed.